SOCIETAL
STRUCTURES
OF THE MIND

SOCIETAL STRUCTURES OF THE MIND

By

URIEL G. FOA
Temple University
Philadelphia, Pennsylvania

and

EDNA B. FOA
Temple Medical School
Philadelphia, Pennsylvania

HM
132
.F62

CHARLES C THOMAS • PUBLISHER
Springfield • Illinois • USA

Published and Distributed Throughout the World by
CHARLES C THOMAS ● PUBLISHER
Bannerstone House
301-327 East Lawrence Avenue, Springfield, Illinois, U.S.A.

© *1974, by* CHARLES C THOMAS ● PUBLISHER

ISBN O–398–02932–6

Library of Congress Catalog Card Number: 73–8925

With THOMAS BOOKS *careful attention is given to all details of
manufacturing and design. It is the Publisher's desire to present books that
are satisfactory as to their physical qualities and artistic possibilities and
appropriate for their particular use.* THOMAS BOOKS *will be true to those
laws of quality that assure a good name and good will.*

Printed in the United States of America

BB-14

Library of Congress Cataloging in Publication Data

Foa, Uriel G   1916–
   Societal structures of the mind.

   Includes bibliographical references.
   1. Interpersonal relations. 2. Social role. 3. Cognition. I. Foa,
Edna B., joint author. II. Title. [DNLM: 1. Psychology, Social.
2. Social behavior. HM251 F649s 1973]
HM132.F62   158'.2   73–8925

PREFACE

When a new book in psychology appears, one usually wonders where it should be classified in terms of its approach, subject matter and methodology. Does the book reflect a cognitive or behavioristic viewpoint? Is it concerned with development, personality, social or clinical psychology? Is its research method experimental or correlational? The present volume presents a theory of interpersonal relations, covering the cognitive structures of social events, their development, dynamics, pathology, and their relationship to the structure of society and to intercultural differences. As such, the book is clearly at odds with the high degree of specialization and compartmentalization prevailing in contemporary psychology. Koestler (1964, p. 252) has noted that "the history of science shows recurrent cycles of differentiation and specialization followed by reintegrations on a higher level; from unity to variety to more generalized patterns of unity-in-variety." In our discipline the end of the specialization stage may have been reached when Sigmund Koch (1969) declared that "psychology cannot be a coherent science," a statement which we optimistically interpreted to indicate that some fundamental changes are needed in psychological theory and research. Indeed signs of a movement toward reintegration appear to be on the increase (e.g., Berlyne, 1965; Bolles, 1970; Cronbach, 1957; Deese, 1969; Halwes and Jenkins, 1971; Kimble, 1971; Levine, M., 1971; Mandler, 1962).

Sharing with Bronowski (1961, p. 27) the belief that scientific progress results from achieving "a new order which gives unity to what has long seemed unlike," we present in this book a theory which strives to integrate a variety of ideas and data from different areas of psychology, as well as from other social sciences. Our approach to the study of social events is cognitive, but we view cognition as an organized record of past learning history. Accordingly, we have attempted to spell out the cognitive representations which mediate between specific stimuli and specific responses. With the behaviorists we share an interest in predicting the outcome under given external conditions, yet we believe that knowledge of mediating cognitive structure improves the accuracy of such predictions. With interpersonal relations as our main concern, we have tried to identify differences between normalcy and pathology by considering the developmental aspects of social cognition and by relating them to the diversity of social experience on the one hand and to those structural aspects that, by being invariant across roles, constitute components of personality.

Both results of laboratory experiments and data from field studies will be reported to provide empirical evidence of hypotheses generated by the theory. Some of these findings stem from our work over almost two decades and from studies conducted by colleagues with whom we were closely associated; other findings were culled from the literature and often reinterpreted into the present conceptual framework. Data from both these sources bear directly on certain aspects of the proposed theory; for some hypotheses there is, however, only indirect evidence, while still other hypotheses await an empirical test. The evidence available to us has been given at the appropriate place in the volume. When no data are given, it means there are none we know of. This way the reader will be able to judge for himself the extent to which the theory presented is supported empirically.

Identification and description of the internal organization of the external social world play a central integrative role in our theory; consequently, it seems essential to discuss and clarify the notions "cognition" and "structure" in the science of psychology. These metatheoretical topics are considered in the introductory chapter. Presentation of the theory itself is organized in three parts, each consisting of three chapters. Part I deals with the development of the structures required for cognizing social events; it begins with a description of basic cognitive classes and their process of acquisition (Ch. 2). Development is seen as a sequence of steps of differentiation, mostly dichotomous, acquired through the mechanisms of imitation and contingent reinforcement. This sequence, and the structural pattern resulting from it, are considered in Chapter 3. The presentation of interpersonal cognitive structures is concluded in Chapter 4 with an analysis of role differentiation in the family, viewed, in turn, as a point of departure for the development of roles in other social institutions.

The function of cognitive structures in the dynamics of interpersonal exchanges is explored in Part II; it begins (Ch. 5) with examining those factors which set the stage for the exchange: the state of the individual, the institutional setting and the properties of the resources exchanged. A person will tend to enter exchanges which reduce his needs and are compatible with his power. Social institutions are seen as channels providing opportunity for exchange, while imposing restraints on the type of transaction which may take place. Other limitations stem from the nature of the resources being exchanged. Some social problems, particularly those of urban life, are considered and interpreted as a conflict between individual needs and environmental demands. Proceeding to interpersonal exchange, various paradigms of transaction are considered in Chapter 6 and their consequences for the participants are examined; both in positive and negative exchanges, some transactions are clearly more satisfactory than others, depending on the cognitive structures. The treatment of exchange is concluded in Chapter 7 with re-analysis and integration of recent research on frustration-aggression, interpersonal attraction and equity, ingratiation and Machiavellism, into the framework developed in the previous chapters.

Part III compares cognitive structures within and between cultures and considers the effects of cognitive differences on interpersonal communication and task performance. It begins in Chapter 8 with an analysis of the communication process, where the concept of cognitive matching is introduced; this notion proves effective in the analysis of leadership and of cognitive deprivation in childhood. Cross-cultural differences in the cognitive structure of interpersonal behavior, as well as problems of cross-cultural training are considered in Chapter 9. In Chapter 10 we turn to explore cognitive differences and resulting communication problems between normal and abnormal individuals; identification of differential deviance patterns in the cognitive structure are suggested as a basis for new ways of diagnosis and treatment. The last chapter examines the practical relevance and application of the theory and data presented in the volume.

Many of the notions discussed in this book will be familiar to the reader, having appeared so often in the psychological literature. We have, however, broken some new ground in our attempt to place each notion into a wider framework, as part of an organized whole. In this attempt towards systematization we have built on the foundation laid by scores of investigators in several decades of work. In spite of our efforts we have probably failed in many cases to give credit to whom it is due. Perhaps the magnitude of the psychological literature will explain, if not justify, this acknowledged shortcoming.

The book is primarily addressed to colleagues in psychology, psychiatry, sociology, education and social work, who have a research or applied interest in understanding social behavior, as well as to students—graduate and advanced undergraduate—in these behavioral disciplines. Nevertheless, even the reader without a previous background in social psychology or related areas will be able to follow our exposition. Familiarity with the simple statistical concepts of mean and correlation coefficient will be helpful in examining empirical data, but, of course, it is not necessary for understanding the theoretical notions presented.

ACKNOWLEDGMENTS

In the course of preparing this book, we have become indebted to many persons and institutions who have helped in our endeavor. The initial version of the manuscript was prepared while both of us were affiliated with the Center for Research in Social Behavior at the University of Missouri-Columbia, fully enjoying the benefit of its facilities. Later work was facilitated by a postdoctoral research fellowship granted to the junior author by the National Institute of Mental Health. Generous financial support for the research on which this book is based was provided by grants from United States government agencies: the National Institute of Mental Health, the U.S. Air Force, the Social and Rehabilitation Services and, more recently, the National Science Foundation.

We are greatly indebted to colleagues and students with whom we had the privilege of being associated in joint research projects. We would particularly like to mention Fred E. Fiedler, Charles E. Osgood, Harry C. Triandis, and—among former students—Martin M. Chemers, Gregory Donnenwerth, Terence R. Mitchell, Roger D. Pigg, Meir and Yona Teichman and Jimmie L. Turner. They all contributed to many of the ideas and empirical data presented in this volume.

For advice and suggestions we thank Paul K. Blackwell, David Davis, John Grunau and Robert E. Lana. Ralph L. Rosnow was generous to us with unfailing support and encouragement. To Widad Bazzoui, Bishwa B. Chatterjee, Henri Collomb, Chantal de Preneuf and Vasso Vassiliou, we are grateful for valuable data which they made available. Empirical work in different institutional settings was facilitated through the help and cooperation of Walter S. De Cloe, Mary Jane Gokbora, Emile Gruenberg, Dorothy Miles, Miriam Mueller, James Ritter, Harold Steere and Wayne Walker.

Jeffrey H. Goldstein and Richard Longabaugh devoted many hours to a careful reading of the manuscript and offered invaluable suggestions for its improvement. Suzanne Adams, Diane Allison and Sherri Watts shared the seemingly interminable task of typing successive versions of the manuscript and provided editorial assistance. Donna DiFurio was of great help in preparing the indices.

For permission to reproduce portions of the text as well as the figures and tables listed below, we are grateful to the copyright holders. The American Psychological Association granted permission for the following articles:

Foa, U.G.: Cross-cultural similarity and difference in interpersonal behavior. *Journal of Abnormal and Social Psychology*, 68:517–522, 1964. (Tables 50, 51 and 52)

Foa, U.G.: New developments in facet design and analysis. *Psychological Review*, 72:262–274, 1965.

Foa, U.G.: Perception of behavior in reciprocal roles: The Ringex model. Psychological Monographs, 1966, 80 (15, Whole No. 623). (Figs. 3, 4 and 6 and Tables 5, 6, 7, 8 and 9).

Foa, U.G., Triandis, H.C. and Katz, E.W.: Cross-cultural invariance in the differentiation and organization of family roles. *Journal of Personality and Social Psychology*, 4:316–327, 1966. (Figs. 8 and 10 and Tables 17, 20 and 21).

Foa, U.G.: Three kinds of behavioral changes, *Psychological Bulletin*, 70:460–473, 1968.

Foa, U.G. and Turner, J.L.: Psychology in the year 2000: Going structural? *American Psychologist*, 25:244–247, 1970.

Turner, J.L., Foa, E.B. and Foa, U.G.: Interpersonal reinforcers: Classification, interrelationship and some differential properties. *Journal of Personality and Social Psychology*, 19:168–180, 1971. (Tables 10, 11, 12, 13, 14, 15 and 28)

The American Association for the Advancement of Science granted permission to reproduce from Foa, U.G.: Interpersonal and economic resources. *Science, 171*:345–351, 1971, (including Fig. 7).

Tables 45, 46, 47 and 59, as well as parts of the paper are reproduced from Foa, U.G., Mitchell, T.R. and Fiedler, F.E.: Differentiation matching. *Behavioral Science, 16*:130–142, 1971, by permission from Behavioral Science.

Table 23 and related test are reproduced from Foa, U.G. and Foa, Edna B.: Resource exchange: Toward a structural theory of interpersonal communication. In Siegman, A.W. and Pope, B. (Eds.): *Studies in dyadic communication*. Elmsford: Pergamon Press, 1972, pp. 293–327, by permission of Pergamon Press, Inc.

Permission to reproduce Tables 30, 31, 32 and 33, as well as related portions of the text from Foa, E.B., Turner, J.L. and Foa, U.G.: Response generalization in aggression. *Human Relations*, 25:337–350, 1972, was granted by Plenum Publishing Co., Ltd.

The British Journal of Social and Clinical Psychology granted us permission to reproduce Tables 64 and 65 and related parts of the test from Donnenwerth, G.V., Teichman, M. and Foa, U.G.: Cognitive differentiation of self and parents in delinquent and non-delinquent girls. *British Journal of Social and Clinical Psychology*, June 1973.

For permission to quote from Foa, U.G. and Chemers, M.: The significance of role behavior differentiation for cross-cultural interaction training. *International Journal of Psychology*, 2:45–58, 1967, and Foa, U.G., Mitchell, T.R. and Lekhyananda, D.: Cultural differences in reaction to failure. *International Journal of Psychology*, 4:21–25, 1969 (including Tables 55, 56 and 57), we are grateful to the International Journal of Psychology and to its publisher Dunod, Paris.

Table 58 and related text was reproduced from Mitchell, T.R. and Foa, U.G.: Diffusion of the effect of cultural training of leader in the structure of heterocultural task group. *Australian Journal of Psychology*, 21:31–43, 1969, by permission.

Finally permission to use portions of Foa, U.G. and Foa, E.B.: Measuring quality of life: Can it help solve the ecological crisis? *The International Journal of Environmental Studies*, was granted by Gordon and Breach Ltd., while with regard to Foa, U.G. and Donnenwerth, G.V.: Love poverty in modern culture and sensitivity training. *Sociological Inquiry, 41:* 149–159, 1971, we are indebted to Sociological Inquiry.

CONTENTS

SOCIETAL
STRUCTURES
OF THE MIND

CHAPTER 1

INTRODUCTION: MAN'S STRUCTURING OF HIS SOCIAL WORLD

HUMAN BEINGS, no matter what they are doing, seek companionship. At work, or while enjoying their leisure, the contact with other people is of primary importance. When this contact is denied, as in the case of a prisoner in solitary confinement, it is a dreadful punishment. Even activities which appear to rest on the skills of the individual may be influenced by the social situation. It has been reported, for instance, that children perform better in intelligence tests when their teachers expect them to be brighter (Rosenthal and Jacobson, 1968). Similarly, workers increase production after becoming the focus of attention (Roethlisberger, Dickson and Wright, 1939).

Man, then, is indeed a social creature, devoting a great deal of time and passion to his dealings with his fellow man. The behavior which is displayed in these encounters varies from explicit transactions involving money, goods, services, and information, to a subtler exchange of words and gestures through which affection and appreciation are conveyed. The need for money, goods, services, or information, as well as the need for the less tangible resources of love and status, are seldom satisfied in isolation. We depend on one another for these resources which are necessary for our well being, and therefore, we seek social situations in which to exchange them through interpersonal behavior.

Although these exchanges are a common occurrence, engaging in even the simplest of them demands complex skills of which we may be largely unaware. To carry out these transactions, then, behaviors must be given meaning and those with similar meaning must be classed together and separated from behaviors with different meaning. Thus, for example, one has to separate behavior of giving from behavior of taking away, behavior of self from behavior of other. Likewise, it is helpful to recognize that norms and actual behavior may differ and that one view of a social event is not necessarily the universal view. These differentiations constitute the dimensions of our picture of the social world, a picture which enables us to understand, predict, and to some extent control the exchange of resources.

Resource theory presents a description of the psychological mechanisms required for these exchanges, specifies their course of development, their parts and dimensions and the function they play in interpersonal encounters. It relates individual structure to the structure of society and provides a basis for classifying differences among individuals and cultures. In examining shared and dissimilar properties of economic and non-economic resources, it establishes a link between economics and other social sciences. Within this theory seemingly disparate notions, such as cognitive dissonance, interpersonal communication, social roles, crosscultural training, leadership, need, power, alienation and psychotherapy are integrated into a coherent whole.

A convenient point of departure for identifying the resource exchange apparatus of the adult is to consider how its basic dimensions become progressively differentiated early in life, when the child interacts mainly with its mother. Then, as the child begins to move beyond the exclusiveness of relationship with his mother, further differentiations are needed for him to be able to participate in the various roles of the family, relate to peers, as well as function in other social institutions, such as school and work. Different resources are, indeed, suitable to each one of these institutional settings, so that institutions provide both limitations and channels for resource exchange: paying for transportation is appropriate in a public vehicle, but not when a neighbor offers you a ride. Even if the neighbor needs money, the loss of status involved in a request for payment would probably keep him from making such a demand. Thus, an institutional setting may prevent a given transaction while facilitating another. An additional condition for an exchange to be satisfactory is that it should be consistent with the participants' previous experience of social events. A person who expects equitable compensation for a big effort will feel dissonance when receiving a small reward. To resolve this inconsistency, he may conclude that the effort he made was not that big and that, in fact, he rather enjoyed it. In this example the restructuring of the dissonant event reduces the feeling of loss, while, at the same time, safeguarding the cognitive organization of the individual. In other instances however, the need for a given resource may conflict with the need to preserve the structure: a person who expects failure may give up status rather than recognize success.

Institutional setting, need-states of the individual, as well as the properties of the resource involved, all affect the likelihood of an exchange to occur. Once an exchange has taken place it is pertinent to inquire how it influences the participants' satisfaction and willingness to enter further transactions. Experiments conducted by us indicate that the appropriateness of the resources exchanged constitutes a significant factor for satisfaction; people seem to have definite preferences about what should be exchanged with what. Serious difficulties in the transaction of resources are likely to arise when the participants do not share similar mechanisms for classifying interpersonal behavior and for assigning meaning to it. These cognitive differences appear indeed to hinder performance, interaction among members of different cultures, and relations with mentally disturbed individuals.

Clearly, identification of the latent cognitive structures underlying interpersonal behavior is a central concern for a theory of resource exchange. Yet the twin notions of "cognition" and "structure" have been subjected to so many different treatments and interpretations that it appears desirable to specify in this introductory chapter the position we take on these issues. We shall begin with a short overview. Cognition is an organized set of categories into which perceived events are classified according to the meaning assigned to them; events having an equivalent meaning are placed in the same class. Cognitive classes are organized into patterns which reflect their similarities and differences; these patterns or cognitive structures provide a representation of self and environment. The significance of studying cognition, for understanding interpersonal behavior, rests on the notion that the reaction to a given message depends on the meaning which is ascribed to it. Since a message has meaning for the sender as well as for the receiver, interpersonal communication is based on the match between their respective cognitions. Uniformity in categorizing social events is facilitated by a common culture. Culture thus constitute a blueprint or template for the classification and organization of social events. This blueprint is acquired by the child in his cognitive development, through exposure to differential reinforcement contingencies. Such a set of contingencies defines a culture, while the reinforcement contingencies of a specific experimental setting may be seen as a miniculture.

COGNITION

Being the psychological mechanism by which meaning is assigned to the external and internal stimuli we experience, cognition indicates the relationship between events, i.e., how one event is "caused" by another. It is through the possession of such mechanism that we are capable of predicting and controlling our environment: the rat which experienced red light followed by shock will soon jump a shuttle box when the light appears; the child who was comforted with candy will soon cry when craving for it. It is indeed through cognition that past experience becomes a guide for operating in the present and for anticipating the future. By cognition we achieve a fairly sensible and ordered view of the world which surrounds us, of the web of interpersonal relations to which we belong and of our position in the community.

In order to accomplish these complex functions cognition must provide some representation of the environment somewhat analogous to a geographical map. Few modern psychologists would, however, consider cognition a passive mirror of reality in which events are merely recorded, a view, this latter, which had enjoyed some popularity in the past. Nevertheless, the debate over the nature of cognition has not disappeared from current thinking, even if it has lost some of its earlier vehemence (Sarbin, Taft and Bailey, 1960, Ch. 2). Major conflicting views are represented by the proponents of materialism and by the idealistic school: for the former, cognition reflects external reality while for the latter reality is constructed by cognition. It is only recently that a third alternative, which came to be known as "structuralism," has emerged. This new development is described by Stent (1972) as follows: "Both materialism and idealism take it for granted that all the information gathered by our senses actually reaches our mind; materialism envisions that, thanks to this information, reality is mirrored in the mind; whereas idealism envisions that, thanks to this information, reality is constructed by the mind. Structuralism, on the other hand, has provided the insight that knowledge about the world enters the mind, not as raw data, but in already highly abstracted form, namely, as structures. In the preconscious process of converting the primary data of our experience, step by step, into structures, information is necessarily lost, because the creation of structures, or the recognition of patterns, is nothing else than the selective destruction of information. Thus, since the mind does not gain access to the full set of data about the world, it can neither mirror nor construct reality. Instead, for the mind, reality is a set of structural transforms of primary data taken from the world" (p. 92).

Selective destruction of information is a necessary operation in the process of categorizing events into classes by which we reduce the complexity of the environment as well as the need for incessant learning (Bruner, Goodnow and Austin, 1956, p. 12). Yet what constitutes important information may vary with the circumstances. The fact that my old friend Joe is wearing a new suit does not make him a different person to me, therefore I do not have to modify my behavior and expectations; his new suit is an irrelevant cue. This same information, the new elegant suit, may constitute quite an important cue for a person who, having never met Joe before, tries to classify him and behave accordingly. Individuals may vary in the cues they select to destroy, so that the same raw data, which originate in the environment, do not always lead to an identical cognitive representation. The simplification of an event by selective suppression is a necessary but not a sufficient condition for processing information. An additional requirement is the fit between cognition and the event.

Congruence between Event and Cognition

When we see an unfamiliar dog we are immediately able to recognize it as a member of the class "dog," although this particular dog constitutes a totally new event for us. Once again, congruence between this event and the class "dog" is achieved by selective suppression of the cues which are specific to this particular dog. We attend only to cues which are common to all "dog" events, according to the previous experience as recorded in our cognition. Suppose now that this dog meows instead of barking; since this sound is not associated with the events of the "dog" class, we shall experience difficulty when attempting to categorize this strange creature. More generally, when the latent structure of an event, as revealed by the shorning of irrelevant information, is congruent with cognition so that it can be assigned to a certain class or cluster of classes then, and only then, the event becomes meaningful.

The concept of congruence between cognition and environment underlies, with varying degrees of explicitness, many theoretical notions in the psychological literature such as reality testing, confirmation of expectation, adaptation level and discrepancy. The idea that these notions involve a comparison between cognition and event was suggested more recently by Foa, Mitchell and Fiedler (1971). Independently, Feather (1971) proposed a distinction between abstract and perceived structures; abstract cognitive structures, being relatively stable, "provide continuity and meaning under changing circumstances, but . . . they are susceptible to change . . . as new and discrepant information is received that cannot readily be interpreted in terms of existing abstract structures." "In contrast, the perceived structure refers to the way information provided by the immediate situation is organized. This type of structure, therefore, is dependent on the immediate situational context and does not have the stable transitual character of an abstract structure" (p. 356). Similarly it was suggested by Stent (1972) that stronger structures are formed from weaker ones through the selective destruction of information. A set of primary data acquires meaning only if its transformation makes its weaker struc-

ture congruent with the stronger structure pre-existing in cognition.
Noting that some important scientific discoveries were ignored by con-
temporaries Stent proposed that the structure of these new ideas was
out of tune with the cognitive structure prevalent at such time among
scientists.

The comparison between cognition and perceived event also constitutes an important aspect of Kelley's (1973) attribution theory, dealing with the manner in which people ascribe causes to behavior. Kelley
proposed two kinds of attribution processes: one is based on pre-
existing casual schemata, such as stereotypes, where a certain "effect"
is associated in cognition with a certain "cause." The second process
refers to the analysis of data from immediate experience. In giving
an example of incongruence between the two processes Kelley quotes
a study in which clinically naive undergraduate students were shown
randomly paired protocols of projective tests and reports on patients'
problems. The students found a relationship between the·two sets
of data. Since protocols and problems were paired at random the
reported association must have originated from the cognition of the
students. Kelley notes that the effect of the pre-existing cognitive state
on the processing of new information also appears in the issues of
primacy versus recency in attitude change, of proactive versus reactive
inhibition and of assimilation versus accomodation.

In spite of its relevance to a great variety of phemomena, the comparison between cognition and event is not sufficient when social events
are considered. A social event originates from people; therefore its
structure should be compared not only with the receiver's cognition,
but also with that of the sender. It is reasonable to expect that in most
cases an event will be congruent with the cognition from which it ensued,
it will in fact be modeled on it. Consequently, a social event will
be incongruent for the receiver when his cognition differs from that
of the sender. In social situations the critical matching is not between
event and cognition, but between the cognitions of the participants;
when they differ—as may be the case in mental disturbances or in
heterocultural contacts—difficulties in understanding and predicting
the behavior of the other person are likely to occur.

For this reason, we shall not focus on the structure of the social
event but rather concentrate throughout this book on the cognitions
of the persons involved in it and on their cognitive matching.

Cognition and Awareness

Before concluding these introductory remarks on cognition its relationship to awareness should be briefly examined; often these two
terms have been considered as synonyns. A.L. Baldwin (1969, pp.

336–337) suggests that learning without awareness is non-cognitive. This view is also pursued by D.R. Peterson (1968, p. 40), who offers the following syllogism: Earthworms learn, they do not cognize—therefore, learning does not require awareness; in the same volume he later notes (p. 75) that ". . . some actions occur under clear and definite cognitive control, while others reel off automatically beyond the reportable awareness of the agent." There is no question that some cognitive activities, such as relating one item to another, often are in the realm of awareness, and thus verbalizing them may facilitate learning (Dulany, 1962). However, other cognitive activities, such as classifying a stimulus according to its attributes, are more likely to be unconscious. Wickens (1970) reported results which suggest that the process of perceiving a word involves some kind of multiple classification, as the word is placed along a number of cognitive dimensions. In proposing that this process is unconscious he comments: ". . . I do not think that the identity of the many encoding attributes or dimensions enter very much into the individual's consciousness. Consequently, we are unaware intellectually of the richness of the encoding of a single word. If we were to consciously recognize this richness, then so much time would be required for the perceptual ingestion of a single word that we would find it next to impossible to listed to a series of words and remember any but the first and last of them. We handle the intellectual and conceptual meaningful reactions to common words with the same kind of automatic skill as the veteran big league outfielder who turns his back to a hard-hit fly ball, runs at top speed, and then without stopping and almost without looking, raises his gloved hand at exactly the right instant and in exactly the right location to grasp the ball.

"The ball player's marvelous competence is the product of his years of experience in the bush leagues, in the training camp, and in the big league ball parks themselves. So, too, our automatic ability to transform the sounds or the sight of a word into many attributes is the product of the many, many experiences we have with words in this highly verbal world of ours. We are more complex and facile in our reactions that we witness ourselves as being, and in our dealing with words, much of an intellectual nature goes on about which we are cognitively blind, deaf, and therefore mute" (p. 1–2).

THE NOTION OF STRUCTURE

The choice of a structuralistic viewpoint in considering the nature of cognition compelled us to introduce the term *structure* before discussing its meaning. Unlike cognition, structure is a notion which occurs not only in psychology but in other sciences as well. Physicists are concerned with the structure of the atom; i.e., with the interrelationship between its subparticles; biochemists investigate the structure of DNA and complex proteins, to locate the mutual position of their component elements. In their investigations of structures these scientists have a big advantage over their psychological colleagues: they use the familiar three-dimensional physical space for determining the place of their units. When Einstein treated time as a fourth dimension, his innovation was hailed as a major intellectual achievement. The challenge faced by the student of cognitive structure is even more radical: physical space is not suitable for ordering his elements, except as a vague and sometimes misleading analogy. Available methods for determining the spatial configuration of a set of psychological variables do not provide identification of the coordinates by which the space is defined, an essential requirement of a structural theory. Attempts in this direction are compounded by the difficulty we experience in conceptualizing spaces, other than the familiar physical one. Our strong dependence on the physical notion of space is clearly apparent in Kurt Lewin's writings: although his theoretical formulation refers to psychological spaces, his examples are mostly drawn from the physical one. This conceptual barrier is also reflected in the frequent use of the expression "psychological dimension" where the term "coordinate" would be appropriate. In the physical space the two notions happen to coincide, since the coordinates are independent of one another. Independence among the various coordinates is less likely to occur in psychological spaces; in this volume we shall indeed present several configurations with three coordinates, which can be adequately described on two dimensions. Bowing to the general custom we shall also use dimensions as synonymous with coordinate. We shall, however, avoid using the term dimension for indicating a variable. This distinction is made clear by defining structure as a *configuration of variables or classes in a space of stated coordinates*. It follows that coordinate and variable coincide only if the space is unidimensional. A virtue of such a configuration is that it indicates parsimoniously the dimensions on which variables are similar or different, as well as the relative similarity of each pair of variables in the given set.

Structure in the Science of Man

At a theoretical level, the study of structures or organized wholes has attracted the attention of psychologists in the past and increasingly so in more recent times. Freud's (1949) notions of Id, Ego and Superego, Lewin's (1936) topological spaces, and Piaget's (1952) schemata are all attempts to provide structural models. Closer to our topic of person cognition is Kelly's (1955) theory of personal constructs, the development of a structural model applied to clinical inference (Sarbin, et al., 1960), and Kelly's (1973) treatment of causal attribution. Persistent interest in this notion is evidenced by recent reviews of its application to child development (Emmerich, 1968) and to psychology in general (Mucchielli, 1966). In disciplines related to psychology the notion of structure is prominent in the anthropological work of Levi-Strauss (1963) and Goodenough (1967), as well as in studies of linguistics (Chomsky, 1957; McNeill, 1966); and recurs often in sociological literature.

In spite of this theoretical interest, the notion of structure had only limited influence in empirical research. Many investigators ignore it altogether. Their work typically consists of investigating the relationship among a few variables; taking three or four variables at a time, it offers an almost endless variety of experimental designs. Consequently, this line of research generates a large amount of data, but also great difficulty in relating the results of various experiments and in attempting broader generalization. This difficulty may be partly due to the fact that in these studies each variable is considered in isolation, rather than in its relationship to a larger organized whole.

Other directions of research have either focused on a single dimension or subsumed the existence of multidimensional structures, without attempting to specify their dimensions.

GENERALIZATION. Most investigations of generalization in experimental psychology involve the notion of dimension but not of structure. The stimuli preferred in these investigations are those which can be ordered on a physical dimension (e.g., light, sound) thus avoiding the problem of spelling out psychological coordinates. This choice of stimuli limits the study of more complex phenomena. For example: displacement of aggression, when formalized as a generalization phenomenon (Berkowitz, 1965), would require specification of the psychological coordinates along which various persons are perceived as similar or different. (The dimensions of role differentiation, presented in Chapter 4, may prove relevant to this problem.)

Stimuli possessing physical properties of order are found quite easily, while responses are unlikely to be so manifestly ordered; consequently stimulus generalization has been studied much more than response generalization. Ignoring the notion of structure, studies of generalization too often deal with unidimensional situations. A pigeon learns to peck a red circle for obtaining food and then it is tested on circles of various colors. Few studies were interested in forcing our pigeon to choose between a green circle and a red square.

COGNITIVE COMPLEXITY AND CONSTRUCT VALIDITY. A third group of studies is concerned with structure, but avoids spelling out its dimensions. Investigations of cognitive complexity belong to this group. Complex individuals are held to have a larger number of differentiated dimensions in their cognitive structure than "simpler" persons: A complex cognition presumedly including all the dimensions which exist in a simpler cognition plus some additional ones. If, however, one person is more complex than another person on one dimension and less complex than him on some other dimension, then it will be impossible to say which of the two is more complex without referring to specific dimensions. Some studies suggest indeed that complexity is not a unitary trait (Scott, 1963; Vannoy, 1965) and thus cannot be divorced from the quest for dimensions. In spite of these limitations, the notion of complexity has generated a considerable amount of research contributing to the understanding of the relationship between cognitive representation and external situation (e.g., Harvey, Hunt and Schroder, 1961; Schroder, Driver and Streufert, 1967).

Another direction in the study of structure without searching for its dimensions is the construct validity procedure. It is used, particularly in the personality area, to validate new instruments for observation and consists essentially in correlating the score provided by the instrument with variables expected on intuitive grounds to be related to it, i.e., to be proximal to it in the unspecified structure.

The difficulties posed by the absence of dimensionally specific descriptions of structures are particularly evident in the investigation of dissonance: dissonance is said to occur when two elements of an event are incompatible (Berscheid and Walster, 1969, p. 131). It appears, however, that for dissonance to occur, the incompatible elements should be cognitively close. Indeed, one way to resolve dissonance is to increase the cognitive distance between the contrasting items. In other words: dissonance implies a discrepancy between the structure of the event and cognitive structure (Feather, 1971). In absence of a specific structural description, the intuition of the investigator remains the only source for deciding whether the elements of the event are incompatible with cognition. This problem, which is not specific to dissonance but applies to consistency models in general, is clearly stated by Pepitone (1966, p. 262): "The wholly unrestricted generality of the dissonance model with respect to the nature and size of the elements of inconsistency can and does create problems on the experimental plane. Without rules or guidelines as to what the elements of dissonance should be, the investigator can only select them on a purely intuitive basis. If he does not know the class of cognitions from which the dissonant ones are derived, he cannot count elements, and this is crucial for obtaining a measure of the strength of dissonance."

Partial or total disregard for the identification of cognitive structures has thus limited the usefulness of investigation in several areas of psychology. Conversely, the study of structures is likely to open new lines of research.

Why Structures Should be Studied

The dictum "the whole is more than the sum of its parts," has a rather long history in psychology: its influence is apparent in the Gestalt school, in the ideographic approach to personality (Allport, 1937) and, more recently, in humanistic psychology (Buhler, 1971).

In studying the "whole," we obtain information about each of its parts as well as about their relationship, i.e., their pattern of organization. Thus only by investigating the whole are we able to specify the structure of the parts. It follows that the study of the "whole" requires the identification of its parts as well as a specification of their relationship.

The terms "part" and "whole" are relative to the level of analysis (Koestler, 1968, pp. 47-49). The part of a molar system becomes the whole of a molecular one. The cell is a part for the student of tissues, but a whole for the microbiologist; "avoidance" is a distinct "part," in the behavior of an experimental animal, but also a complex neuro-muscular pattern in its own right. The nature of the relationship among different levels of observation provides still another reason for investigating structures before attempting to relate variables from different levels. In contrast to this suggestion, a considerable amount of current research in psychology attempts to relate isolated variables from one domain to variables in another domain: psychophysiological variables to behavioral ones, cognitive variables to environmental ones and the like. This line of research tacitly assumes one-to-one correspondence between the variables of one domain and the variables of the other one: for each variable in one system there should be one and only one corresponding variable in the other system. The evidence available seems to militate against this assumption.

In language, for example, different words may have the same meaning and conversely, words often have more than one meaning, so that one-to-one mapping of words and meaning is not always possible. This ambiguity of meaning is usually resolved when the word is seen in the context of an organized whole, a sentence.

A similar situation occurs in the coding of genetic information: each instruction is represented by a specific sequence of three bases, selected from the four found in the DNA structure. The information is provided by the sequence and not by each base taken in isolation, so that the mere frequency distribution of the four bases bears no relationship to the meaning of the instructions. In the era before the identification of DNA as the genetic material, biologists assumed that the heritable differences between organisms must be determined by protein structures, because proteins were the only molecules known to be capable both of sufficient variety of form and specificity of function, as exemplified by enzymes. The structure of DNA, containing as it does only four different kinds of bases, did not seem to offer sufficient potential for either structural variation or specificity. In fact, it was at one time believed that DNA consisted of a mixture of small molecules, containing one of each of the four bases in random sequence, the so-called "statistical tetranucleotide." The discovery in the 1940's that DNA molecules are very much longer than this, and that the genetic material is indeed DNA, was followed by the finding that the frequency distribution of the four bases varies widely among the DNA of different organisms (Strickberger, 1968, pp. 48-59). The elucidation of the structure of DNA by Watson and Crick stimulated speculation in the 1950's on the nature of the genetic code, including the following proposal, which subsequently proved to be correct. By taking the four bases three at a time, 4^3 or 64 different kinds of instructions can be encoded into a linear DNA molecule, and this is more than sufficient to specify a linear sequence of the 20 different kinds of amino acid on which protein structure, and hence enzyme specificity, depend.[1]

This example is particularly instructive because it shows how an unwarranted one-to-one assumption (one base for each instruction) can lead the investigator astray. Again the riddle is solved when the component elements are considered in their structural relationship rather than in isolation. It is not by chance that the breaking of the genetic code followed the discovery of the structure. It could not possibly have preceded it, since the information is carried by the structure.

In an area of more direct interest to the psychologist, the relationship between behavior and brain functioning, the one-to-one assumption is denied in some recent work of Luria (1966). His research on disturbances of higher mental functions in the presence of local brain lesions indicates that more than one brain activity is involved in any given behavior and conversely a given activity participates in several behaviors. For example, a complex activity such as handwriting may be impaired in a manner which is distinctively associated with the location of the brain lesion. Such components as spelling, distortion of the letters, and directionality (i.e., writing on a line from left to right) will be variously affected depending on the localization of the cerebral lesions. Moreover, when a handwriting component such as directionality is impaired, we may also expect to find this component

---

[1] John A. Grunau: Personal communication, 1971.

impaired in other domains of behavior. Social direction (e.g., differentiation between what one does to self and what one does to other) is one example of a behavior which may be defective due to disturbances in the directionality component. More recently Luria and his associates went even further by suggesting, on the basis of clinical observations, that the same behavioral system may be related to different cortical structures at different stages of its ontogenetic development ". . . a psychological operation changes not only its structure, but also its cerebral organization in the course of its functional development," (Luria, Simernitskaya and Tubylevich, 1970). A complex brain-task relationship is also evident in sensory functions. Employing a visual discrimination task, Iversen (1969) found that monkeys with a posterior intratemporal lesion show impairment of pattern discrimination but perform as well as normal monkeys, in color discrimination. These results suggest that more than one brain function is involved in visual discrimination.

Common observation suggests that the assumption of one-to-one mapping is not supported any better in the area of social cognition: behaviors which are quite different in their intrinsic characteristics may have similar meaning and, thus, are cognited into the same class: smiling, waving the hand, saying "hello" or "hi," are all forms of greeting. Conversely, behaviors which are motorically similar may have a different meaning: raising a clenched fist and raising an open hand will probably go into different cognitive classes, as do kissing and biting which are two forms of oral activity. From these considerations emerges what could well be the most important reason for studying structures: understanding the meaning of behavior.

The Study of Meaning

In an interpersonal situation we exchange messages: many of them are verbal, others, no less important, are not: facial expression, gestures, body posture, eye contact and even the distance maintained with the other person (Duncan, 1969; Hall, E.T., 1963), are all interpersonal messages. In either case the significance of the message comes from the *meaning* that the sender and/or the recipient attach to it. The same meaning may be conveyed in quite different ways. If we want to warmly greet the other, we can do it by smiling, raising and waving an arm, or saying "hi;" these various messages are largely equivalent in their meaning, all belong to the same class.

As Bruner, Goodnow and Austin (1956, p. 1) have already noted, one cannot interact with the environment unless he categorizes events. Any perception of events involves the process of categorization, including the scientific conceptualization which always involve the cognitive activity of the scientist, in classifying the subject matter of his investigation. In cognitive studies, however, the subject matter is cognition; thus the task of the investigator of cognition is to cognite about the hidden cognitive structure of his subject. It involves building up hypotheses about the manner in which events are grouped into classes and investigating the order and relations among these classes.

The study of cognition is essentially the study of meaning. Why are we interested in the meaning of behavior? After all, there are other, more explicit, criteria for grouping behaviors, such as the type of organs involved (e.g., verbal vs. nonverbal; Buss, 1961, p. 4). Our choice is determined by the assumption that it is the meaning attributed to a certain interpersonal message or stimulus, which determines the subsequent response, and is therefore crucial for prediction of outcome. In the Far East, for example, a pat on the back is considered as an insult, whereas in Western cultures it will be interpreted as a sign of friendship. Naturally, we will expect different responses to this stimulus depending on the cultural background of the person.

Moreover, the meaning ascribed to the stimulus appears to influence not only the overt response, but also brain activity. John, Shimokochi and Bartlett (1969) trained cats to obtain food when presented with a flicker light of a certain frequency, and to avoid shock when exposed to a different frequency. Subsequently, the cats were presented with a flicker frequency midway between the earliest two. All through the trials, electrical activity in the brain of the animals was recorded by electrodes implanted in the visual cortex or in the lateral geniculate bodies. The shape of the brain wave, following the ambiguous flicker of intermediate frequency, was affected by the meaning attributed to the signal: when this flicker elicited the food response, the wave recorded was similar to the one which was present for the flicker associated with food; likewise, when the avoidance response followed the ambiguous stimulus, the wave shape resembled the one previously produced by the shock avoidance signal. Apparently the same stimulus activated different neuronal activities depending on the meaning attributed to it by the animal. The alternative interpretation, that differential brain activity is related to the forthcoming response rather than to the meaning of the stimulus, is rejected by other studies showing similar results in absence of overt response. Cohn (1971) recorded brain activity in human subjects merely exposed to verbal and nonverbal auditory stimuli. The verbal material evoked activity mainly in the left hemishpere, while the activity for the meaningless noise was always in the right one. The two sets of stimuli differed in meaning, although both belonged to the same physical class of sounds.

From these experiments we learn that: (a) different stimuli may have the same meaning; (b) the same stimulus may have different meanings; (c) response depends on the meaning ascribed to the stimulus. We have also noted that knowledge of meaning requires identification of cognitive structures; thus the notion of structure enables us to relate the stimulus to the response.

Identification of Structures and Factor Analysis

So far the most sustained attack on the identification of structures has been made through factor analysis. There is no essential difference between the notions of factor and dimension, so that factor analysis constitutes a type of dimensional analysis.

Opinions differ as to the value of this approach for the identification of dimensions. On one hand, it is difficult to dismiss such work as the one done by Cattell (1966; Cattell and Warburton, 1967) which produced a sophisticated picture of personality structure. On the other hand, one cannot easily disregard data showing that factorial findings, quite acceptable by current standards, can be obtained from random data (Humphreys, Ilgen, McGrath and Montanelli, 1969). In spite of these disturbing results, factor analysis continues to be widely used, possibly because it is so easily employed: the data are fed into the computer with the analytic program and out come the factorial results. No matter what the data are, some results will be obtained. Consequently there has been an increasing tendency to use factor analysis blindly, i.e., without any theoretical guidance as to which variables should or should not be included in the analysis, and without an hypothesis regarding the structure of the variables. The fact that factor analysis was originally devised as a method for testing structural hypotheses has been often forgotten in current practice. Yet any analytic method can, at best, only reveal the order which is already implicit in the input. An analytic procedure can be compared to a cooking stove: the best stove will not make a good soup out of the wrong ingredients. Even more serious is the suspicion that the factor analytic space rests on metric assumptions which are unsuitable to psychological spaces, and therefore the factors obtained may not necessarily indicate primary dimensions of psychological organization.

In evaluating the factor analytical approach, we should note that even in areas like intelligence, where it has been used most consistently and rigorously, factor analysis failed to yield an acceptable structural pattern. When Guilford (1967) proposed a structural theory of intelligence, he had to follow an intuitive procedure of interpretation and classification of the many factors available in order to develop his dimensional model. A sharper departure from factor analysis is represented by Osgood (1970) who, also using an intuitive approach, has identified ten semantic features for classifying interpersonal verbs and generating structural hypotheses.

Blind reliance on factor analysis in the absence of specific hypotheses has delayed the identification of psychological structures. Another obstacle has been posed by the long accepted dichotomy between structure and dynamics.

Structure and Function

Traditionally, in psychology, "structure" and "function" are considered as separate if not contrasting notions. A structure is characterized by endurance, permanence and stability, while functions are activities or processes, which change in response to environmental stimuli (English & English, 1958). As late as 1968, the Annual Review of Psychology maintained this dichotomy by devoting separate chapters to studies on personality structure and to the work on personality functioning. The fact that this practice has been criticized (Wiggins, 1968) and dropped may indicate that the structure-function dichotomy is becoming less rigid (Vieru, 1969).

The separation between the structure and its function originates in a mechanistic view of the organism. In studying a car engine, it is expedient to become familiar with its parts and their relationship before learning about the functioning of the engine. Separation is justified here because the structure of the engine determines its function, while the only influence functioning has on the structure is that of causing a relatively slow wearing. Non-reciprocal relation between structure and function exists also in conventional computer programs, where the program determines the output but is not modified by it. This is not true of more recent and sophisticated programs devised in studies of artificial intelligence (Slagle, 1971, esp. pp. 130-133). Here the outcome can modify the program thus enabling the computer to capitalize on previous experience instead of proceeding blindly according to the rules set out at the beginning.[2]

Once we accept the view that structure and function are interrelated, not only a major conceptual obstacle in the study of structural dynamics is removed, but also its direction becomes clear. We suggest that the study of dynamics should concentrate on investigating and spelling out the types of changes which occur in structures as well as the conditions under which they occur. With amazing foresight Lewin (1936, p. 155) described three kinds of structural changes: *differentiation*, or categorizing events, which were previously included in the same class, into different classes; *integration* (the opposite of differentiation),

---

[2] Paul K. Blackwell: Personal communication, 1971.

when items, previously classified in different categories, are reunited into the same class; *restructuring*, a change in the relative position of classes. Lewin also suggested some of the conditions in which these changes may occur.

The Lewinian notion of structural change is prominent in modern views of cognitive development (Baldwin, A.L., 1969; Emmerich, 1968; Kohlberg, 1969a). In general, psychological development may be perceived as a process of interaction between cognitive representation and behavioral experiences, a process which does not necessarily terminate in adulthood. Commenting on the fruitfulness of this approach for generating research, Emmerich, Goldman and Shore (1971) single out the following problems: "(a) How changes in social inputs influence the individual's normative structurings, (b) how changes in normative structures influence the individual's social behavior, and (c) how changes in social behavior feed back to influence normative structures." (p. 348)

STRUCTURING AND INTERPERSONAL COMMUNICATION

Behavior must be assigned to a cognitive class to acquire meaning, thus interpersonal communication requires categorization of the interaction. Two cognitions are involved in the transmission of a message—that of the sender and that of the receiver; a successful communication requires a match between these two cognitions. When will a message be received as intended? First, the receiver should have the class appropriate for the message; and second, the sender and the receiver should both recognize the message as belonging to the same class. When these conditions are missing, communication will be impaired. There are several ways for reducing misunderstanding. A common one is redundant communication, where several messages from the same class are sent in succession. Often we combine verbal and nonverbal messages to enhance our intention: when we want to convey friendship, we may follow the message "I like to be with you" with a smile or a warm look. In addition there are messages which intend to clarify the meaning of previous ones, such as "I was really joking," "I did not mean to insult you," etc. The most powerful factor for reducing misunderstanding is, however, a shared culture.

The Cultural Blue-Print for Meaning

Culture provides a template or model for the cognitive structure of its members, so that persons belonging to the same culture tend to have similar structures, and are able to communicate more effectively. The same idea is conveyed by Bruner, et al. (1956, p. 10), "The categories in terms of which man sorts out and responds to the

world around him reflect deeply the culture into which he is born."
Culture also determines which message goes into which class—it
determines the meaning of messages. In consequence, we can compare
different cultures in terms of how different their blue-prints are. Certain
characteristics of cognition may well be common to different cultures
and perhaps to all human beings, as well as to certain higher animals,
enabling us to communicate with people from other cultures and even
with animals, such as dogs. These pancultural aspects of cognition
are probably present from birth, while the culture-specific ones are
learned in childhood by interacting with other individuals, especially
the parents, who are carriers of the cultural blue-print. Thus, while
cognitive structures are acquired through early interpersonal experiences, once developed they become determinants of later experiences
by affecting their meaning.

Reinforcement Contingencies and Culture

   Reinforcement contingencies provide a mechanism for learning the
cultural model, quite similar to the one used in laboratory experiments:
"correct" responses are rewarded, while "wrong" ones are punished;
usually communication failure results in an inappropriate response
followed by punishment. Suppose, for example, that a person behaves
in the same way in two different situations when his culture dictates
that behavior A is appropriate for the first situation and behavior B
for the second one. The culture demands that in each situation the
behavior should come from different classes, while our person uses
the same class in both cases. He might be taught to discriminate
between the situations in the way a white rat learns that when green
light is on, pressing left bar releases food, pressing right bar produces
shock; when red light is on, pressing left bar produces shock, pressing
right bar releases food.
   This simple experimental paradigm demonstrates the fact that reinforcement contingencies in a learning experiment constitute a pattern
of interrelated events which is comparable to the cultural blue-print
from which the child learns to structure his cognition. Solomon, Turner
and Lessac (1968) noted the fruitfulness of laboratory learning situations that can be extrapolated to conditions of socialization and provided
a good example of them. In an experiment they did, dogs were punished
for eating "forbidden" and highly preferred food; some of the animals
received immediate punishment as soon as they touched the taboo
meat, while for others punishment was delayed so that they had a
chance to eat some of the forbidden food. Compared to quickly-
punished dogs, those in the delayed punishment group were less resistant to temptation, appeared more frightened during and after violation

of the taboo, and their attraction for the permitted food was lower. These findings may be applicable to socialization of the child, and they illustrate the usefulness of regarding reinforcement contingencies as artificial mini-cultures. As such, they serve the same purpose a culture does, in developing and modifying the structural arrangements of experimental work, it will be necessary, however, to devise contingencies that replicate specific cultural patterns. Interest in conceptualizing reinforcement contingencies as an organized pattern has already been evidenced by some modern learning theorists (see e.g., Jenkins, 1971). Even more significant is the fact that a model of a non-culture (i.e., a random or disorganized schedule where no contingencies exist, has been proposed as a control procedure in classical conditioning (Rescorla, 1967). According to our reasonong, a random schedule will result in structural disorganization of the subject. Indeed, this procedure produces powerful negative effects, such as stomach ulcers, loss of weight, defecation, absence of response. These destructive effects, while impairing the effectiveness of the random schedule as a control procedure (Seligman, 1969), emphasize the interplay between organization of the environment and organization of the organism.

Individual Deviance from Culture

Learning of the cultural model is unlikely to be perfect: some deviations will occur, thus generating individual differences in structure, which in most cases, will be only minor. The cognitive organization acquired by the child may, however, differ considerably from the cultural blue-print when the parents themselves deviate, when the child is unable to receive or process the information communicated to him, or through some subtle interaction of both. Whatever the cause, a severe deviation from the typical structure of society will produce difficulties in interpersonal communication, since it will result in attributing uncommon meaning to messages. Suppose, for example, that a cognitive deviation consists of mixing up feelings and behaviors pertaining to self with those directed toward other (as it happens to schizophrenics), instead of sorting them into separate classes. Then the message "*I* am tired," will be decoded as "*We* are tired." If the deviant recipient is not tired and in fact intends to read a book, interpretation of the message as "We should sleep rather than read" will result in distress.

Various types of disturbances in interpersonal communication may be characterized by specific deviance patterns in the structural arrangement of classes. Treatment would then be specific to each pattern of deviance and would consist of an attempt to modify the structure in the direction consistent with the culture, through the use of suitable reinforcement contingencies. Experimental work on learning, focusing on the cognitive effects of various reinforcement contingencies, would offer a rich source of information for solving therapeutic problems of structural change; this research would indeed provide the mini-culture therapeutically indicated for specific structural deviances.

TOWARD AN INTEGRATED PSYCHOLOGICAL THEORY

The considerations developed in this introduction to the subject matter of our book propose an important conclusion: The cognitive structure of social events, used as a central concept, leads to convergence and integration for different areas of psychology, which have tended to grow increasingly apart. In this framework, development becomes the process through which the structure of society is acquired by the individual member; abnormal psychology becomes concerned with the patterns of structural deviance; experimental psychology investigates the effects of environmental structures on the organization of the individual and thus provides techniques for structural change which can be applied to psycho-therapy. At the same time, cross-cultural comparison of various structures may indicate what aspects of the structure are basic and invariant and what are the differentiating aspects. Thus, while deviance patterns of individuals may provide a taxonomy of psychopathology, cross-cultural comparison leads to a classification of cultures on the basis of their different structural characteristics. Through the following chapters of this volume we shall consider the interdependence among these various aspects of the social environment. We begin by describing the development of its cognitive representation.

PART I

STRUCTURAL

CHAPTER 2

THE DEVELOPMENT OF BASIC
SOCIAL CONCEPTS

Overview

MUCH OF THE WORK on child development and on the socialization process deals mainly with *how* the child acquires
social behavior (e.g., Aronfreed, 1969; Bandura, 1969; Gewirtz, 1969).
A typical procedure in this line of research consists of choosing a given
behavioral class, such as aggression or self-criticism, and investigating
the mechanisms (imitation, reinforcement) by which this behavior is
acquired, as well as the conditions facilitating or hindering its
acquisition. The cognitive organization (along psychological dimensions) of the behaviors learned is at most noted as an open problem.
Thus Gewirtz (1969, p. 74) refers to "dimensional learning" and
Aronfreed, more explicitly, states that "It is the cognitive structures
which are transmitted in the verbal communication of socializing
agents, rather than the cues which are immediately inherent in overt
behavior. . . . These concepts and standards can be used to make
complex discriminations within and among large classes of behavior,
along cognitive dimensions which represent the properties of the
behavior . . ." (1969, p. 183).

The present chapter specifies those concepts which are transmitted
through socialization. It describes *what* classes of social behaviors are
acquired by the child as well as their organization along psychological
dimensions. Occasionally we may offer hypotheses as to the conditions
which facilitate or inhibit the acquisition of a structure, but most of
our attention will be devoted to a description of the basic social concepts
which constitute the course of development of social cognitive structures. We shall first examine some general notions pertaining to cognitive development. The processes of differentiation and generalization
will be discussed in their relationship to cognitive growth, and the
notion of boundary will be elaborated. Then, we shall proceed with
specifying the differentiations which underlie elementary forms of

25

social behavior, namely, differentiation between acceptance and rejection, between self and other and among resources exchanged in interpersonal transactions. The differentiation between actual and ideal level, i.e., what is perceived as done and what ought to be done, will complete this review of the basic notions in social interaction. The last portion of the chapter takes up the problem of the developmental sequence among these differentiations, in the process of cognitive development.

SOME REMARKS ON COGNITIVE DEVELOPMENT

In the previous chapter an intuitive notion was given about some properties of a cognitive structure. The classes are ordered so that those containing similar messages are nearer to each other, while messages in the same class are equivalent in meaning. Whether any two messages are similar enough to enter the same class or different enough to go into separate classes is learned by interacting with members of a particular culture. When, for example, expressions of affect (love) and expressions of esteem (status) occur in separate occasions, or lead to different outcomes, two classes are needed for handling communications of love and of status in an efficient manner. Conversely when these behaviors have a high frequency of joint occurrence and/or lead to similar outcomes, they will be considered as equivalent. Consequently, contrary to a fairly common assumption (e.g., Capehart, Tempone and Hebert, 1969), equivalence in meaning does not necessarily reflect similarity of physical properties but rather depends on similarity of consequences.

At the beginning of his social life an infant will have very few categories, his classes of interpersonal behavior will be largely *undifferentiated*. He will not, for example, interact with a stranger differently than with one of the parents. But slowly, through successive steps of differentiation among social events, the structure will grow, and new classes will become available for sorting incoming and outgoing messages. Later on, a reverse process takes place: the child may behave in a similar way toward two persons to whom he previously behaved differently. Therefore, social development is conceived as a process of differentiation and generalization of social events. This view is similar to Piaget's conceptualization of cognitive development: "accommodation" is essentially a process of differentiation, while "generalizing assimilation" corresponds to generalization; the latter should not be confused with "recognitory assimilation," the assigning of a new stimulus to a pre-existing class, an operation which does not modify the cognitive structure. By contrast, cognitive structure does change in generalization: the emergence of a new dimension, on which previously differentiated classes have the same value, makes them more similar to one another. Closer to the viewpoint proposed here are Harvey, Hunt and Schroder who state that "learning occurs through a process of differentiation and integration, during which time the person breaks down the environment into parts relevant to his current conceptual structure . . ." (1961, p. 4).

Differentiation and Generalization

If generalization consists of discovering some common attributes between previously discriminated stimuli, then it should occur after differentiation between these stimuli has been established. Furthermore generalization is obtained when a successive differentiation, along a new dimension, takes place; the previously differentiated classes are then found to be similar on the newly established dimension. It is precisely this added dimension which allows generalization to occur. This relationship between differentiation and generalization may be clarified by the following example. The child first learns to interact differently with father and mother; later on he realizes that these two interactions have some common elements which differentiate them from interactions with siblings. Thus father-mother generalization, expressed by the term "parent," is based on the new differentiation between parents and siblings. To discover that two classes of social events have common features it is first necessary to recognize then as different and then to contrast them with a third class without the features. In a similar vein Harvey, Hunt and Schroder (1961, p. 88) suggest that any developmental stage is characterized by a new differentiation, which in turn requires a transitional stage of integrating the previous differentiation. Conceptualizing generalization as integration avoids confusing it with the undifferentiated state which precedes differentiation. This point is well made by R.W. Brown (1958) who states: "The child who spontaneously hits on the category four-legged animals will be required to give it up in favor of dogs, cats, horses, cows, and the like. When the names of numerous subordinates have been mastered, he may be given the name quadruped for the superordinate. This abstraction is not the same as its primitive forerunner. The schoolboy who learns the word quadruped has abstracted from differentiated and named subordinates. The child he was abstracted through a failure to differentiate. Abstraction after differentiation may be the mature process, and abstraction from a failure to differentiate the primitive. Needless to say, the abstractions occurring on the two levels need not be coincident, as they are in our quadruped example."

The literature on learning often treats non-discrimination and generalization as equivalent phenomena since behavior resulting from generalization may appear to be non-discriminative. Recent studies, however, suggest that non-discrimination yields flat gradients whereas generalization results in steep ones. Furthermore it seems that a generalization gradient cannot be established unless there is previous discrimination among the generalized stimuli. Peterson (1962) reared ducklings in a monochromatic light from the moment of hatching, and trained them to peck at a key that was also transilluminated by the same light. In a later generalization test these ducklings were exposed to other wavelengths of which they had no previous experience. No generalization gradient was established for this group. Similar results were obtained by Ganz and Riesen (1962) showing that macaque monkeys reared in darkness, later yielded a flat generalization gradient of wavelength. The gradient becomes, however, steeper through repetitions of the same generalization test. Jenkins and Harrison (1960) have further shown that exposure to a range of stimuli is not sufficient for obtaining generalization gradients and that an actual differential training should take place beforehand. Since, however, Jenkins and Harrison tested tone-frequency generalization while the other studies tested wavelength generalization it could be that, for a given species, discrimination between certain stimuli may be obtained by sheer exposure while for certain other stimuli an actual differential training is necessary in order to establish discrimination. All these studies, however, indicate that discrimination should occur before generalization can take place.

Differentiation and Cognitive Growth

We have proposed that cognitive development results from the twin processes of differentiation and generalization. Since generalization has been interpreted as an eventual by-product of a successive differentiation, the growth of social competence can be conceptualized as a sequence of differentiations, which increases the number of cognitive classes available for categorizing social events and provides a behavioral repertoire appropriate to each class. This view has been repeatedly advanced in the past: Kurt Lewin (1936, p. 155) stated that "the development of the life space from infancy to adulthood can be characterized to a large extent as a process of differentiation"; R.W. Brown (1958) said that "cognitive development is increasing differentiation"; and Parsons (1955) conceptualized socialization as a series of differentiations.

Cognitive growth begins when the first differentiation partitions the undifferentiated class of "all social events" into two compartments. The next differentiation subdivides the previous partition and results in four classes of events. Parsons (1955, pp. 395–399) has noted the similarity between this pattern of cognitive development and the early embryological stages; both develop by binary divisions: like cognitive classes, a cell divides into two, then each is again divided into two, and so on. Perhaps this parallelism between tissue growth and psychological growth is just a matter of curiosity. On the other hand, as Piaget (1952) has suggested, psychological functions may be modeled on pre-existing biological functions. Accepting the notion that nature is parsimonious, we expect a basic mechanism such as the binary division to serve more than one system. Such parallelism in functions cannot be proved or disproved; however, it is an assumption which is supported by some observations. It has been found (Cone, 1968) that some cancer cells are undifferentiated: a stimulus applied to one cell diffuses to the others as well; this does not happen in normal tissues. Similarly we have found (see p. 353) that underdifferentiation. among certain cognitive classes is found in schizophrenics. Thus in both cases underdifferentiation is associated with a pathological state.

In psychological structures, partitions are not tight, so that what happens in one class influences the state of neighboring compartments, although it may not affect the state of remote classes. Thus instead of defining a given social event as belonging to one, and only one class, it would be more appropriate to say that it belongs *mainly* to a given compartment but to a lesser degree it also belongs to proximal compartments. When somebody, for example, runs a personal errand for us we classify his behavior as "giving services," but also as a sign of friendship ("giving love"). These interrelationships of neighboring classes are reflected in language as well. Verbs pertaining to social interaction can be categorized into more than one behavioral class; "advising" definitely belongs to the class of "giving information," but it also may convey some loss of status for the advisee. In general we would expect to find many words expressing meaning which pertain to two *neighboring* classes and few words which will cover two *remote* classes. Thus semantic analysis provides a way for investigating the relative proximity of classes. A promising beginning in this direction has already been made. Osgood (1970) has proposed a scheme of *semantic features* for analyzing the language of interpersonal behavior. Wickens (1970) analyzed a series of experiments on short-term words recall; the results support the view that ". . . when a person hears or sees a word, the process of perceiving this word consists of encoding it within a number of different aspects, attributes, or conceptual psychological dimensions." He also noted that: "The results of the experiments indicate that different dimensions vary in their effectiveness for proactive inhibition release. In general, semantic dimensions (taxonomic categories or semantic differential) are highly effective, whereas physical characteristics such as word length or figure-ground colors of the slide presentation are relatively ineffective in releasing proactive inhibition."

Another approach to the study of mutual influences among classes consists of applying a stimulus to a given class and then observing the extent to which other classes are affected by it; obviously proximal classes should show a stronger effect than those which are remote from the stimulated class. Such gradient of effect has been repeatedly reported, sometimes under the different labels of *irradiation, diffusion,* and *response generalization* (Rosnow, 1968).

Boundaries

Since differentiation does not result in complete independence among differentiated events, the partitions between classes can be perceived as boundaries which are more or less permeable. Again, comparison of cognitive classes to cell tissues seems appropriate. The conceptualization of psychological structures as having permeable boundaries among their elements is well rooted in psychology though not always explicitly. The idea that psychological events (such as memories and emotions) may move from the unconscious to the conscious has been advanced by Freud, Jung and many others; it implies a permeable boundary between awareness and non-awareness. Lewin's notion of the nature of psychological boundaries is more explicit; for him the barrier (defined as a boundary which offers resistance to psychological locomotion) is like a more or less permeable membrane (1936, pp. 124–125).

In discussing various types of boundaries Ruesch (1956, p. 341) notes: ". . . Many terms in psychiatric practice essentially refer to boundaries. The term dependent, which is used psychiatrically in many different ways, refers to people who eliminate certain boundaries. If you have two people who are mutually interdependent, both have formed a symbiotic system in which they function as a unit. Consider the case of compulsive people who stick to rules and rituals and do things just so. They seem to classify, order and divide, and they see boundaries where others do not see them. Informal people, in contrast, by mutual consent omit formalities and temporarily discard existing boundaries." Later, in the same paper (p. 343), he states: "Perceptual boundaries exist where the stimulation changes. If there is continuous stimulation, there is no boundary. If it stops, or becomes more intensive, or decreases, or changes in nature, there we detect a boundary . . . whenever there is a change of discontinuity, the chances of finding boundaries increase."

It is easy to conceptualize the notion of boundary in physical terms. When one steps out of the door, he has just crossed the boundary between the house and the back yard. Similarly the boundary between two cells is marked by a visible membrane. But what is a *cognitive* boundary? Events are categorized into classes according to specific criteria which consist of dividing a given dimension or coordinate into parts. This division is the product of differentiation. We shall call the cognitive dimension along which a differentiation occurs *facet*, and the notions differentiated *facet elements*. The conceptual difference between two elements is a cognitive boundary. A class of events is defined by a combination of elements from different facets. Thus any two classes may have one or more boundaries, depending on the number of elements in which they differ. The differentiation between domestic and wild animals provides a boundary between the class of cats and the class of jaguars, although both are feline; dogs and cats are both domestic but only the latter is a feline.

The weaker the differentiation between the facet elements the more permeable the boundary is. Empirically a weak boundary will result in: (a) high relationship between events belonging to the two classes, which differ in the elements of a given dimension; (b) when one such class is manipulated, the other class will also be affected. For most purposes cats and dogs are considered more similar than cats and jaguars, so that the boundary between canine and feline is more permeable than the one between wild and domestic. On the other hand a jaguar and a cat are more similar than a bird and a cat, the last pair having more than one boundary between them. Thus the relationship between two classes is dependent on the number of boundaries between them as well as on their permeability.

In conclusion, social growth is a process by which more and more classes are added to the cognitive structure of an individual by a sequence of differentiations along given dimensions or facets. Often, but not always, each successive differentiation occurs along a new dimension, thus resulting in the subdivision of the classes which previously existed according to the dimension newly introduced. Hence the facets of differentiation are not specific to one or few classes, but cut across all the classes of a given domain. Consequently a few facets are sufficient to produce a large number of classes, an arrangement which is most economical. For example: six facets, with two elements each, will bound or define 64 classes. The number of classes is simply obtained by multiplying across all facets the number of elements of each facet. Thus the many classes used for categorizing social events can be described by a relatively small number of facets, differentiated into their elements. To these differentiations we now turn.

DIMENSIONS OF SOCIAL INTERACTION

In the remaining part of this chapter we shall be concerned mainly with describing the dimensions or facets which, by being differentiated,

lead to a classification of social events. Because of the strong relationship between the developmental sequence of these dimensions and
the structural properties of social cognition, a systematic discussion
of the sequence will be given in the next chapter, which deals with
cognitive structures. However, since each successive differentiation
rests on previous ones, a presentation of the dimensions cannot be
entirely divorced from their sequence. We shall thus begin with the
earliest development.

The Foundation: Acceptance and Rejection

Observation of a new-born infant suggests that he possesses at least
one differentiation, so that from the first minute of his life he can
classify events into the two classes of comfort and distress; a stimulus
may be pleasant or unpleasant. Accordingly he has two gross types
of behaviors: he can either take the nipple (*accepting*) when it adds
to his comfort or he may refuse (*rejecting*) it when it disturbs his pleasant
sensation; he will swallow the milk or he may throw it up. This inborn
differentiation is purely physiological. However, it constitutes the basis
for cognitive differentiation. In the first months of life the infant is
mainly enlarging these two classes of acceptance and rejection or
"pleasure and pain" (Anna Freud, 1965, p. 58), by including in each
class more and more stimuli. Now it is not only the milk and warmth
of the mother's body which makes him feel pleased but also certain
colors and certain objects (toys); unfamiliar objects or noises are incor-
porated into the unpleasant class.

It is convenient to have a term for each dimension and we shall
indicate this first one as differentiation of *mode* or *direction*. The labels
of acceptance and rejection are suitable for naming the two poles of
this dimension at the early stages of cognitive development: they provide a link to physiological mechanism and implicitly convey the notion
that affect is a prominent resource in early transactions with mother.
Acceptance of a child is expressed by *giving* him affection and care;
rejection is deprivation of both or *taking away*. Later on, when
resources other than love and care become differentiated, it will be
more appropriate to denote the elements of the mode by giving and
taking away, rather than by acceptance and rejection.

Self-Other Differentiations

Self and not-self are standard terms in immunology (Burnet, 1969)
by which the organism's rejection of foreign cells and acceptance of
its own is indicated. Thus, like acceptance and rejection, the cognitive
distinction between self and not-self may have a physiological
forerunner. Unlike the former, however, it is not manifested behaviorally in the first few months of life and consequently the idea that

the newborn infant does not differentiate between self and other is widely accepted. J.M. Baldwin (1894) described this state by the term "adualism" where no consciousness of the self exists; Freud talked about a state of "primary narcissism," which was later elaborated by Anna Freud (1965) as lack of differentiation between self and other. There is considerable agreement that the differentiation between self and non-self is the basis for social growth. When such differentiation is achieved the child is able to observe an action and say whether it was emitted by him or by somebody else and whether it was directed toward him or toward the other. Moreover, the child may realize that his interpretation of a certain event may not correspond to the other's interpretation. These examples suggest that the distinction between self and other occurs on more than one dimension. It might refer to the person doing the action, to the target of it and to the viewpoint taken.

The first two differentiations between self and other are primed by sensoric and motoric perceptions. When the child is fed he gets sensoric feedback coming from tasting the food. Later on when he becomes able to grasp the food with his hands and put it into his mouth, the previous sensoric feedback is combined with the motoric feedback of him putting the food in his mouth. Now the child starts to differentiate between self and non-self as *actors*. When mother is the actor only sensoric feedback is experienced; when he himself is the actor both motoric and sensoric stimuli are present. The child comes to differentiate self from non-self as actors on the basis of the fact that sometimes sensory and motor feedback are correlated (when self is actor) and sometimes they are not (when other is actor). Behavior toward self thus precedes differentiation between actors. However, when a preference for one of the two behaviors (feeding himself or being fed) is manifested and extended to other behaviors of the same type, we are justified to state that differentiation has been established.

Observations made on an eight month old baby girl revealed that acquisition of the skill to feed herself was almost immediately followed by refusal to take food from others. Thus acceptance was linked to the behavior emitted by self, and rejection to the behavior of other. We interpret this pattern as a device for strengthening the newly-acquired differentiation between actors by pairing it to the pre-existing differentiation between acceptance and rejection. For this particular linkage to occur, the motoric feedback should be pleasant for the baby. Imagine how difficult it would be for the baby to acquire new behaviors if self as an actor was linked to rejection. The idea that being an actor is a source of pleasure has already been advanced by Piaget (1952) in the concept of "circular response." Piaget conceives of a sort of sensuous satisfaction in the exercise of schemas, especially those that are not yet fully adapted to the circumstances (Baldwin, A.L., 1967, p. 197). As Kohlberg (1969a, p. 450) aptly notes: "At this point, the desire for mastery is reflected in the need to do things oneself. A typical incident is a two-year-old's frustration at putting on his coat, followed by a temper tantrum if his mother tries to help him. The temper tantrum indicates that the child clearly differentiates what he can cause from what others can do, and as a result only what he can do leads to a sense of mastery."

The differentiation between actors provides the baby with perception of himself as an actor. At this stage the baby mostly does things for himself, i.e., he is the object of his own behavior. Some time later a new kind of behavior appears: he begins to put food in the mouth of the other. This new behavior signals the occurrence of yet another differentiation: this time between self and other as *objects or targets* of behavior. Once again the same behavior (feeding by self) leads to different sensations. When the baby feeds himself he gets both kinesthetic and gustatory feedback whereas feeding the mother results in kinesthetic feedback only. Often we observe that a baby alternates between feeding himself and feeding the other "one spoon to Jimmy and one spoon to mommy"; this behavior may be interpreted as an exercise in the newly acquired differentiation between objects—feeding *himself* and feeding the *other*.

Initially, both differentiation (of actors and objects) are linked to acceptance and rejection: there is an acceptance of the other as an object when the self is an actor—and rejection of the other as an actor when the self is an object. When the two differentiations are established their linkage to acceptance and rejection is loosened, and the whole range of combinations of the three differentiations, resulting in eight classes, becomes available for sorting interpersonal events. Figure 1

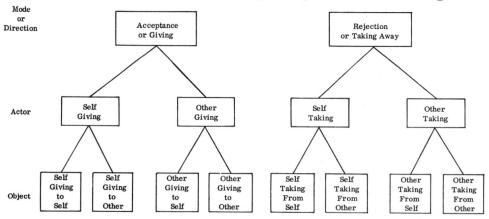

Figure 1. A schematic representation of eight classes of social events resulting from three successive differentiations.

represents the eight classes in a schematic way. This scheme is merely a way to summarize the differentiations discussed so far and should not be interpreted as reflecting the structural relationship among classes. The reasons for this note of caution will become apparent in the next chapter.

Some of the classes are self explanatory; observation of giving things to the other or taking away things from him are very common. Even the behaviors of giving to self may be intuitively understood, but when does the self take away from self? Concepts such as self-rejection or self-criticism represent examples of this class; the child takes away love from himself when he addresses himself by saying: "Johnny is a bad boy," "Johnny is mean." Behavior toward oneself, such as talking when alone, is not uncommon among young children, but tends to disappear with age, probably because it violates cultural norms. Even in the absence of overt behavior one does continue to relate to self.

The emergence of the differentiations between actors and between objects has the important effect of enabling the child to relate his own behavior to the behavior directed by other toward him and to develop contingent expectations regarding the probability that a given proaction will be followed by a given reaction. Establishment of the proaction-reaction sequence, in turn, provides the ground for two further developments: the notion of norm or ideal and the notion of reciprocal roles, roles of self toward other and of other toward self. Both these notions will be considered later.

The proaction-reaction sequence also provides a basis for imitative behavior. Moreover, the cognitive classes acquired offer a classification of the various types of imitation:

1. The child does to himself what mother does to him—feeds himself.
2. The child does to mother what mother does to him—tries to help her dress up, combs her hair.
3. The child does to mother what mother does to herself—puts jewelry on her.
4. The child does to himself what mother does to herself—puts make-up on his face.

The last class has been often termed as "taking the role of the other" (O'Toole and Dubin, 1968) rather than imitation proper.

Imitation is extended also to interaction with other people and to objects such as dolls, thus providing the beginning of role differentiation. The examples of imitative behavior illustrate the fact that we can hardly talk about any behavior without specifying its content. To specify *what* is given or taken away, we shall turn to discuss a further series of differentiations which results in formation of resource classes.

Interpersonal Resources

In the previous section we discussed the development of two aspects of an action: *who* is doing the action and towards *whom* it is directed. Earlier we have proposed that an action results in a gain (giving) or in a loss (taking away) for the object. Thus social action has been conceptualized as a behavior through which the actor increases or decreases the amount of *something* possessed by the object, by giving to or taking it away from him; in short, interpersonal behavior is a channel for resource transmission. Accordingly, a resource is any commodity—material or symbolic—which is transmitted through interpersonal behavior. In a similar vein, Levinger (1959, p. 84) defines a resource as "any property of an individual which he makes available to persons in his environment as a means for their positive or negative need-satisfaction."

The messages exchanged between adults present a great variety and several classes are needed to classify them adequately. There are messages dealing with love or affect such as "your company is very pleasant," or "you are charming." There are messages of status, like "well done," "I am honored by your presence here." Other messages deal with information which does not refer to either love or status: "It is five o'clock," "The door is on the left side," "Two and two make four." Goods, material things of any sort, and money are also resources exchanged in interpersonal situations. Finally, one may give services, increasing the recipient's physical comfort, by running an errand for him, doing something to his body (cutting his hair), or to his belongings (cleaning his clothes). Altogether we have listed six classes of resources: *Love, status, information, money, goods* and *services*. The usefulness of this classification and its fitness to people's perception of social behavior will be discussed later. For the time being let us accept it provisionally and turn to the development of these classes in childhood.

The resources received by an infant at the beginning of his life constitute an undifferentiated bundle of love and service: the flowing milk, the warmth and softness of the mother's body and her care for him are all presented simultaneously. The differentiation between love and services becomes possible after the child has acquired some psychomotoric skills, sufficient for serving himself, like feeding himself, washing hands, etc. At this time mother can give him love without services, by requesting him to serve himself and at the same time encouraging him to do so. "The child then is to her no longer alone the object of her care, but also the object of her *love* . . ." (Parsons, 1955, p. 70). Thus differentiation between love and services is again built on the previous differentiation between self and other as *actors;* mother gives love (to the child), the child gives services (to himself), so that love is linked to the "other as an actor" and services is linked to "self as an actor." In both cases the child is the object of the action. Again, when the boundary between love and services is established all possible combinations of self and other as actors and as objects with respect to these two resources occur. The child provides services not only for himself but also for other persons, and "he not only is loved, but he actively loves" (Parsons, 1955, p. 43).

A situation in which love and services were provided by different actors from the onset, was experimentally devised by Harlow (1958): infant monkeys were placed with two mother surrogates, a cloth surrogate—warm and soft (giving love) and a wire surrogate—hard and cold. Only one of the two mothers lactated; thus in the group where the wire mother provided milk (service) the two resources of love and service were given by different mothers. The monkeys developed affection (giving love) for the soft mother, independently of whether she lactated or not. These results show that attachment or giving love to the other is related to receiving love and not to receiving services. However, three of the four monkeys nursed by the cloth mother preferred to spend most of the time being close to the surrogate rather than to a gauze-covered heating pad that was on the floor of the cages (Harlow and Zimmerman, 1959). It seems that it is precisely the initial non-differentiation between services and love, which is responsible for the amazing attachment to the mother.

Subsequently to the differentiation between love and services, goods are differentiated from services and status from love. Consumption goods, like food, are hard to differentiate from service because they appear simultaneously with service and are used only once. It is only when the child realizes that some objects disappear (the notion of "all gone") while others can be used again and again that the differentiation between services and goods becomes feasible. The differentiation of esteem or status from love requires some acquisition of language since most behaviors which pertain to status ("gee you did it") are verbal. In many cultures distinction between status and love overlaps with differentiation between mother and father as social objects, which we shall encounter later: love is often given mainly by mother and status by father (Parsons, 1955, p. 45; Zelditch, 1955). It is interesting to note that evolvement of status from love is also evident in some species; submissive gestures of dogs contain certain friendly elements which arise directly from the relation of the young animal to its mother, and the submissive behavior of baboons evolved from the female invitation to mate (Lorenz, 1966, pp. 135–136).

In the last stage of resource differentiation, money is differentiated from goods and information from status. For a two-year-old child money is perceived as a shiny object or a piece of paper. It gets its distinctive meaning when the child realizes that money may be exchanged for goods. Rarely is a child able to get goods immediately after receiving money, so that the perception of money as a resource requires the ability to delay rewards and anticipate an event which will take place in the future. Close relationship between differentiation of money from goods and ability to delay rewards is supported by experiments in behavior modification. Children have been trained to regard tokens as reinforcers (a type of money) by pairing them with appreciable goods, like M & M candies (Hamblin, Buckholdt, Bushell, Ellis and Ferritor, 1969). The notion that money is exchangeable for most other resources and thus has a generalized and intrinsic value, comes only later.

Parents usually expect their two-year-old child to repeat the information they give him (e.g., parents point at an object, call it by name and ask the child to repeat it). A successful repetition is usually followed by a praise. Thus information is almost always paired with status, and consequently these two classes are hardly distinguishable. When the child broadens his social world and enters a peer group, he discovers criteria for status, other than information, such as physical strength. This new situation facilitates differentiation of information from status.

A schematic representation of the differentiation of resource classes is given in Fig. 2. In this figure a newly differentiated class is indicated by a double frame.

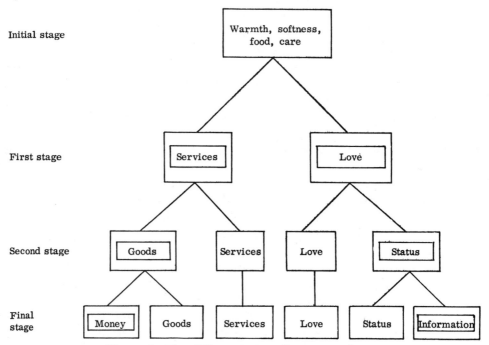

Figure 2. The differentiation of resource classes.

We have already noted that differentiation does not result in complete independence; since boundaries among classes are permeable, some relationship still exists. Children insist on receiving services from others long after being able to serve themselves, since being served is interpreted as being loved. Similarly an adult may prefer a restaurant where "service is good" (i.e., where love and concern is given in addition to service). The original non-differentiation of love and service is maintained to a large extent in sex, although some sexual relations are mainly viewed as an exchange of services while in some others, the exchange of love dominates. These examples suggest that service and love are not fully differentiated. The same is true for the second class which is differentiated from love, namely status. Messages such as "I am very proud of you" contain both love and status elements; more often than not, we tend to respect the people we do love. The close relationship between status and love is reflected in the fact that often they are combined together in psychological studies under the variable "attraction," or "liking." However some investigators like Jones, Bell and Aronson (1972) noted that the notion of "attraction" contains two distinct classes: social attractiveness which is equivalent to love, and competence which we call status.

The relationship between status and information is reflected in the common expectation that high status individuals are perceived as a more reliable source of information and advice than low status ones. Some evidence to this effect is provided by the finding that children tend to imitate more high status adults (Baldwin, A.L., 1967, p. 431). The same phenomenon seems to take place among monkeys (Hall, K.R., 1963), and in experiments on conformity where statements attributed to prestigeful individuals were more likely to be accepted (Asch, 1948; Lewis, H.B., 1941; Sherif, 1935b). Informal observation suggests that wise men are honored and the humble are assumed to be ignorant.

The less differentiated the resources the more likely they are to be conveyed together in the same behavior: rare is an expression of love which does not include some connotation of status or services, while a gift—the simultaneous giving of love and goods is a less common occurrence, often reserved for special occasions.

The degree of permeability of any given boundary between two resources depends on the developmental sequence. Resources which are proximal in this sequence are more related, more likely to occur jointly, and will tend to be perceived as more similar than remote ones; love and status, for example, have more in common than love and money. This partial differentiation leads to an order among resource classes whereas complete differentiation would have resulted in independence among the classes and the structure of resources which will be presented and discussed in the next chapter would not have been developed.

Giving and Taking Away Resources

In discussing the development of resource classes we mainly referred to examples of behaviors in which resources are given by an actor to an object. We shall recall however that even when resources are still undifferentiated the infant already possesses the differentiation between acceptance and rejection; thus a resource can be taken away, as well as given. *Giving* is then defined as *increasing* the amount of resources available to the object; conversely, *taking away* is a *decrease* in the amount of resources available for the object. Thus giving love is expressing acceptance, friendship and liking; taking away love means rejection, expressing disliking or hate. Giving status means expressing esteem and respect while taking away status is done by indicating disesteem by belittling or by giving a low rating. Cheating, misleading and deceiving are examples of taking away information: the deceived is left with less information than he had beforehand, while when being given information the amount of knowledge one possesses is increased. Taking away and giving goods or money are self-evident notions. For services, taking away means damaging the body (e.g., spanking) or the belongings of the object, while giving services would increase the object's physical comfort, or save him expenditure of energy, such as running an errand for him.

For taking away, as for giving, the boundaries between resources proximal in the developmental sequence are more permeable than those between remote resources. Thus the probability of taking away, simultaneously, two proximal resources is higher than a joint occurrence of taking away two remote resources. One may hit physically the hated person; the word "insult" conveys the taking away of both love and status; the confidence man is likely to take away both information and money. On the other hand the thief is unlikely to express hate for his victim and physical assault does not go well together with cheating.

Having differentiated between giving and taking away between self and other as objects and actors and among resource classes, the child is equipped with the necessary tools for classifying social actions. These differentiations yield a $2 \times 2 \times 2 = 8$ types of behaviors for each resource, or a total of $8 \times 6 = 48$ classes of interpersonal behavior. The ability to classify actions does not terminate social development, neither does it provide sufficient equipment for becoming a member of a given society. One should be able to tell whether a given action is appropriate and one should also realize that different people may hold different opinions about a given action. To the development of these notions we now turn.

Norms and Viewpoints

In the previous section we have covered all the concepts necessary for classifying actions emitted in a given dyad, such as child-mother. Having acquired the differentiation between modes, actors, objects, and resources the child is able to attribute a meaning to what is actually done by himself and by his mother. He is also able to relate his behavior to the behavior of his mother. But any given dyadic relationship, or a role, includes more than the emission of actions. There are also expectations and wishes which characterize this relationship. They may be presented in terms of "what does mother want me to do"? "What do I want mother to do?" and then "What should I do?" and "What should mother do?" These questions provide a hint to an additional differentiation between self and other.

While the previous differentiations of actors and objects were based originally on sensoric-motoric feedbacks the new differentiations depend on social feedback, i.e., on the reaction of the parent to the behavior of the child. It is precisely the previous development of the notions actor and object, which has provided the cognitive tools necessary for relating the behavior of self to the behavior of other. In fairly normal conditions the reaction of the adult will tend to be contingent upon the proaction of the child. Certain proactions of the child will be followed by love giving behavior of the parent while certain other proactions will usually be followed by taking away behavior. If there is a certain consistency in the reaction of the adult, the child will come to expect this reaction. An attentive observer will notice that one-year-old or slightly older children often probe the proaction-reaction relationship by looking for the expected reactions as soon as they have initiated the proaction. Many little children's games, like peek-a-boo or superimposing hand, have the same goal: exercising the proaction-reaction sequence. To the grown-up these games may look somewhat boring, because of their utter predictability. For the young child their outcome is still uncertain and each confirmation becomes a source of delight.

Predictability of the reaction means essentially that proaction is classified according to the reaction which follows it. Two important classes are: behaviors which are followed by mother's acceptance and those which are followed by rejection. This is the beginning of the notion of normative or *ideal behavior*. The occurrence of this development requires a certain consistency in the reactions to the child's behavior. When the reaction of the grown-up depends on his mood or on his relations to a third individual rather than on the actual behavior of the child, the child is not provided with an opportunity for differentiating between what ought to be done and what ought not to be done; proaction and reaction will tend to statistical independence, creating a random environment similar to the control condition in Rescorla's (1967) experimental design. But consistency alone is not a sufficient condition for differentiation to occur. When every action of the child is followed by punishment consistency is very high, but contingency is missing, and all the behaviors will be classified into one class of "ought not to be done." Perhaps the catatonic is the perfect example of such one-sided classification of behaviors. Through the process of consistent and contingent reaction, ideal or normative behavior becomes differentiated from actual behavior so that what ought to be done (in order to receive a reaction of giving) may or may not be identical with what is actually done. When such differentiation is possessed by the child, he is able to perceive himself tearing a book and at the same time classifying this behavior as "should not be done." On the basis of the two classes, *ideal* and *actual*, which emerge from the differentiation between levels of perception, we can define the concepts of expectation and aspiration. Both these notions are merely a projection of the actual and ideal levels into the future. Expectation refers to future actual behavior while aspiration is the future ideal behavior.

Again, this new differentiation between actual and ideal is linked to a previous differentiation—between self and other as actors. The ideal behavior is linked to the other as an actor, since it emerges from the mother's contingent behavior, while the actual is linked to the behaviors of the self; and again when differentiation between actual and ideal becomes more established it separates from the previous one and all four combinations take place. There is the actual behavior of self and the actual behavior of the other; i.e., what mother does and what I do. There is also the ideal behavior of the self and the ideal behavior of the other, i.e., what mother should do and what I should do.

An additional level of perception is the *desire* or the *wish*. Very early in his life the child becomes familiar with the experience that what *actually* happens does not always correspond to what he *desires*. For an infant, however, what he wishes is pleasurable and accepted; what he does not wish is painful and rejected. Hence the experience of a discrepancy between actual and wished for overlaps with the differentiation between acceptance and rejection. Moreover the discrepancy between actual and desired usually occurs when the other is the actor and the self is the object, since the infant is likely to do what he wishes, while mother may not always do what he wants. It is only with the onset of the ideal level that the child begins to do something against his own wishes. The child wants to wet his pants but his mother wants him to sit on the pot. In order to get mother's approval the child will sit on the pot, and now *he* is doing something that he does not wish to do. When this happens the early identity between wish and pleasure becomes untenable and the wish level emerges in its own right, as distinct from the actual and ideal ones.

When mother imposes her wishes on the child, the child realizes that what he wishes does not always correspond to what mother desires and a new differentiation begins to develop: the differentiation between the *viewpoint of the self and the viewpoint of the other*. When this differentiation is established the child becomes able to realize that other individuals may differ from him in the way they see a given actual behavior, or in what they believe to be an appropriate behavior, i.e., the ideal level. This differentiation enables the child to develop and construct an internal model of the other individual. Any event has two perspectives now, and thus is classified twice; from his own point of view and from the other's point of view.

Differentiation between actual and ideal levels permits the evaluation of what is being done by comparing it to what ought to be done, and thus provides the individual with internal standards of behavior. It would hardly be possible to exaggerate the pervasive importance of moral judgment for the functioning of the individual and of human society as well. It is therefore not surprising that this topic has attracted the attention of theoreticians and investigators and has resulted in a very large body of literature. Some recent and comprehensive treatments have been provided by Aronfreed (1968) and Kohlberg (1969b).

The acquisition of the viewpoint of the other has often been considered as the hallmark of mature social communication, enabling a person to take into account the other's perceptions, feelings and needs. Asch (1958) stated that "the study of person cognition is, in good part, the study of the ways in which we observe and take into account perceptions, intentions, thoughts, and passions of others." In Heider's discussion on perception and communication (1958) differentiation between viewpoints is perceived as the core of the difference between persons and non-persons interaction, since it is only on the basis of this differentiation that we become aware of the fact that as much as we perceive, we are also the objects of the other's perception.

Investigating the development of the ability to take the viewpoint of the other, P.H. Miller, Kessel and Flavell (1970) found an increase from the first to the fifth grade, leveling off afterward. While relatively little research was devoted to the development of the differentiation between viewpoints, there have been many studies of "assumed similarity" in which the perception of the subjects was compared with the perception they attribute to the other. The results (Byrne, 1969, pp. 42–44) suggest that differentiation between viewpoint is rather weak so that the perception ascribed to the other is more likely to be similar to the perception held by the self, than to this perception as reported by the other (i.e., real similarity).

With the differentiation between viewpoints we have concluded the review on the development of basic concepts of interpersonal communication in a child. Starting from the differentiation between modes, giving and taking away, we have discussed differentiation by actor and object, then differentiation of resources into six classes and, finally, the differentiations by level and viewpoint. In three of these differentiations, by actor, object and viewpoint, the differentiated classes have been indicated by the same terms of "self" and "other." In everyday language the structure of the sentence or the situation usually clarifies who is self and who is other in each one of these differentiations. If one says for example: "He thinks he was nice to me," it is clear that the actor is the other, the object is the self and the viewpoint is the other's. However, when these terms are considered in isolation there may be some ambiguity as to who is called self and who is called other. Viewpoint of the "other," for example, may mean either the viewpoint of the actor or the viewpoint of the person observing the action, when observer and actor are not the same individual. To avoid confusion let us agree on the following convention. With regard to the actor the term "self" indicates that the action is done by the individual observing the action, the observer, while the term "other" pertains to the non-observer. When a subject reports about his own behavior, he is the observer and the actor and therefore his report pertains to behavior of the "self." For example when mothers are interviewed with respect to their children's behavior, the mother is the observer and she reports on the other's (her child's) behavior, so that the actor is the "other." When she reports on her behavior she refers to behavior of "self."

As to the differentiation by object, the term "self" pertains to behaviors of the actor which are directed towards himself while the term "other" denotes behaviors of the actor towards the non-actor. In both the following statements the object is the self: "My son usually considers himself as an excellent student" (my son gives status to himself); "I consider myself a competent mother" (I give status to myself). For the differentiation by viewpoint the terms "self" and "other" are denoted with respect to the actor. When the actor's point of view is reported we refer to it as the self's point of view while the term "other" refers to the non-actor's perception. Thus "Ron thinks he is doing fine at school" and "I think I did a good job" both pertain to the self's point of view. "Dan thinks his father would not like his new painting" and "I think my husband would approve of my approach" are both reports about the other's point of view.

In summary, the term "self" is equivalent to the observer, for differentiation by actor; it denotes the actor in object and viewpoint differentiations, while the term "other" will be equivalent to non-observer and to non-actor, respectively.

ENVIRONMENTAL CONDITIONS AND THE DEVELOPMENT OF BOUNDARIES

So far we have described the essential dimensions required for the emergence of a mature person, who is capable of communicating efficiently with his social environment. Although it is not in the scope of this book to describe the mechanisms by which these differentiations are acquired we do have some thoughts in this line which we would like to share with the reader before leaving the topic of development.

As we have already stated, differentiation among conceptual elements (e.g., self and other) never results in complete independence. It follows that the child should learn an *appropriate degree* of differentiation rather than a complete one.

For any differentiation to occur, the child should be exposed to a great number of events belonging to the different classes. First he learns to discriminate between specific instances of the classes, so that when the events are slightly changed discriminative behavior disappears. It is only after being exposed again and again to different instances of the same classes, that the child's discrimination becomes associated with the relevant elements which differentiate between the two classes. For example, the child is praised when sharing a cookie with another child and punished when taking it from him; then praise is contingent upon giving a toy, a kiss, etc., and punishment comes after hitting or taking a toy from the other. Gradually the elements of "taking away" and "giving" any resource become relevant. At the same time the child is being hugged strongly when getting love from parents, the hugging may sometimes be an unpleasant experience and the kisses may be pleasant—he learns that as much as "giving" and "taking away" behaviors results in differential reaction, they still sometimes appear simultaneously so that differentiation is not complete.

In this acquisition of boundaries with an appropriate degree of permeability, there is an interplay between the mechanisms of learning: imitation and differential reinforcement. The child imitates the differentiating behaviors of the adult by perceiving the appropriate situational cues which are associated with different behaviors. At the same time the child's own behavior is followed by differential rewards and punishment, a contingency which also facilitates differentiation. Parents will, for example, punish the child for taking away behaviors and will reward him for giving behaviors. In this manner they provide models of giving (reward) and taking away (punishment) behaviors, while, at the same time, exposing the child to differential reinforcements of these behaviors when emitted by him.

The relationship among behavioral classes, or the appropriate degree of differentiation, is learned by imitation and reinforcement. The child observes that certain classes of behaviors are emitted simultaneously or successively by the model while the joint occurrence of certain other classes is rare. Likewise, certain behaviors emitted by himself result in similar responses while certain others produce differential responses. Reinforcements as well as punishments are mostly administered by parents on an intermittent schedule. More than this, the same behaviors may sometimes be punished and sometimes rewarded, although some behaviors would be reinforced most of the time and some others would mostly result in punishment. These "errors" in the schedule leave some relationship between differentiated classes while at the same time serve to stabilize the degree of differentiation, in its reflection on the frequency of emitting differential behaviors in different situations (Aronfreed, 1968, p. 23).

The two learning models, imitation and reinforcement, may lead to opposite predictions about change in the child's behavior. Consider, for example, a child who has been punished for beating his younger brother (taking away services). The imitation model predicts an increase in taking away behavior of the child, who will imitate the aggressive punitive parent. The reinforcement model, on the other hand, predicts a decrease of the punished behavior. A solution to this dilemma may be provided by the findings of Sears, Maccoby and Levin (1957, Ch. 7). Their results suggest that if the child takes away a service (e.g., beating) and he is punished by his parents by taking away the *same* resource from him (physical punishment) the imitation model will prevail and the child will show high frequency of taking away services. If, on the other hand, punishment consists of taking away from the child a *different* resource, such as status ("you are a bad boy") then the reinforcement model will operate, with consequent low frequency of the punished behavior. This interpretation of Sears' findings suggests that imitation is more resource-specific than reinforcement. Both mechanisms, however, require that the differentiation to be learned by the child pre-exists in the adult. If, in the behavior of the parents, giving and taking away are not well differentiated, it will be difficult for the child to acquire such a differentiation, since both imitation and differential reinforcement will produce poor differentiation. Evidence on this point is provided by McDavid and Schroder (1957). These authors subjected delinquent and non-delinquent adolescents to a test of interpreting interpersonal events in terms of success and failure or positive and negative. They found that normal boys differentiate well between positive and negative events, while delinquent boys did not differentiate at all. The author explains this difference in differentiation as a result of inconsistency of discipline. Other dimensions are similarly affected by parent-child interaction: when the behavior of the parents is determined by their own needs, rather than by those of the child, differentiation between self and other as objects may be impaired; likewise a child receiving money or goods where love and status would be appropriate, and vice versa, may experience difficulties in differentiating among resources.

Frustration and Delay of Reinforcement

We have suggested that several differentiations are linked, at their onset, to the basic differentiation between giving and taking away. In particular, we have said that self as an actor toward self is linked to giving or acceptance (a pleasurable sensation) while other as an actor toward self is rejected. The differentiation between ideal and actual is related to giving behavior of the other toward self and non-ideal consists of all behaviors which are followed by taking away reactions by the other toward self (i.e., punishment administered by the parents). At this point the ideal of the other and the ideal of the self are not differentiated. It is only when the child realizes that the viewpoint of the other may be different from his that the other may be perceived as having a different ideal.

Viewpoint is a most abstract notion which cannot be differentiated either by imitation or by differential reinforcement. If the parent reinforces behavior which is appropriate from his point of view this is perceived by the child as an ideal behavior, but not as a difference in opinion. It is only in situations of conflict between the parents and himself that the child may realize different viewpoints. When the child asks for candy just before mealtime and the mother refuses, the child is exposed to different opinions about having candy. If he does not get the candy he is frustrated, if he gets it there is no confrontation with a different viewpoint. Thus, through repeated instances of frustration and conflicts with other people, the differentiation between viewpoints is acquired. Moreover, the schedule of differential reinforcement and punishments exposes the child to many frustrations so that other differentiations involve frustration as well. We may conclude then, that exposure to frustration is a necessary condition for differentiation to develop and strengthen. A child who is never exposed to refusal will not develop differentiation between actual and ideal and between his viewpoint and the other's viewpoint. Children at the age of one to three years old are said to be negativistic. They reject almost any request coming from other persons. One has the impression that they are "seeking" a disapproval from the parents; they do things that they know would result in negative response. This negativistic behavior may be interpreted as an exercise for establishing the differentiation of the self viewpoint from that of the other. In Piaget's terminology a new schema is developed and there is an intrinsic motivation to exercise it until it is established. Indeed, past the third year negativistic behavior decreases and the child does not deliberately confront himself with frustrating situations. Still many situations embed frustrating elements for children as well as for the adults. Any situation in which reinforcement is delayed is frustrating (Bandura and Walters, 1963). We do see, however, an increased ability in children to accept a delay of reinforcement without too much distress. For this to happen the child should have accumulated the resources of love and status, so that he may constitute an independent source of resources for himself. He should be able to give love and status to himself, as intermediate reinforcement, while working toward a delayed reward. The separation of the ideal behavior from the other's reaction (i.e., internalizing it) is a necessary condition for such self-reinforcement, and thus is a prerequisite for long-term delay of reward.

SUMMARY

Cognitive growth consists of a sequence of differentiations and generalizations, the latter being a by-product of the former. Generalization, which follows differentiation, is altogether different from the initial state of non-differentiation. Basic cognitive elements for interpersonal relations are acquired mainly through a process of binary division. These elements, however, are never fully differentiated, so that some relationship between them remains. Consequently the boundaries among cognitive classes are permeable. The closer two classes are in the developmental sequence the more permeable will be the boundary between them.

Six basic dimensions or facets, each differentiated into elements, underlay the development of the classes essential to the cognition of social events. The first dimension, *the mode or direction*, appears differentiated from the beginning of the infant's life; it contains the two elements of *giving* (acceptance) and *taking away* (rejection). Consequently the new born infant is capable of sorting events into two classes: events which are pleasurable are categorized into the class of giving while painful events are classified as taking away. The existence of cognitive classes in the infant is inferred from the fact that certain events are followed by the same or similar responses while certain others are met with different reactions.

The second dimension, the *actor* (who is doing the action), is differentiated into the elements of *self* and *other*. Its acquisition is based on the motoric feedback that the infant gets when he is the doer of the action, and which is missing when the other is the actor. Within a short period of time a third differentiation occurs resulting in acquisition of the notion *object* or recipient of behavior; again the elements are *self* and *other*. This dimension is based on a sensoric feedback. When the infant is feeding himself he can taste the food, when he feeds his mother, the motoric feedback still exists, but no gustatory sensation follows. These two differentiations between self and other as actors and objects are exercised and sharpened by attaching their elements to the previously established elements of acceptance and rejection. Self as an actor and other as an object are accepted; while other being the actor and self being its object are rejected. This attachment results in the "negativistic" period, evident in children age one to three years.

On the basis of the differentiation between self and other as actor, a new dimension starts its development when the child is required to do things, i.e., to serve himself, and at the same time these actions are reinforced by the mother's love. Thus *interpersonal resources* start to be formed into distinct classes with the differentiation between *love* and *services*. Next, *goods* are differentiated from services and *status* from love. Later on, *information* and *money* become distinct classes. Altogether six classes of resources become available for classifying social events.

The four dimensions of mode, actor, object and resources result in $2 \times 2 \times 2 \times 6 = 48$ classes of social actions in a dyad. But any given social interaction consists of more than emission of actions. There are wishes, expectations and norms of each person. To account for these aspects two additional dimensions are developed: the *level* of an event may be either *actual* (what is actually done) or *ideal* (what should be done). For the infant, the wished and ideal are equivalent. They become differentiated when the child is required to do things (to be the actor) against his wishes.

The last dimension, the *viewpoint*, results from yet another differentiation between *self* and *other*; the child learns that an event may be perceived differently by him and by the other; having candy before a meal may be a desirable event for him but not for his mother. These two last dimensions increase the number of social cognitive classes to 192, each defined by one element from each dimension.

None of the notions proposed here to account for the cognitive development of social interaction is novel. They are all current in psychological literature and have been the object of many studies.

Yet there is some virtue in bringing them together in a systematic manner and in showing that a large number of classes can be accounted for by the combination of a few basic notions. Laying bare the component elements of cognitive classes does more than just provide more parsimonious definition; it also reveals their similarities and differences. Consider, for example, the notion of self-esteem, central to the brilliant study of Coopersmith (1967), who investigated both its social consequences and its socialization antecedents. For the reader of this chapter it will be clear that self-esteem is a complex notion involving an actor, a mode (giving), a resource (status) and an object (self). Translating self-esteem into "the actor gives status to self" may appear as merely pedantic, but immediately it invites hypotheses regarding the relationship between this cognitive class and similar ones, differing from it in actor, mode, resource or object, such as getting status from other or taking away status from self. Such relationships among cognitive classes are considered in the next chapter.

CHAPTER 3

FROM DEVELOPMENTAL SEQUENCE TO ADULT STRUCTURE

Overview

HAVING DEFINED "structure" as "a configuration of classes in a space of stated coordinates" (Ch. 1), we have, in Chapter 2, proceeded to spell out basic cognitive classes of social events by identifying the coordinates along which they become differentiated. We have thus considered two of the notions appearing in the definition of structure—classes and coordinates. In the present chapter we turn to examine the third notion: the configuration of classes. In this configuration certain classes are nearer to each other while certain others are more distant. We are already familiar with a psychological interpretation of distance: the nearer two classes are, the more likely they are to be similar in meaning, to influence each other and to occur jointly in interpersonal situations.

We propose that the spatial arrangement of the classes originates from the sequence in which various differentiations develop in the child. In this chapter we shall derive structural hypotheses from the development sequence and then examine pertinent results. The instruments and the procedures by which these data were collected are described in Appendix A. The reader who is interested in methodology may wish to consult this appendix before proceeding with the findings.

The sequence of differentiations has been mentioned in the previous chapter only to the extent that this was necessary in describing the various dimensions. However, in view of its importance in determining the adult's structure, it becomes appropriate to begin this chapter with a more systematic treatment of the developmental sequence.

DIFFERENTIATION SEQUENCES

It was already noted that for some differentiation to develop, certain others should have already been established, so that the latter should occur in an earlier age than the former. It seems improbable that all social dimensions develop in a single sequence, one after the other. Most likely, some differentiations occur almost simultaneously and fairly independently of one another. Therefore we shall first consider some partial sequences and then discuss the relationship among them. For purposes of convenience and clarity we treat each differentiation as an all-or-none phenomenon, as if it were established at a given point in the developmental sequence. Obviously this presentation grossly simplifies the developmental process. It is more accurate to conceive each differentiation as a process in time, consisting of a gradual and slow build up of a boundary between classes, through the repeated occurence of events which reinforce the boundary, until it becomes well established and its permeability stabilizes. Thus the statement that differentiation B follows differentiation A should be understood to mean that the onset of B follows the onset of A; it is quite likely, however, that the beginning of B will occur *before* the stabilization of A.

Let us first examine and describe separately two partial sequences of differentiations, and then link them into a more complete picture. The first sequence includes the differentiations by mode, object, and resources (love and status). The second, involves the differentiation by actor, level and viewpoint. We shall refer to the first sequence as a *behavioral* one; the second will be called a *perceptual* sequence.

The Behavioral Sequence

The initial differentiation in this sequence results in the two classes of giving and taking away, which first appear in the primitive form of accepting and rejecting at a physiological level. Observation on neonates suggests that positive responses or approach behavior is present from the first minute after birth while withdrawal or rejection develops later on. Schaller and Emlen (1962, cited by Salzen, 1970) have found that avoidance responses are absent at first in precocial birds and appear by about ten hours after birth. They also find that for an altricial species, all objects were accepted and given positive rather than negative response until several days after birth. The observation that approach precedes avoidance response is also evident in imprinting (Lorenz, 1935) when precocial birds follow any object present immediately after emerging from the egg. As to the human neonate, the Darwinian reflex appears shortly after birth and when it disappears, intentional grasping starts to develop with a chronological overlapping of the two (Halverson, 1936). Little is known about early avoidance behavior. On a rational level, one should approach objects in order to survive and only later reject those things which interfere with survival. Thus the neonate approaches the nipple and swallows the milk; it is only when he is satiated that he drops the nipple or gets rid of an excess amount of milk.

The elementary classification of events in terms of pleasant-unpleasant (acceptance and rejection) is necessary before the notions of actor and object become relevant and then meaningful. At the same time the development of the notion to *whom* (self or other) an action is directed precedes the differentiation of the resources involved. While differentiation by object can develop in the dyadic interaction of infant-mother, the latter differentiation between status and love requires the additional infant-father role. It is only with the ability to differentiate between same-sexed and different-sexed roles that the differentiation between love and status can be developed. (A more detailed discussion on this point is provided in Chapter 4.)

In view of these considerations it is suggested that in the behavioral sequence differentiation between giving and taking will occur first, followed by differentiation between self and other as objects, while status and affect are the last to be differentiated. The three stages of this proposed sequence are represented, schematically, in Figure 3. In this figure each successive binary division is built on the previous one. The inner circle represents the first differentiation between giving and taking away. At the next stage (second circle from the center of

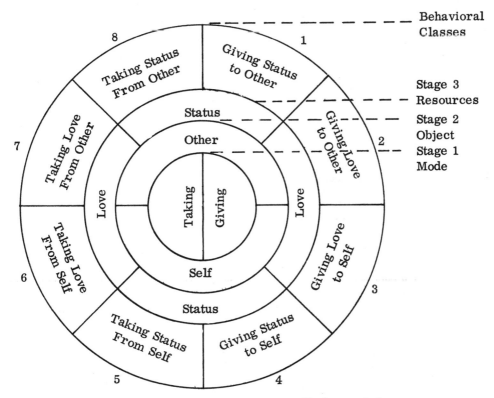

Figure 3. Differentiation sequence of behavioral classes.

the figure) the differentiation between self and other as objects is superimposed on the previous one. Thus, while in the first stage only the two simple classes of giving and taking away are available, at the completion of the second stage the repertoire of behavioral classes is doubled to four: giving to and taking from other, giving to and taking from self. At this second stage the differentiation of resources has probably yet to begin so that the four behavioral classes involve a single undifferentiated resource. When the first differentiation between resources occurs, the number of behavioral classes is doubled again to eight. The differentiation between status and love is represented in the third circle of Figure 3. The eight classes of behavior, resulting from the three stages are given in the outer circle of the figure.

The reader will probably wonder why we have chosen love and status as an example for resource differentiation, even though the distinction of services from love was said to appear earlier. The only reason for this choice was the fact that the relationship between status and love had been studied intensively by the first author before the classification of resources was developed. Consequently the order among the behavioral classes, represented in the outer circle of Figure 3, was empirically studied mainly with respect to love and status. Its extension to other resources will be discussed later.

Let us now turn to the next partial sequence, the perceptual one.

The Perceptual Sequence

The perceptual sequence consists of differentiations by actors, levels and viewpoints. As suggested earlier the differentiation between self and non-self, as actors, begins when the child acquires the ability to perform actions that had been previously performed by the mother. He then realizes that his behavior and his mother's behavior are not one and the same thing. Actors differentiation provides the child with his first two roles: his role toward his mother and the role of the mother toward him. The differentiation between actual and ideal level could not be easily made before actors are differentiated. Ideal behavior, in its elementary form, is that behavior of the child which is followed by acceptance behavior of the adult. It requires an ability to distinguish between the two actors, the child and the adult. The realization that "what mother wants me to do" may be different from "what I want to do," provides the beginning of the third differentiation between the viewpoint of the actor and the viewpoint of the other. If indeed, differentiation by level requires prior differentiation by actor and contains the beginning of differentiation by viewpoints, the following sequence of development will be sustained: Nonself as actor is differentiated from self, then ideal behavior is differentiated from actual behavior and, finally, the viewpoint of the other becomes differentiated from the point of view of the self. Initially, the child perceives himself as the actor of everything being done, so that self, as actor, and his viewpoint are primary elements of the perceptual dimensions; so is the actual level which precedes the ideal one.

These elements, however, become meaningful only after they become differentiated from the other, secondary elements. As Piaget (1954, p. 237) has noted "Precisely because he feels omnipotent, the child cannot yet contrast his own self with the external world."

The three stages of the perceptual sequence are represented in Figure 4. The inner circle indicates differentiation by actor, between self and other or, more precisely, between the actions of the observer

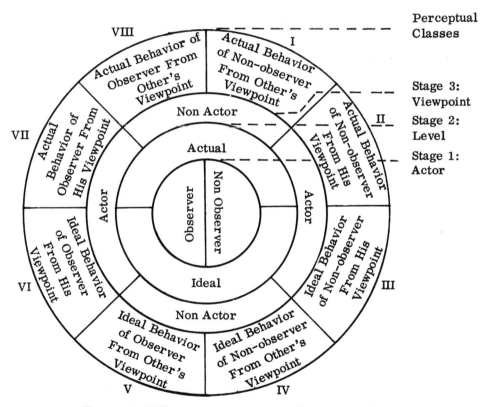

Figure 4. Differentiation sequence of perceptual classes.

Observer as actor =	the action is emitted by the person who reports it.
Nonobserver as actor =	the action is emitted by the "other," not by the person reporting it.
Viewpoint of actor =	the viewpoint of the person emitting the action.
Viewpoint of nonactor =	the viewpoint of the "other," the person who did not emit the action.

and those of the non-observer. Moving away from the center, the next circle shows how the differentiation by actor subdivides according to the level—actual and ideal, so that four perceptual categories are now available: the actual and ideal behavior of self as well as the actual and ideal behavior of the other. The third circle indicates the further subdivision by viewpoint: the point of view of the person doing the action, the actor, becomes discriminated from the viewpoint of the other, the non-actor. The outer circle represents the eight perceptual classes, resulting from the three-stage-process of successive binary divisions.

The concept of observer is not included in this developmental scheme. A child learns to differentiate between actors, objects, modes, etc., only after *becoming* an observer. But no differentiation between observers occurs at any stage of development. What in common parlance is often described as differentiation between observers is in fact differentiation between points of view of the same observer. The realization that so very many classes of observations are all possessed by one observer provides a commom denominator to the various differentiations. Accordingly, we can perceive the notion "observer" as the source of a certain degree of unity and integration maintained by the individual with respect to the enormous variety of social events that are perceived by him.

Each behavioral class results from the combination of mode and object with one of the resource classes. A perceptual class, on the other hand, is the combination of actor, level and viewpoint. This division of the various interpersonal dimensions into behavioral and perceptual sequence is useful for analytic purposes; it should not, however, obscure the fact that they are both parts of the same interpersonal structure. Each cognition of a social event results from the combination of a given behavior, a given resource and a given perception. In view of this unity it appears justified to consider the differentiation sequence as a whole. This is done in Table 1. Differentiations are listed according

Table 1

DEVELOPMENTAL SEQUENCE OF DIFFERENTIATIONS IN THE
INTERPERSONAL DOMAIN

Behavioral Dimensions	*Resources*	*Perceptual Dimensions*
Mode (giving vs. taking)	Love	Actor (observer vs. non-observer)
	Services	
Object (self vs. other)	Status	Level (actual vs. ideal)
		Viewpoint (actor vs. non-actor
	Information	
	Goods	
	Money	

to their approximate time of occurrence, those at the top appearing earlier than those at the bottom of the table.

Some Other Models of Developmental Sequence

Before proceeding to the next step of deriving structural hypotheses from the sequences depicted in Figures 3 and 4, let us pause briefly to compare our developmental model with some other models of sequence.

Stimulated by Piaget's ideas, investigations have been designed to show that a child is not capable of performing task B before being successful in task A; likewise he cannot respond to situation B before mastering situation A, or emit response B before the appearance of response A. A and B are chosen by the investigator because, intuitively, they meet the following two conditions: (a) both tasks or situations involve the same cognitive, sensory and/or motoric area; and (b) B is more complex than A, i.e., it involves the same processes which are required by A plus additional ones.

A sophisticated example of this line of research is provided by Uzgiris and Hunt (1972) who constructed ordinal scales for studying specific areas of infant development. For one of the areas investigated—"Visual pursuit and the permanence of objects" the development sequence underlying scale construction is described by the authors (Ch. 8) as follows: "This development begins with the ready-made scheme of looking. The orienting response and looking behavior may be elicited in a situation which presents the infant with a change in his on-going visual input. First accommodative changes in the looking scheme are manifest in the visual pursuit of slowly moving objects. Development proceeds through progressing accommodative changes in the looking scheme to permit following objects moving faster and faster, through wider and wider arcs. In this development of visual pursuit, a certain degree of ordinality is built in, for pursuit through a full arc of 180°, which requires a coordination between looking and head-turning, clearly implies the ability to follow through lesser arcs. Even when an infant becomes able to follow an object through 180°, however, there is a period when his gaze immediately leaves the place where the object has disappeared. When, later, the infant begins to hold his gaze at the point of disappearance, this holding of gaze implies that the central processes which have presumably developed out of his repeated encounters with his visible surroundings begin to endure. The fact of visual following and of holding the gaze at the point where an object has disappeared implies some desire for contact with the object. At a later point in psychological development, this desirability becomes even more obviously indicated by the coordination between visual following and reaching for the object. Then comes a point when the infant responds as if to the whole object from seeing but a small portion of it, and this is manifest in his efforts to reach for and to grasp with his hands desired objects which have been partially hidden. Infants will reach for a desired object, partially covered, however, when that same object totally covered elicits no effort whatever on their part. Later, however, they search for and remove the covers from desired objects which have been covered completely, and thereby completely removed from view. This implies the beginning of object permanence and of the persistence of central processes allowing a limited construction of perceptually absent events. A little later, the fact that infants will persist in their search for desired objects long enough to remove several covers implies an increased endurance of these central processes. In each of these eliciting situations, termed *visible displacement,* the examiner places a cover directly over an object, for which the infant has demonstrated a desire, while it is in full view of the infant. Still later, infants manifest a higher level of object permanence by following desired objects through *invisible displacements.* Here the eliciting situation is elaborated further: the examiner places the desired object into a container of some sort (a box, a cup, or the hand), he then places the container under a cover, releases the object, and withdraws the container empty. Following an object through such an invisible displacement implies a new level in the central processes representing the object which must permit the infant to consider the object separately from the container and to infer the location of the object from observing the displacements of the container. Even later, infants follow an object through a series of such invisible displacements. The eliciting situation consists of having the examiner place the desired object in the container and then hide the container under several covers in a sequence. At one level, infants search for the desired object under the several covers in the order in which the container was placed under them. Eventually, infants are able to reverse the order of search and start their search under that cover where the container disappeared last, then next to last, etc. This reversal in the order of search implies central processes which can run off in the opposite as well as in the same direction as the sequence represented."

The first, most simple, testing situation of the scale is as follows:

1. Visual pursuit of a slowly moving object—multi-colored ring. Take the multi-colored ring and hold it in front of the infant, about 12 inches from his eyes, until he focuses on it (E may shake the ring in order to attract the infant's attention). Move the ring slowly

through a lateral arc of 180° and observe whether the infant follows it with his eyes.

Does not follow_____

Follows through part of arc_____

Follows through 180° with jerky accommodations_____

*Follows through 180° smoothly_____

Then the complexity of the situation increases gradually; one of the most complex tasks presented is thus described:

8. Finding an object after successive hidden displacements by following the route of the displacements.

Take a small toy in which the infant shows strong interest, cover it with your hand, making it visible to the infant, and slide the hand holding the toy under the cloth, scarf, and pillow successively, leaving the toy under one of the screens. Vary the starting point and the screen under which the toy is hidden by making the last screen of one trial the first screen of the next trial. Show the infant your empty hand after the last move and encourage him to look for the toy. Observe the infant's manner of search. If the infant does not stay still long enough to watch the entire procedure, ask the mother or an assistant to hold the infant, urging him to watch the procedure, until the hiding is completed. The infant must have followed the movements of the hand in order for the observations of his search to be valid. Repeat about 5 times or until the infant's manner of search is clear.

Searches in E's hand_____

Searches under the first screen only_____

Searches haphazardly under all screens_____

*Starts search under first screen and continues along the course that E's hand followed until he finds toy_____

The last response, indicated by an asterisk is, of course, the best one.

In this sequence successive tasks require increasing use of cognitive representation with consequent decreasing dependence on immediate perceptual cues. The cognitive development which makes possible the performance of increasingly complex tasks is left, however, largely unspecified. By contrast the development models we proposed spell out the dimensions of differentiation which enable the child to become increasingly discriminative in his interpersonal relations. Once the cognitive sequence is known it becomes simple to devise situations of increased complexity. For example: a situation requiring giving of status without giving love is more complex than a situation where avoidance of ambivalence between giving and taking is required. We have indeed proposed that the differentiation between giving and taking precedes the one between love and status.

A quest for the dimensions of complexity is also found in other areas of development. Breznitz and Kugelmass (1967), for example, investigated the development of using intentionality by adolescents. They presented subjects with 12 variations of a transgression and examined the role played by the intention of the transgressor in the moral judgment attached by the subject to his action. In building the different levels of intentionality, proceeding from less to more mature usage, these authors considered three aspects of using intentionality: mere usage vs. verbalization; recognition vs. recall; and crudeness vs. refinement. They hypothesized that verbalization is more mature than usage, recall more mature than recognition and refinement more mature than crudeness. They further proposed that verbalization is necessary for recall, and that both are necessary for refined application of the notion of intentionality. By specifying the elements of intentionality, the authors were able to define four stages. The least mature is Usage-Recognition-Crude, and the most mature is Verbalization-Recall-Refined. This sequence of three dichotomous steps bears a close formal similarity to the models presented here. There is however an important difference: the six notions employed by Breznitz and Kugelmass refer to gross characteristics of the observed responses, rather than to elementary differentiation in the underlying cognitive structure; verbalization, recall and refinement are complex notions in their own right and, as such, they can hardly be acceptable as bases for a developmental model.

The work of Kohlberg (1969, b, esp. pp. 381–389) approaches the requirements of a cognitive sequence. He proposes six stages of motives for engaging in moral action. Each successive stage involves a cognitive differentiation which is not required for the preceding one. Some of these differentiations are similar to those presented at the beginning of this chapter. Kohlberg's stage 2, for example, is characterized by differentiation of one's own fears, pleasure or pain from punishment consequences; this appears to be a differentiation between self and other as actors. In stage 3 disapproval is differentiated from punishment, probably indicating the emergence of status as a distinct resource class. In stage 4 the differentiation between guilt (taking away from self) and disapproval (others taking away from subject) appears, indicating the distinction between self and others as objects. Stage 5 and 6 involve differentiation among different roles which are treated later in this volume. Kohlberg found a close relationship between stages and age of subjects, a relationship which justifies the notion of "sequence." Even more interesting are the results suggesting that the same sequence occurs in different cultures, although in some of them the highest stages may not be reached. We shall return to the topic of cultural constancy or invariance in the developmental sequence when comparing different societies (see Ch. 9). For the time being, having completed this short digression on the study of sequence let us go back to the models presented at the beginning of this chapter and examine the structural hypotheses to which they lead.

THE BEHAVIORAL STRUCTURE

Let us begin with a very simple structure, which is obtained by combining the *mode* of an action (i.e., the direction) and its *object* in a dyadic interaction for a given constant *resource*. The mode has two elements—giving and taking away; the elements of the object are self and other. Thus four behavioral classes are obtained by all the possible combinations of the four elements: giving to other, giving to self, taking away from self and taking away from other, *one* given resource (love, status, etc.). Each one of the four classes has one element in common with two of the other classes, and no element in common with the fourth class. For example, "giving to self" has the *mode* in common with "giving to other" while sharing the *object* with "taking away from self." Between "giving to self" and "taking away from other" neither mode nor object are shared. By keeping the resource constant and varying only mode and object we are, in effect, considering the first two stages of the sequence depicted in Figure 3 and ignoring the third stage of differentiation between the resources of love and status. The pattern obtained by considering only one resource is shown in Figure 5. The upper part represents the pattern for love and the lower part, for status. Similar patterns could, of course, be considered for other resources as well.

The circular arrangement of the two figures reflects the fact that each class shares one element with its two neighboring classes, and has no elements in common with the non-neighboring class. Neighboring classes may either share the object and differ in the mode, or they may share the mode and differ in the object. Thus, the similarity between two given classes may be due either to the mode or to the object. When the object changes and the mode is shared, the relationship between two classes indicates how much similarity is perceived, by a given observer, between behavior toward self and the behavior toward the other. A high positive relationship (measured by correlation coefficient) will indicate weak differentiation between self and other as objects; low correlation will be taken as indicator for strong differentiation.

SELF AND OTHER. The idea that in interpersonal situations one relates to himself as well as to other persons is reflected in the literature by concepts such as self-acceptance (giving love to self), self-hatred

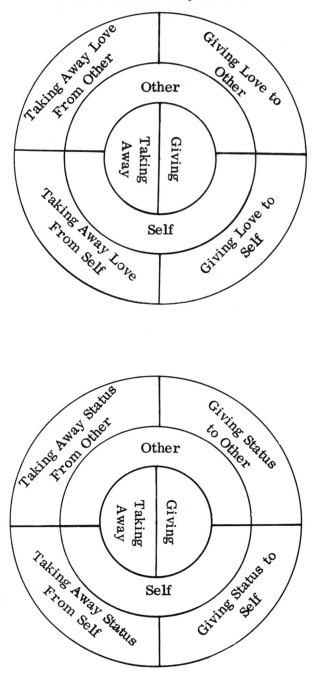

Figure 5. Behavior types for the resources of love and status.

(taking away love from self), and self-esteem (giving status to self). Considerable attention has been devoted to the relationship between attitudes toward self and toward other. There seems to be an agreement among clinicians that a person who accepts himself will also accept others (Fromm, 1939; Horney, 1939; Rogers, 1951). Adler (1926) adds that those who feel inferior depreciate others. Indeed, Berger (1952), Crandall and Bellugi (1954), Omwake (1954) and Stock (1949) all report a positive relationship between self-acceptance and acceptance of others; Henry (1956) found a positive correlation between tendencies toward blaming one's self and blaming others. Similar results are reported by Wylie (1961, pp. 235–240), in a review of twenty-one studies on the relationship between acceptance of self and of other. It is, however, unfortunate that no data were provided in these studies for the relationship between acceptance and rejection, as well as for love and status. Another interesting point which deserves attention is whether the size of the correlation tends to change systematically in accordance with different "others." In the studies reported by Wylie, subjects were asked to rate a wide range of "others"—from parents to strangers. Since, however, they used different instruments, such comparison is not possible. We would hypothesize that the more intimate the relationship the weaker the differentiation between self and other; therefore the higher the intimacy with the other, the higher will be the correlation between the relation toward him and toward self.

GIVING AND TAKING. When the object of an action is kept constant while the mode changes, the correlation between the two classes will indicate the amount of differentiation between "giving" and "taking away." Low differentiation results in ambivalence, defined in Webster's Dictionary as "simultaneous attraction toward and repulsion from an object, person or action." In the case of complete lack of ambivalence, the relationship between loving and hating the same person (or self) would be perfect and negative. To avoid negative correlations which are inconvenient to analyze we can simply correlate the degree of *presence* of love with the degree of *absence* of hate. Then a complete absence of ambivalence will be indicated by a positive correlation of 1, and a negative coefficient will indicate that the more we love a person the more we hate him.

Although the notion "ambivalence" recurs in theories of personality and psychopathology we do not know of empirical studies on it. On the contrary, research tools such as personality inventories and questionnaires were constructed with the implicit assumption of non-ambivalence. Acceptance and rejection are usually used as two poles of the same dimension. Thus, when the subject is asked to indicate how much he likes a person, on a scale which ranges from dislike to like, by definition the more he likes the less he dislikes. It is only when two separate scales are provided, that the relationship between liking and disliking can be studied.

The intercorrelations of the four basic behavioral classes provide us with the possibility to investigate the amount of differentiation between objects as well as between modes. To complete the analysis we should also consider the relationship between the classes which do not share any elements, i.e., between giving to other and taking away from self, as well as between giving to self and taking away from other.

First we shall concern ourselves with the structural hypothesis that empirical results follow the order suggested by Figure 5. We have predicted that classes sharing one element, which thus are neighbors in the circular order, will be correlated more than classes which have no element in common. This prediction is supported by the intercorrelations among the four behavioral classes for love as well as for status, which were obtained from different samples. (See appendix A for a description of instrument and procedure).

Table 2

EXAMPLES OF INTERCORRELATION AMONG TYPES OF BEHAVIOR FOR
LOVE AND FOR STATUS IN DIFFERENT ROLES AND CULTURES

Population of Subjects and Role	Sample Size	Mode	Object		Love 1 2 3 4	Status 1 2 3 4
Columbia, Mo. High School male pupils. Role of father to son. Actual level, viewpoint of subject.	46	Giving to Giving to (Not) Taking from (Not) Taking from	Other Self Self Other	1 2 3 4	— 66 13 39 66 — 27 31 13 27 — 53 39 31 53 —	— 12 02 46 12 — 05 02 02 05 — 37 46 02 37 —
Jerusalem, Israel Married females. Role of wife to husband. Ideal level, viewpoint of other.	633	Giving to Giving to (Not) Taking from (Not) Taking from	Other Self Self Other	1 2 3 4	— 23 01 20 23 — 08 00 01 08 — 14 20 00 14 —	— 19 03 30 19 — 15 01 03 15 — 25 30 01 25 —
Dakar, Senegal females. Role of father to daughter. Ideal level, viewpoint of subject.	50	Giving to Giving to (Not) Taking from (Not) Taking from	Other Self Self Other	1 2 3 4	— 43 29 40 43 — 40 67 29 40 — 37 40 67 37 —	— 10 -17 -07 10 — 01 00 -17 01 — 22 -07 00 22 —

(Samples of Normal Subjects)

In Table 2 examples from three different cultures, Missouri, Israel, and Senegal, are given. As indicated in the left column, the samples differ with respect to the roles, level (idea actual), and viewpoint (actor, non-actor). In spite of these differences, the hypothesis that classes which share the same element correlate higher than classes differing in all elements, is confirmed in all samples. Consequently, we may conclude that the structure of behavioral classes is constant across cultures, roles, levels and viewpoint.

In each row the highest correlations are situated on either side of the main diagonal, while the coefficient which is most removed from the diagonal is usually the lowest in the row. There is one deviation from this pattern in the first example, and a couple of them in the third one. These examples were chosen because they provide good illustrations of the predicted structural pattern. Nevertheless, the total frequency of deviation in all data available so far remain well below chance level: the hypothesis is confirmed in 529 out of 640 intercorrelations.

Relationship between Giving to and Taking away from Self and Other

Earlier we suggested that it would be interesting to investigate separately the relationship between acceptance of self and of other and between rejection of self and of other. Re-examination of Table 2 does not indicate any differences. Out of six possible comparisons, three coefficients are higher for "giving," and three are higher for "taking away."

Another interesting question is whether people are more ambivalent toward others or toward themselves. Again we can answer this question by re-examining the six patterns of intercorrelations in Table 2. The intercorrelation between variables 1 and 4 represents the amount of ambivalence toward others, and the intercorrelation between variables 2 and 3 indicate ambivalence toward the self. We shall remember that the *higher* the coefficient the *lower* the ambivalence. In the Missouri and Israeli samples all correlations between giving to, and taking away from, self are lower than the corresponding ones pertaining to attitudes toward other. There is more ambivalence toward self than toward other in these two samples, although there is a considerable amount of ambivalence directed toward significant others (the correlations are far from approaching 1.) In the Senegal sample a similar amount of ambivalence is directed toward self as toward others.

Relationships between Love and Status

In the literature concerning the relationship between self and other, status and love are often treated as equivalent notions. Measures of regard, esteem, liking, evaluation and rating, are all considered to tap the notion of "acceptance." Since we consider status (esteem, regard) and love (acceptance, liking) as two different interpersonal resources, we shall examine the similarity and difference between behavioral classes involving each one of them.

The data of Table 2 suggest that the structure of behavioral classes remains essentially the same for status as for love. There are, however, certain fairly systematic differences between the correlations for love and those for status, which are implicitly suggested by the development sequence depicted in Figure 3. In this figure behavior toward self and behavior toward other are proximal for love but more apart for status. If we interpret proximity as indicating less differentiation or stronger relationship, it follows that the correlation between self and other should be higher for love than for status. A quick glance at Table 2 shows that this is usually the case. There is, however, one exception in the Israeli data where the correlation between taking away from self and from other is higher for status than for love. In the set of data available, 55 out of 80 possible comparisons confirmed the hypothesis that differentiation between self and other as object is higher for behaviors involving status than for those involving transmission of love. The probability of getting this result by chance is .0014 as computed by Sign Test.

The sequence of development depicted in Figure 3 also suggests that the correlation between giving and taking away will be higher for status than for love, since giving and taking away status are neighbors in the figure, while giving and taking away love are removed from one another. Higher correlation indicates less ambivalence, so that ambivalence would be more profound for love than for status. Indeed, the term ambivalence, in the psychological literature mainly refers to expressions of love and hate. There is no support for this hypothesis in the examples given in Table 2. Other data of this type show a slight tendency in the predicted direction, but not strong enough to be significant.

We have repeatedly suggested that the structure of the adult reflects the pattern of development in childhood. Thus, a developmental explanation should be provided for the noted difference between the behaviors of love and status. Status, as a distinct resource class, became differentiated from love, and therefore emerged later in the developmental sequence. The boundaries between love and status appear after the differentiations between giving and taking away, as well as between self and other as objects, have begun to be firmly established. Therefore these differentiations are stronger for status than for love. Apparently each resource picks up the degree of differentiation between behavioral classes which exist when this resource becomes an autonomous class. If this is the case, one can expect that resources like information, goods and money, which occur after status, will exhibit even a stronger differentiation among behaviors. Support for this prediction is found in a study done by Meir Teichman. The subjects were 30 advanced undergraduate and graduate students from the University of Missouri, who were participating in a group task required by their coursework. They were asked to state their expectations regarding the behavior of two co-workers, the one they preferred most and the one they preferred least as a partner. Six classes of behavior were studied: Giving and taking away love, status and information (See Appendix E). The correlation between giving and taking away of each resource are presented in Table 3. For both the most and the least preferred co-worker

Table 3

CORRELATION BETWEEN GIVING AND TAKING FOR VARIOUS RESOURCES IN THE EXPECTED BEHAVIOR OF MOST AND LEAST PREFERRED CO-WORKER

Resource	Most Preferred Co-Worker	Least Preferred Co-Worker	Difference (Least less Most)
Love	−.13	.21	.34
Status	.11	.36	.25
Information	.39	.40	.01

the correlation is lowest for love, increases for status and is highest for information. Remembering that giving has been correlated with not-taking so that the higher the correlation the less the ambivalence, these results indicate that the strongest ambivalence is found in love, followed in decreasing order by status and then by information. There is more ambivalence (lower correlation) in the expectations toward the most preferred co-worker than toward the least preferred one; this difference, given in the right-most column of Table 3, is largest for love, declines for status and closely approaches zero for information. The stronger ambivalence toward the most preferred co-worker supports the previously suggested hypothesis, that the more intimate the relationship to other the stronger will be the ambivalence.

Love and Status Behaviors Combined

We have discussed the structure of four behavioral classes for a given resource and noted similarities and differences in this structure for different resources. Comparing the behavioral patterns of love and status has prepared the way for considering the larger structure which includes both, and was suggested by the three-step sequence of Figure

3. Once again we shall expect those behavioral classes which are nearer to each other in the figure to be more related than classes farther apart. Let us now see whether this hypothesis is supported by data.

Table 4

EXAMPLES OF INTERCORRELATION AMONG BEHAVIORS OF LOVE AND STATUS

Mode	Object	Resource		633 married males, Jerusalem, Israel. Role of husband to wife. Actual level viewpoint of other.								47 high school female pupils. Role of daughter to father. Actual level, viewpoint of subject.							
				1	2	3	4	5	6	7	8	1	2	3	4	5	6	7	8
Giving	Other	Status	1	—	76	44	34	11	17	41	51	—	71	64	48	16	02	23	37
Giving	Other	Love	2	76	—	40	27	07	17	34	38	71	—	71	39	15	00	10	15
Giving	Self	Love	3	44	40	—	59	14	20	11	19	64	71	—	50	30	11	14	25
Giving	Self	Status	4	34	27	59	—	19	13	00	01	48	39	50	—	16	15	00	02
Taking	Self	Status	5	11	07	14	19	—	45	31	29	16	15	30	16	—	67	28	37
(Not) Taking	Self	Status	6	17	17	20	13	45	—	34	34	02	00	11	15	67	—	42	46
(Not) Taking	Other	Love	7	41	34	11	00	31	34	—	65	23	10	14	00	28	42	—	66
(Not) Taking	Other	Status	8	51	38	19	01	29	34	65	—	37	15	25	02	37	46	66	—

Table 4 contains two examples out of the many available matrices of correlations for the eight behavioral classes of love and status. These two examples are again chosen from different cultures and roles. The order resulting from the developmental sequence is well reflected in both matrices. Behavioral classes which are close in the order correlate higher than remote classes. The coefficients are high near the main diagonal; they decrease and then increase again. Let us examine the first row of the left matrix (Israeli subjects): the coefficients decrease as one moves from the first column to the right, reach the lowest point in column 5, then increase again gradually. Thus class 1 correlates most with its two neighbors, classes 2 and 8. In the second row, the highest correlations are again situated next to the diagonal cell, and again the pattern of gradual decreasing and increasing is sustained. The same is true for all other rows, as well as for the second matrix (Missouri subjects) on the right side of the table. There are four deviations from the predicted order of size of correlations in the Israeli sample and six in the Missouri sample. These two examples differ not only with respect to the culture but also in sex and age of subjects, as well as in the role and in the viewpoint. Apparently, these differences do not change the cognitive structure of behaviors involving love and status. Later on we shall examine some aspects of the structure which are influenced by these factors; the order of the classes, however, remains constant for all the normal subjects that were investigated. It follows the pattern emerging from the developmental sequence of differentiation illustrated in Figure 3.

Some Metatheoretical Considerations

This point in our exposition appears appropriate for a brief methodological aside. The reader who is not interested may skip this section without loss of continuity.

We have predicted the relationship among the four behavioral classes (for a given resource) from their similarity in the facet elements defining these classes. Thus classes having the same mode or the same object were predicted as more related than classes having neither in common. In doing so we have applied the *principle of contiguity* (Foa, 1958a and 1965) which states that variables more similar in their conceptual elements will be more related empirically. This principle does *not* assume that all the coordinates will have a similar degree of differentiation. If the differentiation among elements of facet A, for example, is much stronger than for the elements of facets B and C, then variables differing in the elements of A but alike in B and C will correlate less than variables alike in A but differing in both B and C. Therefore, a structure predicted from the principle of contiguity is assumed to have as many dimensions as the number of facets which define the variables. In our case this principles was adequate for proposing a circular, i.e., a *two*-dimensional structure for the four behavioral classes defined by the elements of *two* facets.

When, however, behaviors of love and of status were considered together, three facets (mode, object and resource) were involved in the definition of the eight classes. The contiguity principle would have then suggested a three-dimensional structure. Yet in Figure 3 the eight variables are ordered in the two-dimensional space of a circle rather than in a cubical one. A three-facet structure yields a situation in which any given variable shares two elements with *three* other classes, while in a circular order each variable has only *two* neighboring classes. Thus some criterion is required for deciding which of the three classes will be neighbors and which will not; according to the contiguity principle, they all would be neighbors. Such a criterion is provided by the notion of *semantic principle components* (Foa, 1961 and 1965) which brings into the picture the notion of a hierarchial relationship among the facets.

SEMANTIC PRINCIPAL COMPONENTS. Let us consider a set of eight variables defined by three facets, each facet having two elements. One element of facet A will be indicated by a_1, and the other element by a_2; in the same way we can indicate the elements of facets B and C, and denote the variables as follows:

1. $a_1b_1c_1$
2. $a_1b_1c_2$
3. $a_1b_2c_2$
4. $a_1b_2c_1$
5. $a_2b_2c_1$
6. $a_2b_2c_2$
7. $a_2b_1c_2$
8. $a_2b_1c_1$

There are several different ways to order these variables in a circle. The problem is how to predict a particular order. Let us suppose, for the sake of argument, that we predict the above order. In this order, Facet A behaves as the first semantic principal component; it changes value only once. Facet B behaves as the second component; it changes value twice. Facet C behaves as the fourth component; it changes value four times.

Reversing the argument, one can now say that knowledge of the facet components tells a good deal about the order of the variables, but not everything. An alternative order, which preserves the components, may indeed be obtained by interchanging, in the above order,

Variable 1 with Variable 2, Variable 3 with Variable 4, and so on, as follows:

2. $a_1b_1c_2$
1. $a_1b_1c_1$
4. $a_1b_2c_1$
3. $a_1b_2c_2$
6. $a_2b_2c_2$
5. $a_2b_2c_1$
8. $a_2b_1c_1$
7. $a_2b_1c_2$

To determine a unique order it is also necessary to identify the first variable of the order. If the first variable is $a_1b_1c_1$, then the alternative order given above is ruled out. Identification of the first variable is also required for differentiating between the first and the second components. Since the proposed order is circular, one could otherwise start, for example from the third variable; then Facet A would behave as the second component and Facet B as the first one.

The first variable cannot be identified simply by indicating the subscripts of its facet elements. If these subscripts are assigned arbitrarily, any one of the variables can be indicated by $a_1b_1c_1$ or by any other combination of subscripts we wish. It is therefore necessary to assign subscripts to the elements of the facets in a meaningful manner.

In conclusion: to predict a unique two-dimensional order, for the eight variables defined by three dichotomous facets, it is necessary and sufficient to identify the principal component of each facet and the first variable in the order. The position of each facet in the differentiation sequence suggests the principal component appropriate for it: the component shall be higher for later developing facets. In this way the first criterion for a single order is satisfied. The second criterion, determination of the first variable in the order, can be satisfied by the following steps: (a) In each facet the two elements are ordered from the more to the less interpersonal, in the manner shown later in this chapter (see p. 75), or according to some other suitable notion of order; (b) subscript 1 is consistently assigned to the element of each facet coming first in the order; (c) the variable defined by $a_1b_1c_1$ will then be considered the first one (Foa, 1965).

THE NOTION OF ORDER. Both the principle of contiguity and the semantic principal components provide rules for predicting the configuration of variables in a psychological space, in which more related variables will be found nearer to each other than less related ones. Familiarity with the physical space may lead us to make assumptions which are not appropriate to a psychological space. The configuration of variables in the latter space does not necessarily reflect the absolute strength of the relationship between any two variables, but only its relative value in respect to other relationships. In consequence the ordering of the variables in the configuration is not necessarily a linear function of the strength of their relationships; for the order to be meaningful a monotonic function is sufficient. Thus, for example, variable 1 will be more related to its neighbor variable 2 (which is only one step removed from variable 1) than to variable 3 which is two steps removed; likewise variable 1 will be more related to 3 than to 4. The decrease in relationship when moving from 2 to 3 does not, however, have to be the same as the decrease occurring when moving from 3 to 4.

An intuitive way to grasp these limitations in the notion of order, as used here, is to imagine that a structure of classes, such as the one shown in Figure 3, is not represented on paper but on rubber which can be stretched in different directions. Pulling it will make distances between certain variables larger while shortening the distance between other variables. But no matter how much and in which direction we pull, the order among the variables will not change: variable 2 will still be between 1 and 3, variable 4 between 3 and 5 and so on. After this methodological digression we shall continue to examine our substantive structures.

THE PERCEPTUAL STRUCTURE

Let us now consider the structure of perceptual classes, i.e., the pattern of intercorrelations between the behaviors of two actors in a dyad, between actual and ideal, and between the viewpoint of the actor and the viewpoint of the other person, *as perceived by one observer*.

In Figure 4 (p. 55) a proposed developmental sequence of perceptual classes has been presented. By using the same considerations as for the behavioral structure, namely the developmental order and the component principle, we arrived at an hypothesis of the order among the eight classes of perception. Again, classes nearer to each other in the model should correlate higher than distant ones. An example of a correlation pattern for perceptual classes is given in Table 5. These data were obtained from a study of 633 married couples in Jerusalem, Israel, and this particular matrix refers to the wife's perception of the behavior "Giving love to the other." The eight perceptual classes are defined in Figure 4.

The order of the intercorrelations follow the predicted structure of Figure 4. The highest coefficients are situated along the main diagonal, and for each row the coefficients decrease and then increase again

Table 5

AN EXAMPLE OF THE INTERCORRELATIONS AMONG
PERCEPTUAL CLASSES

Class	I	II	III	IV	V	VI	VII	VIII
I	—	71	59	42	00	26	45	52
II	71	—	67	55	14	30	40	51
III	59	67	—	61	26	34	31	44
IV	42	55	61	—	53	46	32	36
V	00	14	26	53	—	47	33	33
VI	26	30	34	46	47	—	56	47
VII	45	40	31	32	33	56	—	61
VIII	52	51	44	36	33	47	61	—

as they approach the other side of the diagonal. There is only one deviation: the correlation between classes 3 and 4 in the third row is lower than expected.

Two characteristics of the perceptual structure may be briefly noted, both involving comparison of the viewpoint of the observer with the viewpoint he ascribes to the other: the other is seen as differentiating less between actors and more between levels than the observer does.

The behaviors of the two actors are closer to each other (or less differentiated) for the viewpoint of other than for the viewpoint of self. Conversely, actual and ideal behaviors are closer to each other for the viewpoint of self than for the viewpoint of other. Compared to self, the other is assumed to perceive greater discrepancy between actual and ideal behavior and more similarity in the way the two actors behave.

The Structure of Behavioral and Perceptual Classes

We have proceeded from the simple four-class structure to more complex, eight-class behavioral and perceptual structures. Let us now turn to describe a larger structure of sixty-four classes which combines the perceptual and behavioral structures. In this way we are presenting a hierarchy of structures, proceeding from simple to complex units.

So far we have considered the relationship among the same perception of different behavioral classes, as well as the relationship among different perceptions of the same behavioral class. Thus, for example, in the perceptual structure we considered the relationship between actually giving love to the other and how much love one should give to the other. In the behavioral structure, the perception was kept constant while the relationship among the behavioral classes was investigated. For example, the actual giving of love to other was correlated with the actual taking away of love from other, but from the actor's point of view. By combining the perceptual and behavioral structures we now turn to investigate the relationship among classes, when both the perceptual and the behavioral elements are different. Thus, this structure involves relationships such as what the other gives to us and what we give to ourselves.

The sixty-four interpersonal classes (or variables) are given in Table 6.

Table 6

INTERPERSONAL VARIABLES RESULTING FROM THE COMBINATION OF PERCEPTUAL AND BEHAVIORAL CLASSES

Perceptual Class				Behavioral Class							
			Mode	**Giving**				**Taking Away**			
			Object	**Other**		**Self**		**Self**		**Other**	
Actor	Level	Viewpoint	Resource	Status	Love	Love	Status	Status	Love	Love	Status
			Type	1	2	3	4	5	6	7	8
Nonobserver or other	Actual	Nonactor	I								
		Actor	II								
	Ideal	Actor	III								
		Nonactor	IV								
Observer or self	Ideal	Nonactor	V								
		Actor	VI								
	Actual	Actor	VII								
		Nonactor	VIII								

Each row of the table defines a perceptual class, indicated by a Roman numeral from I to VIII. Each column of the table defines a behavioral class, numbered from 1 to 8. Each cell of the table, at the crossing of a given row with a given column, defines a variable which is composed of the perceptual class of its row and of the behavioral class of its column. Therefore, for indicating a given variable it is sufficient to specify the numerals of its perceptual and behavioral classes. For example, Row I, Column 1 defines the Variable I, 1 "To what degree does the observer perceive, from his point of view, that the other (nonobserver) gives him status."

Some other examples are: Variable V, 2 "To what degree, according to the observer, does the other think that he (the observer) ought to give him love." Variable VII, 5: "To what degree does the observer feel that he is taking away status from himself." Variable VI, 7: "To what degree does the observer feel that he ought to deny love to the other."

The upper half of the table refers to the role of the other toward the observer, the lower half contains the role of the observer toward the other. This classification of variables can easily be interpreted in terms of social exchange. Variables in Rows I-IV, Columns 1-2 and 7-8, refer to what the nonobserver gives to the observer; that is, they indicate what the observer receives from the other. Variables in Rows V-VIII, same columns, are concerned with what the observer gives to the other. The remaining variables refer to what each actor gives to himself. Only two resources, love and status, are included. What *is*, and what *ought* to be *given* and *denied* is recorded from the *point of view* of the observer as well as from the point of view of the other.

In the eight variables of any given column the behavioral class is constant, only the perceptual type changes. Conversely, variables of the same row share the same perception, while the behaviors change. Thus, for example, the variables of Row VII indicate the degree to which each one of the eight behavioral classes appears in the observer's perception of his own actual behavior from his own point of view.

The prediction of the relationship between variables taken from different rows and columns of Table 4 seems to require some understanding of the manner in which the set of 64 variables is organized as a whole. Such understanding may be acquired by considering the position of each variable in the set, indicated by the multiple correlation of each variable with the other variables. Some of these multiple correlations will be higher than others. Essentially this is the problem of communality in factor analysis (Foa, 1963). It has been recognized that the communality of a variable depends on the set of variables to which it belongs; it is not a property of the variable itself. The set of variables considered in this study is interpersonal behavior. Thus all the variables are interpersonal, but, to paraphrase George Orwell, some variables may be more interpersonal than others. Consequently, we may expect that the multiple correlation of the more interpersonal variables will be higher: they belong to the set more than the other, less interpersonal ones.

To decide the degree to which a variable is interpersonal, we should consider its elements. Each dimension has two elements. These pairs of elements are: self-other; love-status; giving-taking; and actual-ideal. In each pair one of the two elements appears to be more interpersonal than the other one. Relations with *other* are characteristic of interpersonal behavior, while relations with self are not. *Status* has stronger interpersonal connotations than love. Some degree of *acceptance* is necessary for the interpersonal relationship to continue, while rejection leads to the cessation of the relationship. There is no interpersoanl situation without *actual* behavior, but an ideal can be maintained without reference to the other. Thus, the elements status, other, giving, and actual, are more closely associated with interpersonal behavior than the elements love, self, taking, and ideal.

The variable containing only interpersonal elements is Variable I, 1, situated at the upper left corner of Table 1: the actual giving status to the other from the viewpoint of the other. The variable containing none of these elements is V1, 6: the ideal amount of taking away love from self, by self, from the viewpoint of self. It is predicted that multiple correlation will be high for the most interpersonal variable and will decrease as one moves toward the least interpersonal one. To test this hypothesis the multiple correlation of each variable with all other variables of the same behavioral structure was computed, using the data of the Israeli study already mentioned (Foa, 1966). These multiple correlations are given in Tables 7 and 8.

In these two tables the variables are ordered in the same way as in Table 6, which showed their conceptual composition. Now we can interpret this order as going from the most to the least interpersonal

Table 7

MULTIPLE CORRELATIONS OF THE 64 VARIABLES
FOR THE OBSERVER WIFE

Perceptual Class	Behavioral Class							
	1	2	3	4	5	6	7	8
I	78	78	65	70	52	45	75	74
II	77	75	73	72	49	47	63	61
III	79	78	66	68	47	44	61	64
IV	71	67	66	65	46	46	51	56
V	68	63	56	55	51	48	47	52
VI	70	63	56	58	49	44	47	51
VII	71	68	57	60	52	51	61	64
VIII	80	77	72	68	49	56	63	67

Table 8

MULTIPLE CORRELATIONS OF THE 64 VARIABLES
FOR THE OBSERVER HUSBAND

Perceptual Class	Behavioral Class							
	1	2	3	4	5	6	7	8
I	78	74	63	66	51	45	72	75
II	78	76	70	68	52	39	67	68
III	76	71	68	66	52	46	66	64
IV	67	63	67	63	46	33	58	59
V	67	67	65	62	63	60	64	62
VI	67	63	65	67	59	59	50	52
VII	73	70	67	65	49	45	64	69
VIII	82	77	66	64	52	53	68	73

variable. The coefficient of multiple correlations are high in the top left corner; they decrease moving to the right or down, until the sixth column or row is reached, and then start increasing again. Along the diagonals of each table this trend is even more regular. Since the more interpersonal variables have a multiple correlation higher than the less interpersonal one, their position in the configuration should be more central than the position of variables which are less specifically interpersonal.

In this manner we have gained some information with regard to the structure of the variables: it should be shaped in such a way as to permit a distinction between the center and the periphery. It should also account for the intersecting circular orders of behavioral and perceptual classes. The anchor ring or torus, a figure shaped like the inner tube of a car, fulfills these requirements. In an anchor ring the points situated in the inner part of the surface are more central than those situated in the outer part. We have called this structure a *ringex*. The proposed ringex structure of the 64 variables is portrayed in Figure 6.

This figure is an attempt to represent the empirical relationship among the variables of Table 6. The large eight circles of the figure

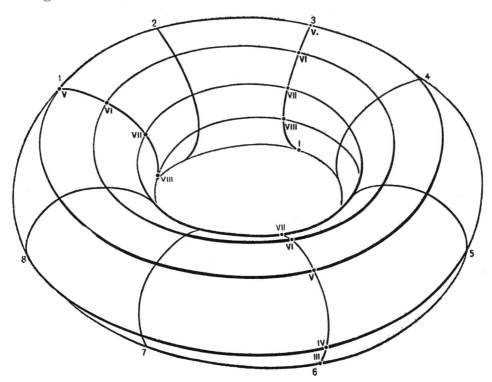

Figure 6. A representation of the ringex model.

are the behavioral structures and correspond to the rows of Table 6: each of these circles contains the same variables which are found in a given row of Table 6. The small circles represent the perceptual structures, each one of them corresponding to a given column in Table 6. Each behavioral circle crosses each perceptual circle once, and this point of intersection defines the position of a given variable with respect to the other ones. It corresponds indeed to a cell of Table 6. Thus, Figure 6 depicts the proposed empirical interrelationship among the variables while Table 6 depicts their relationship in terms of the conceptual elements. It is remarkable how closely these two representations correspond to one another. In effect the ringex structure can be obtained by folding Table 6 so that the bottom row will join with the top row and then folding it again in the other dimension so that the first and last columns will also become neighbors.

If the ringer of Figure 6 is a correct portrayal of the interrelationship among the variables, it will also be expected that:

1. The average correlation among variables belonging to the same behavioral circle will be highest for the circles in the internal portion of the surface and will decrease gradually as one moves toward the external part. Internal circles are indeed smaller than the external ones. The smaller the circle the larger the correlation, on the average, among its eight variables, since they are closer in the space, and the size of correlation is inversely related to distance.

2. The average correlation of each behavioral structure will always be lower than the average correlation of perceptual structures. Perceptual circles are, indeed, always smaller than even the smallest behavioral circle so that their variables should correlate higher.

The average correlations for each circle and for each observer are given in Table 9.

Table 9

AVERAGE CORRELATION AMONG VARIABLES SHARING A GIVEN
PERCEPTUAL OR BEHAVIORAL CLASS

Shared Class	Behavioral		Perceptual	
	Wife	Husband	Wife	Husband
1	27	29	54	60
2	25	28	44	53
3	23	25	64	70
4	21	24	59	65
5	18	21	48	58
6	18	23	54	58
7	27	26	57	65
8	28	31	47	58

For simplicity's sake the circles of Table 9 are all indicated by an Arabic numeral. It would have been more correct to denote a behavioral structure by the Roman numeral of the perceptual class which is constant in it. Both hypotheses appear well supported. The average correlations for the behavioral structures, given in the first two left columns of Table 9, are larger for the smaller circles found in the inner portion of the ringex (a large correlation indicates a small circle) and decrease in size as one moves to the outer portion where circles are larger. On the other hand, the differences in size of the average correlations for the various perceptual circles (two right-most columns of the Table) do not appear to be related to their order position. In fact, there is nothing in the ringex structure to suggest such a relationship.

The lowest correlation of the perceptual circles is .44; the highest one of the behavioral ones, .31. Since a large correlation indicates a small circle, this finding supports the suggestion of Figure 6 that the perceptual circles are always smaller than the smallest behavioral one.

Different perceptions of the same behavior are, on the average, more interrelated than the same perception of different behaviors. This may not be surprising considering that perceptual classes relate actual and ideal behavior from the point of view of self and other. Realizing that the perception or norm of the other is different from our own, or that there is a discrepancy between actual behavior and the corresponding norm, may generate stress and set in motion mechanisms for reducing the gap. As a result, correlations between actual and ideal level, as well as between points of view, tend to be relatively high. Differences among behaviors, on the other hand, may be less conductive to strain. Perceiving a discrepancy between status and love, between behavior toward self and other, and between acceptance and rejection, may not necessarily produce strain. Thus, differentiation among behavioral classes is stronger than among perceptual classes.

We have presented a picture of the cognitive organization a person has of his relationship to another person in reciprocal roles. The proposed cognitive organization is essentially based on two rationales: the developmental and interactive ones. The ringex suggests which of the two will be prevalent in determining a particular interrelationship pattern. The developmental rationale proposes that the relationship among variables is determined by the sequence in which these variables become differentiated during the cognitive development of the child. We have seen that this rationale leads to the prediction of the order of perceptual and behavioral classes. The interactive rationale, on the other hand, proposes that the relationship between variables is determined by the interpersonal situation. According to this rationale the variables can be ordered from the most interpersonal or overt to the least interpersonal or covert. It follows that a covert or intrapersonal variable will be more closely associated with an overt one than with another covert variable. In this context the process of maturation may be conceptualized as moving away from the organization pattern determined by the developmental sequence, toward a pattern more attuned to the interpersonal situation.

All the cognitive structures discussed by now, deal only with two resources: love and status. In this sense they can be perceived as examples of interpersonal structures, but they do not contain all the elements of social communication. For completing the structural picture, let us now turn to consider the relationship among the various interpersonal resources.

INTERPERSONAL RESOURCES

In addition to love and status, the development of four other classes of resources, information, money, goods and services, has been discussed in Chapter 2. Status and service are differentiated from love. The notion of goods is an off-shoot of services; money, in turn, derives from goods and information from status. Implicit in this differentiation sequence is the notion that resource classes which are derived from one another will have more permeable boundaries, will be perceived as more similar, and will be more likely to occur jointly. Thus, once more, developmental assumptions generate structural hypotheses: resources consecutive in the differentiation sequence will also be nearer in the structure of resource classes and, as we shall see later (see Ch. 6), share similar exchange properties. Services and status, for example, will be more similar or related to love than money, and services and money will be more related to goods than status. If resources may be ordered with respect to their relative similarity, one should be able to specify the nature of these similarities and differences. *What* makes love similar to status and services, and different from money? This question points to the need for specifying the coordinates on which resources may be ordered, independently of their differentiation sequence and of the empirical relationship among them.

Two attributes on which the six resource classes can be compared are particularism and concreteness. The coordinate of *particularism* derives from the writings of Parsons (1951) and Longabaugh (1966) and is similar to Blau's (1967) notion of intrinsic and extrinsic rewards. This attribute indicates the extent to which the value of a given resource is influenced by the particular persons involved in exchanging it and by their relationship. Changing the bank teller will not make much of a difference for the client wishing to cash a check. A change of doctor or lawyer is less likely to be accepted with indifference. One is even more particularistic with regard to a friend, a spouse, or a mother. Indeed, Harlow and Suomi (1970) showed that when the facial features of a surrogate mother are altered, the baby monkey reacts with fear, refusing to accept the change. In some animal species certain communications are more target specific than others. Mating calls are more particularistic than status signals and the latter are less general than distress or alarm signals (Johnsgard, 1967, pp. 71-72).

In operant terminology this coordinate may be thought of as the extent to which variables associated with the agent of reinforcement are important discriminative stimuli affecting the salience of the reinforcer. At one extreme of this coordinate is love, the most particularistic resource. Money, the least particularistic resource, is situated at the other extreme. It matters a great deal from whom we receive love as its reinforcing effectiveness is closely tied to the person-stimulus. Money, however, is most likely of all resources to retain the same value and meaning regardless of the relation between, or characteristics of, reinforcing agent and recipient. Services and status are less particularistic than love, but more particularistic than goods and information.

The attribute of *concreteness* ranges from concrete to symbolic and suggests the form or type of expression characteristic of the various resources. Some behaviors, like giving an object or performing an activity upon the body or the belongings of another individual, are quite concrete. Some other forms of expression, such as language, posture of the body, a smile, a gesture, or facial expression, are more symbolic. Services and goods involve the exchange of some overtly tangible activity or product and are classed as concrete. Status and information, on the other hand, are typically conveyed by verbal or paralinguistic behaviors which are more symbolic. Love and money are exchanged in both concrete and symbolic forms, and thus occupy an intermediate position on this coordinate.

The plotting of each resource class according to its degree of particularism and concreteness, produces the structure of resources presented in Figure 7.

This order is identical with the one suggested in the previous chapter (p. 38), although this time it has been derived independently of developmental considerations. Therefore, the two coordinates, particularism and concreteness, may suggest the cognitive criteria along which the differentiation of resources develops. For example, both status and services are differentiated from love and are less particularistic than this class. Services, however, are more concrete and status is less concrete than love. Thus while the general path of differentiation is from more to less particularism, in each stage, another boundary is superim-

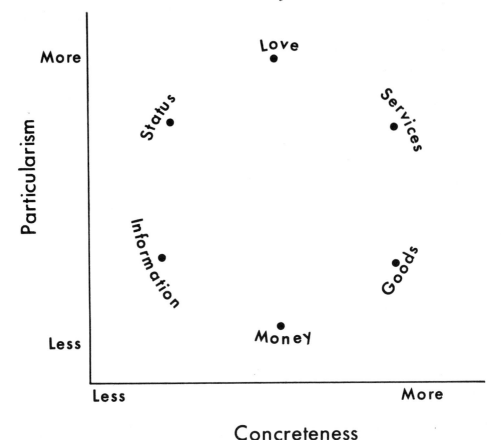

Figure 7. The cognitive structure of resource classes.
Copyright 1971 by the American Association for the Advancement of Science.

posed on the previous differentiation—the boundary between more and less concreteness.

In the structural model presented in Figure 7, resource classes are shown as discrete and neatly separated one from the other. It would be more accurate, but also more confusing, to present each resource class by a segment which merges gradually into its neighboring classes on both sides. We should remember that the resource classes are categories of the *meaning* assigned to actions and not a classification of actions. Consequently, each class covers a wide range of actions all conveying the same resource. For example, one can convey his liking for the other by verbal means, by a smile, a kiss, etc. Thus, for any given resource, there are some forms of expression which are closer to one neighbor while other expressions will be closer to the other neighboring resource. A verbal expression of love such as "I like you very much" is symbolic and thus is more similar to status than to services. Conversely, fondling and kissing are concrete ways of expressing affection, and are closer to services than to status. Services to the body are proximal to love, while services to one's belongings are nearer to goods. Likewise, consumption goods are closer to services than durable goods. A credit card can be considered a kind of money, but it is more particularistic than currency; not every merchant will honor a credit card, and the card is not issued to everybody. This form of payment is also more symbolic than currency; although nothing concrete is given in a credit card payment, currency actually changes hands. Thus a credit card will be nearer to information than currency. In fact, the card provides information on the solvency of its holder.

In general it appears that for each resource class some specific forms are more similar to one neighbor while other forms are nearer to the second neighbor. These similarities are responsible for the permeability of the boundaries among resource classes, and for the structural relationship among them. However, one might question the usefulness or the accuracy of the proposed classification if boundaries are so permeable. The answer is an empirical one: as long as events of the same class tend to be more similar one to the other, than to events of different classes, it will still be possible to obtain empirical evidence for the order. Let us now turn to examine some of this evidence.

EMPIRICAL TESTING OF THE ORDER AMONG RESOURCES

We have repeatedly said that one of the psychological meanings of the distance between two classes is the degree of similarity between them. Accordingly, the first study which will be reported here deals with the relative similarity of the six resource classes. The second series of studies deals with the relative differentiation among preferences for the six resources under various conditions. It is predicted that the nearer two resources are in the theoretical structure, the less differentiated they will be. Other studies which bear evidence for the structure will be discussed later, under the topic of resource exchange (Chapter 6).

Similarity among Resource Classes

A study conducted by Jim L. Turner (Turner, Foa and Foa, 1971) tested the hypothesis that the more two given resources are proximal in the structure the more they will be perceived as similar. Conversely, the more two given resources are distal in the order, the more they will be perceived as different. Subjects, 37 undergraduates (23 female and 14 male) were volunteers from introductory classes in psychology and education at the University of Missouri, Columbia. They were solicited ostensibly to participate in a study of "Dyadic interpersonal communication under conditions of minimal cues." Participants received a series of messages each of which represented a particular resource class. Their task was to return, from a prearranged array of resource messages, the message most similar, as well as the one most dissimilar, to each message received. Experimental manipulation of their alternatives denied subjects the option of returning a message from the same resource class as the stimulus card.

The items used to represent the six resources consisted of short statements which were individually typed on 3×5 index cards. Examples of these items are: I feel affection for you (love); you do things very well (status); here is my opinion (information); here is some money for you (money); here is a package for you (goods); I ran that errand for you (services). Three messages were provided for each resource, giving a total of 18 different card-messages (see Appendix B for the complete set of messages). Each message was phrased to imply that a particular resource was being given to the other. Every effort was made to provide messages which were as general as possible and to avoid phrasings which suggested a particular form or quantity of the resource. We also sought to avoid statements whereby the giving of one resource might imply the giving or taking away of another resource, thus expressions like "favor" or "advice" were eliminated.

All messages representing a given resource were pretested on another group of subjects to see whether they were perceived as belonging to the same class. These subjects (N=11) sorted the total deck of 18 cards into as many different categories as they thought appropriate. Only one subject used more than six categories in performing this task. Although several subjects initially used less than six categories, in each case this was a result of combining neighboring resources into the same category. The most common tendency was to use six categories of unequal N's. Here again, it was always neighboring resources that were combined. The most common "error" was to combine love with status and/or goods with money. When further instructed to sort the cards into six different categories of three cards each, there was substantial agreement across subjects that each triplet of messages belonged to the same distinctive class.

The sequence in which messages were received from the "other subject" (actually a confederate of the experimenter) was randomized prior to the experimental session. The decks of messages, available for the subject to choose from, were also previously randomized (within resources). Each deck contained five messages, one from each resource, except the one which the subject was to receive on that trial. An experimental session consisted of 18 trials, i.e., one trial for each message, 3 trials for each resource. The subject's responses were recorded by the confederate.

Table 10 presents the percentage frequency for which the various resources were returned as being most like the resource received. Since the proposed order is circular, the highest frequencies should be in the two cells bordering the main diagonal. Lower frequencies were predicted for the cells which are two steps removed from the diagonal and the lowest frequency for the cell which is three steps removed, or most distant from the diagonal. Examining both rows and columns in the matrix reveals that, with the exception of three deviations, this is precisely the order obtained.

Table 10

PERCENTAGE FREQUENCY DISTRIBUTION OF RESOURCE
RETURNED AS BEING *MOST LIKE* RESOURCE RECEIVED

| | | | Resource Returned | | | | |
		Love	Status	Infor-mation	Money	Goods	Ser-vices	All Resources
	Love	—	65	10	0	2	23	100%
	Status	62	—	20	10	3	5	100%
Resource	Information	17	34	—	11	24	14	100%
Received	Money	0	16	8	—	60	16	100%
	Goods	6	5	21	55	—	13	100%
	Services	41	18	7	16	18	—	100%
All Resources		21	23	11	15	18	12	100%

Table 11

PERCENTAGE FREQUENCY DISTRIBUTION OF RESOURCE
RETURNED AS BEING *MOST UNLIKE* RESOURCE RECEIVED

| | | | Resource Returned | | | | |
		Love	Status	Infor-mation	Money	Goods	Ser-vices	All Resources
	Love	—	4	19	44	26	7	100%
	Status	3	—	17	24	28	28	100%
Resource	Information	18	10	—	18	22	32	100%
Received	Money	51	9	19	—	3	18	100%
	Goods	39	16	24	5	—	16	100%
	Services	11	18	33	24	14	—	100%
All Resources		20	10	18	19	16	17	100%

Table 11 presents the percentage distribution of subject' judgements as to which resource was most dissimilar to resource received. In this table the predicted order of frequencies is the converse of that obtained in the previous one. The highest frequency should fall in the cell three steps removed from the diagonal with a corresponding decrease in frequency as one approaches the diagonal from either direction. Again, with the exception of two minor deviations, the predicted order was obtained. Moreover, any other ordering of the resources produced many more deviations than the predicted one. The Friedman two-way analysis of variance by ranks, for rows and columns of both tables, provided levels of significance between .029 and .00013, indicating that the obtained distributions of frequencies did not arise by chance and that deviations from it are insignificant.

It is of some interest to note that in the post-session interview a substantial number of subjects volunteered the information that judgments about which message was most similar were considerably more difficult to make than judgments as to which message was most unlike the one received. Since the circular order suggest two neighbors for each resource but only one resource which is farthest away, these subjective reports are consistent with the circular order, and lend credence to its relevance as a model for the cognitive structure of resource classes.

Differentiation among Resources

We have seen that resources proximal in the structure are more likely to be perceived as similar than remote ones. It follows that the boundaries between neighboring resource classes are more permeable than boundaries between distant ones. If the order reflects the relative differentiation among resources, then we could also predict that preferences for resources proximal in the structure will intercorrelate more than preferences for distal resources. For example, if one wishes to receive love in a given situation, his preference for status will be higher than his preference for money. Consequently, the correlation between preference for love and for status will be higher than the one between love and money. Moreover, if the order among resources constitutes a basic cognitive structure, it is further proposed that the circular pattern of intercorrelations among resource preferences will remain invariant across exchange situations.

To test these two hypotheses an instrument called "Social Interaction Inventory" was devised and administered to 120 college freshmen.

In this inventory, given in full in Appendix C, the subject is presented with six situations, in each of which he assumedly gives a certain resource to another person. For love the situation is described as follows: "You convey to a person that you enjoy being with him and feel affection for him." For status, the situation is: "You convey to a person your respect and esteem for his talents." For goods, it is as follows: "You give a person certain objects that you possess." Similar descriptive statements were provided for the other resource classes. After each statement a series of items pertaining to various resources was given, and the subject was requested to rate the desirability of the item, in return for the resource he had assumedly given, on a five point scale ranging from very desirable to very undesirable.

Examples of the items are as follows: For love: "The person indicates that he wants to be your friend." "The person says he is fond of you."

For status: "The person praises you." "You are told that the person has confidence in your abilities."

For information: "The person gives you the benefit of his familiarity with a certain subject." "The person makes you familiar with new facts."

For money: "You receive payment from the person." "You receive cash from the person."

For goods: "The person gives you some merchandise." "The person gives you a certain product."

For services: "The person runs an errand for you." "The person makes himself available to do some work for you."

For each resource three statements were rated. The score on each resource was obtained by adding the points of the three statements pertaining to it. This rating procedure was repeated for the six stimulus situations, i.e., for each resource given by the subject to the hypothetical person. Thus each subject received 36 scores, each one indicating the desirableness of a particular resource in exchange for the resource assumedly given by him to the other person. The scores were then intercorrelated. Two sets of 6 × 6 intercorrelation matrices were compared. In each matrix of the first set, the resource given was kept constant while the resource desired varied (e.g., when the subject gives love how much each resource is desired in return). In the other set, the resource given varied, while the resource desired remained constant within each matrix (e.g., how much love is desired in return for each of the six resources, given by the subject). From each set of matrices two examples will be presented and discussed.

Table 12

INTERCORRELATION AMONG PREFERENCES FOR STATUS
WHEN DIFFERENT RESOURCES ARE GIVEN

Resource Given	Love	Status	Info.	Money	Goods	Services
Love	—	61	40	29	46	52
Status	61	—	52	26	54	45
Info.	40	52	—	42	56	51
Money	29	26	42	—	66	57
Goods	46	54	56	66	—	69
Services	52	45	51	57	69	—

Table 12 shows the intercorrelation of preferences for receiving status when various resources are given. For example, the coefficient of .61 in the first row, second column, indicates the correlation between the desire to receive status when love is given and the desire to receive status when status is given. The relative sizes of these coefficients are as predicted: they are higher for resources which are proximal in the order and lower for more distant resources. In the first row of the table, for example, the correlation between preference for love and status, two neighbors, is quite high. It then decreases for information and still more for money. With goods the correlation begins to increase and is even higher for services. This pattern is repeated in the other rows, with only two deviations from the predicted order: the correlation between status and goods is higher than expected and the correlation between information and money is lower than expected. The lowest correlation, however, is not usually between resources two steps removed in the order. More often it is between resources one step removed, going in counter-clockwise direction.

Table 13

INTERCORRELATION AMONG PREFERENCES FOR GOODS
WHEN DIFFERENT RESOURCES ARE GIVEN

Resource Given	Love	Status	Info.	Money	Goods	Services
Love	—	67	53	42	45	49
Status	67	—	74	52	42	45
Info.	53	74	—	69	55	54
Money	42	52	69	—	65	61
Goods	45	42	55	65	—	77
Services	49	45	54	61	77	—

Table 13 gives the intercorrelation among preferences for goods in exchange for the various resources given. It is readily apparent that this matrix also preserves the predicted pattern of higher coefficients for resources proximal in the order and lower ones for more distant resources. In this table there are no deviations and the lowest correlation is usually found between resources two steps removed from one another. The remaining four tables for the other resources present a similar pattern, although sometimes with a few more deviations. Thus the interrelationship among resources given follow the order, irrespective of the resource desired.

We turn now to the second set of matrices where preferences for different resources were intercorrelated for each resource for different resources were intercorrelated for each resource given by the subjects. Again we shall give two examples out of the six available.

INTERCORRELATION AMONG PREFERENCES FOR
DIFFERENT RESOURCES WHEN LOVE IS GIVEN

Resource Preferred	Love	Status	Info.	Money	Goods	Service
Love	—	71	17	−04	22	26
Status	71	—	23	17	44	50
Info.	17	23	—	25	41	46
Money	−04	17	25	—	74	48
Boods	22	44	41	74	—	68
Services	26	50	46	48	68	—

Table 14 shows the correlation among preferences for various resources when love is given; in Table 15 the constant resource given is money. In both tables the relative size of the coefficients follows the pattern previously noted.

Table 15

INTERCORRELATION AMONG PREFERENCES FOR
DIFFERENT RESOURCES WHEN MONEY IS GIVEN

Resource Preferred	Love	Status	Info.	Money	Goods	Services
Love	—	56	40	−22	22	21
Status	56	—	38	−11	26	36
Info.	40	38	—	−04	35	33
Money	−22	−11	−04	—	49	32
Goods	22	26	35	49	—	65
Services	21	36	33	32	65	—

There are, however, a few more deviations: four in each table. Half of the deviations involve again the class of information. The order of resources is also sustained by the remaining matrices, suggesting that the interrelationship among preferences of resources remains the same irrespective of the resources given.

In conclusion all twelve tables of intercorrelations follow the proposed structure among resources, thus providing evidence for the order of resources as well as for its invariance across the exchange situations considered.

With the analysis of the relationship among resource classes we have concluded the presentation of cognitive structures of interpersonal communication. These structures reflect the way an individual classifies and orders social events which take place in any interpersonal situation where *two people*, himself and another person, interact. So far we have been concerned with structures within one role pair (e.g., mother-daughter, husband-wife). Let us now take one step forward and widen our theoretical framework by considering the relationship among social events in different roles. Our next topic is thus the structure of family roles.

SUMMARY

The elements underlying classes of social events are differentiated in parallel partial sequences, rather than in a single sequence. Within each sequence, for some differentiations to develop, other dimensions should have already been established.

The *behavioral* sequence starts with differentiation between giving and taking away in the primitive form of acceptance and rejection. This elementary classification of events in terms of pleasant and unpleasant is necessary for the notion of object to become relevant and meaningful. Thus the second stage in the behavioral sequence consists of differentiation between self and other as *objects* of an action. This differentiation is developed in the two-role-system of infant-mother interaction. When the child interacts differentially with the two parents, then "status" starts to emerge as a distinct resource class, different from "love." Thus, the third stage in the behavioral sequence consists of differentiation between the *resources* of love and status.

Another partial sequence is the *perceptual* one. It starts with the differentiation of self and other as *actors*. This first stage is based on motoric feedback while the basis of the behavioral sequence was sensoric feedback (pain, pleasure). The second stage of the perceptual sequence consists of differentiation between actural and ideal *level*. It could not emerge before the actors are differentiated, since ideal behavior in its elementary form is the behavior of the child (self) which is followed by acceptance behavior of the adult (other). The third perceptual stage emerges with the differentiation between the *viewpoint* of the actor, and that of the non-actor. This dimension is based on the previous differentiation by levels; it starts with the realization that "what mother wants me to do" may differ from "what I want to do," which is a differentiation between two ideals.

The developmental sequence determines the cognitive structure of the adult, so that the relationships among classes of social events could be predicted by developmental considerations. The relative distance between any pair of classes in a given structure was tested by correlating their frequency of occurrence in a given dyadic interaction. The higher the coefficient of correlation the less differentiated two classes are; therefore, the smaller the cognitive distance between them.

Five models of circular structures were constructed and then empirically validated. The most simple and elementary structure is composed of the four behavioral classes, giving to—and taking away from—self and other, a given resource (love or status). The combination of the two structures for love and status, which corresponds with the behavioral sequence, was also tested and confirmed. The third circular structure is composed of the eight perceptual classes, one for each behavioral class. It relates the behavior of the subject to the behavior of the other, actual to ideal level and viewpoint of self with viewpoint of other. The fourth structure is the combination of the perceptual and behavioral structure, and thus contains $8 \times 8 = 64$ cognitive classes.

Starting from very simple structural units of four classes, we have proceeded toward more complex structures in a succession of hierarchical steps. In all these four structures only the two resources of love and status were included. In the fifth structure we examine the relationship of these two resource classes to other resources. The six interpersonal resources of love, status, information, money, goods and services, are ordered on two coordinates: *particularism* and *concreteness*. Particularism indicates the extent to which the value of a given resource is influenced by the particular persons involved in its exchange. At one extreme of this coordinate is love, the most particularistic resource; it matters a great deal *from whom* we receive love. Money is the least particularistic resource, since most likely of all resources, it retains the same value regardless of the relationship between the giver and the receiver. Services and status are less particularistic than love, but more particularistic than goods and information.

The coordinate of concreteness ranges from concrete to symbolic and suggests the form of expression characteristic of each resource class. Services and goods involve the exchange of overt activity or of product and therefore are the most concrete. Conversely, status and information are typically conveyed by verbal behaviors which are more symbolic. Love and money are exchanged in both concrete and symbolic forms and thus occupy an intermediate position on this coordinate. The plotting of each resource class according to its degree of particularism and concreteness, results in a circular structure. Data on perceived similarity among the six resources, as well as on preferences for each one, support the theoretical model.

The structures examined in this chapter refer to the cognitive recording of behavior within *one* given role-pair. In the next chapter, the differentiation and interrelationship of various roles in a specific institution, the family, will be discussed.

CHAPTER 4

THE DEVELOPMENT AND STRUCTURE
OF FAMILY ROLES

Overview

IN INTRODUCING THE structure of family roles we shall follow the previous presentation paradigm. First, the cognitive dimensions of family roles, as well as their differentiated elements,
will be identified and their developmental sequence specified. Again,
this sequence of differentiations provides the basis for constructing
a structural model which will be empirically tested. We shall start
with investigating the roles acquired by the child in his family of
birth or orientation. These roles are developed through a sequence
of differentiations which are based essentially on the child comparing
himself with other members of the family. Three criteria for such comparison become successively focal: first, the comparison between actor
and non-actor, with which we have already become familiar, is made.
Then the child compares his own sex with that of other members,
realizing that some dyadic relationships are same-sex while others are
different-sex. Finally the comparison by power becomes relevant;
power is "same" for interactions of siblings, and "different" for child-
parents interactions. Thus in the family, differentiation by power overlaps differentiation between generations: interaction between two
generations are characterized by difference in power, while interactions within the same generation are marked by equivalence in power.
This identity between generation and power may not necessarily be
replicated in institutions other than the family, therefore we have chosen the latter term.

The presentation of the relationship among roles in the family of
orientation provides the ground for considering some topics of wider
scope: the structure of self, differentiation among various "others,"
and the relationship between differentiation and generalization.

When a person marries and establishes a family of his own, he
acquires the new roles of spouse and parent. The derivation of these
roles and their integration into the previous structure is discussed in
the second part of this chapter.

FAMILY OF ORIENTATION

In the previous chapters we have discussed the cognitive concepts necessary for categorizing social events in a dyadic interaction. We then proceeded to describe the relationship among these categories. Thus, so far, we have dealt with cognitive structures of social events which take place within a pair of persons. Although these structures might be valid for any dyadic relationship, most of the data presented pertains to interactions within family pairs (e.g., son-father, husband-wife). This choice of data was not accidental. When one aims at studying basic elements of social interactions, it is best to start with primary relations. For the same reason, in the present chapter, extending the analysis to groups larger than a dyad, we will be concerned with the structure of the family. "The family is significant as a type (of organization) that in its internal structure represents very elementary level of roles..." (Parsons, 1955, p. 37).

The notion of "role," although very popular in many writings, was subjected to disagreement and dispute. It is not within the scope of this book to review the various definitions and usages of this notion. We should, however, clarify how this term is used in the present context. Several writers consider "role" as the set of *norms* about the behavior of a particular social position (Biddle and Thomas, 1966, p. 29), while Emmerich (1961) defines it as "the behaviors (performances) of the incumbent of one position toward the incumbent of another position in a social structure." We prefer the view that both norms and behavior (i.e., ideal and actual levels) should be covered under this concept. Following Parsons (1951, pp. 38–39) and Merton (1967, pp. 41–45) we conceive a role as a set of behaviors and norms, pertaining to a specific "actor" in the context of his relationship to a given "object." It follows that for designating a given role, both participants should be specified. For example, the role of "Father-Daughter" consists of behaviors directed by the father toward his daughter and towards himself, as a father of his daughter. In our terminology this role contains the giving to—and taking away from—himself and his daughter certain resources, both on ideal (norms) and actual levels.

Several points emerge from this specific conceptualization of the notion role. First, if a role is confined to a dyadic interaction, then each person in the family has several roles. The role of father-to-daughter is different from that of father-to-son, so that the four-role paradigm, suggested by Parsons (1955), is not sufficient for describing the family organization. Support for our view is given by findings indicating that fathers behave differentially to their sons and daughters (Biller and Weiss, 1970). Secondly, roles go by pairs. For each role there is a reciprocal one, in which the "other" becomes the actor and the previous actor becomes the other. For example, the reciprocal role for Father-Daughter is Daughter-Father; it consists of all behaviors of a daughter towards her father and towards *herself*, as a daughter of her father, as well as of the norms for these behaviors.

If a role contains the *giving to* and *taking away* from *self* and *other* certain *resources* by a specific actor, it follows that any particular role may be perceived as a profile of normative and actual frequencies for emitting social behaviors. Role differentiation thus becomes synonymous with acquisition of different frequency profiles for the various social interaction in which one is engaged.

Common observation of newborn infants indicates that their behavior remains invariant across interactions with different people. Soon they learn to differentiate between familiar and strange faces; still their behavior to all familiar persons remains invariant. Only later, in the second year of life, babies start to behave differentially towards the various members of the family; it is then that differentiation among roles starts to develop.

We know from the previous discussion of developmental processes that boundaries between classes are created through differentiation of basic elements, by a process of binary division. If this is a general rule of cognitive-social development, then it becomes our task to specify the sequence of differentiations which provides the boundaries among the various roles. We shall begin from the roles a child acquires in the family in which he is born, his family of orientation.

The Foundations of Family Roles

ACTOR. As we have already said roles go by pairs. One does not just behave, he acts towards a specific other. Moreover, even when one relates to himself (e.g., "I could do it better") he does it within the conceptual framework of a specific role. Indeed one may have high self esteem in his relationship with his boss and low self confidence when interacting with his wife. If a role is defined by specifying the actor and the other (non-actor), then differentiation between self and other as *actors* is a basic requisite for its development. Differentiation by actors results not only in acquisition of self-other role. By being able to observe what he is doing in contrast to what the other is doing, the infant acquires also the role of the other towards him, i.e., he develops expectations and later on also norms regarding the frequencies which each behavior is emitted by the mother towards him. Thus at the same time that his role is acquired there is also a cognitive representation of the reciprocal role (Cooley, 1902, p. 120). By acquiring both the role of himself and the role of the other, the child is able to notice the contingencies between his actions and the reciprocal other's actions, so that acquisition of roles is followed by a cognition of exchange. The child realizes that if he gives love to his mother there is a high probability that his act will be reciprocated by getting love from her, whereas mean acts will be met with unpleasant reactions.

At the first stage of role acquisition, the stage of self-other differentiation, the infant is a one-role creature, being a member only in the infant-mother pair. This does not rule out interactions with other members of the family. However, babies are treated more or less invariantly regardless of the actor or even the infant's sex (Barry, Bacon and Child, 1957). Interactions with babies are restricted to providing them with services and love and not much room is left for noticeable variations across interactions with the various members of the family. If a role is a distinct profile of frequencies of actions, the invariance among members of the family in interaction with the infant makes all of them representatives of mother-infant role. The baby realizes that members of the family are different persons, he even calls them by different names. Yet this recognition does not provide him with new roles. It is only when communication with the infant expands to include additional resources that variation in frequency-profiles of actions and contingencies becomes feasible. These variations, in turn, enable the child to make new differentiations. He enters the second stage in role development with the onset of boundary between sexes.

SEX. There is considerable agreement that sex constitutes a relevant dimension in acquisition of roles. Less clear is the nature of the behavioral cues which constitute the basis for differentiation between the two conceptual classes of "male" and "female." Parsons (1955) has stressed the differences between mother's and father's behaviors. Mother, having the expressive role, mainly uses the particularistic resources, while father is responsible for providing the instrumental or non-particularistic ones. In addition, mother's behavior is characterized by high frequency of giving, whereas father, being the punishing figure, has higher frequency of taking away behaviors. Cross-cultural evidence for these differences in parent's behavior has been reported by Zelditch (1955). Some support for such resource specialization in parent's roles is also provided by data obtained from the Role Behavior Test (see Appendix A). If the father's behavior is mainly characterized by giving or taking status, while mother mainly gives and takes away love, then the correlation between the two roles should be lowest for these two behaviors. Indeed, this prediction is confirmed for subjects of both sexes, differing in culture and age (juveniles from Missouri and young adults from India).

Except for a minor deviation for Indian men, the correlation between the behavior towards the child, ascribed to father and to mother, is

Table 16

INTERCORRELATION BETWEEN THE BEHAVIORS OF FATHER AND
MOTHER IN GIVING TO OR TAKING AWAY FROM THEIR
OFFSPRING LOVE AND STATUS

Behavior of		Correlation for			
		Missouri		India	
Father	Mother	Boys	Girls	Men	Women
Giving Love	Giving Love	30	62	49	33
Giving Status	Giving Status	63	57	68	19
Giving Love	Giving Status	35	59	43	25
Giving Status	Giving Love	25	45	44	14
Taking Love	Taking Love	43	25	53	39
Taking Status	Taking Status	34	22	53	58
Taking Love	Taking Status	51	22	51	44
Taking Status	Taking Love	07	10	44	29

Note—Decimal points omitted.

lowest when the father gives (or takes) status and mother gives (or takes) love.

A somewhat similar picture emerges from a study conducted by Devereux, Bronfenbrenner, and Rodgers (1969). The subjects were English and American sixth-grade boys and girls, who were asked to report how their parents behave toward them. Children in both cultures report higher frequency of every behavior for their mother. The only behavior in which the father received higher score than the mother was encouragement of autonomy and initiative in their children. Moreover, the mother's activity is especially high in the areas of nurturance, control (expression of worry for physical well-being) and protectiveness. Father becomes relatively more active in urging children towards achievement (status) and in the use of deprivation of privileges to enforce discipline (taking away behaviors). Besides confirming to some degree the hypothesis about resource specialization in parental roles, this study also brings to the fore the fact that the expectations held by the father with respect to their children's behavior are different from those held by the mother. In other words parents differ not only with respect to their roles towards their children but also in their norms of how should their children behave. It seems that this difference is not so much in how should the child behave towards the parents, but mainly in how should the child behave towards himself, as well as in other roles. Fathers, for example, expect their children to become a provider of resources earlier, i.e., to become autonomous whereas mother tends to delay independence. These differential expectations are likely to result in differential contingencies: an autonomous behavior may be rewarded by father while punished by mother.

The literature on effects of parents' absence bears relevance to the differential contingencies hypothesis. There is evidence that father-absence is associated with boys being overdependent (Tiller, 1958) more feminine (Hatherington, 1966; Lynn and Sawrey, 1959) and less aggressive (Sears, 1951; Sears, Pintler and Sears, 1946). Santrock (1970) found all three characteristics in preschool father-absent boys. The effects of father-absence on girls is less clear. While Santrock (1970) did not find any differences between father-absent and father-present girls, Sears, et al. (1946), reported higher aggression for the former group. The differential effect of father-absence on boys and girls points to still additional difference in parental roles. Parents' expectations vary with respect to their child's sex. There is a large body of results showing that fathers behave differentially to sons and daughters by employing different resources (i.e., rewards and punishments) contingent on different behaviors. Johnson (1963) cites many direct and indirect results which show that the father differentiates his roles toward children of the opposite sex whereas mother does not. She suggests that the mother is expressive to both son and daughter while the father is instrumental towards the son and expressive towards the daughter. Indeed, Mussen and Rutherford (1963) found that fathers of highly feminine girls reinforced their daughters more in feminine activities than did fathers of non-feminine girls. Even more relevant to this discussion are the results reported by Tasch (1952, 1955). Fathers perceived their daughters as more sensitive than their sons, they used more physical punishment with their sons and expected different activities from sons and daughters. More symmetry for mother and father differentiation relative to the sex of the child is suggested by Devereux, et al. (1969). When both the sex of the parent and the sex of the child are taken into account simultaneously, parents in English and American cultures tend to behave differentially toward same-sex and opposite-sex children. "In matters of control and discipline as well as in companionship, for example, fathers are more concerned with sons, while mothers are more concerned with daughters. However, precisely the reverse is true for variables such as indulgence and protectiveness; here fathers receive the higher rating from daughters and mothers from sons." In translating these results in terms of resource transmission, we could say that mothers use high frequency of love exchange with boys and status exchange with girls. The reverse is true for fathers. Thus instrumentality is more prominent within "same-sex" relationships whereas love is used more in "opposite-sex" relations. The same position regarding symmetrical interaction is held by Rothbart and Maccoby (1966) who state that differences in parent-child interactions seem to be both a function of child's sex as well as sex of parent. It follows that the boundary of sex differentiation is based on the sex of the two participants in the role relationship—the child and the parent. The acquisition of the notions of "male" and "female" is not appropriate in role differentiation since it does not take into account the interaction of each member's sex. We therefore suggest that what the child learns at this stage is the differentiation between *different sex* and *same-sex* roles. This new boundary is imposed on the previous differentiation between actors. Thus at this second stage of role acquisition the child possesses cognition of four roles: child-mother, mother-child, child-father, and father-child.

POWER. An interesting point in the development of boundaries among roles is that each differentiation is based on the comparison between the two persons (actor and object) of the role. The first differentiation is based on the observation of who constitutes the source of action, self or other. The second differentiation is based on comparing the sex of the two participants: same sex or different sex. There is still another comparison that is pertinent in describing the relationship between reciprocal roles: the comparison between the frequencies of actions that are emitted by each actor. Such comparison leads to the realization that in both roles towards parents, the child is more a receiver than a provider of resources. In this sense the parents have more power than the child (see Ch. 5 for the notion of power). That the parents have control over resources is made clear to the child by having their provision or denial contingent upon his behavior. Since the child has very few resources to give, his ability to control the parents rests mainly on taking away behaviors, either towards the parents (e.g., crying) or towards himself (e.g., refusing food). It has been suggested that the perception of power difference between self and parents motivates parental identification (Lynn, 1969, p. 10). Indeed, Bandura, Ross and Ross (1963) have clearly demonstrated that it is the perception of the other as a possessor of resources that enhanced imitation.

At the age when sex differentiation starts, about 18 months (Brown, D.G., 1958; Money, 1961), and even later, differentiation by power mostly overlaps with differentiation of self and other. In his roles with both parents the child possesses a lower degree of power, so that "other" is powerful and "self" is powerless. Indeed, Barker and Wright (1955), in their survey of actual parent-child interactions, found that dominance and nurturance are the most frequent parent behaviors, whereas appeal, submission and resistance are the most frequent child behaviors. It is only when siblings enter the social scene that the differentiation by power departs from differentiation by actor. By observing the relationship of parent-sibling the child realizes that the latter are more similar to him than the former, in terms of power. This realization leads to the perception that there are powerful others and powerless others besides him; the powerless are children and the powerful are parents.

Emmerich (1961) studied two dimensions of role differentiation: relative power and attitudinal direction (positive and negative or giving and taking away). The subjects were asked to attribute different statements to either one of the following persons: boy, girl, father or mother. The statements which reflect high power are concerned with the actor giving to and taking away a resource from an anonymous object (e.g., "you made that very well," i.e., giving status to other; "you didn't make it very well," i.e., taking away status from other). The low power statements belong to several cognitive classes, such as request to get a resource, submissive or disobedience and giving to as well as taking away status from self ("I made it very well," "I can't make it very well"). The results indicate that children used the power dimension not only to differentiate between generations, but also between the parental roles, as more power is assigned to the father than to the mother. Interestingly, but not surprising, the attitudinal direction did not discriminate between generation. As noted before it is the *power to give* that differentiates between the child and the adult. The power to take away is possessed by both generations as it does not require a previous possession of resources, except in the particular form of withholding.

THE SEQUENCE. We have outlined a three-stage sequence in the acquisition of boundaries between the roles in the family of birth. The first stage is characterized by differentiation between self and other as actors. The second stage consists of differentiation between "same sex" and "different sex." In the third stage, the relative power of each reciprocal role is differentiated, resulting in still another binary division: "Same power" and "different power." This sequence results in the development of the eight roles in the family of birth, as shown in Figure 8 for a male child and in Figure 9 for a female child. The two figures are identical; only the names of the family roles, which are given in the outer circle, differ for boys and girls.

Formally the sequential model delineated in these figures is just like those depicting the development of behavioral and perceptual structures (see Figures 3 and 4). Indeed it represents an additional cognitive configuration, the structure of family roles. As such, it suggests an hypothesis of order among the roles: the nearer two roles are in the circle, the more similar they are in terms of their behavioral profiles. Two properties of the order can be noted: (a) The roles toward family members of same and opposite sex are more similar when power is

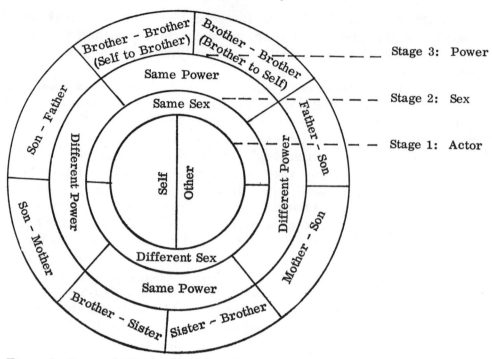

Figure 8. Stages of differentiation of roles in the family of orientation of a male child.

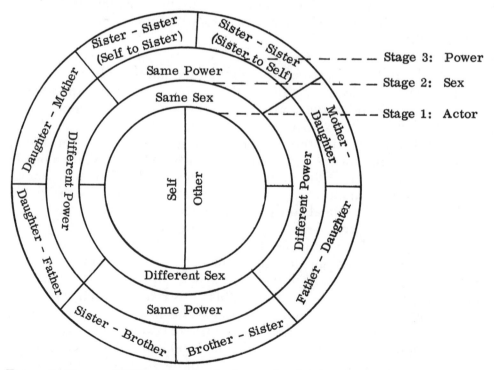

Figure 9. Stages of differentiation of roles in the family of orientation of a female child.

different than when power is the same. Indeed the roles toward mother and toward father are neighbors whereas roles toward brother and toward sister are farther apart, it follows that the former boundary is more permeable than the latter. This would lead to the prediction that children are more apt to behave differentially toward brother and sister than towards father and mother. (b) The reciprocal roles of self and other are more similar when power is similar than when it is different. This means that there is more similarity between reciprocal roles of siblings than between the behavior of the child to parents and the reciprocal behavior of the parent toward him. Indeed brother-sister and sister-brother, for example, are neighbors in the order while the roles of child to parent and parent to child are further apart.

The empirical data that were presented for the previous structures were collected by the first author after the theoretical models had already been developed. By contrast, evidence on the structure of family role was obtained by several investigators, independently of the present developmental model (see Foa, Triandis, Katz, 1966). Unfortunately this fact resulted in several limitations when testing the family structure.

1. Subjects were young adults rather than children.
2. No separate observations were made for the roles of the subject and the reciprocal roles of the others.
3. The different resources in the observed actions were not discriminated.
4. Several roles were not included.

With these limitations in mind let us now turn to examine the empirical evidence for the family structure.

The Structure of Family Roles in Four Cultures

The first set of data presented here was obtained by the Behavioral Differential Instrument (Triandis, 1964). Subjects were instructed to indicate whether in their culture, a given action is appropriate for a particular role pair. A culture was defined as "the circle of people who are most like yourself—in race, religion, social class, neighborhood, nationality, region of the country, etc." The example given was:

Male-Female

Would   Would not

_____ , X , _____ , _____ , _____ , _____ , _____ , _____ , _____

Let go first through a door

The first member of the role pair was specified to be the actor; the second is the object or recipient of the act.

The behaviors were obtained through a sentence completion technique and included actions such as "admire," "hate," "hit," "be commanded by," "treat as a subordinate," "protect," "accept gift of," etc. The 100 roles times 104 behaviors required 10,400 judgments. Since the number of judgments was very large, the total set was divided into 17 groups, leaving 620 judgments for each subject. Each group of judgments was given to 13 S's, so that the total study employed 17 × 13 or 221 S's. In addition, *all* S's made 50 judgments on a common list of actions. The judgments made by each group of 13 subjects were summed. Thus, from each group 620 sums were obtained, plus the 50 sums that correspond to the "common" pool of judgments. The subjects' judgments were then arranged in a 100 by 104 table involving the roles and the behaviors. A 100 by 100 matrix of intercorrelations among the roles was then obtained, based on 104 observations per role. From this large set of intercorrelations the ones referring to family roles were selected. The S's were male students at the University of Illinois, about 20 years old. The study was then repeated with Greek male students (Triandis, Vassiliou and Nassiakou, 1968). The behaviors used in the Greek study were generated by identical procedures as in the American study. The lists of the specific actions were different for the Greek and American studies; both were obtained by sentence completion technique, but each study employed for this task members of the particular culture studied.

Using a similar procedure, Charles E. Osgood collected data on role behaviors from Hawaiian students of Japanese ancestry, and from Japanese students. These two groups of subjects included both male and female with a slight preponderance of the latter group. In the American and Greek studies the subjects were male, therefore only the roles of a male can be analyzed. The structure of the female's roles is discussed only with regard to the Hawaiian and Japanese samples. One or two roles are missing in some of these sets of data, as will be noted in the presentation of the findings.

The data obtained in all these studies do not differentiate between self and other as actors, when the two interacting persons are of the same sex. In the father-son role, for example, the respondent based his judgment on the behavior of a generalized father toward a generalized son, which does not specify whether the respondent is the "actor" or the "other," in the role. Thus, with regard to male-to-male or female-to-female roles the same coefficient is given twice in the same table, once for the self to other role and once for the reciprocal role of other to self. An arbitrary coefficient of 1 has been assumed between the two roles. This arrangement seems preferable to leaving certain rows and columns empty, as it facilitates inspection of the correlation matrices. Furthermore at the normative level one's judgments of how his son should behave toward him is more likely to be similar to his perception regarding his behavior as a son towards his father. Obviously at the actual individual level these two sets of judgments may differ.

The procedure adopted in the analysis resulted in the elimination of the variance due to individual differences. This may explain the high correlations obtained. Furthermore, all the roles considered here are family roles so that they may be expected to have a common core of behavior.

THE STRUCTURE OF ROLES IN THE FAMILY OF BIRTH

The correlation matrix of Table 17 obtained from the Illinois subjects supports the model of family structure given in Figure 8.

Table 17

Facet								
				Elements of Facet				
Actor	Other				Self			
Sex	Same		Different		Different		Same	
Power	Same	Different	Different	Same	Same	Different	Different	Same
Role	1	2	3	4	5	6	7	8
1. Brother-Brother	—	90	89	78	76	78	82	100
2. Father-Son	90	—	93	71	78	79	80	90
3. Mother-Son	89	93	—	80	84	84	82	89
4. Wife-Husband	78	71	80	—	93	81	79	78
5. Husband-Wife	76	78	84	93	—	81	77	76
6. Son-Mother	78	79	84	81	81	—	95	78
7. Son-Father	82	80	82	79	77	95	—	82
8. Brother-Brother	100	90	89	78	76	78	82	—
(Sister-Brother)	86	88	89	75	79	81	82	86
(Brother-Sister)	87	92	90	74	79	82	83	87

Notes – The available data do not differentiate between role of the Subject-to-his-Brother and the reciprocal role of the Brother-to-the-Subject. Therefore, the same correlations are given for both roles.

Decimal points omitted.

As predicted, the correlations near the main diagonal are high. Moving away from the diagonal cell, the coefficients decrease and then increase again. For example, in the first row of the table, the coefficient in the second column is .90. Moving to the right, the coefficient decreases systematically, and then increases again, thus supporting the hypothesis that the nearer two roles are in the order, which results from the development sequence, the more similar they are in terms of their respective behavior profiles. There are only three deviations from the predicted pattern.

But although the circular pattern itself was confirmed for American subjects, there is an interesting divergence between the theoretical and the empirical structure. The reader will note that in Table 17 the roles of brother-sister and sister-brother have been relegated to the bottom of the table and their rightful place has been taken, respectively, by the roles of husband-wife and wife-husband. These two pairs of roles are identical in terms of sex and power dimensions, since both are defined as "different sex" and "same power." The latter pair does not occur, of course, in the family of birth; a son becomes a husband only when he leaves his family of birth, marries and becomes a member of his family of procreation. The results indicate that the spouse roles displace the position of the sibling roles, in the cognitive structure of the adult (the subjects were undergraduate students). Moreover, the correlation coefficients between the role of siblings and the other roles (given in the last two rows of the table) indicate that these two roles do not belong to the circular order. Nevertheless they are systematically related to the structure of the other roles. Starting from the highest correlation and moving along the row, the correlations of these two roles decrease and then increase regularly with one deviation only; the correlation between sister-brother and wife-husband is lower than expected. Despite these systematic relationships between role of siblings and the cognitive structure of the remaining roles, there is no position in the circular pattern in which they fit. It is of interest that the role most closely related to sister-brother is mother-son, and the closest role to the brother-sister is the father-son. In both these pairs of closely related roles the actor is of the same sex (brother vs. father and mother vs. sister) but the power relationship changes. Not less interesting is the finding that spouse roles have the lowest empirical relationship to sibling roles, although sharing with them identical elements: both are "same power" and "different sex." According to these results the brother-sister and sister-brother roles appear displaced from their original position in the circle by the spouse roles. It may be suggested that this displacement is made necessary by the special situation of these two roles with respect to the incest taboo: sexual relations between persons belonging to different generations and/or the same sex, are not readily accepted by society. However these two criterion for incest taboo are not applicable to the brother-sister and sister-brother roles since the sex is different and the generation is the same. To sustain the taboo, cognitive differentiation between spouse and sibling increases while the differentiation between siblings and parental roles decreases. For an adult male, his sister becomes a mother figure and, in turn, he becomes a father figure for her.

We have established that for the American young male our developmental model predicts the cognitive structure of family roles. Will this be true for other cultures as well? In the Greek group, the husband-wife and brother-sister roles were missing. In spite of this, there are eight deviations from the proposed order. The number of deviations is reduced to four when we accept the alternative sequential hypothesis that power differentiation precedes differentiation by sex in the Greek culture, and when the siblings' roles are replaced in their original position. This replacement tends to suggest that the displacement of the sororal role by the spouse role occurs in this culture at a later age. Indeed Greek students do not marry as early as do American students. In addition, incest taboo may be more severely punished by the relatively traditional Greek culture so that over-differentiation is not necessary.

The structural model of family roles is well supported for males in the Hawaiian-Japanese culture. There are three deviations only: father-son and wife-husband as well as son-father and husband-wife correlate too low, while the correlation between son-mother and mother-son is too high. Here again, sister-brother and brother-sister are outside the circle, away from the spouse roles and near to the son-mother and mother-son roles. For the Hawaiian culture we were able to test the family structure of female subjects although no data were collected on mother-daughter and daughter-mother roles. The data on all other roles fit the order, except for the correlations between sister-sister and daughter-father, as well as between father-daughter and husband-wife which are lower than predicted.

The structural model was again verified for Japanese males and females. For the male role there are four deviations from the predicted pattern, all due to the fact that husband-wife and wife-husband tend to interchange their respective positions. This tendency exists also in the Hawaiian data, but to a lesser extent. As to the Japanese females, again the two roles of mother-daughter and daughter-mother are missing. No deviation from the predicted pattern was found in the remaining female roles.

An Indian Study

Further evidence for the proposed structure of family roles comes from data obtained by Professor Bishwa B. Chatterjee from the Gandhian Institute of Studies in India. The subjects were 100 normal adults, in the age range between 16 and 50 (most subjects were 20–40 years old), with nearly an equal number of males and females. They were administered the Role Behavior Test (see Appendix A) for the role pairs of parents-child and spouse, but not for sibling roles. More specifically the test for male subjects included the son-to-father, son-to-mother, husband-to-wife roles of self as actor, and the reciprocal roles for other, father-to-son, mother-to-son and wife-to-husband. Likewise for female subjects the self-roles were: daughter-to-mother, daughter-to-father, wife-to-husband; the reciprocal roles of other were: mother-to-daughter, father-to-daughter, husband-to-wife. For each role, data were collected on eight different classes of behavior (giving to and taking away from, self and other, love and status) at the actual and at the ideal level (see Ch. 2 for these notions). Thus the relationship among the six roles could be studied separately for each behavioral class, on normative as well as on actual levels.

Each subject was asked about 300 questions and the interview lasted almost three hours; covering the sibling roles as well would have lengthened the interview to five hours. As Professor Chatterjee remarked half-seriously, after such an interview subjects could no longer be considered normal.

The present data differ from those we have previously examined on several points. They were, of course, obtained in another culture; the instrument used was different—Role Behavior Test rather than Behavior Differential; they pertain to specific behavioral classes and not to interpersonal behavior in general; finally the subjects' responses refer to the behavior and norms of specific individuals—themselves, their spouse and parents—rather than to the typical behavior of sons, mothers, and husbands in the culture of the subject. Precisely because of these differences from the data previously considered the Indian results are particularly valuable in further validating the structure of family roles; one has more confidence in an hypothesis which is supported by different methods and in various populations.

Intercorrelations among the six roles were computed separately for each specific behavioral class and level, for both female and male subjects. It was expected that for each behavioral class, as well as for each level, correlations will be higher the nearer the two roles are in the structural model of Figures 8 and 9. Two examples of the intercorrelation matrices thus obtained are given in Tables 18 and 19.

Table 18

INTERCORRELATION FOR BEHAVIOR OF TAKING AWAY
STATUS FROM SELF (ACTUAL LEVEL) AMONG FAMILY
ROLES OF NORMAL INDIAN MALES

Role	Roles of Self			Roles of Other		
	SF	SM	HW	WH	MS	FS
Son-Father	—	43	43	12	10	14
Son-Mother	43	—	43	34	30	10
Husband-Wife	43	43	—	21	45	37
Wife-Husband	12	34	21	—	31	01
Mother-Son	10	30	45	31	—	27
Father-Son	14	10	37	01	27	—

Table 19

INTERCORRELATION FOR BEHAVIOR OF GIVING LOVE TO
OTHER (IDEAL LEVEL) AMONG FAMILY ROLES
OF NORMAL INDIAN FEMALES

Role	Roles of Self			Roles of Other		
	DM	DF	WH	HW	FD	MD
Daughter-Mother	—	49	20	−10	27	38
Daughter-Father	49	—	54	15	46	27
Wife-Husband	20	54	—	35	10	10
Husband-Wife	−10	15	35	—	40	15
Father-Daughter	27	46	10	40	—	32
Mother-Daughter	38	27	10	15	32	—

These two matrices are as different as possible. One refers to male subjects and the other to female subjects. One is at the actual level and the other at the ideal one. Also different in the two tables are mode (giving vs. taking), object (self vs. other) and resource (love vs. status). The order of family roles is supported in both matrices; roles nearer in the structure tend to correlate higher than distal ones. There are four deviations in Table 18 and two in Table 19. In the matrix for male subjects all deviations are in the spouse roles, whereas in the female structure both deviations result from high correlations between daughter-father and father-daughter roles. In matrices for the other behavioral and perceptual classes, the predicted order among family roles is maintained with approximately the same number of deviations, occuring mostly in the relationship to spouse.

These deviations being fairly systematic, tend to suggest that in the Indian culture the reciprocal relationship with spouse is somewhat weak, as compared to the relationship towards parents. Perhaps in this culture, spouse roles tend to develop relatively late. There were indeed consistently fewer deviations from the order in the female group, whose median age was slightly higher than the median for the males (28 vs. 24 years).

SOME IMPLICATIONS OF A MULTI-ROLE STRUCTURE

By considering structural relationship among family roles we have extended the cognitive model from a dyad to a larger group. This extension provides some insight into issues of wider scope, having implications which go beyond the present topic.

Relationship between "Several Others"

The behavioral and perceptual structures, discussed in Chapter 3, involved only two persons, the "self" and the "other"; both were considered as actors and as objects of the actions which occur within their particular dyad. In studying the structure of family roles we have considered a situation which involves several "others" as well as several "selves." Thus while in the dyadic structures, the relationships between one "self" and one "other" were in the fore, here the similarity among various others is considered. In the Indian study, separate observations were done for roles of self and the reciprocal roles of others, therefore it provides a clearer illustration of the relationship within each group of roles. An example of the cognitive similarity among "others" is provided by the correlation matrix of Table 19. In this table three "others"; husband, father and mother, are considered as actors towards our subjects (in the lower right quadrant) and as objects of the subject's behavior (in the upper left quadrant). The correlation in the two quadrants indicate the degree of perceived similarity among these "others" as actor and as objects, for the behavioral class of giving love to other. The correlations, being well below the value of 1, indicate that these various others are differentiated. Yet, since the coefficients are above zero, these others are related and therefore may be considered collectively as a "family."

In the interrelationship among others illustrated in Table 19 each entry refers to a specific pair of roles and thus the possible effect of one role upon the relationship between two others is not taken into consideration. It is, however, a common experience that the presence, actual or potential, of a third individual may modify the relationship between or the behavior of two persons: A married couple, for example, is unlikely to engage in intimate expressions of love when their child is present; a mother may become more attached to her son after losing her husband. In general, changes in the frequency of emitting behaviors of a given class may be caused by the presence or absence of a third individual; however, the structural order of the classes is not likely to be modified. In fact, the order of the classes, or the relative cognitive distance among them, is remarkably stable. Before discussing this structural stability, let us examine the structure of the different "selves" and observe its similarity to the structure of "others."

The Structure of Selves

In everyday language we rarely use the plural form of the word "self." We conceive our personality as having one unified self. It was George Mead (1964, p. 207) who noted that when interacting with different individuals we not only behave differentially towards them, but our self-perception also changes as we move from one role to the other. Hence it is appropriate and more accurate to consider the various "selves" of an individual rather than implying a single unitary self.

If there are as many selves as roles, it becomes relevant to examine their interrelationship, or relative similarity. An example of such relations among three "selves" in the family is provided by Table 18. In the upper left quadrant of the matrix, the subject is *both* the actor and the object. The correlation coefficients indicate the degree to which the relationship towards self is similar in the three roles, for the specific behavioral class of taking away status. The correlations in the first row, second column, for example, indicate the degree of similarity between self-derogation as son of father and self-derogation as son of mother. In Table 18 the three correlations happen to be identical; this is not the case in other behavioral classes and therefore we cannot consider this result as typical. Since the coefficients are far from approaching 1, there is considerable differentiation among these three selves, although some relationship does exist. The correlations in the other rows and columns are quite low as they indicate the relationship between self-perception of different individuals, the wife, mother and father of the subjects.

Considering the matrix as a whole, we notice that the structure of the selves in Table 18 is equivalent to that of the others in Table 19. It followed that the order among roles remains constant across actors and objects as well as across the different behavioral classes. The generality of this structural uniformity deserves some further comments.

Structural Constancy

We have considered so far the four structures of behavioral classes, resources, perceptual classes and family roles. It would be more accurate to term each one as a substructure, since they are all interrelated parts of the same organized whole, the cognitive representation of social events. In a matured cognition, each event is classified simultaneously into a given role, a given behavioral and perceptual class as well as into a given resource class. However, in the cognition of a child some of the previously discussed dimensions will be missing or rather, from an adult viewpoint, they will have only one value. An infant, for example, has only one role as he is the sole actor; for him the notion of role does not yet exist. In investigating cognitive structures it is more precise to consider the undifferentiated dimensions as single-valued.

Much like children we have kept some dimensions constant when we wanted to present an empirical example of a particular structure, but unlike the child, we did spell them out. When, for example, we examined the interrelationship among behavioral classes (see Table 2) we could hardly do it without specifying the constant resource, the perceptual class and the role pair to which each set of behavioral classes referred.

At the theoretical level we employed the convenient abstraction of considering each structure as a separate entity. We were able to do it because of structural constancy: the relationship among classes remains the same in different contexts. We have seen that the structure of behavioral classes remains the same for actual and for ideal level, for behavior of self and of other and for different viewpoints. Likewise the structure of perceptual classes remains the same for different types of behavior; as we have just noted, the structure of family roles is constant across behavioral and perceptual classes.

It seems, therefore, that each substructure is independent of the other substructures, to which it is linked as a part of a larger inclusive structure. One cannot help wonder at the ingenuity of this property which provides for both flexibility and parsimony in cognitive representation. The same structural pattern is applied to a great variety of purposes. At the same time a relatively small number of substructures yield a complex network of cognitive classes, sufficient for handling social events.

The notion of structural constancy refers to the *order* of proximity among classes. In the structure of resources, for example, love is nearer (or more similar) to status than to information; a structural change would occur when love would become nearer to information than to status. As we have said, such change is unlikely to occur in normal individuals. However, constancy in the order of proximity does not preclude changes in the degree of differentiation among classes. In fact we have already noted some systematic differences in the degree of differentiation existing in various structures. The differentiation among behavioral classes, for example, is weaker at the actual than at the ideal level (see Table 9), yet the order of the classes is identical for the two levels. Systematic changes in the degree of differentiation do occur in the course of cognitive development; of particular interest is such increased permeability among classes due to generalization.

Generalization and Discontinuity in Differentiation

The differentiation sequence of family roles depicted in Figures 8 and 9 provides a clear illustration of the relationship between differentiation and generalization, which are often considered as contrasting processes. During the second stage of this sequence father becomes differentiated from mother, while in the third stage parents are differentiated from siblings. Thus in the last stage the two parents, previously differentiated, are now found to have something in common: mother and father are classed together as those who have more power. The term "parent" comes precisely to indicate what is common to father and mother, but not to siblings. In a similar fashion parents and siblings share characteristics which are not found in a stranger; this sharing is indicated by the term "family" as opposed to "non-family" (Parsons, 1955, p. 60–61).

These examples point out that a later differentiation may induce generalization of a previous discrimination, thus, in effect, weakening it. The discovery that mother and father are alike in several respects reduces the differentiation between them. Paradoxically, however, we cannot find common aspects between classes unless we first realize that they differ. In consequence, the addition of a new coordinate to the cognitive representation may result in decrease of differentiation along a previously existing coordinate. The number of dimensions and the degree of differentiation within each dimension are two different phenomena often confused under the same term of "cognitive complexity"; H. Miller and Bieri (1963), however, have pointed out the distinction between them.

If generalization does follow a new differentiation, we shall expect that cognitive development will be characterized not only by increased differentiation but also by its decrease. Evidence on this point is provided by Emmerich, Goldman and Shore (1971), in a thoughtful study concerning the development of social norms. They investigated 680 subjects aged 8 to 17 years, from a middle-class background, with an equal representation of boys and girls and a similar number of subjects in each age group. Their findings show that differentiation between parents and peers (equivalent in the family to power differentiation) decreases after reaching a peak in late childhood; differentiation between sexes (male vs. female) also decreased but to a lesser degree. Particularly interesting is their findings that "brighter children discriminated more sharply between parent and peer objects at an earlier age and then reduced this differentiation earlier than less bright children" (p. 350). By contrast no systematic changes were found in the differentiation of behavioral contents for these 8–17 year old subjects, a result which was interpreted by the authors as supportive of our hypothesis that the differentiation of behavioral classes precedes differentiation of roles.

Emmerich, et al., point to some results suggesting that, contrary to the sequence we proposed (Figures 8 and 9), "Differentiation by generation precedes that by sex, at least with regard to sex typing within the child's own generation." The Greek data previously discussed also raise this possibility. We concur with Emmerich's remark that for a direct attack on the problem of sequence the best strategy is to investigate young children at the onset of the differentiations by sex and by power, which probably occur in the third year of life. Paradoxically, however, the study of young adults appears more appropriate than the investigation of subjects in late childhood and adolescence. As the study by Emmerich, et al., has shown, the strength of differentiation may change in both directions during development before eventually reaching a fairly stable level in adulthood: hence it is rather unreliable to make inferences about the sequence from observation during this dynamic phase. There is little we know of in the literature which can contribute to the clarification of this sort of problem, in spite of the very large amount of research on parents-children interaction and, to a lesser extent, on siblings' interaction (e.g., Brim, 1958; Leventhal, 1970; Sutton-Smith and Rosenberg, 1965; Wohlford, Santrock, Berger and Liberman, 1971). Typically these studies investigate the influence of various family conditions (e.g., father absence, sex and age of siblings) on specific aspects of role acquisition, while disregarding the problems raised here: differentiation sequence and cognitive organization of family role. With the clarification of these latter problems, however, it becomes feasible to study the developmental and structural effects of various family situations.

After having examined the cognitive structure of the family of orientation and some of its theoretical implications, let us turn to the new roles which are acquired in the family of procreation.

ROLES IN THE FAMILY OF PROCREATION

When individuals leave their parents' home and establish their own family they acquire new roles: first one becomes a spouse and then a parent. It is widely accepted that these roles are developed through modifications of some pre-existing roles in the family of birth. In attempting to be more specific in advocating the "transference" view, let us note that after marriage six new roles will be required, three for self as actor and three reciprocal roles of the other as the actor. For the male the new roles are: husband-wife, father-son and father-daughter (when self is the actor), and the corresponding reciprocal roles of the other: wife-husband, son-father and daughter-father. The equivalent six roles for the female are easy to figure out.

The key to the development of these new roles is provided by the mechanism of taking the role of, or identifying with, the parents. This process is facilitated by the fact that roles go in pairs, so that when acquiring the role of self one also acquires the reciprocal role of the other. The existence of cognitive representation for the role of the other is an obvious advantage when one begins to assume it for himself. Yet, knowing the role is not sufficient for performing it accurately. This is probably the reason why little girls play at being a mother with their dolls, distributing love and personal services, while in games played by boys status is prominent as they act in prestigeful occupations, such as doctor, tractor-driver, etc., depending on the values of their own culture. Much of children's games are thus training sessions for their future roles.

When the little girl takes the position of her mother in the family structure, the mother "becomes" a daughter and the father "is" a husband and a son. It follows that the parent of the same sex is modeled by the child for the future role of a parent toward a child of the same sex, both these roles are characterized mainly by exchange of status and information. On the other hand, the opposite-sex parent provides a model for *both* the future spouse role and the role toward a child of the opposite sex; these three roles are characterized by exchange of love. In essence, the newly acquired roles of the family of procreation are modeled after roles which already exist in the family of birth; roles of others become roles of self and, conversely, roles of self become roles of others. Consequently, the young adult acquires higher-power roles, whereas in the family of birth he either possessed a lower or the same power, but never more power.

This paradigm for role acquisition abandons the idea that boys model after their fathers and girls after their mothers. Instead each parent becomes the model for different roles. Moreover, if opposite-sex parent influences the development of four roles (two for the self as an actor, and the reciprocal roles for the others) whereas the same-sex parent influences only two roles, then the former is more important for the future adequacy of the child, in assuming the proper roles as an adult. This view was advocated by Freud in stressing the importance of satisfactory termination of the Oedipus conflict for achieving mature social relationships in adulthood.

The Structure of the Adult's Roles

The emergence of the new roles, resulting in a total of 14 roles, requires a *reorganization* of the previous cognitive structure which had only 8 roles. We suggest that this structural change takes the following form: the original circular structure of the child's roles (see Figures 8 and 9) splits into two semicircles; one contains roles when the "self" is an actor and the other semicircle consists of the reciprocal roles of the "others." Each semicircle is then reformed into a complete circle by adding the appropriate new roles of the family of procreation. Thus while the *child's roles*, his own and the reciprocal ones of the other, are all ordered in *one circle*, the *adult's* structure contains *two circles* of roles, one for the roles of self and one for the reciprocal roles of others. (The brother-sister and sister-brother roles will occupy positions outside the two circles.)

Since the two circles of the adult are parts of the same structure we hypothesize consistent relationships across circles: the two roles which are alike in terms of sex and power will be nearest to each other, i.e., they will occupy corresponding positions, each in its own circle. This relationship between the circles bears relevance for the role-derivation paradigm: each "new" role will be near to the "original" role, from which it was derived.

The complicated model for the structure of the adult's family roles is depicted in Figure 10.

For the purpose of indicating graphically the relationship between roles which belong to different circles (in terms of relative distance), and because the figure is presented in a two dimensional space, the two circles have been presented one inside the other. This should not be taken as a suggestion that they are in the same plane, or that one of the circles is smaller than the other. In fact, as the data will show, the circles are facing each other on a three dimensional space.

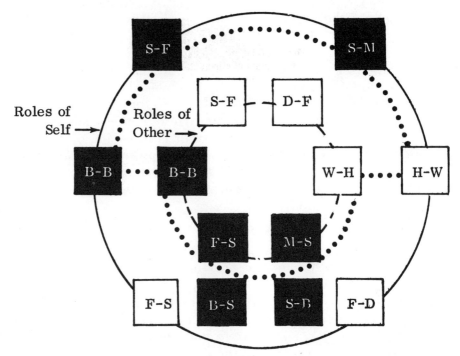

Figure 10. Organization of family roles in the adult male. (Roles are indicated in the figure by the initial of the actor and object. Thus, S-F means son-father; S-M, son-mother; H-W, husband-wife; B-B, brother-brother; B-S, brother-sister, etc. Role in the family of orientation is indicated by a black square; role in the family of procreation, by a white square; circle of roles with self as actor in adult is indicated by unbroken line; circle of roles with other as actor in adult by broken line; circle of roles in the family of orientation, by dotted line.)

In Figure 10 the outer circle portrays the proposed order of the six roles in which the actor is self: a full line connects these roles in the figure. The inner circle portrays the six reciprocal roles in which the actor is the other: these roles are connected by a broken line. It is interesting to note that the eight roles of the family of orientation maintain their original circular order: this order is indicated by a dotted line in the figure, which connects the upper half of the outer circle with the lower half of the inner circle. In the adult, however, each one of the original semicircles had been completed by including the roles of the family of procreation, thus forming a circle in its own right. As noted before, the husband-wife and wife-husband roles have occupied the place of the brother-sister and sister-brother roles, leaving them out of both circles.

Empirical Evidence

To test the structural model of Figure 10, we shall turn again to the same source of data from four cultures (Foa, Triandis and Katz, 1966) used for testing the structure of the family of birth. The relevant coefficients of correlation, for the American subjects, are given in Table 20.

The upper left quadrant of the table shows the intercorrelations among the six roles of self as an actor, and therefore corresponds to the outer circle in Figure 10. The lower right quadrant gives the inter-role correlations for the reciprocal roles, where others are actors and

Table 20

INTERCORRELATIONS AMONG BEHAVIORS IN THE FAMILY ROLES OF A MALE (AMERICAN SUBJECTS)

Actor	Role	Self						Other					
		SM	HW	FD	FS	BB	SF	SF	BB	FS	MS	WH	DF
	Son-Mother	—	81	63	79	78	95	95	78	79	84	81	79
	Husband-Wife	81	—	83	78	76	77	77	76	78	84	93	69
Self	Father-Daughter	63	83	—	93	83	75	75	83	93	94	75	63
	Father-Son	79	78	93	—	90	80	80	90	100	93	71	67
	Brother-Brother	78	76	83	90	—	82	82	100	90	89	78	69
	Son-Father	95	77	75	80	82	—	100	82	80	82	79	85
	Son-Father	95	77	75	80	82	100	—	82	80	82	79	85
	Brother-Brother	78	76	83	90	100	82	82	—	90	89	78	69
Other	Father-Son	79	78	93	100	90	80	80	90	—	93	71	67
	Mother-Son	84	84	94	93	89	82	82	89	93	—	80	72
	Wife-Husband	81	93	75	71	78	79	79	78	71	80	—	72
	Daughter-Father	79	69	63	67	69	85	85	69	67	72	72	—
	(Brother-Sister)	82	79	88	92	87	83	83	87	92	90	74	73
	(Sister-Brother)	81	79	87	88	86	82	82	86	88	89	75	68

Note - Decimal points omitted.

the self is the object. This quadrant represents the inner circle of Figure 10. The remaining two quadrants give the intercorrelations among the roles of the self and the reciprocal roles of the other, and as such they indicate the relationship between the two circles.

The circular order in the intercorrelation among the roles of the self as well as among the roles of reciprocal others is clearly maintained, supporting the hypothesis about the two-circle structure. There is only one deviation from the predicted order in the upper left quadrant, and two deviations in the lower right quadrant. Although the lowest correlation is not always in the cell three-steps removed from the main diagonal, the predicted cognitive "map" of the roles was confirmed. For example, the role of a man towards his wife is most similar to his role towards his mother and his role towards his daughter. The role least similar to the husband is the brother role. The latter, in turn, is closest to the role towards the father, on one side, and to the role towards the son, on the other side.

The circular pattern is also apparent in the remaining quadrants, as expected, if the two circles are facing one another. This systematic relationship between roles of self and roles of others enables us to predict the relative cognitive distance between any role in the outer circle and all other roles in the inner circle, and vice versa. For example, let us consider the role of husband-wife for self as an actor (outer circle), and predict its relationship to the roles of others in the inner circle. According to Figure 10 the closest role to husband-wife is wife-husband, followed by mother-son, father-son, etc. We now can turn to Table 20 and check whether these predictions are supported. The right-most half of the second row contains the relevant correlations between the self-role of husband with all roles of others. Husband-wife role correlates highest with wife-husband role, followed in decreasing order by mother-son, father-son and brother-brother roles. The correlation then increases again for son-father since the pattern is circular. According to Figure 10 the coefficient should further increase for daughter-father but it fails to do so. There are three such deviations from the predicted order between the two sets of roles.

The last two rows of Table 20 give the intercorrelations of the brother-sister and sister-brother roles with the rest of the roles. These coefficients confirm what has been noted previously: the roles of opposite-sex siblings are systematically related to the family structure but they are outside the circles.

In the corresponding intercorrelations for the Greek data there are nine deviations: one in the roles of self, four in the roles of the other, and four across self-other roles. Of these nine deviations, six are accounted by the fact that the correlation between brother-brother and son-mother, as well as between son-father and mother-son, are higher than expected. In the correlations between roles of self and roles of others the highest one is always in the diagonal cell, as predicted, except for the correlation between son-mother and daughter-father, which is too low. Even a better fit between the model and the empirical data is provided by the Hawaiian males. There is no deviation in the roles of others and only two in the roles of the self: husband-wife correlates too low with son-mother and father-daughter. Two other deviations are found across the two circles. More deviations exist in the corresponding Hawaiian data for the female roles. Out of a total of nine deviations, seven are due to the fact that sister-sister correlates too high with the spouse roles. A perfect fit is supplied by the Japanese data for both male (see Table 21) and female roles, as no deviations from the predicted order were found in this culture.

Derivation of the Adult's Roles

The correlations among the two circles provide the data for testing the role-derivation paradigm, which was suggested earlier. This paradigm contains two hypotheses:

1. The original role with opposite-sex parent provides a model for the new opposite-sex roles; likewise the same-sex parent is the model for the newly developed same-sex roles.
2. There is a switch in actor-object between the derived and the original roles. New roles of the *other* are modeled on the original role of *self,* and conversely, new roles of *self* are derived from original roles of *others.*

Table 21

INTERCORRELATIONS AMONG BEHAVIORS IN THE FAMILY ROLES
OF A MALE (JAPANESE SUBJECTS)

Actor		Self						Other					
	Role	SM	HW	FD	FS	BB	SF	SF	BB	FS	MS	WH	DF
	Son-Mother	—	84	75	66	64	82	82	64	66	82	89	88
	Husband-Wife	84	—	90	87	69	71	71	69	87	90	90	72
Self	Father-Daughter	75	90	—	97	90	57	57	90	97	93	78	67
	Father-Son	66	87	97	—	90	54	54	90	100	90	74	62
	Brother-Brother	64	69	90	90	—	51	51	100	90	85	69	57
	Son-Father	82	71	57	54	51	—	100	51	54	69	83	90
	Son-Father	82	71	57	54	51	100	—	51	54	69	83	90
	Brother-Brother	64	69	90	90	100	51	51	—	90	85	69	57
Other	Father-Son	66	87	97	100	90	54	54	90	—	90	74	62
	Mother-Son	82	90	93	90	85	69	69	85	90	—	88	74
	Wife-Husband	89	90	78	74	69	83	83	69	74	88	—	86
	Daughter-Father	88	72	67	62	57	90	90	57	62	74	86	—
	(Sister-Brother)	83	76	71	69	72	84	84	72	69	80	89	90
	(Brother-Sister)	82	79	85	78	81	67	67	81	78	90	78	73

Note - Decimal points omitted.

A combination of the two hypotheses lends to the following predictions:

1. For the adult male, the new roles of self, *husband-wife* and *father-daughter*, are derived from the original other's role of *mother-son;* therefore they will correlate higher with the latter than with father-son role. The new roles of the other, *wife-husband* and *daughter-father*, are modeled on the *son-mother* role, and therefore will correlate higher with the latter than with the son-father role.

2. For the adult female, the new roles of self, *wife-husband* and *mother-son*, are derived from the *father-daughter* role, and the new roles of other, *husband-wife* and *son-mother*, are derived from the *daughter-father* role.

For the American male subjects, the derivation paradigm is confirmed for all new roles except daughter-father which correlates higher with son-father rather than with son-mother. However, if only the first hypothesis is considered, i.e., that the opposite sex parent provides the model for all four new opposite-sex roles (both for the self and the other as actors) then all four predictions are confirmed. Indeed, father-daughter, daughter-father, husband-wife and wife-husband roles, all correlate higher with mother-son than with father-son.

The data of the Hawaiian-Japanese males confirm the entire paradigm: all four new roles of opposite-sex correlate higher with mother-son than with father-son. Moreover, the hypothesis of a switch in actor and object in the derived and modeled roles, is also confirmed. Wife-husband and daughter-father roles are nearer to son-mother than to son-father; husband-wife and father-daughter are nearer to mother-son than to father-son.

The derivation paradigm is confirmed in the Greek subjects for the daughter-father and wife-husband roles; both correlate higher with son-mother than with son-father. Father-daughter role is equally distant from mother-son and son-mother. Data on husband-wife role were not available.

The paradigm of role derivation is only partially confirmed for the Japanese male subjects. Daughter-father, wife-husband and husband-wife, all correlate more with the original role of mother-son, as predicted. However, contradicting our hypothesis is the stronger relationship between the new role father-daughter and the original role of father-son.

We could not test the derivation paradigm for the same-sex roles of males, since as noted before, no separate observations were made for self as son-to-father and self as father-to-son. Unfortunately there were no data on mother-daughter and daughter-mother roles, consequently we could not test the derivation hypotheses for female subjects.

The second hypotheses—role reversal was well supported for the parental roles: so in the male the role of father-to-daughter is always closer to mother-son than to son-mother, while the contrary is true for the role of daughter-to-father; likewise, in the female, the role of mother-to-son correlates higher with father-daughter than with daughter-father, and the finding is reversed, as expected, for the role of son-to-mother. With regard to spouse roles, however, the data leave in doubt whether role reversal occurs: in the male the spouse roles correlate about the same degree with son-mother as with mother-son. In the female father-daughter and daughter-father are nearly equally related to the spouse roles.

Family Roles in Modern American Literature

The results discussed so far refer to the cognition of living persons. How different from their's is the cognition of fictitious persons, populating novels and short stories? A partial answer to this question is provided by a study of Evelyn Walker Katz (1964), who did a content analysis of 50 American contemporary short stories and computed indices of similarity among the role behaviors of the male and female personages of these stories. All family roles were included except brother-brother, brother-sister and sister-brother, which did not appear with a sufficiently high frequency of interaction in the stories. The data for the available roles fitted quite well into our structural model for both male and female figures. There was, however, an interesting difference: in the short stories the husband-wife role replaced the position of brother-brother while wife-husband took the position of sister-sister role. Thus the closest neighbors of the husband are father-son and son-father; the neighboring roles of wife-husband are mother-daughter and daughter-mother. In the structure of real individuals, spouse roles are also between parent and child, but of the opposite sex. Thus, in this fictional material differentiation by sex was obscured, perhaps heralding a trend which appears later in real people of the American culture: the tendency toward reduced differentiation between male and female in behavior, dressing, occupational activities and the like.

From the Family to Other Institutions

We have seen that the development of family roles rests mainly on differentiations by sex and by power. Both dimensions have implications with regard to the resource exchange: in roles where self and other are of the same sex, status is prominent, whereas in opposite-sex roles, love appears to be the prominent resource. Likewise, the notion of relative power refers to the degree to which one actor controls a resource needed by the other. The power criterion for role differentiation appears also in other institutions: the boss is more powerful than the worker, and the teacher more powerful than the pupil. Thus the boss-worker role in the work institution corresponds to the father-son role in the family. There is however an important difference between these two roles: the resources which are prominent in father-son interaction are different from those transacted between a boss and the worker. In general, institutions differ with respect to the resources exchanged within their realm. It follows that the notion of power, although applicable to all institutions, change its resources: mother may be powerful in the family by having control over dispensation of love; in the stock market, power refers to money and possibly to information, but certainly not to love. These remarks suggest that the cognitive structures described in the first part of this book may be extended to cover interpersonal situations other than family interaction.

We shall return to this topic in the second part of the volume, when dynamic aspects of resource exchange are discussed.

SUMMARY

The acquisition of family roles is achieved through three successive differentiations based on comparisons made by the child between himself and other members of the family. The three criteria for this comparison are:

1. Who emits the action, the actor, self or other.
2. Is the sex of the other same or different from the child's sex? Son-father is a same-sex role; son-mother is a different-sex role.
3. What is the power of the self relative to the other's power? Again power can be the "same" for sibling roles, and "different" for parent-child roles. Thus in the family, unlike other social institutions, power difference overlaps the distinction among generations.

The three-step sequence of differentiations predicts the relative similarity among eight family roles, in terms of the behaviors emitted in each. Intercorrelations among the behaviors of the various roles were computed for four cultures, American, Hawaiian, Greek and Japanese. The data confirm the structural model of family roles based on the developmental sequence of differentiation by actor, sex and power. However, the brother-sister roles were found alongside the same-sex parent, displaced from their theoretical position in the structure.

Further support for the structural model of family roles was obtained in an Indian sample, using a more detailed method of observation.

In this study the subjects' self-perception in three different family roles was recorded, in addition to their perception about father, mother and spouse. As Mead suggested, the self perception changes for different roles; it is more similar for roles which are closer in the structural model than for more remote ones. This order among different "selves" is the same as for different "others." More generally, we found that each structure tends to remain constant in different contexts, although the permeability of the boundaries among its classes may vary from one situation to another. Permeability seems to decrease rapidly at the onset of differentiation and then to increase again when generalization takes place.

A turning point in the structure of family roles is reached when one acquires the new roles of spouse and of parent, required in the family of procreation. This transition is facilitated by the fact that parental roles are already represented in the cognition of a child, albeit as roles of the other. Thus the role of the same-sex parent provides a model for the role toward the child of the same sex. The roles toward spouse and toward a child of the opposite sex are derived from the relationship to the parent of different sex. The emergence of these new roles requires a reorganization of the structure, which takes the form of two circular patterns facing each other; the original circular structure splits into two semicircles, one for the roles of "self" and one for roles of "others." The derivation of new roles and the structure emerging from it were supported by empirical data.

A brief comparison between family roles and roles of other social institutions suggests that the basic concepts of social cognition discussed so far can be extended without difficulty to cover the full range of interpersonal situations.

We have thus concluded the first part of this book, in which cognitive development and structures of social events have been presented. The notions acquired so far will serve us in understanding processes of social interaction, to which we now turn.

Part II:

INTERACTIVE

CHAPTER 5

PRELUDE TO RESOURCE EXCHANGE

Overview

AFTER HAVING DESCRIBED the growth and organization of the basic cognitive elements in social behavior, we now turn to explore the function of these cognitive structures in the dynamics of interpersonal interaction. Social experiences are interpersonal encounters in which resources are given and/or taken away. Whether or not an exchange will take place depends on conditions which will be explored in this chapter. In essence, there are two sets of conditions, which we shall consider: One pertains to the motivational state of the potential exchangers, their need to receive and capacity to give; the other set refers to the appropriateness of the environment for an exchange of a particular type.

We shall begin by proposing that for each resource class there is an optimal range; when the amount of a given resource possessed by the individual is within this range, he feels comfortable and is not motivated to induce a change. When the amount falls below the lower bound of the range, the situation will be subjectively perceived as a *need* for this particular resource and the person will be motivated to increase the amount in his possession. Contrariwise, when the amount exceeds the upper limit of the optimal range, one will be motivated to "get rid" of some of the resource, through suitable exchange behaviors. By accumulating an amount beyond his need, the individual acquires *power* in this specific resource class.

These definitions of need and power suggest that an optimal condition for exchange exists whenever a person who needs resource A and has power in resource B meets a person needful of B and powerful in A. Yet, the intrapersonal state of the exchangers constitute only part of the requirements for an exchange to take place. The institution within which the exchange occurs and the role of each participant are important factors for enhancing or abating it. We have already noted briefly that exchanges appropriate to one institution may not be permissible in another one. In this chapter we shall expand on the function of institutions in channeling and limiting exchanges and shall consider transactions in two institutional settings: psychotherapy and a task group.

Another significant element of the exchange situation is the particular resources involved, since resources differ in their exchange and environmental properties. If two persons who need money, exchange dollar bills with one another, neither of them will benefit much. On the other hand, an exchange of love increases the amount of it possessed by both participants. The reason is that in love, unlike money, giving to the other is positively related to giving to self; consequently, one cannot reduce his amount of love by giving it to other, as he could do with money, since by giving love to the other he also increases the amount possessed by him. This positive relationship is also reflected in negative exchange: when one takes away love from the other he simultaneously takes away from himself. Lovers' quarrels may have this homeostatic function: keeping the amount of love below the upper limit of the optimal range. Resources also differ in the environmental conditions in which they can be best exchanged: lovers will seek solitude, shoppers a crowded marketplace. Thus both exchange and environmental characteristics of resources will influence the feasibility of a particular transaction. These properties will be discussed in the last part of this chapter and their eventual significance for problems of modern society, particularly urban society, will be explored.

In summary, the present chapter examines factors influencing the occurrence of an exchange: The motivational state of the participants in terms of optimal range, need and power; the facilitation and limitations imposed by social institutions; the consequences of resource properties. The latter factor includes both individual and social aspects and thus provides a link between the motivational state of the person and the environmental conditions.

MOTIVATIONAL STATE OF THE INDIVIDUAL

The term motivation usually refers to internal states of the individual which spur the emission of a certain behavior. When discussing social motivation, we aim at answering such questions as: what drives a person to interact with others? what determines the type of this action, it direction and vigorousness?

We shall focus here on two basic mechanisms which motivate social behavior. The first is the strive to maintain the amount of each resource within an optimal range, and the second is the strive to maintain the cognitive structures.

The Optimal Range[1]

In physiology the concept of homeostasis or normal range of the organism's parameters was proposed by Cannon (1939). He saw it as the tendency for an orgamism as a whole to maintain constancy, or to attempt to restore equilibrium if constancy is disturbed. Need was defined, in turn, as a condition arising from the lack of something essential to the organism and motivation as a state existing from a desire to maintain equilibrium or homeostasis. When the homeostatic balance of a particular factor is disrupted, an aversive and motivating state develops. It seems likely also that a need may be present at times other than during disequilibrium and that the unbalanced state does not directly produce motivation but instead gives rise to a need, an intervening process which, once established, in turn produces the motivation by which energy is expended and the system moves once again to equilibrium. That is, disequilibrium produces a need within the system; as the system becomes aware of the need through action of the homeostats, motivation arises and instigates action. Shortly after equilibrium is restored, the need disappears, motivation is removed and activity ceases. From the early ideas of Cannon, a large body of research has developed. For example, McClelland (1955) has suggested that an individual's personality characteristics are determined in large part by the efficiency of *his homeostatic system*. And Tomkins (1962), who notes that the homeostatic system is silent and unconscious in its operation, adds (Tomkins, 1965) that if a drive state (a state that is instigated by homeostatic imbalance) is not reduced within the tolerance limits of the organism, the drive becomes stronger. Other researchers (Pribram, 1960; Benzinger, 1961) delving into the physiological aspects have provided evidence that the regulatory mechanisms necessary for maintaining physiological balance or homeostasis are located in the hypothalamus.

From Tomkins' (1965) notion of "tolerance limits," it follows that either too much or too little of a particular necessary factor may destroy homeostasis and consequently motivate the organism to act in order to restore the system's balance. For example, too little water will lead to dehydration and death, just as too much water within a system will produce bloating and death. Homeostasis is that tolerable range of deviation (for any factor) within which behavior remains unmotivated for that particular factor.

Before a homeostatic model may apply to any dimension, whether physiological or psychological, certain necessary conditions must be met. The dimension or factor being considered must exist on a con-

---

[1] We are indebted to Roger D. Pigg for his contribution to this section.

tinuum where the possibility exists for the system to have either a zero amount of it, some greater amount, perhaps infinite, or any amount in between. There must be the possibility of variation as to the amount of the factor "held" by the system in question. And there must exist some upper and lower "tolerance limits" upon the continuum such that no need will be experienced by the system when the amount held by it falls within these limits. Beyond these tolerance limits, however, needs arise and motivated behavior will result.

The notion of optimal level is found in several theoretical models of motivation. The classical drive reduction paradign (e.g., Hull, 1943) mainly emphasizes this internal state which occurs when the amount of resource possessed by an organism is *below* a certain limit. Lack of food induces unpleasant physiological stimulation; the organism's activity is then directed towards reducing such stimulation. Yet, under the notion of avoiding pain or discomfort one can easily include the state of having "too much." Hunger and oversatiation both produce unpleasant physiological cues, and as such both can be accounted for in the drive-reduction paradigm. More explicit in postulating an optimal range is Berlyne (1960) who suggested that the organism strives toward maintaining an optimal level of arousal; any state below or above this level activates a search for a change so that there are stimulus-seeking behaviors as much as stimulus-reducing ones. One may argue that a state of too-little arousal produces cues of discomfort and therefore behaviors directed towards increased arousal are again drive reducing. It seems that the argument between these two formulations (Lana, 1960 and 1962) boils down to the question of what the optimal range arousal is. While the drive reduction theory assumes lack of internal stimulation as the optimal level, Berlyne suggests a higher and wider range.

By applying the homeostatic model to resources, the nature of the discomfort that is aroused in the organism and drives him toward a search for change is specified. The amount of resources one possesses at any given time can be described on a continuum. Let us consider "love" as an example. The system may potentially "hold" no love at all, or some amount which may vary from time to time. There are obviously times when love is actively sought for by a system; at other times even when available, the opportunity to receive love is ignored and even rejected. Gewirtz and Baer (1958) found that children previously deprived of companionship learned faster than non-deprived ones a discriminative task which was reinforced by social approval. The slowest learning occurred in those who were previously satiated with social interaction. Reformulating these results, the isolated children possessed an amount of love and status below the optimal range;

for them the learning task provided an opportunity to acquire these resources in exchange for the correct response. On the other hand, the potential exchange did not prove attractive to those who already possessed a sufficient amount of the resources offered.

In general, it appears reasonable to assume that for every resource there is a lower limit below which motivational arousal will occur. The upper limit, however, varies for the different resources and consequently the optimal range also differs from one resource to another: it will be smallest for love and practically infinite for money. The optimal range of the remaining resources will follow the structural order. The closer they are to love the narrower will be their optimal range, while resources closer to money will have a wider range. The proposed Relative range of resources is depicted in Figure 11.

When the optimal range is narrow, the balance is upset frequently and requires constant restoration by increasing or decreasing the amount held by the system. We feel miserable being far away from those who love us, but when close to them, we sometimes want to be alone. Similarly, it is pleasurable to dine in a good restaurant where service is prompt; yet, in those exclusive restaurants with several waiters in constant attendance, one may wish they would disappear. It is only with regard to those resources that can be stored outside the system (mainly money, but also goods and information) that we can own large quantities without being disturbed.

Obviously there are individual differences in the optimal range. It seems that at least for the more particularistic resources, the range will be narrower for those who received little of them in early childhood

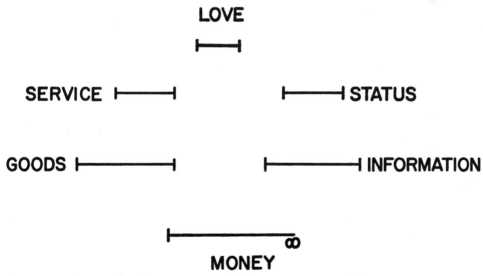

Figure 11. Proposed relative width of the optimal range of the various resources.

(see Ch. 8). A person who had not received enough love will probably feel unbalance when suddenly confronted with the necessity to absorb large quantities of it. He may react to this disturbance of his homeostasis with hostility, in order to get rid of the overdose of love smothering him.

Below the Optimal Range: Need

Need is defined as a state of deficiency in a given resource; it occurs when the individual possesses an amount below the lower bound of the optimal range. It follows that there are six classes of need, one for each resource class.

Table 22

SOME NEEDS REFERRING TO ONE RESOURCE
OR TWO NEIGHBORING ONES

Resource	Need	Reference
Love	Love	(Tolman, 1951)
	Affection	(Schutz, 1958)
Love and Status	Approval	(Crowne and Marlowe, 1964)
Status	Achievement	(McClelland, Atkinson, Clark and Lowell, 1953)
	Recognition	(Murray, 1938)
Status and Information	Competence	(White, 1959)
Information	Curiosity	(Berlyne, 1960; Harlow, 1953)
	Exploration	(Stagner and Karwosky, 1952)
Goods and Money	Acquisition	(Cattell, 1950; McDougall, 1932; Murray, 1938; Stagner and Karwosky, 1952)
Services and Love	Succorance	(Murray, 1938)
	Comfort	(McDougall, 1932)

Several of the needs recurring in the literature on motivation refer to a specific resource or to a combination of two neighboring resources; some examples are given in Table 22. Other needs found in the literature cover a wider range of resources. The need for affiliation (Schachter, 1959), for example, appears to include all the resources which are exchanged in face-to-face contact: love, status, information and services; the desire to be with another person represents an expectation to receive some resource rather than an end in itself. Such expectation for resources is also embedded in the similar notions of "social instinct" (Young, 1936) and gregariousness (Cattell, 1950; McDougall, 1932; Tolman, 1951). Still other needs focus on additional aspects of resource acquisition; the need for security (Stagner and Karwoski, 1952) indicates a desire to assure *future* supplies of unspecified resources; one may need security for love, status, money etc. The need for independence (Rotter, 1954, p. 132) represents a wish to have many alternative sources, thus avoiding reliance on any specific individual for obtaining resources; the need for dependence, in turn, implies a tendency to maintain supplies only from specific others. Once more these needs may apply to any of the six resource classes: one may have many sources of money but few persons from whom to receive love. Indeed, the more particularistic the resource, the less one is likely to be independent in it; since for particularistic resources, the giver is relevant, it becomes more difficult to secure alternative sources of supply. Quite often a person is independent and secure with regard to one resource while manifesting dependency and insecurity in another. Thus it is necessary to specify the resource as well as the patterns of behaviors connected with it. Moreover, we sometimes accept a loss in one resource in order to secure a supply of another, which is needed more. Staub and Sherk (1970) provided children with their favorite candies; they could eat and share them with another child while listening to a recorded story. High need approval children ate less and gave less to the other. Presumably they expected that such a restrained behavior would be approved by the experimenter; approval was more valuable to them than eating their favorite candy.

All the needs discussed here, although different with respect to resources, share a common characteristic: they all refer to a situation where the object is "self", the behavior—"giving," and the actor is mainly "other." A resource is sought after by the individual in order to reduce a present or future deficit, and to maintain the amount held by his system within the optimal range. However, the term "need" has also been used to indicate situations where the potential object is the "other" and behavior is either giving or taking. The mother "needs" to give love and care to her infant; the aggressive individual "needs" to express hostility, i.e., to take away love from the other. What deficits are behind such needs? Let us consider first the need to give to the other by analyzing the outcomes of these "needed" behaviors. The most obvious explanation for the urge to give evolves from the notion of optimal range: when the amount of a given resource exceeds the upper limit, one would be motivated to "get rid" of it by giving to the other. In spite of its simplicity, this explanation is ruled out by theoretical considerations, which are, however, different for particularistic and non-particularistic resources. When one dispenses money, he indeed becomes poorer. But we did propose that no upper limit exists for money, hence there should be reasons other than discomfort for such behavior. As to love, excessive amount does indeed cause discomfort, but giving love to other increases rather than decreases the amount possessed by the self, and therefore is not a successful way to restore balance. It seems more plausible to perceive "generosity" (giving to other) as a device for obtaining access to needed resources. It is quite uncommon for a person to give away money indiscriminately. Benefactors are usually quite choosy: they will give for a "worthy" cause which will bring them honor or self-respect. Often the donation is part of an exchange situation: beggars are likely to reciprocate the alm with a blessing for the giver. The benevolent mother is likely to be praised by her family and friends besides increasing her self acceptance. In general, three exchange paradigms, which are *not* mutually exclusive, provide access to needed resources through benefiting others: (1) A gives to B and is reciprocated by him with a needed resource. (2) A gives to B and is reciprocated by giving to himself. (3) A gives to B and is reciprocated by a third person, C. Thus giving behavior, even when it appears unconditional, provides access to some needed resource so that one's own balance is restored. But what is achieved by taking away behaviors? How is balance restored by aggression? The effect of taking away from the other is reversed in comparison to giving. Taking non-particularistic resources may increase the amount held by the taker and thus serve to satisfy his deficit. Yet sometimes the aggressor purposely destroys the other's possessions, without any obvious gain to himself. Common observation indicates that some satisfaction is derived from such destruction. By reducing the amount in possession of the victim, the aggressor decreases the difference between himself and the victim. If a poor, desperate person sets afire the house of the well-to-do, he indeed does not become richer absolutely, but will be less poor in comparison to the other. We shall consider this relative increase resulting from social comparison later in this chapter.

While taking away non-particularistic resources serves to increase the amount possessed, taking away love from the other has the effect of decreasing the amount in one's possession, thus reestablishing equilibrium when the amount previously held exceeded the upper limit. In summary, taking away from the other non-particularistic resources reestablishes a balance by increasing the absolute or relative amount held by the self; taking away particularistic resources reduces the amount possessed by the taker and thus reestablishes the balance when this amount was excessive.

The foregoing discussion of the effects of taking away focused on dyadic relationship. As in giving behavior, often a third party joins the exchange and rewards the taker for his aggressive behavior with a needed resource. When taking away behavior is directed toward an outgroup, often the group reacts by rewarding the aggressor; taking from the "foe" of the group results in receiving from the group members. The hero who killed many enemies is hailed; he receives status from his comrades.

ACTUAL AND POTENTIAL NEEDS. We have already briefly noted that the optimal range may be altered by cognitive operations. Reducing the amount of resources possessed by the other eliminates the discrepancy between one's own possession and the other's belonging. Thus, although the *potential* need is still high, the *actual* need has been decreased. The distinction between actual and potential need is even clearer on a physiological level: a person who has been starving for a long time needs a great amount of nourisment. Yet he will not be able to digest large quantities at once; in fact he may become seriously ill if he does. Potentially his need for food is high, but his actual need is rather limited. Likewise, a person who has received little love, particularly in early childhood, may have a strong potential need, but little ability to actually absorb it.

The potential need can be reduced only by receiving the appropriate resource. An actual need, on the other hand, can be modified by cognitive manipulations. One way of changing an actual need is by social comparison (Festinger, 1954), which, as we have seen, may influence the *lower* bound of the optimal range for non-particularistic resources. TV advertisements obviously serve to raise the lower bound by exposing the individual to "all the people" who own luxurious goods, have better education and earn more money; sibling rivalry has the same effect of increasing demand with regard to particularistic resources. The influence of social comparison on the upper limit is more obscure: will one be able to receive more love if he is among people who are much beloved?

Similar questions can be raised with regard to expectation; the latter differs from social comparison in that there the need is modified by past experience of the subject, while in the latter the modification results from past experience of others. It is well known that failure to receive an expected resource produces discomfort as it is receiving an unexpected one. We do not know, however, whether these effects are due to changes in the optimal range or result from the motivation to maintain the structure, which shall be considered later in this chapter.

We have attempted to show that many of the psychological needs and motivational states proposed in the literature can be seen in function of the six resource classes. As the structure of these classes has already been established, hypotheses about the relationship among needs and their interchangeability can be suggested: needs pertaining to proximal classes will be more related than needs which refer to distal resources. A person exposed to loss of love will also feel, to a lesser degree, a need for status. The positive correlation of .55 between need for approval and the TAT measure of need for affiliation (Crowne and Marlowe, 1964, p. 163) could be predicted, for example, on the grounds that the two needs share common resources.

The dilemma between too many and too few motives is well described by Madsen (1961, p. 313): "According to the usual scientific principle of economy it is *practical to presuppose as few motives as possible.* One must therefore avoid using a list of motives which is so long that the notion of motive does not explain anything. If the list becomes too long the result is that the explanations employing these motives as their basis do not really explain anything. . . . But it would also be a mistake to try to explain everything from a single or a few motives. The explanations would then either be too vague and imprecise, or they would become too artificial and *speculative* because so many hypothesis would have to be assumed that simplicity would be lost." We believe that parsimony can be achieved not only by limiting the number of needs, but also by determining the structural relationship among them.

Within the Optimal Range: Power

As noted by Cartwright (1959b, pp. 1–2) the study of power has been neglected by social psychologists. Yet, this notion generated theoretical interest, which is reflected in the many definitions proposed in the literature (Cartwright, 1959a, pp. 185–187). Common to several of these definitions is the idea that power implies control over others, or as proposed by Blau (1967, p. 117), the ability to influence the behavior of others. These definitions seem inadequate as they focus on the effect of power rather than on what constitutes power; to define power as the ability to induce behavioral changes is like defining rain as the ability to make wet. Certainly such a definition is not helpful in predicting its occurence or classifying its various types. More enlightening are Thibaut and Kelley (1959, p. 101), who define power as the amount of reward and punishment one can administer to the other. This definition implies two types of power: the power to give a certain resource and the power to take it away. So rephrased, Thibaut and Kelley's definition invites a further classification of power according to the resources involved in the punishment and the reward. Indeed, as Cartwright and Zander (1968, Ch. 17) have noted, a close relationship between the notion of power and resources has been frequently implied in the literature. Such relationship is reflected, to a certain degree, in the classification of power proposed by French and Raven (1959). Two out of the five powers suggested by these authors, reward and coercive power, correspond to Thibaut and Kelley's definition. French and Raven, however, proposed three additional classes: legitimate, referent and expert power. Legitimate power stems from the values held by the person that the other has the right to influence him. This notion clearly introduces the self as a source of reward and punishment:

compliance to a legitimate power results in self-esteem or as stated by Berkowitz (1969a, p. 73) "the individual following the powerful person obtains the satisfaction of doing what is 'right' and he avoids the guilt often arising from norm-deviating actions." The last two bases of power refer to specific resources. In "referent power" the resources of love and status are implicit. The powerful person, by being highly attractive and his opinions and actions appealing, serves as a model for the other. French and Raven held that imitation does not have to be followed by the external reward, but rather the act of imitation is rewarding in itself, or, as we would say, it provides the imitator with a reason to give love and status to himself. It is likely that the model himself is perceived as possessing a considerable amount of those resources. Power as possession of a specific resource becomes explicit in the last type, expert power, which is also labeled "informational power" (Deutsch and Gerard, 1955). It indicates knowledge or information in a specific area, *possessed* by the holder of power and *needed* by the other individual. This formulation provides an exchange paradigm which can be extended to other resources as well.

We shall thus define power as *the amount of a given resource that is available to an individual for eventual giving.* This definition suggests six basic classes of power, one for each class of resources. Possession of power is not necessarily reflected in influencing other's behaviors or opinions as often suggested. More generally, the powerful person is in a position to enter an exchange in which he offers some resource and, in turn, expects to be reciprocated.

By defining power in terms of resource possession, some hypotheses about the relationship among the different types of power can be developed. The structure of resources suggests that proximal types will be more related than distal ones. A person powerful in money may easily possess valuable goods, but not always status and certainly can be quite "poor" in love. The specificity of power with respect to resources has been obscured by the fact that a person having great power in a particular resource may acquire other resources through exchange (Benoit, 1966): an individual possessing a large amount of money may acquire status by donations to appropriate institutions such as educational, medical, religious, etc. This possibility of exchanging one class of power with another is limited. One cannot buy genuine love with money, at most he buys personal services; likewise the "nouveau riche" is often rejected by those circles he most wishes to join, although they may possess less money than he. In many instances, the "self made man" achieves the desirable status only through his offspring whom he helps to possess information, a proximal resource to status. Again, the limitations in exchanging one type of power with another may be predicted from the structure of resources.

ACTUAL AND POTENTIAL POWER. As Cartwright and Zander (1968, pp. 216–217) have pointed out, power cannot be exercised unless there is a corresponding need on the part of the receiver. A person may have great potential power and little actual power when there is scarce demand for the resource he possesses in abundance. No matter how much love one can give, he may not attract the girl who has an already highly satisfactory relationship with another person. Likewise, the expert in aeronautics has little actual power when the airplane industry is in crisis. Thus the distinction between actual and potential, already applied to needs, holds for power as well. Potential power is an attribute of a single agent, whereas actual power is "a relationship between two agents" (Cartwright, 1959a, p. 213), the one who can give and the other who needs the specific resource.

The reciprocal relationship between need and power is well illustrated by Levinger's experiment (1959) dealing with the resource of information. Sixty-four subjects were requested to work with a partner (the experimenter's confederate) in solving some town-planning problems. In one group the confederate presented himself as ignorant and as lacking self confidence. In the other group he introduced himself as having considerable expertise and as a self-assured person. Each group was further exposed to differential treatment: in half of the cases the confederate most often accepted the proposals of the subject, while rejecting the ideas of the other in the remaining cases. Subjects felt more powerful when they believed they had more information than their partner, i.e., when the other needed their information. Levinger also found that this effect of the initial presentation decreased over the 24 trials, depending on the reaction of the confederate to the subject's proposals: when acceptance was prevalent, the feeling of power increased. In rejection there was some decrease, particularly for those who were previously led to believe they were superior. Since most of these changes occurred in the first half of the trials, it seems that interaction tends to stabilize on a definite power relationship. Subjects who felt more powerful were more likely to be assertive, to attempt influencing the other and to reject his attempts to influence.

SYMMETRY OF POWER. This experiment illustrates a situation where only one resource is involved so that the power relationship is likely to be asymmetric: one of the participants possesses this resource in an amount larger than the one possessed by the other. In most interactions, several resources are exchanged; then, A may be more powerful in one resource and B in another, so that symmetry does occur, and both partners may gain the needed resource. Obviously the notion of symmetry (Cartwright, 1959a, pp. 197–198) refers to actual power; in a satisfactory exchange situation, each participant is powerful in the specific resource the other needs.

THREAT. When summetry is absent the power of the other is more likely to be perceived as a threat: when the other possesses a resource we need, and we do not have any resource that he needs, he gains control without us being able to limit it by withholding what we own. Consequently, individuals or groups possessing a large amount of resources, are often perceived as threatening; contemporary examples are the big corporation, the big union, the big government.

Cohen (1959) investigated two conditions which may influence the perception of threat: ambiguity of the situation and self-esteem. In the ambiguous situation, the subject was presented with vague and contradictory cues as to what was expected of him, a manipulation interpreted by us as reduction in the information available to the subjects. This information was necessary for performing adequately on the assigned task and thus obtaining status from the powerful person, the "supervisor." It was found that subjects who received ambiguous information perceived the powerful person as more threatening than those exposed to structured and clear tasks. Low self-esteem subjects perceived more threat in the structured situation than did high self-esteem ones. However, in the ambiguous situation, the degree of self-esteem did not influence the perceived amount of threat. It seems that the amount of need for status is a relevant factor only when there is an access to this resource, i.e., when the type of information available is sufficient for successful performance. On the other hand, when there is no way to reduce the need, the situation is equally threatening for both high- and low-need persons. The interpretation of threat as absence of symmetry in the power relationship suggests that the feeling of being threatened will decrease when several opportunities for exchange are opened for the powerless person. Evidence on this prediction was provided by Stotland (1959). Subjects under "threat" who were permitted to meet another subject in a similar condition, were better able to stand up against the threatening figure and particularly so when they developed an "interest" in the other subject, i.e., when they had meaningful exchanges with him. As Stotland (1959, p. 67) perceptively noted, "by establishing a positive relationship with one person, the subject was protected from having to establish a similar relationship with another, less satisfactory person." Stotland's experiment presented exchanges among three persons. The asymmetry between the powerful and the powerless persons decreased when the latter, through symmetrical relations with a third party, increased the amount of resources available to him. This relationship among several exchanges of one individual introduces the problem of transitivity.

TRANSITIVITY OF POWER. In analyzing the various properties of power, Cartwright (1959a, pp. 198–199) asks: "If A has power over B and B has power over C, does it necessarily follow that A has power over

C?" Although stated in terms of actual power, this problem of transitivity pertains as well to potential power: if A *has more* power than B and B has more power than C, does it follow that A has more power than C? Cartwright's examples suggest that power may be transitive when the various power relationships are within the same institution; when different institutions are involved, power is intransitive. But we already know that resources tend to differ in various institutions, so that the property of transitivity can be stated, more precisely, as follows: Both potential and actual power are transitive within each resource class even across different roles and institutions. When different classes are involved, the power relationship is intransitive, particularly when the resources involved are distal. The boss is powerful over his employee as a source of money; if, in turn, this employee retains power over his wife, *only* through the provision of material resources, then the boss is more powerful than the the employee's wife in *this* resource. When, however, the husband's power is rooted in his ability to give love, his boss will have no power over the worker's wife.

ACCUMULATION OF POWER. One could argue that the power possessed by an individual will increase in proportion to the amount of a given resource he receives. This way of achieving power seems to fit those resources which can be stored outside the individual, mainly money and goods; with regard to other resources, some qualifications are needed. We have already stated that there is an upper limit to the optimal range of resources which are stored within the organism. Any amount that exceeds this limit results in satiation (Gewirtz and Baer, 1958). The upper limit, in turn, depends on previous experience in receiving and possessing resources. When little was received in the past, satiation will occur after absorbing a small amount; consequently, a rapid increase in power is not feasible. The finding (Eldred, Bell, Sherman and Longabaugh, 1964) that schizophrenics appear unsuccessful in obtaining resources from other persons, even after making allowances for their resource bankruptcy, is significant in this respect. A person possessing little power seems to be less able to increase it, not only because he has little to offer in exchange, but also because he is less able to receive what is given to him for the little he has to offer. Paradoxically, such inability to receive limits also the power of the giver. This may explain the feeling of helplessness sometimes experienced when interacting with an emotionally disturbed individual.

The Power of the Powerless

We have defined power as possession of resources. Certainly without "owning" the resource, it cannot be dispensed to others; likewise, a threat to withhold it is meaningless unless the resource is available for dispensation. Yet, one can threaten to take away or actually create a loss without previous possession of it. One can deceive the other without having the right information, as well as stealing without having money. With regard to particularistic resources, especially love and status, such power is limited. To be insulted by a low status person is less damaging than being degraded by a high status individual. However, the amount of money owned by the thief does not affect the amount of loss he may inflict on his victim. This may be the reason why social and legal sanctions are imposed on acts of taking away less particularistic resources. As we shall see later (Ch. 6), taking away is likely to be followed by retaliation: the victim, on being deprived, acts to inflict a loss on the taker. If, however, the taker possesses very little resources, the possibility of retaliation is reduced. Thus, the state of having little confers to the "desperate" a sort of quasi-power, the power of the powerless.

A different kind of quasi-power, possessed by the weak individual is noted by Parsons (1955, pp. 46–47): The child, although being dependent on his parents, may be able to influence their behavior; often children gain control over their parents, not by taking away from them, but rather by creating a loss to themselves. Refusal to eat or hitting the head on the floor constitute examples of such behaviors. This quasi-power depends, however, on the love of the parents for their child. Those parents who are indifferent towards their child would probably not be influenced by the latter inflicting loss on himself. Only the mother who is powerful in love may feel incompetent when confronted with the self-depriving behavior of the child. This behavior would not be equally effective with strangers and, in fact, children usually reserve it for their parents. Grown-ups may also resort to this technique, as in hunger strikes. But again, they are unlikely to succeed unless the party they attempt to control has some positive attitude toward them, either directly or through a third party: the jailer may be indifferent to the prisoners refusal to eat, but would lose status by ignoring public opinion sympathetic to them. In summary, there are three techniques for controlling the behavior of the other: (a) threat to deny him a resource he needs and cannot obtain elsewhere; (b) threat to take away from him a resource he possesses; and (c) taking away from self.

By examining the notions of need and power, we have dealt with one motivational mechanism: the strive for maintaining an optimal amount of resources by giving what we have and receiving what we need. We now turn to consider a second motivational mechanism.

Preservation of Structure from Dissonant Events

In the introductory chapter we have noted the significance of cognitive structures as a frame for ordering perceived events, without which one would be overwhelmed and confused by the richness of environmental stimuli. If cognitive structures are essential to our well-being, we need means for protecting them from events which challenge their validity.

The need for maintaining cognitive structures has been acknowledged by many scholars under various labels, such as "drive for understanding" and "drive for meaning." In reviewing the area of cognitive consistency, Berkowitz lucidly states that " 'understanding' entails knowledge of the relations among stimuli, or possession of a 'coding system' which enables the person to predict what leads to what, or what goes with what" (1969a, p. 88). The drive for understanding is then an attempt to maintain cognitive patterns of relationships. A threat to the structure occurs when one is confronted with an event which contains dissonant components. Indeed, the notion of dissonance and cognate concepts, such as imbalance and incongruity (Zajonc, 1960) are usually taken to indicate the coexistence of incompatible elements.

The threat to the structure posed by incongruent elements is not explicit in the original formulation of dissonance. Festinger (1957, p. 13) proposed that two elements are dissonant when "the obverse of one element would follow from the other." To borrow one of Festinger's examples, the element "I smoke cigarettes" is incongruent with the element "cigarette smoking produces cancer." To reduce the discomfort created by dissonance, some behavioral and/or cognitive change will take place (Festinger, 1957, p. 3).

In spite of the varied and exciting research generated by dissonance theory, even benign critics have recognized its lack of precision (Aronson, 1969; Zajonc, 1968). The main criticism has turned on the following points:

1. No clear-cut rule is provided by dissonance theory for determining when two elements of a situation are psychologically inconsistent. Aronson (1969, p. 7) asks, for example, whether dissonance would occur after learning that my favorite novelist beats his wife.

2. Even in the simplest situation, more than two elements are likely to be involved; whether or not two of them are dissonant may depend on a third one (Aronson, 1969, pp. 24–26). Smoking and danger of cancer will be dissonant only if one wants to avoid the possibility of getting cancer.

3. There are various ways in which dissonance may be resolved: one can either stop smoking or disbelieve the information that

smoking produces cancer. Yet no specific criteria for predicting which alternative will be chosen in a given situation are offered by the theory.

4.   Some results predicted by dissonance theory appear to contradict the ones derived from reinforcement theory. According to dissonance theory, a person advocating a view he opposes will tend to accept it more after receiving a smaller compensation. Conversely, reinforcement theory would predict that the larger the compensation, the greater will be the change in attitude. Some experiments have supported the first prediction, while others have corroborated the second one. The critical question is, then: what are the conditions leading to each of the two outcomes?

A more precise definition of dissonance may contribute to the solution of these problems.

DISSONANCE REDEFINED. We have proposed earlier (Ch. 1) that an event reaches cognition as a structure, displaying a relationship pattern among its component elements. This pattern may or may not be homologous to the appropriate cognitive structure; a consonant event is readily absorbed into cognition; indeed, it provides additional confirmation to the validity of the cognitive structure. On the other hand, an event which does not fit cognition constitutes a threat to its structure. It seems, then, that dissonance involves a comparison between two structures, the structure of the event and the cognitive structure onto which it is mapped. Dissonance is thus defined as the condition in which these two structures do not match. A similar conceptualization has been independently developed by Feather (1971).

Consider, for example, events which involve receiving love and losing status, or vice versa. Such events will produce dissonance, since—as we have seen in Chapter 3—love and status are positively related in the cognitive structure. A negative relationship between love and status was indeed produced by Sampson and Insko (1964), who manipulated the subject's liking for another person, as well as the degree to which he disagreed with him on judging the movement of light in an autokinetic situation. The results are summarized by Berkowitz (1969a, p. 94): "Relatively great cognitive imbalance existed in this study when (1) the subject liked the other person and initially held a dissimilar opinion, or (2) there was a dislike for the other person but the subject's initial judgment was similar to his. This imbalance caused a greater tendency for the subject to alter his judgments of the light movement (toward increased balancing), and also to feel anxious while making these judgments, than did the more balanced conditions."

Other dissonance experiments involve a manipulation of the

exchange paradigm (see Ch. 6). In cognition, giving a resource is positively related to receiving one; consequently, a situation where the subject experiences a loss which is not compensated by an acquisition will be perceived as dissonant. In a classic experiment, Festinger and Carlsmith (1959) found that subjects who were paid little for expressing an opinion they did not share tended later to accept it more than those who were paid a larger amount of money. By being hypocrites, subjects lost status or self-esteem; this loss was compensated when a large sum was received in exchange. On the other hand, when only one dollar was paid, imbalance was restored by reduction of the status loss; this was obtained by agreeing with the opinion they had previously stated. It should be noted that a status-money exchange is not common (see Ch. 6) and consequently, the cognitive relationship underlying the assumed dissonance might not be particularly strong: indeed, later replication did not support the original outcome (Sampson, 1971, pp. 113–114). Perhaps more clear-cut results would have been obtained by using exchanges which were more firmly established in the learning history of the subjects.

A formalization of the dissonance situation and its resolution is presented in Figure 12. This figure depicts the positive relationship between two classes (e.g., amount of resource taken and amount of resource received) embodied in the experience of past events represented in cognition. In the deviant event the relationship is negative (high giving is associated with low receiving). Dissonance is then reduced by decreasing the value of one element (the resource given), thus bringing

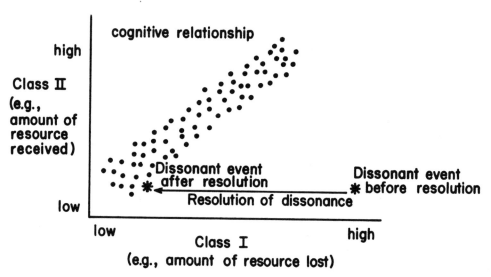

Figure 12. Schematic representation of the cognitive relationship between classes and of the dissonant event.

the event into line with cognition. In other experiments (e.g., Aronson and Mills, 1959) resolution was obtained by an increase in value of the resource received: harsher initiation made the group discussion more attractive. Here the dissonant event is resolved by transferring it to the upper right corner of Figure 12. This figure shows, indeed, that even in relatively simple situations there are at least two ways to increase the fit between event and cognition. Sampson and Insko's subjects could have changed their liking for the other (love), rather than their judgment of the light movement (status). Subjects paid one dollar would have convinced themselves that they had received a large amount of money, rather than modifying their attitude (status). Finally, in the Aronson and Mills experiment, participants could have considered the initiation "ritual" milder than it was (services), rather than finding the group topic interesting (information). In all three experiments dissonance was resolved by modifying the perceived value of symbolic resources—status or information—rather than of love, money, or services, which are more concrete. Perhaps the more symbolic the resource is, the less it may be resistant to a perceptual change of its value. Further support for this hypothesis will provide a basis for predicting the way in which dissonance is reduced.

The reanalysis of these experiments suggests that, once the cognitive structure is known, it becomes possible to predict whether a given event will create dissonance. Earlier in this book (Ch. 3 and 4) we have examined basic structures of social relations which appear quite stable, not only across roles and individuals but also across cultures, as we shall see later (Ch. 9). This stability facilitates the prediction of dissonance. Many dissonance investigations capitalized, indeed, upon the invariance of the structure: the experimenter relied implicitly and intuitively on his own cognition in deciding whether an event would or would not be dissonant. This method was successful when the experimenter's structure resembled that of his subjects—a common occurrence when both parties were normal individuals from a common culture; it tended, however, to exclude from experimentation cases in which the event was not perceived as dissonant by the experimenter but would create dissonance in individuals who, for one reason or another, possessed a different structure. We shall return to this problem later in the discussion.

DISSONANCE VS. REINFORCEMENT. Quite often the prediction of reinforcement theory is contradicted by the outcomes in dissonance experiments. Indeed, it was found that agreement or liking are higher when the reward is smaller or punishment stronger. Aronson (1969, pp. 20–24) has provided a brilliant review of those investigations where dissonance prediction was supported under certain conditions while reinforcement prediction appeared to prevail under different ones.

1. Subjects who had performed a dull task were requested to describe it as interesting; later they expressed their opinion of the task. When the positive description was given face-to-face, thus committing the subject, a smaller reward resulted in a more favorable opinion of the task (dissonance effect). When the description took the form of an anonymous essay, the contrary was found: higher reward resulted in a more positive opinion (reinforcement effect). (Carlsmith, Collins and Helmreich, 1966.)

2. Subjects were requested to write an essay favoring close paternalistic supervision of students by college authorities. Later on they expressed their opinion on the topic. Subjects left free to choose whether or not to write the essay expressed more favorable opinions the smaller the reward (dissonance); those who were not left with such a choice expressed a more favorable opinion when the reward was higher (reinforcement). (Linder, Cooper and Jones, 1967.)

3. Subjects were asked to record a short statement which they did not believe, ostensibly to be played to a large student audience; later they gave their opinion regarding the statement. When the recording was on videotape, along with personal details of the subject, those who received a smaller reward became more favorable (dissonance). When the recording was on audio and anonymous, those who received a larger reward expressed a more favorable opinion (reinforcement). (Helmreich and Collins, 1968.)

4. Freedman's (1963) subjects were asked to evaluate a dull task they had previously performed; some subjects were told that the data would be of no value, since they were too late to be used by the experimenter; other subjects were informed that the data would be of great value. When this information regarding the value of the data had been given *before* the task was performed, subjects in the no-value condition enjoyed it more than those in the high-value condition (dissonance); however, when the same information was given *after* task completion, the results were reversed (reinforcement).

5. Gerard and Mathewson (1966) exposed subjects to strong or mild electric shock before admitting them to an ostensible group discussion, which was, in fact, pretaped. Those told that receiving shock was a requirement for joining the group rated the taped discussion as more attractive when shock was higher (dissonance); subjects who simply received shock before listening to the tape, but not as a condition for participation, found the discussion somewhat more enjoyable when shock was milder (reinforcement).

Clearly, as suggested by Aronson (1969, p. 24) the variable responsible for the reversal of results is the degree to which the subject had previously committed himself, by public endorsement of the view, by freely choosing to perform a task or to join a group. The question is, then, how does commitment operate as contingent variable?

Commitment appears to have two effects:

1. It produces a loss of status for the subject who endorsed a view he opposes, a dull task, or a boring discussion;
2. It changes the connotation of the attitude or evaluation expressed by the subject in the final stage of the experiment. In the absence of commitment, attitude change or positive evaluation gives status to the experimenter who presented the view or the task (see Ch. 7 for a discussion of conformity). On the other hand, for committed subjects the same behavior avoids a further loss of status for himself, which would occur if he disagreed with the position previously taken.

With these two effects in mind, let us examine differences in the exchange situation for committed and uncommitted subjects. The loss of status incurred by the committed subject is counterbalanced when compensation is large: he lost status but gained a rather substantial amount (in money or in the status derived from doing something of high value). However, when compensation is small and incommensurate to the loss, support of the previous position reduces the perceived amount lost. For the uncommitted subject, the exchange situation is simpler: the amount of status he gives the experimenter, by agreeing with him, is commensurate to the amount of whatever resource he received: he agrees more when the experimenter was generous in his reward, or as in the Gerard and Mathewson's investigation (1966), moderate in the punishment he inflicted.

There is no real contradiction between the two sets of results and no need for two different theories. Resource theory provided an explanation for both sets. In cognition, loss and gain are positively related; therefore, an event displaying a different relationship will create dissonance. Such discrepancy may be experienced by committed, as well as by uncommitted subjects: receiving a small compensation for a large loss is not more dissonant than gaining a large compensation for a minimal loss. The committed subject reduces dissonance by limiting his loss, while in the absence of commitment the reduction of dissonance is obtained by giving status to the experimenter.

INDUCING DISSONANCE BY COGNITIVE CHANGE. Most dissonance investigations consist essentially of comparing subjects confronted with a dissonant event with others experiencing a non-dissonant situation. In devising these two types of event, the experimenter relies intuitively on his own cognition; the cognitive structure of the subjects does not appear in the experimental design, although it is tacitly assumed to resemble that of the experimenter; hence, the manipulation of the event constitutes the independent variable. In a radical departure from this traditional design, Bramel (1962) kept the event constant while manipulating differentially the cognition of his subjects. By increasing the self-esteem in half of the subjects and decreasing it in the other half, he modified the relationship between actual and ideal self. Subjects were then exposed to a situation indicating that they had homosexual tendencies. A bogus machine, to which they were hooked, showed "physiological arousal" when they observed pictures of nude males. The machine was, of course, controlled by the experimenter and not by the reactions of the subject. Bramel correctly predicted that those with increased self-esteem will experience more dissonance. Indeed, high self-esteem denotes a strong positive relationship between actual and ideal self—the notion of actual self covaries with desirable traits; by contrast, actual self is associated with an undesirable characteristic in the event "I have homosexuual tendencies". Hence, such event is particularly dissonant when self-esteem is greater.

Bramel's experiment shows that the same event—evidence of homosexual tendencies—may be more or less dissonant, depending on the cognitive structure of the subject. Thus, a prediction of dissonance should consider both the event and the cognition of its observer. As Aronson (1969, p. 28) notes, being untruthful is not dissonant for a psychopathic liar; but then, wouldn't he experience dissonance when telling the truth? Limiting the investigation of dissonance to cognitions which are widely shared and thus more readily predictable by the experimenter has obscured the relationship between dissonance and some other areas of psychological study.

DISSONANCE AND PSYCHOPATHOLOGY. Consider a person with an extremely low self-esteem; for him, the event of succeeding in a task would create dissonance: he would either tend to downgrade his success or he will ascribe it to some factor unrelated to his abilities. Situations of this type have not been recognized as cases of dissonance, although they are well-known to students of psychopathology. For a long time it has been noted that some individuals court failure, become upset when things go too well, refuse love and are embarrassed by praise. For them, receiving status and/or love are dissonant events, threatening their cognitive structure; they will seek interpersonal relations in which they can be consonantly deprived of resources. This type of behavior has been widely discussed in the literature. Mechanisms for the maintenance of a congruent self-image to avoid tension have been investigated by Secord and Backman (1961, 1965); Leary

(1957) has propounded the notion that interpersonal behavior is also an invitation to the "appropriate" reaction from the other; thus, for example, hostility wards off the threatening possibility of receiving love. Jackson (1957) has shown how disturbed individuals may have a stabilizing effect in disturbed family systems, in which somebody else gets worse when the "patient" gets better.

The basic unity of these phenomena has been often obscured because of the different terminology used by various authors. Carson (1969) has provided an integrated treatment of this area, summarized in his view of psychotherapy; ". . . the strategic task of the psychotherapist is to change his client's self-in-relation-to-world image . . . An image is changed through the provision of experience that is both new *and* assimilable in terms of existing, accessible cognitive categories. Cognitive categories, especially perhaps those relating to self, cannot be bludgeoned into change; they tend to repel experiences that do not "fit them" (p. 275).

For disturbed individuals, the need for resources and the motivation to preserve the structure are often in conflict as resource-providing events may be incongruent with their cognition. This conflict between resource accumulation and structure preservation has originated rival hypotheses, regarding the effect of criticism and praise on their recipient, summarized by S.C. Jones (1973). The consistency hypothesis suggest that ". . . For individuals with high evaluations of themselves or some aspect of self, positive evaluations from others are consistent, whereas for individuals with low self-evaluations, positive evaluations are inconsistent and negative evaluations are consistent. Therefore, the prediction from the self-consistency theories is that high self-evaluators will react more favorably to approval than to disapproval and that low self-evaluators will react more favorably to disapproval than to approval (p. 186)." By contrast, the self-esteem hypotheses proposes that ". . . low self-esteem individuals are predicted to respond more favorably to positive evaluations from others and more unfavorably to negative evaluations from others as compared to high self-esteem individuals. This prediction . . . follows from the assumption that low self-esteem people have greater needs for esteem enhancement and are therefore more satisfied by the approval of others and more frustrated by the disapproval of others than are high self-esteem people" (p. 187). It is not by chance that the two hypotheses differ mainly with regard to low self-esteem subjects. Those are the people who find themselves in a conflict: if they absorb criticism and ignore praise, their need for status becomes greater with every encounter; if they accept praise and reject criticism, they experience inconsistency between their cognitive structure and the external event. S.C.

Jones (1973), in reviewing relevant evidence, reported more support for the self-esteem hypothesis. This finding, however, may be due to a characteristic of the subjects in the investigations he considered. The analysis presented here suggest that the lower self-esteem is the more dissonance is experienced by the individual when praised. Therefore, a person possessing very low self-esteem will tend to reject praise in favor of maintaining the structure. Such extreme individuals are rare in the college population from which subjects in psychological research are usually obtained. Among them one is more likely to find persons of moderately low self-esteem who fulfill their need for status, since the threat to their structure is not very great. Stronger support for the consistency hypotheses is likely to be found in a clinical setting, where cases of extremely low self-esteem are more common.

Conceptualizing dissonance as a contrast between past experience of the organism (as represented in the cognitive structure) and current experience reveals its relationship to other notions which have been considered unrelated to it.

EXTENDING THE NOTION OF DISSONANCE. A threat to the preservation of structure may come, not only from an event with a different structure, but also from a series of unstructured events. Such random environment, in which the conditioned and unconditioned stimuli would be statistically independent (i.e., the probability of their joint occurrence is equal to the product of their marginal probabilities) was proposed by Rescorla (1967) as a control for classical conditioning experiments. This suggestion was criticized (Seligman, 1969) on the ground that a random environment produced disruptive side effects. These effects may be due to the threat posed to the cognitive structure by the random events. It is interesting to note that any learning experiment involving a change in reinforcement schedule produces some dissonance: after the organism had learned to associate response A with reward and response B with punishment, it is presented with a contrasting situation. Since the learning period is usually short, the schedule is unlikely to become firmly established in cognition and the dissonant effects are weak. Even "superstitious behavior" (Skinner, 1953, pp. 84–87) when contrasted by future events may create dissonance. A pigeon fed small amounts at frequent intervals may acquire the habit of repeating whatever it was doing when food was first administered, although food release was regulated by the clock independently of the pigeon's behavior. When, in future trials, the coincidence between emission of behavior and provision of food will disappear, dissonance may occur.

So far we have considered dissonant events characterized by elements which deviate from the relationship among their respective cognitive classes. Incongruence may also occur when a person is presented with an event which belongs to class A according to one cue, but should be classisfied into class B according to another cue. For example, a person having a beard but wearing a female dress represents an incongruent event; the dress suggests that this person should be classified as "female", yet the beard provides a cue for the "male" class. A similar situation arises when the experience of one sense is not supported by other senses. Seeing a person but being unable to feel him when touched is a strange experience; such apparition is likely to be labeled ghost. But again, incongruence will be experienced only when sight and touch are cognitively related; one does not feel uncomfortable because he can see but not touch the images appearing on a TV screen.

DISSONANCE AND VISUAL ILLUSIONS. Our re-definition of dissonance also suggests the interpretation of perceptual constancy and spatial illusions as special cases of dissonance reduction. It is well known that an object moving away from the observer is not perceived as shrinking in size, although its image on the retina becomes smaller as the distance increases; likewise a coin tilted at 45 degrees is perceived as round rather than eliptical in spite of the fact that the shape seen by the observer is eliptical. Perceptual constancy thus consists in modifying perception to fit the relevant cognitive image, a process which also occurs in dissonance reduction.

Spatial illusions, systematically misjudging the size, shape or other properties of objects under certain conditions, have often been considered a class of phenomena distinct from perceptual constancy; Day (1972) has, however, proposed that illusions occur when stimuli that normally preserve constancy are present while the image of the object does not change. Clearly events presenting this combination are dissonant, as they deviate from the common experience recorded in cognition; dissonance reduction produces the illusion: the perceived size of the object is modified as it should be when constancy stimuli are present.

DISSONANCE AND COGNITIVE GROWTH. Classes are positively related in cognition when their elements tended to occur jointly in the events previously experienced by the organism; thus the structure reflects past experience. A dissonant event contradicts the wisdom accumulated in the cognition, or it disconfirms an hypothesis held by the observer. Being an isolated instance, its perception is modified to fit cognition. If the same deviant event continues to occur, one would expect a permanent modification of the structure, as it happens during cognitive development. Both dissonance and cognitive development are characterized by a discrepancy between events and cognition. In dissonance, however, the deviant event is an isolated case and the solution involves perceptual modification to fit the structure. In development, on the other hand, dissonant events tend to be repetitive and eventually result in a modification of the cognitive structure.

Having examined aspects of the motivational state of the individual which influence his propensity and ability to enter an exchange of resources, we now turn to consider the facilitations and restrictions imposed on transactions by social institutions.

THE INSTITUTIONAL SETTING

For an exchange to eventuate, a person needing a given resource and powerful in another should meet an individual who is in a complementary motivational state, i.e., who needs what the other offers and can give what the other needs. It sounds like a complicated task, yet we are constantly involved in resource exchanges, mostly occuring as a matter of routine. Indeed, society has developed mechanisms for facilitating the meeting of individuals having reciprocal needs and powers. The first function of these mechanisms, which are called social institutions, is to provide suitable settings for the different exchanges. When a person wants to exchange money for goods he obviously goes to a shop; when he intends to get money for his labor or services he turns to a work institution. The institution not only specifies the type of exchange, but also determines what resources each party should give and what he should receive in return. A salesman, for example, provides the goods while the customer provides the money; likewise the employee provides the service and the employer the money.

The second function of institutions is to dictate the proper pairs of resources to be exchanged. The guest is about to leave after having been treated to a very good dinner. What shall he give in exchange? In a private house he would probably thank the hostess profusely, expressing his pleasure for the pleasant evening (giving love) and his admiration for her cooking skills (giving status). In a restaurant he will pay the bill and leave a tip on the table. It is easy to imagine what would happen if our guest would give money for the meal he had at his friend's home and would express his pleasure at the restaurant, leaving without paying. In both cases he is likely to find himself in trouble. It appears, therefore, that not every type of exchange is permissible in a given institution; a resource appropriate to the commercial catering institution may be highly unsuitable for the hospitality institution, and vice versa.

The influence of the institutional setting on exchange patterns is demonstrated in a number of investigations. Kiesler (1966) found that in a cooperative situation, subjects liked more the confederate who shared the money with them, while in a competitive situation, the one who did not share was liked better. Weinstein, DeVaughan and Wiley (1969) arranged pairs of subjects in such a way that one member of the pair would contribute to the joint task more than the other. An opportunity for establishing equity was then offered in a second interaction. Repayment varied according to the institutional situation: to a friend, it was made by giving him status; when the partner was a stranger, however, debitor partners invested more effort in the joint task at the second interaction and assumed leadership. Other studies (Brehm and Cole, 1966; Schopler and Thompson, 1968) briefly described later (see Ch. 7), have shown that when the resource given is institutionally inappropriate, there is less reciprocation.

For each institution there are certain resources which are more typical and more frequently exchanged. The exchange of money with services is typical of the work institution; information is exchanged with money in school institution, if private, and status is exchanged for information in public schools; money-goods exchange is found in the trade institution; and in the family, love and status are the crucial resources. In all these examples, the resources exchanged tend to be proximal in the structure of resources; it suggests that each institution focuses on a particular segment of the structure. It is difficult to think of any institution where the crucial resources exchanged are most distal from one another, like love and money, goods and status, or services and information. The family is probably the institution where the widest range of exchange is found, but even here not every exchange is permissible or customary: one is not supposed to give money for a service received in the family. A colleague's wife asks money for shining her husband's shoes; her explanation for this seemingly strange request is that shoe shining is not part of the normal housewife's duties.

Although certain exchanges are characteristic to a given institution, other exchanges may also take place in it, but only as accessory to the main one. It is quite possible to accompany goods-money exchange with minor expressions of friendship toward the salesman. To enter a shop for the sole purpose of exchanging affect would probably raise some eyebrows. In general, institutions make exchanges easier and more predictable: if a person appears in a doctor's office, it is a safe bet that he wants medical treatment rather than applying for a loan. On the other hand, institutions also constitute limitations and barriers to exchange. One should address himself to the appropriate institution for a given exchange, yet he may not have an access to it. A person who does not satisfy certain educational requirements cannot become a college student; an introvert individual will be barred from exchanges of friendship. Not having access to the appropriate institutions, one may seek the needed resource in inappropriate settings: a person in need of status may prefer to buy in a small shop where he gets personal attention, rather than at the big department store where prices are lower but no status is given; some people go to the doctor, not because of poor health, but to receive support and love (Shuval, 1970).

The requirement of institutional access is much stronger for exchanges of giving than for exchanges of taking away. There is no need for formal introduction before robbing a person of money or goods, hitting him or insulting him. Could it be a reason why exchanges of taking away (aggression) are more frequent for those who have little access to the existing institutions?

Institutional differences in resource exchange will be illustrated by analyzing two settings, psychotherapy and a group task in college. The analysis of resource exchange in various schools of psychotherapy is speculative, being based on generally accepted notions about these schools; however, the conceptualization of psychotherapy as an institution is not new (Levine, 1969). The analysis of the second setting, task group in college, is based on empirical data.

Psychotherapy as a Social Institution

The psychotherapeutic setting can be seen as an institution, in the sense that it provides an opportunity for the exchange of certain resources, while barring certain others. Furthermore, as resource exchange appears to vary, in theory and perhaps also in practice, for different therapeutic schools, each school may be perceived as a different institution. Consider three different schools: the behavioristic, the Rogerian and the orthodox psychoanalytic. In each one of them it might be possible to specify the resources involved in the behavior of the therapist toward the patient, as well as in the behavior of the patient toward the therapist and toward himself. The behavior of the therapist toward himself is not included, since little information about it can be found in the theory of the respective schools, and one is led to presume that it should not be much in evidence in the therapeutic situation. The "learning analysis" of the therapist, required in psychoanalysis, is indeed meant to free the analyst from concern with his own problem, i.e., to reduce the frequency of his behavior toward himself. On the other hand, the behavior of the patient toward himself appears to be very relevant to psychotherapy. When therapy is behavioristic, for example, the patient is quite likely to be rewarded for doing some service to himself, such as feeding himself, whereas the patient's giving love to self is desirable in client-centered therapy. As already noted, this kind of exchange occurs also between parents and child in training for independence.

Selectivity of Schools

Each school appears to prefer certain resources and to exclude certain others. In behavior therapy the rewards given by the therapist to the patient are often money or tokens and goods, like M & M candies. Love and status seem to be in little use and, according to some reports (Hamblin, et al., 1969), giving status or approval has not proved very effective. Punishment, when used, frequently involves taking away a service such as mild electrical shock. Information does not seem to play much of a role in behavior therapy. There are apparently no resources that the subject ought to give to the therapist, but he is expected to give himself certain services, such as keeping clean, assuming a certain posture, and the like. Often the behavior rewarded may be toward a third individual and, in this case, most resources may be involved.

In Rogerian therapy the client is to receive love and status from the therapist and to give these resources to himself. Some results given later suggest that this exchange may run into difficulties with schizophrenics in regard to love and with neurotics in regard to status, since the respective correlations between receiving from other and giving to self are rather low for these patients. The sole resource the client is expected to give the therapist is information, talking about himself. The resource exchange of client-centered therapy appears, therefore, to be different from the one of behavior therapy.

Still another picture is presented by orthodox psychoanalysis. Here the therapist is expected to give information to the patient, in the form of interpretation of material (free association, dreams, etc.) supplied by the latter. The therapist appears also likely to take away status from the patient by putting him in a position of inferiority; lying on the couch, without being able to see the therapist is indicative in this respect. The analyst should be perceived as a stern and superior father image. It seems also that taking away money from the patient, making him pay for the treatment, is considered a relevant aspect of the psychoanalytic treatment. The therapist is not expected to give love to the patient (counter-transference is indeed discouraged), nor to give goods or services. The administration of services such as shots and other forms of physical treatment may, however, occur irrespective of school, when the therapist is a psychiatrist.

In orthodox psychoanalysis the patient should give information and money to the therapist, as already noted. He is also expected to give him love (transference) and status, by recognizing his superior position in the situation. At the same time the patient is expected to take away status from himself. The existence of defense mechanisms is assumed to lead the patient to rationalize and misinterpret his behavior, thus taking away information from himself, in the terminology adopted here.

This attempt to describe three schools of therapy in terms of resource exchange is summarized in Table 23. In this Table "giving" is indicated

Table 23

RESOURCE EXCHANGED IN THREE PSYCHOTHERAPEUTIC SCHOOLS

Behavior	Resource	School		
		Behavioristic	Rogerian	Orthodox Psychoanalysis
Therapist to Patient	Love	?	+	0
	Status	?	+	−
	Information	0	0	+
	Money	+	0	−
	Goods	+	0	0
	Services	−	0	0
Patient to Therapist	Love	0	0	+
	Status	0	0	+
	Information	0	+	+
	Money	0	0	+
	Goods	0	0	0
	Services	0	0	0
Patient to Self	Love	0	+	0
	Status	0	+	−
	Information	0	+	−
	Money	0	0	0
	Goods	0	0	0
	Services	+	0	0

by a plus sign and "taking away" by a minus sign. A zero indicates absence of both giving and taking away. No sign has been used to indicate ambivalence or joint occurrence of giving and taking, as we were unable to find prescriptions for it in the theory of the various schools. This does not mean, of course, that ambivalence cannot occur in practice. A question mark has been used when we felt unable to reach even a tentative decision with regard to the use of a particular resource. In Table 23 resources are listed in their structural order (see Fig. 7). It should be remembered, however, that this order is circular so that the first and last resources in the list are also proximal.

SELECTIVITY AND ORDER. Listing the resources in their order reveals an interesting property: identical signs appear next to each other in the order. The pluses, minuses and zeros are grouped together. The sole exception is in the behavior of therapist to patient in psychoanalysis, where the taking of status is separated from the taking of money by a giving of the intervening resource, information. The position of the zeros in the behavior of the patient toward himself for psychoanalysis, and in the behavior of the patient toward the therapist, for Rogerian treatment, may give the false impression of deviating from the order. The order is, however, circular, services being closer to love, so that the zeros are actually grouped together. The grouping of the resources in all three schools suggests that in each school, similar or neighboring resources are likely to be treated in a similar manner. This manner appears to be different in each school; indeed the profiles of signs in Table 23 differentiate among the schools. In fact, the patient's behavior toward himself with regard to status would be sufficient to differentiate among schools: status is taken away from self in the Freudian, given in the Rogerian, neither given nor taken in the behavioristic school. Another difference among the schools regarding exchange which does not appear in Table 23, is the degree to which the behavior of the therapist toward the patient is contingent upon the behavior of the patient toward the therapist, himself or a third individual. The strictest contingency is likely to be found in behavioristic treatment, where reward and punishment administered by the therapist are determined by the behavior of the patient. At the other end, the Rogerian therapist is assumed to keep his behavior independent of the patient's behavior; his giving of love and status is unconditional. Orthodox psychoanalysis probably occupies, in this respect, an intermediate position: the analyst may, for example, modify his behavior if the patient manifests resistance.

To summarize, we suggest that the resources exchanged in the various schools of psychotherapy are different, and that each school tends to treat similarly resources which are proximal in the structure. In this respect, these three schools appear to constitute different institutions: like social institutions, each school prescribes particular exchanges and bars certain others.

When a comparison among the three therapeutic approaches is made, the strongest contrast is provided by the Rogerian and behavioristic ones. Love and status are prominent in the former and absent in the latter. Data presented in Chapter 10 suggests that deviations in the cognitive organization of mental patients are likely to impair their ability to exchange love and/or status. For this reason, these resources may not be effective in behavior therapy where the provision of resources by the therapist is strictly contigent upon the patient's behavior. Using love and status as rewards would be somewhat like attempting to train a pigeon by rewarding it with dollar bills. In client-centered therapy, on the other hand, the very absence of contingency permits the provision of these resources, hoping to modify the cognitive structure of the patient toward normalcy through such an unconditional giving.

Resource Expectation in Task Groups

Teichman (1970) studied expectations for resources in small groups which were assigned to write joint papers. Obviously, the most prominent resource in such a setting is information, but love and status are always exchanged to some degree in small groups (Bales and Strodtbeck, 1951). The expectations regarding these three resources were studied with respect to two roles: the most and the least preferred co-worker (Fiedler, 1967, Ch. 3).

The subjects were 30 undergraduate students (16 females and 14 males) enrolled in the course "Racial Problems," offered by the Sociology Department at the University of Missouri. The class was divided into groups of 4–6 students. As part of the requirements for the course, each group was asked to reach agreement on the topic of a paper they should submit to the instructor; the work of preparing the joint paper was divided among the group members. The students were to meet several times during the semester in order to report about their progress, to consult with their partners, and to exchange relevant information. After the groups had met at least once and not more than twice, their expectations regarding the most and least preferred partners were investigated; a measure of the amount of love, status, and information they expected to receive from—and be deprived of—by each of the two partners, was obtained.

The instrument devised by Teichman is given in full in Appendix E; it consisted of 24 statements covering the three resource classes of love, status and information; in each class, four items pertained to expected gains (giving behaviors), and four to expected deprivation (taking away behaviors). Examples of the items are as follows; receiving love: "Would give you the feeling that you are very likeable;" Losing love: "Would be unfriendly toward you;" losing status: "Would let you understand that you do not do things well;" receiving information: "Would make you familiar with new facts;" losing information: "Would tell you things that would lead you to the wrong decision."

The subject was instructed to rate each item, as to the likelihood of its occurrence, on the following scale: almost always (4), often (3), sometimes (2), seldom (1), and almost never (0). Since four items were presented for each behavioral class, the highest possible expectation score was 16; it was obtained when every item of the class was expected to occur "almost always." The lowest expectation yielded a score of zero. Separate scores were obtained for receiving and losing love, status and information by the most and least preferred co-worker; hence each subject obtained 12 expectations scores.

FREQUENCY OF EXPECTED EXCHANGE BY RESOURCES. The means and standard deviations of these scores, for all 30 subjects, are given in Table 24. The mean difference between most and least preferred co-worker is also given for each behavioral class. With regard to positive (giving) behaviors, the results indicate that: (1) The expectation from both co-workers was lowest for love, higher for status and highest for information. (2) The most preferred co-worker was expected to give *more* of all three resources than did the least preferred one. (3) The difference between the expectations from the two co-workers was lowest for love, higher for status and highest for information. Thus, in the institutional situation of an intellectual task, the expectation to receive information out-paces the expectation of more particularistic resources, particularly so with regard to the most preferred co-worker.

Table 24

MEANS AND STANDARD DEVIATIONS OF EXPECTED GAIN AND LOSS
FROM MOST AND LEAST PREFERRED CO-WORKER, FOR EACH RESOURCE.

Resource	Giving Behavior					Taking Behavior				
	Most Preferred		Least Preferred		Diff. of Means	Most Preferred		Least Preferred		Diff. of Means
	Mean	S.D.	Mean	S.D.		Mean	S.D.	Mean	S.D.	
Love	7.10	3.48	3.24	2.24	-3.88	2.10	2.26	5.07	3.08	4.30
Status	9.10	3.11	4.44	2.81	-4.66	2.04	2.14	4.80	2.87	4.24
Information	11.97	2.74	5.74	3.51	-6.23	1.07	1.17	2.80	2.52	3.46

This picture was reversed for taking away behavior: (1) The expectation of being deprived by either co-worker was highest for love, lower for status and lowest for information. (2) The most preferred co-worker was expected to deprive *less,* in all three resources, than did the least preferred one. (3) The difference in expected deprivation between the two co-workers was highest for love, lower for status and lowest for information. In a task group setting, members expected to be most deprived of love, particularly so with regard to the least preferred co-worker. Among friends (see Ch. 6), love is the most prominent resource. It follows that the task group setting considered here differs from the friendship institution with regard to giving behavior, but not in behaviors of taking away. In both modes, however, the results conformed to the structure of resources; classes proximal in the structural order were less different in terms of their means than were remote classes. The structure was also reflected in the standard deviation: its value for status was always intermediate between those for love and information. Moreover, except for expectation regarding gain from the least preferred co-worker, the standard deviation was always lowest for information. Low variance indicates high agreement among the subjects, hence more consensus was found in expectation for information than for love and status.

RELATIONSHIP AMONG BEHAVIORAL CLASSES. The structure of behavioral classes in each role can be predicted from two notions which have already been established: (1) The structure of resources predicts that behavior involving love is more related to behavior involving status than to one which involves information. (2) Mutual exclusiveness between giving and taking (i.e., lack of ambivalence) will increase as one moves away from love towards money (see Ch. 3, p. 63). These two notions served as criteria for ordering the six behavioral classes of each role. Within each mode (giving and taking away) the classes are ordered according to the structure of resources. Between modes, the order was determined by the second criterion: for the most mutually exclusive resource—information, giving and *not* taking are neighbors. Table 25 gives the intercorrelations among the six behavioral classes in the role of the least preferred co-worker. The reader will notice that this matrix is identical with the behavioral structure presented in Chapter 3 (see Fig. 3), except that the resource of information was added here. The pattern of the intercorrelations, indeed reflects the circular structure. In each row, the size of the correlations decreases as we move away from the diagonal cell; there is only one deviation, in the last row, which stems from the high ambivalence in behaviors of love.

Both predictions, which served to determine the structure, were also supported; within each mode, love correlated higher with status

Table 25

INTERCORRELATIONS AMONG THE CLASSES OF BEHAVIORS
EXPECTED FROM THE LEAST PREFERRED CO-WORKER

Expected Behavior	1	2	3	4	5	6
1. Giving Love	—	.70	.26	.00	.12	.21
2. Giving Status	.70	—	.65	.33	.36	.39
3. Giving Information	.26	.65	—	.40	.38	.33
4. (Not) Taking Information	.00	.33	.40	—	.87	.76
5. (Not) Taking Status	.12	.36	.38	.87	—	.77
6. (Not) Taking Love	.21	.39	.33	.76	.77	—

than with information, thus additional evidence for the structure of resources was provided. The relationship between giving and *not* taking away was highest for information (.40) and lowest for love (.21), with status occupying an intermediate position (.36). Here again, giving was correlated with not-taking, so that the more positive the correlation, the lower the ambivalence; complete absence of ambivalence will yield correlation of plus 1.

A similar but less regular pattern of intercorrelations was obtained for the most preferred co-worker. The correlations tended to be lower than those in Table 25, suggesting that the role of the most preferred co-worker is more differentiated than the role of the least preferred one. To gain further insight into the difference between these two roles, their corresponding behavioral classes were intercorrelated. It was found that the expectation from the two roles differ most in information, which is the most relevant resource to this institutional setting. They also differ more in behaviors of giving than in behaviors of taking away, in each one of the three resources.

Resources in Different Roles

In another study Teichman investigated the proposition that the expectation of resources varies for roles in different institutions although resources proximal in the order will have similar expectations. He administered to 50 undergraduate students at Fairmont State College in West Virginia a modified form of the "Social Interaction Inventory" (see Appendix C); it contained 24 items, each resource class being sampled with four items. Subjects were asked to rate on a five point scale their expectation that the actor in each given role would engage in the behavior described in each item. The following six roles were presented: mother's behavior to child (love); child to father (status); supervisor to worker (information); bank teller to customer (money); salesman to customer (goods); and barber to customer (services).

Teichman predicted that the resource indicated in brackets after each role would be the most expected one in this role; he further predicted that the expectation of other resources would decrease the less close they were in the structure to the most expected.

Table 26
MEANS OF EXPECTED BEHAVIORS IN SIX SOCIAL ROLES

			Role			
Resources Given	Mother to Child	Child to Father	Supervisor to Worker	Bank Teller to Customer	Salesman to Customer	Barber to Customer
Love	14.14	12.32	7.84	6.08	5.92	6.70
Status	12.98	12.74	9.22	6.37	7.42	7.05
Information	12.73	7.74	11.35	7.00	8.54	7.00
Money	7.40	4.14	7.33	10.68	2.82	2.10
Goods	10.26	10.26	5.73	8.91	9.78	5.90
Services	11.30	11.30	6.55	4.94	6.46	11.68

The mean expectation for each resource and role, given in Table 26, well support the hypotheses: the resource most expected is always the predicted one; the expectation for other resources tends to decrease according to the structure. For example, in the first column—mother to child role, the highest mean is for giving love to the child, the means then decrease gradually as the resource becomes more distal from love, then increase again as love is approached from the other side of the structure. There are only two deviations from the circular order in the whole table.

In summary, the theoretical analysis of resource exchange in psychotherapy and the results obtained from empirical studies support the view that the structure of resources remains constant across different institutional settings, while the relevance of each resource changes. Let us now turn to discuss the third factor which influences exchange, the properties of resources.

STRUCTURE-RELATED PROPERTIES OF RESOURCES

On various occasions we have noted that resource classes differ systematically on some characteristics; in Chapter 3, for example, we have proposed that the relationship between self and other is stronger for love than for status, and mutual exclusion between giving and taking is least pronounced in love, increases for status, and more so for information. Another characteristic was suggested earlier in this chapter; the optimal range is smallest for love and increases gradually as one moves towards money in the structure of resource classes.

A more comprehensive review of resource properties will be given here. The characteristics we shall consider seem to be related to the cognitive structure of resource classes, so that the values proximal resources assume on any of them will be more similar than the values of remote resources. The value taken by each resource on any property may depend on the cognitive and environmental conditions existing at the time this particular class became differentiated. We shall discuss this point after considering the various properties. Finally, we shall examine the consequences of these differential characteristics for resource exchange.

In view of their effects on transactions, it seems appropriate to consider resource properties before we turn to interpersonal dynamics in the next chapter. Some of these properties pertain to environmental conditions (or institutional settings) facilitating or hindering the exchange: a small group, for example, is more suitable for exchanges of love; a large group facilitates the exchange of money. Some other properties bear upon the effects of resource exchange on the motivational state of the individual: giving to self and to other, for example, are related positively for love and negatively for money; consequently, when one gives love he becomes richer, while after giving money he is poorer. This property reflects a cognitive state (self and other are less differentiated for love than for money), which, in turn, determines differential rules of exchange for the various resources. As noted earlier, reduction in the amount of love one possesses requires *taking it* away from the other, while a decrease in one's bank account would be accomplished by *giving* some money to the other.

There are probably properties which have not yet been identified. Of those we know, love and money differ most; this suggests that the particularistic dimension may be the more relevant one, as love and money are at its opposite poles. By stating the values that love and money assume on each characteristic, we shall provide also an approximate idea about the values of other resources. Services and status will be more similar to love, while information and goods will assume values proximal to money. Let us start with those properties which bear on rules of exchange.

Properties Affecting the Motivational State

We have identified six properties which influence the balance of resources after the exchange had taken place.

RELATIONSHIP BETWEEN SELF AND OTHER. It is proposed that the relationship between the amount of resource given to the other and the amount left to self is positive for love, decreases and becomes negative as one moves along the structure toward money. We have already seen that the relationship between giving to self and to other (as well as between taking away from self and from other) tends to be weaker for status than for love, although both are positive. The more we give love or status to the other, the more is left for ourselves. Giving information to another does not appear to reduce or increase the amount possessed by the giver. It can be argued, however, that sharing may reduce the value of the information if the situation is competitive (e.g., industrial or military secrets). On the other hand, transmission of information may also result in some increase of information available to self, as for instance when repressed information is brought to the surface during a psychotherapeutic session. Likewise, misleading another person (i.e., taking away information from him) does not change the amount of information possessed by the deceiver, except for the eventual knowledge that the victim has been hooked. On the whole, it seems that the amount of information left to the giver is independent of the amount he had given, so that information is characterized neither by positive nor by negative relationship between self and other. Strong negative relationship is characteristic of money and goods, where giving to other definitely reduces the amount left for self. Services may show a more moderate but still negative relationship: performing a service for another person usually results in physical discomfort for the performer, as it involves expenditure of energy. In general, the relationship between giving to other and to self appears to change gradually for the various resources, along their position in the structure: love has the most positive relationship; status is less positive; information, independent; money and goods most negative. Service is again less negative.

THE RELATIONSHIP BETWEEN MODES. A positive relationship between giving and taking, denoted by the term "ambivalence", usually refers to love exchange. It is inconceivable to describe money transactions as ambivalent. Indeed the relationship between giving and taking are most positive for love. One can love and hate the same person simultaneously. We have already seen data suggesting that in love there is a considerable amount of ambivalence, even among normal individuals. We also noted some ambivalence for status, although lower than for love. Ambivalence in status is well exemplified by expressions such as "to pay respect grudgingly." Still less ambivalence has been found in information; yet some erroneous, misleading or ambiguous item may be included in a given transmission of information. Likewise, an information mainly erroneous may contain come correct items. Sometimes one tells "half the truth." Results for love, status, and information, supporting this hypothesis of a progressive decrease in ambivalence, were given in Table 24. Money suggests absence of ambivalence; giving money appears to exclude taking it away. Even counterfeit money is just not given, but neither is it taken away. Ranking of resources by decreasing degree of ambivalence has so far followed the structural order. If this rule is also valid for the remaining resources, ambivalence will now increase as we are approaching the most particularistic resource, love, from the other side of the circle. For goods, the extent to which giving and taking occur jointly may be slightly higher than for money: defective goods may actually cause damage. The "ambivalence" of services may be higher than for goods. It happens that some damage is done in the performance of a service: the barber may cut the client's skin, the physician may cause some damage to the patient's body in the course of treatment, the mover may damage the furniture, and the housewife may burn the roast. These considerations suggest that the joint occurrence of giving and taking away will follow the circular structure of resources, being highest for love and lowest for money.

The preceding analysis of the relationship among behaviors proposes that different resources do not obey the same rules. The change from one resource to another appears, however, to be gradual and to follow the order. At one extreme there is money, where giving to self excludes giving to other and taking away excludes giving. For money, therefore, each transaction can be described by a single value: if A gives five dollars to B, A has five dollars less and B five dollars more. As any accountant knows, the amount credited to an account should be the same as the amount debited to another account. At the other extreme there is love: our accountant would probably tend his resignation if requested to keep books on love exchanges. Here, giving to the other often increases the amount left for self and giving does not necessarily rule out a certain amount of taking away. It should be noted, however, that the same types of behavior occur for money as for other resources. It is only the *relationship* among these behaviors that varies for different resources. Attempts to extend the rules of money transactions to other resources have caused some difficulties in applying the notion of exchange to other forms of interpersonal communication, since the fact that one can give without reducing the amount in his possession has been considered contradictory to the very notion of exchange (Cartwright and Zander, 1968, p. 233).

Building on the notion that information, unlike goods, can be transmitted without loss to the giver, Rosen (1966) predicted that the monetary price demanded for information would be lower than for goods. To test this hypothesis, Rosen gave his subjects control over a box which contained three pieces of a jigsaw puzzle needed by another person in order to complete his picture and win points. Some subjects were given a key for the lock; others were told the combination for opening it. Both groups of subjects were asked to set a price for giving the key or the combination to the other person. The price demanded for the key was, on the average, higher than for the combination. This differential property of goods and information was neutralized in other experimental groups by stipulating that: (a) the key would be used and then returned; and (b) the information on the combination would not be given to a third individual. In these conditions, the prices for key and combination tended to equalize, particularly when the other person was expected to comply with these limitations.

VERBALIZATION OF NEED. We propose that the easiest need to express is that for money and the one most difficult to communicate is the need for love. Statements such as "I demand an increase in salary" or "I have to raise the price" are quite commonly heard, particularly in times of inflation. A straightforward bidding for love is relatively rare, even among intimates. This difference may be related to the degree to which verbal communication is suitable for the various resource classes. Language appears quite appropriate for money dealings; love, on the other hand, is more easily expressed by paralinguistic communication: touching, expressions of the face, eye's contact, body posture, or physical proximity. We often say that we have no words for expressing our feelings. Indeed it takes a poet to accomplish this feat; for common mortals, a misty look is more handy.

This property affects the resources exchanged and their substitution. In expressing a need, or in bidding for a resource, there will be a tendency to "skid" toward less particularistic ones. A child in need of love may ask for a toy, some candy, or will complain of pain. A lovelorn adult may settle for professional success, for information and perhaps even for money. On the other hand, a person who needs money is unlikely to ask for sympathy. Thus, substitution of one resource for another is not a two-way street; a less particularistic resource is more likely to be substituted for a more particularistic one than the other way around.

EXCHANGE OF SAME RESOURCE. A lonely individual, needing love, will wish to meet another lonely person, so that they would be able to exchange love. But meeting another pauper will not help the person who is short of money. Thus, the more particularistic a resource, the higher the probability that it will be exchanged with the same resource, while nonparticularistic resources will tend to be exchanged with different ones.

In a study of exchange preferences, to be described in the next chapter (see p. 182 and Table 28), it was found that the preference for exchanging love with love was maximal, 32 percent (because of the way the questionnaire was constructed, no preference could be higher than 33 percent in this study). Following the structure of resources, the preference for same-resource exchanges decreased gradually: status 27 percent; information 25 percent; money 22 percent and goods 18 percent; then the figure went up again for services, 25 percent. Although these data are restricted to exchanges in a specific social institution—friendship—they support the notion that exchanges within the same resource are more likely for particularistic than for non-particularistic ones.

RANGE OF EXCHANGE.[2] This property refers to the number of resources with which a given one may be exchanged. It is related to the self-exchange property, but does not necessarily follow from it: a given resource, although not often exchanged with itself, may be transacted only for a specific other resource. We propose that the more particularistic a resource is, the narrower is the range of resources with which it can be exchanged. Few resources can be exchanged with love, but several can be obtained for money; in consequence, money appears as an appropriate means of exchange in several social institutions, while love is suitable only in a few.

To test this hypothesis, the data from the exchange preference study (see pp. 181–183 and Table 28) were used again, in spite of the fact that they were obtained in only one institution. We reasoned that when a resource is exchangeable with several others, there should be little variance among all the possible transactions involving this resource; on the other hand, variance will be larger when one or two resources are preferred as an exchange for a given resource. To provide a test which is independent of the previous property, the preference for exchanging the resource with itself was excluded from the computation of variance; the following values were obtained: love 57; status 75; information 45; money 13; goods 17; and services 18. Although, unexpectedly, the variance for status was higher than for love, these values follow the structure of resources without deviation. More to the point, they support the notion that there are more possibilities of exchange for non-particularistic resources; many things can be obtained with money, but few in exchange for love.

RELATIONSHIP BETWEEN INTERPERSONAL SETTING AND EXCHANGE. Transmission of money does not require a face to face interaction; it can be sent conveniently through a third person. Moreover, money may be kept for future exchange. Exchange of love, on the other hand, can hardly be separated from the interpersonal situation, and love cannot be kept for a long time in the absence of actual exchange, or transmitted by an intermediary without incurring loss. This property is closely related to the *locus* of storage of the resource. Love is stored (but not for long) in the "heart"; money is kept at the bank or under the mattress. Some other resources can be stored either inside or outside the individual. Information, for example, can be memorized or recorded

---

2. This property was proposed by Meir Teichman.

in writing, tape, punch cards, etc. Food can be stored in the refrigerator or inside the body as fat.

The relationship between the interpersonal setting and the resource exchanged influences the outcome of the exchange and, in turn, is influenced by the environment or, more precisely, by the level of technology. In cultures which do not possess a written language, information must be memorized, i.e., stored inside. Where food cannot be kept long enough to assure a steady supply, being fat is considered an advantage, while overweight constitutes a problem when freezing and canning are within easy reach. Thus, in a sense, this property mediates between the motivational states of the individual and his environment. Let us turn now to some of the properties which are more clearly influenced by environmental conditions.

Properties Affected by Environment

These properties indicate characteristics of the environment or institutional setting which will enhance or inhibit the exchange of a given resource.

TIME FOR PROCESSING INPUT. Giving and receiving love cannot be done in a hurry; it requires time and even some leisure. Money, to the contrary, can change hands very rapidly. In an environment providing an overload of stimuli, those resources which require a longer processing time are more likely to receive low priority. Such selection will thus favor the less particularistic resources.

An experiment done by Meir Teichman showed that subjects allotted 15 minutes for affective exchanges were significantly less satisfied than comparable subjects who had 25 minutes available for the interaction. The number and content of love messages received by the subject was the same in both conditions so that subjects who interacted longer did receive the same amount of affection as those in the other group; for the former participants the remaining time was filled by neutral messages. By contrast, increasing the time available did not alter satisfaction when the resource exchanged was money. These results support the notion that time available is a significant factor in love exchanges but not in monetary transactions.

DELAY OF REWARD. Love is a relatively long term investment, with rewards being reaped only after several encounters; a friendship needs to be "cultivated" and a girl needs to be courted. Therefore exchanges of love require the possibility of repeated encounters and trust, i.e., high expectation that the transaction will be completed. On the other hand, an exchange of money with goods can be consummated in a single encounter and, at least in cash payments, does not require trust in the buyer. In an environment where most encounters are with strangers and are non-repetitive, the less particularistic the resource, the more likely it is to be an object of exchange.

OPTIMUM GROUP SIZE. It has been noted that in animal species living in groups, such as monkeys and apes, there is an optimum group size (Carpenter, 1963). When the group becomes too large, behavior which disrupts its normal functioning appears to increase (Calhoun, 1962). The work of Bailey (1966) suggests that such negative effects are obtained even when the increase in group size does not result in higher density; in Bailey's experiment, density was kept constant by increasing the space available to the animals in proportion to their augment in number. The sheer effect of group size, as distinct from crowding, may be explained by limitations in the cognitive capacity of the animals to handle an overly large number of mates.

As for human beings, it appears that the more particularistic a resource is, the heavier are its demands on cognitive representation for the following reasons:

1. The very notion of particularism implies that the uniqueness of the exchange partner as an individual is important; hence there is a desire to obtain a large amount of information about him and to provide him with information about ourselves. Indeed, the significance of self-disclosure, particularly in relationship with intimates, was stressed by Jourard (1964). One of the first things lovers do is to exchange intimate information; and Mowrer (1964) has held that avoidance of self-disclosure is a major source of alienation from the group. Perhaps not by chance, the verb "to know" is used in biblical Hebrew to indicate sexual intercourse, a highly particularistic form of behavior.

2. The more particularistic a resource, the less it is amenable to external conservation and therefore it depends more on internal, cognitive storage: the very idea of a lover taking notes on the self-disclosure of his beloved sounds ridiculous.

Since the amount which can be stored within the system is limited, small group setting should be more suitable for particularistic exchanges than large groups. Evidence for this prediction is reported in the literature. Zimet and Schneider (1969) observed discussion groups who met over a period of three or four years. Group composition remained the same over the total period, but the actual number of participants varied between two and five at different meetings because of absences. The frequency of direct personal expressions referring to a group member decreased as the group size increased; communication—apparently—became less particularistic when more people were present.

Nye, Carlson and Garrett (1970) investigated the relationship between family size and interpersonal exchanges among its members. Instead of direct observation, as in the Zimet and Schneider study, they relied on self-reports of family members, obtained partly by mail and partly by direct interviewing. A large sample from the state of Washington participated in this study. Among the variables investigated, the following are relevant to our topic:

1. Adolescents' perception of their parent's affect toward them.
2. Adolescent's affect toward their parents.
3. Mutual affect of spouses as perceived by the wife.
4. Mutual affect of spouses as perceived by adolescent children.

In all four variables, the same general trend appeared: there was a slight increase of reported affection as the number of children in the family rose from one to two; affective exchanges decreased steadily as the number of children became larger. Hutt and Hutt (1970, pp. 151–152) found that normal children reduced their social contacts as the size of the group increased; results for brain-damaged and autist children were, however, open to various interpretations, although the frequency of their contacts was below normal in every group size. In summarizing results of studies on group size and particularistic exchanges, Goldstein, Heller and Sechrest (1966, pp. 340–341) noted the following effects of larger groups: (1) "Sense of belonging" decreased (Miller, N.E., 1950); (2) Affectional ties among members decreased (Coyle, 1930; Kinney, 1953); and (3) The tendency to form subgroups and cliques increased (Hare, 1962).

Latané and Darley (1969) conducted a series of experiments to identify variables influencing the willingness to help or to safeguard the well being of another individual in an emergency situation. In our classification, helping belongs to the class of services, a neighbor of love. Latané and Darley varied the number of persons present in the emergency situation; they consistently found that the probability of helping behavior decreased when the number of by-standers increased.

All these investigations indicate that exchanges of particularistic resources are more likely to occur in a small group than in a large one. By contrast, economic transactions appear to be facilitated by larger groups: access to a wide market is considered advantageous by businessmen; shoppers will tend to prefer a store where sales are brisk; and one will prefer a stock or commodity exchange where many people convene. We can thus expect that in an environment of large size groups, non-particularistic resources will be exchanged more than particularistic ones.

Properties and Cognitive Development

We have considered certain characteristics of resources bearing on the outcome of the exchange and on the environmental conditions suitable for its occurrence. We have also proposed that these characteristics are related to the position of the resource class in the structure and, especially, to its particularistic dimension; partial evidence has been presented supporting the relationship between properties and structure. It should be remembered that their structure has been derived from a sequence of differentiation among resource classes (see Ch. 3). If resource properties also originate in the development sequence, then this sequence will provide the link between the properties and the structure. It is indeed proposed that the value assumed by a resource class on each property reflects the cognitive and environmental conditions which had existed when the class became differentiated.

Love develops early, before the differentiations between giving and taking, as well as between self and other have become firmly established; its development precedes the acquisition of language, as well. Therefore, in love, there is ambivalence between giving and taking, high positive relationship between self and other, less amenability to verbal expression, and less opportunity for exchanging it with a wide range of other resources. Money, on the other hand, acquires its meaning much later after one has acquired some mastery of language, has learned that giving is not taking and other is not self, and has already differentiated a full range of resource classes. Furthermore, love begins to be exchanged in the small and relatively stable family group, while money, even at an early age, is mostly used for exchanges outside the family. In summary: (1) Resources are best exchanged in environmental conditions that resemble those under which they had been developed in the past. (2) They reflect the cognitive state which existed at the time of their differentiation. (3) The closer two resource classes are, the more similar are the values they assume on each one of the properties.

SOME IMPORTANT IMPLICATIONS OF PROPERTIES

It is perhaps too early to judge the impact that the identification of resource properties will have on the understanding and control of human affairs; neither is it possible to discuss all social phenomena which are related to them. At this stage we can only attempt to outline some of the consequences that look particularly important.

Differential Laws of Exchange

We have seen that in exchanges of love, unlike economic transactions, someone's profit does not have to be another's loss. Consider for example sexual relationship, an interpersonal exchange at the borderline between love and services; it would be rather difficult to specify costs and rewards in such a situation. Thus the rules of economic exchange apply to only one subset of resources, while other resources follow different rules. Consequently, attempts to interpret non-economic exchanges in terms of profit and loss would meet with considerable difficulties.

The difference between love and money exchanges has always been realized intuitively: accountants were never renowned for their expressions of love, nor poets for their ability to keep books. Yet the fact that in love, two and two do not make four but rather five or six, and the non-verbal forms of expressing it have lent a phantomatic quality to this resource class; serious, hard-minded people like economists, engineers or social planners are not supposed to be concerned with exchanges of love. With the realization that the exchanges of more particularistic resources are just as lawful as economic transactions, although their laws may differ, the resistance to consider their importance and significance to human welfare may decrease, leading us to a fuller and more integrated view of the role played by the various resources in individual and societal functioning.

Effects of Urban Environment

The environmental properties of resources, i.e., time for processing input, delay of reward and optimum group size, combine to hinder the exchanges of some resources from urban society. Very succinctly, an environment in which there is strong competition among inputs, encounters are brief and non-repetitive, and where every person engages in numerous contacts, constitutes an obstacle to the exchange of particularistic resources, while facilitating non-particularistic transactions. When these conditions appear concurrently, their effects will be cumulative. Often, in a large crowd there are many more competing stimuli than in a small group and less opportunity for repeated encounters. Yet there are situations where the group is small but unlikely to meet again: it is improbable that patients in the doctor's waiting room, visitors to an art gallery, or buyers in a fashionable boutique will maintain personal contacts. These examples suggest that the size and stability of a group can vary in different social institutions: although a family may be similar in size to a group of friends, the former is more stable; groups at work are likely to be larger and less stable, and in commercial setting one can usually find large crowds and non-recurrent encounters.

The conditions within a particular institution, in turn, are influenced by the wider social setting. In a small town, for example, one is likely to meet frequently the same group of people at the corner drugstore; in a large metropolis these encounters are most often non-recurrent. In general, in the urban environment, the conditions are less conducive to particularistic exchanges, beyond any specific institutional setting. Milgram (1970) has proposed that reducing the time allocated to each input is an adaptive response to the overload of interpersonal stimuli which characterizes an urban center; if processing a love stimulus requires longer time, it follows that in the city these stimuli will be filtered out more than stimuli pertaining to less particularistic resources. It is hardly necessary to point out the existence of large crowds in the city and to the non-repetitiveness of many encounters.

The selective influence of the urban setting in resource exchanges contributes to the understanding of some of the less savory aspects of city life. We shall briefly consider three of them: crime, alienation and drugs.

CRIME. It is unnecessary to note that crime is on the increase, particularly so in densely settled areas. Some interesting aspects of it are revealed in an experiment reported by Zimbardo (1970). A car with license plate removed and hood open was left in the Bronx near the New York University campus. Another car in the same condition was left for an identical time in Palo Alto, near the Stanford University campus. All the movable parts were stolen from the New York car within the first day. Nothing was removed from the Palo Alto car during the whole period. In New York the pilferage occurred in broad daylight when other people were present and was done also by middle-class-looking white adults. In a small community these same individuals would probably behave as pillars of law and order, but there, antisocial or asocial behavior would entail loss of status long before any eventual legal punishment. The relative scarcity of particularistic exchanges in the city deprives society of powerful informal instruments of social control, particularly the giving and taking of status. The law enforcement system is built on the assumption that for most people the threat of status deprivation by other and by self, which are positively related, is a sufficient deterrent against the violation of social norms. Even the arm of the law becomes less effective when particularistic means of social control fail. When one does not care about the opinion held by his neighbors about him, sitting in jail becomes merely a temporary loss of freedom and not a permanent loss of face. Moreover, the judicial procedure becomes inefficient and cumbersome when attempting to take care of all those cases that previously had been handled by non-formal means.

ALIENATION. We have already learned that the relationship between self and other is positive and highest for love. Thus, it is through love exchanges that we relate to other persons. Scarcity of particularistic transactions is subjectively experienced as loneliness and estrangement. In consequence, alienation will be more frequent among the large city crowds than in rural areas.

Alienation has often been interpreted to mean self-estrangement, a notion which was criticized for its apparent lack of rigor: how can one be alienated from himself? The puzzle is solved when we reflect that only in the particularistic resources giving to other also implies giving to self, so that the self is *both* actor and object, rather than being *either* actor or object. Thus a worker that does his job only to get his wages is more likely to be alienated than a worker who takes pride in what he does, i.e., who gives *himself* status in addition to receiving money from the employer. Seeman (1959) came close to this interpretation when stating that ". . . what has been called self-estrangement refers essentially to the inability of the individual to find self-rewarding . . . activities that engage him" (p. 790).

DRUGS. It seems that in modern society the use of drugs has increased with scarcity of particularistic resources. When something is scarce, there are two alternative solutions: increasing its supply or reducing the need. This is not a world-shaking thought, yet it suggests that certain drugs may facilitate particularistic exchanges in unfavorable environmental conditions, while certain others may reduce the discomfort caused by the shortage of particularistic resources. Investigating the effects of marihuana, Halpern (1968, pp. 381–382) administered several psychological tests to 45 subjects, when they were under the influence of marihuana and when free from its influence. In comparing results from the Thematic Apperception Test in the two conditions, she reported a reduction in needs in the drugged condition, with the exception of the need for dominance, which increased. All the needs analyzed were in the service-love-status range and thus quite particularistic. While these results may suggest that the need for particularistic resources is reduced under the influence of marihuana, more recent work on marihuana[3] (Hollister, 1971; Weil, Zinberg and Nelsen, 1968) did not provide data which are directly related to the hypothesis proposed here.

Reports on the effects of LSD seem to suggest that this drug may facilitate exchanges rather than reduce the need. Mogar and Savage (1964) reported that after a single strong controlled experience with LSD, a subject "values human brotherhood more . . . tends to be less distrustful and guarded with others, warmer and more spontaneous in expressing emotions . . ." (Mogar, 1966, p. 102). According to some investigators (Harman, McKim, Mogar, Fadiman and Stolaroff, 1969,

---

[3] We are grateful to David Davis for bringing these works to our attention.

p. 457; Stafford and Golightly, 1967, pp. 61–93), subjects who were administered LSD reported improved ability to relate interpersonally. In a study of drug use in nonliterate societies (Blum, 1969, pp. 150–151), it was found that hallucinogen drugs, similar to LSD, were used in a group situation almost as often as in private; marihuana and opium, on the other hand, were taken mainly in private. Although these results are based on a small number of cultures, they again tend to suggest that while certain drugs increased interpersonal sensitivity, other drugs reduce the need for friendship. There is little in the literature which bears on these hypotheses: in spite of the widely accepted assumption that drugs constitute a response to emotional problems, studies of drugs often deal with their effect on other variables, such as intellectual abilities and task performance.

City Life: Selection and Training

The growth of large metropolitan areas with their high population density, the increased institutional specialization and the opportunities for physical and social mobility, is a rather novel feature of human society. It has greatly facilitated economic exchanges, while hindering particularistic transactions. The parallel with physical environment is striking: in both cases technology has created new problems in the process of solving old ones. The private car is a great means of transportation; it also pollutes the air. D.D.T. has increased food production; it also poisons the environment. Modern society, and particularly urban society, has provided new opportunities for trade and work; it also reduces the exchange of particularistic resources. As suggested here, certain negative features of modern society may be due to this reduction.

We know next to nothing about the minimum level of these resources necessary for proper functioning of the individual, although there is solid evidence on the negative effects of resource deprivation in early age (see Ch. 8). There are probably considerable individual differences in the tolerance of deprivation. Those having a lower minimum level, the "cold," "distant," "manipulative" individuals, may adjust more to conditions of city life. They may constitute the "urban type," better fitted to operate in the urban environment.

THE APPEARANCE OF NEW INSTITUTIONS. For those who cannot endure the lack of particularism, new institutional forms are created for the exchange of particularistic resources in spite of unfavorable environmental conditions. What is common to these institutions is that their norms call for the exchange of love and sometimes also sex, which is on the borderline between love and services. These norms endorse spontaneity, expression of feelings, touching and other forms of nonverbal behavior. The various institutions differ mainly in the size and the stability of the group; the innovative aspect of these attempts consists of introducing love exchange in conditions which are usually considered to be unfavorable to it, such as extended and/or temporary groups. Size is relatively large, but there is considerable stability in communes and in group sex. Youth festivals of the Woodstock type are characterized by large and temporary groups. Temporary, but smaller in size, are groups having the purpose of training a person in particularistic exchanges, with the expectation that he will be able to perform these transactions in other situations as well. These groups go under different names such as sensitivity training, encounter, marathons; some stress touching, body movements and other forms of nonverbal communication; some demand nudity of the participants. They all constitute recognition of the fact that in the environment provided by modern society, particularistic exchanges are hindered and thus special training and opportunities are necessary in order to surmount these obstacles. When successful, these types of training may reduce the negative aspects of city life which have been previously briefly noted.

SUMMARY

Social experiences are interpersonal encounters in which resources are given or taken away. Whether or not a particular exchange will take place depends on three sets of conditions: the motivational state of the potential exchangers, the appropriateness of the environment and the properties of the resources to be exchanged.

The individual tends to steer his interpersonal contacts to maintain an optimal amount of resources. Possessing too little as well as too much is experienced as discomfort, which the organism wishes to eliminate. For each resource there is a lower limit, below which a motivational arousal occurs; the upper limit, however, varies for the different resources. Consequently, the optimal range differs from one resource to another. It will be smallest for love and practically infinite for money. The optimal range of the remaining resources will follow the structural order. The closer they are to love, the narrower will be their optimal range; resources closer to money will have a wider range.

When the amount of a given resource possessed by the organism at a given time falls below the optimal range, it is experienced as a need. It follows that there are six classes of needs, one for each resource.

Most of the needs refer to situations where the object is the "self" and the behavior—"giving." A resource is sought after by the individual in order to reduce a present or future deficit and to bring the amount held by his system within the optimal range. Even the need to "give" may be perceived as means for increasing the amount possessed by the giver. Particularistic resources are accumulated by the giver through the positive relationship between self and other; when one expresses love towards the other, he simultaneously accepts himself. When one dispenses non-particularistic resources, he expects to be reciprocated. But what about the need to destroy or to take away? Again, for particularistic resources, there are positive relationships between self and other; while rejecting the other, one also rejects himself to a certain degree. Thus the urge to express hostility may reflect a state of satiation. When the amount of love possessed by an individual exceeds the upper limit, he cannot get rid of it by giving some to the other, as giving love will further increase the amount possessed by him. By expressing hate, he also rejects himself, thus decreasing the amount of love within the optimal range. For non-particularistic resources, taking them away from the other reestablishes a balance by increasing the actual or perceived amount held by the self.

While need is a deficit in a particular resource, power may be defined as the amount of a given resource that is available to the individual for an eventual giving. Again, there are six classes of power, one for each class of resources. A powerful person is in a position to enter an exchange in which he offers some resource and in turn expects to be reciprocated. Yet, power cannot be exercised unless there is a corresponding need on the part of the receiver. A person may have great potential power and little actual power when there is scarce demand for the resource he possesses in abundance.

The power to give requires a possession of a certain amount which is beyond the lower limit of the optimal range. Yet even the poorest person may create a great loss. With regard to particularistic resource, such power of the powerless is limited. To be insulted by a low status person is less damaging than being degraded by a high status one. However, the amount of non-particularistic resources that can be taken away is independent of the amount possessed by the taker; therefore, formal punishment is exercised to protect the owner, where expressions of hostility are handled by non-formal means.

Beside the strive to maintain an optimal amount of each resource, the individual's behavior and perception is directed towards protecting his cognitive structure. An event containing relationship among elements which differ from the relationship among the relevant cognitive classes, will create dissonance. The perception of such event will be distorted so that it will fit the structure. However, when a dissonant event will occur frequently, the structure would have to be altered.

For an exchange to take place, a person needing a given resource and powerful in another should meet an individual who is in a complementary motivational state. Since exchanges take place so often, society has developed mechanisms for facilitating the encounter of individuals having reciprocal needs and powers. These mechanisms are called social institutions. They provide a suitable setting for the exchange and determine what resources each party should give and what should be received in return. Each institution specializes in certain resources, which tend to be proximal in the structure of resources; it follows that each institution focuses on a particular segment of the structure. Indeed, there are no institutions where money is exchanged with love or status with goods. While institutions facilitate the exchange process, they also constitute limitations and barriers. One should address himself to the appropriate institution for a given exchange. Yet he may not have an access to it, and he may have to invest more for getting the same amount of resource in an inappropriate institution.

Beside the motivational state of the potential exchanger and their access to the appropriate institutions, the completion of an exchange and its consequences are influenced by the properties of the particular resources exchanged. Some of these properties affect the motivational state of the participants after the exchange had taken place; other properties dictate the differential environmental conditions for each resource, within the appropriate institutions. In general, these properties are related to the cognitive structure, so that proximal resources are more similar with respect to the values they assume on each property than do remote ones. Moreover, the value assumed by a resource class on each property reflects the cognitive and environmental conditions which had existed when the classes became differentiated. Indeed, resources are best exchanged in environmental conditions that resemble those under which they had developed. Since the cognitive structure is a developmental product, the sequence of development constitutes a link between the structure and the properties of resources.

The environmental properties of resources combine to reduce particularistic exchanges in modern society. An environment in which a person is exposed to a large amount of stimuli and many contacts is not suitable for exchange of love. Many encounters are not repeated, and groups, although sometimes small, are often unstable in urban environments. Moreover, the highly specialized institutions of modern society do not provide a frame for exchanges of love as an addition to other exchanges. Consequently, people in such environment suffer from alientaion and love deprivation. Criminal behavior increases as the criminals are not afraid to lose status and love from their neighbors; the latter do not provide these resources even when one behaves properly. Usage of drugs increases to overcome the feeling of alienation, either by reducing the need for human companionship, or by facilitating these exchanges in spite of unfavorable environmental conditions. Still another consequence of particularistic poverty is the development of group encounters; those are new institutions with the sole function of exchanging love.

CHAPTER 6

THE EXCHANGE AND ITS AFTERMATH

Overview

AFTER HAVING DISCUSSED some of the intrapersonal and environmental conditions influencing resource exchange, we now turn to consider various exchange paradigms and to examine their consequences. A paradigm specifies the mode of the proaction and the mode of the reaction. Most common are the two paradigms in which the mode—giving or taking—is alike in proaction and in reaction. In the first one, a person gives to the other a resource and the other participant reciprocates by giving him the same or a different resource. In the second paradigm a person takes a resource from the other, who, in turn, retaliates by taking away one of the resources from the person. Both types of exchange raise two interrelated problems, the first being concerned with the relationship between the resource of reaction and that of proaction. A number of studies and experiments, which are described here, suggest the existence of definite preferences for the resource of reaction, both for reciprocation and for retaliation. The identification of these preferences raises the other question: what are the consequences of preferred and unpreferred reactions? This problem is examined in two experiments dealing, respectively, with exchanges of taking and of giving. The effect of previous loss on a successive exchange of giving is considered in another investigation. The last experiment to be described in this chaper also involves both types of exchange and investigates the choice of partner for the transaction as well as the type of resource chosen for reaction.

PARADIGMS OF INTERACTION

Let us consider some interpersonal behaviors such as the following ones: Person A embraces (gives love to) person B; A assaults (takes away services from) B; A misleads (takes away information from) B; A pays (gives money to) B; A reprimands (takes away status from) B. In all these examples the object behavior is always the "other."

178

However, as noted earlier, one can act toward himself so that the following examples are also forms of interpersonal behavior: A shaves himself (gives service to A); A feels guilty (takes away love from A); A solves a problem (gives information to A); A deludes himself (takes away information from A).

It is easy to recognize that all these examples of behavior are composed of four constituent elements, all of which have been discussed at length in the first part of this volume. There is an *actor*, the person who performs the act, there is an *object* or a recipient of the behavior, who may or may not be the same person as the actor; there is a *mode* of behavior, either giving or taking away; and, finally, there is the class of the *resource* which the actor gives to, or takes away from, the object. Thus a unit of exchange is defined by any given combination of an actor, an object, a mode and a resource class. For our present purposes it is convenient to consider this unit from the point of view of the actor, at the actual level. The function of the ideal level and the viewpoint of the non-actor will be discussed later in this section. We can further simplify the exchange paradigm by considering the case where actor and object are different individuals. We have already seen (Chapter 5) that the relationships between behavior toward the other and behavior toward self is influenced by the resource involved, being positive for love and becoming lower and the negative as one moves in the order of resources from love toward money. When mode and resource class are both known for the behavior towards the other it is possible to make some prediction with regard to the behavior toward self; this self-other relationship offers some justification for limiting the present discussion to behavior toward the other.

A typical interaction is constituted by two units of transaction, following one another in time. It is convenient to call the first unit proaction and the second one reaction. By varying actor, mode, and object and leaving the resource unspecified, several paradigms of interaction can be constructed. Some of them are given in Table 27. In most of these paradigms the actor of proaction becomes the object of reaction, while the object of the proaction becomes an actor in the reaction.

In each paradigm there will be a resource class involved in the proaction and the same or another class in the reaction, so that each

Table 27

PARADIGMS OF INTERACTION

Type of Paradigm	Proaction	Reaction
1. Giving	A gives to B	B gives to A
2. Taking (Aggression)	A takes from B	B takes from A
3. Restitution	A takes from B	A gives to B
4. "Turning the other cheek"	A takes from B	B gives to A
5. "Ingratitude"	A gives to B	B takes from A

paradigm offers $6 \times 6 = 36$ possible combinations of resources. Some of these combinations might be more likely, more satisfactory or more appropriate than others. The problem of an appropriate match between the resource of reaction to the resource of proaction is of great practical significance and involves consideration of both individual need and of institutional norms. If somebody plays a musical instrument at a gathering of friends, it is appropriate to compliment him for his skill, but inappropriate to offer him money. On the other hand at a public performance, it is not enough to clap hands energetically, one must also pay the admission price. In these two examples the resource of the proaction is the same, but the appropriate resource for reaction is determined by the institutional situation. Within a given institution, the individual needs may influence exchange preferences. A person who needs status may prefer a lesser paying but prestigeful job to another where salary is higher but status is lower; a small shop may attract shoppers (who need to be loved) by giving them the individual attention they miss at the less expensive but more impersonal department store.

The most desirable exchange is that which fulfills the needs of the participants in an appropriate institutional setting. When planning such an optimal exchange one should consider the two aspects of interpersonal behavior which have been disregarded in describing the unit of exchange: ideal level and viewpoint of the other. The ideal level indicates whether the proposed exchange is institutionally appropriate, according to the norms of a particular society. For example the ideal level will indicate that giving good grades in exchange for money is inappropriate to the roles of teacher and pupil in spite of the fact that the teacher may need money and the pupil may prefer good grades to cash. Considering the viewpoint of the other provides information about the other's needs, i.e., about the likelihood that the proposed exchange will be accepted. When one tries to hire the services of a person who is in need of money by offering him a high status position which does not pay much, the transaction may not be successful.

The ideal and other's viewpoint influence not only the degree of satisfaction but also the initial willingness or readiness of a person to enter a given exchange situation, even when it might be suitable for his own needs. Expectation of rejection, especially when generalized ("nobody cares for me") and possible violation of institutional norms may block the expression of needs. Thirsty for approval a person may still insist that he could not care less about others' opinion of him. We have already seen (see Ch. 5) that the more particularistic the resource the stronger the difficulties in verbalizing the need for it; furthermore, an experiment done by Meir Teichman, and described later in this chapter, suggests that expression of particularistic demands may devaluate the person in the eyes of the exchange partner, an effect which is likely to discourage verbalization of such needs. For all these reasons a direct assessment of needs presents certain difficulties, particularly so for the more intimate ones; often an expression of preference for a given resource may be influenced not only by the individual's need for it but also by expectations regarding the partner and consideration of the institutional situation.

EXCHANGE OF GIVING

In considering the paradigm of giving we are interested in questions such as: if A gives a certain resource to B, which resource would he prefer most in exchange, what will be his second preference and which resource will be least preferred by him? Will the decrease in preference follow the order of resources? If a given resource of reaction is preferred most for a resource of proaction, for which other resource of proaction will it be preferred next?

The following study (Turner et al., 1971) was conducted to explore some of these questions. One hundred sixty freshmen at the University of Missouri, Columbia, were administered a modification of the "Social Interaction Inventory," which was described in Chapter 4 and is given in full in Appendix C. In this inventory the subject is presented with six situations, in each of which he gives a certain resource to another person. Each situation is followed by fifteen pairs of items, where each item in the pair belongs to a different resource class. Since there are six classes of resources, the 15 pairs allow for the combination of each resource with every other one. In each pair the resource is presented by a different item, so that there are five items for each class. The subject was instructed to choose in each pair the item which he preferred in exchange for what he had given. To balance sequential effects both the order of presentation of the situations across subjects, and the order of presentation of paired comparison within each situation, were randomized. Table 28 presents the percentage with which each resource was preferred in exchange for each resource given. Since in each stimulus situation a specific resource appeared only five times in the 15 paired alternatives, it could not be chosen more than one third of the time. Consequently, the highest possible percentage is 33 percent, while the lowest is, of course, zero.

The reader will remember that the structure of resources, depicted in Figure 7, has already been empirically established; in Chapter 3 we saw that resources proximal in the structure are perceived as similar and reacted to in a similar manner. Here again we predicted that for

Table 28

PERCENTAGE NUMBER OF CHOICES OF RESOURCES
CONTIGENT UPON RESOURCE GIVEN

Resource Given	Resource Chosen in Exchange						All Resources
	Love	Status	Info.	Money	Goods	Services	
Love	32	24	18	2	9	15	100%
Status	26	27	21	2	8	16	100%
Info.	23	21	25	5	10	16	100%
Money	11	14	15	22	16	22	100%
Goods	21	17	16	9	18	19	100%
Services	20	17	18	9	11	25	100%
All Resources	22	20	19	8	12	19	100%

each resource given, the frequency of the resources desired in exchange will follow the structural model. This prediction is, indeed, supported by the data. In the first row, for example, where the resource given is love, this resource is also the most chosen in exchange. Moving from left to right on the first row, the frequency in choice decreases for status, still further for information and reaches the lowest point for money. Then it increases again for goods and more so for services. Thus, starting from the resource with the highest frequency the pattern shows a decrease and then an increase, as the most preferred resource is approached from the other side of the circular order. The same pattern is also found in the other rows of the table, with three deviations: the frequencies of love in exchange for information, services for money, and information for services, are all higher than predicted. Here, as well as in the first study, deviations generally involve information, suggesting that this class of resources may require a closer scrutiny.

We have seen earlier (Table 10) that resources two steps removed from each other are perceived as least similar. In the exchange pattern of Table 28, however, the resource which is least exchanged is usually money, independently of the resource given. The only exception is when money is given: here the least likely exchange is with love, the opposite of money. Although this feature of the exchange pattern does not alter the order, it requires some explanation. The situations of the Social Interaction Inventory implicitly refer to an exchange between friends. In the institution of friendship, as in any social institution, certain resources are more appropriate than others. We have already noted that resources suitable for one institution may be scarcely used in another institution (Ch. 5; see also Foa and Donnenwerth, 1971) so that each institution may be characterized by its own profile of the relative frequency of resources. The profile obtained for friendship is given in the bottom row of Table 28: the highest frequency is for love and the lowest for money. The remaining resources fell between these two extremes, decreasing and then increasing gradually, according to the structure. The profile of resource frequencies would be different for other institutions. In banking, for example, one would expect money to have the highest frequency, while the frequency of the other resources would decrease as one moves toward love. Thus the distribution found in each row of Table 28 depends not only on the resource given, but on overall institutional constraints as well. These constraints are also reflected by the *most* frequent resource in each row. Among friends it might be appropriate to reciprocate information with information or with services. At the drugstore, however, the appropriate exchange for the information contained in the daily newspaper is a coin. While institution and role may prescribe which exchanges will occur most and least often, the frequency of the remaining exchanges appears to follow the cognitive structure. The institutional effect may account for the fact that the marginal distribution of resources in Table 28 is somewhat different from the one in Table 10, where no particular institutional setting was specified. Both distributions are given in Table 29.

Table 29

PERCENTAGE FREQUENCY DISTRIBUTION OF RESOURCES
FROM TWO STUDIES

	Love	Status	Information	Money	Goods	Services
Friendship Institution	22	20	19	8	12	19
No Institution	21	23	11	15	18	12

If we were to repeat the study for a different institution we would predict that the frequency distribution will change again, but the order will be preserved. In fact the frequency distribution changes, even within the same institution, depending upon the resource given. By virtue of its invariance, the notion of order appears to be more general and useful than the hierarchy of frequencies proposed by Premack (1965). In a very specific situation order and hierarchy of frequencies are identical. But, while the order appears to remain invariant across situations, the frequency distribution does change. Consequently the combined distribution of two or more institutional situations is unlikely to reveal the order. The combined distribution of the institutions of friendship and trade, for example, will probably be bimodal with peaks at love and money. Such distribution would suggest the wrong conclusion that love and money are closely related.

These data aimed at exploring the cognitive structure of resource exchange and did not investigate overt behavior. Will a person, prevented from expressing love, be more likely to give status than information? Will an individual, barred from physically assaulting somebody, be more likely to insult than to deceive him? A main contention of this book is that cognitive structure mediates between stimuli and overt responses. Therefore we expect the order of resources to be reflected in overt exchanges as well. A comparison between the cognitive and behavioral levels is possible by considering the following two studies which investigate the second paradigm of interaction, exchanges of taking: the first study is concerned with probing cognitive structures, while the second deals with overt behavior.

EXCHANGE OF TAKING

Frustration and aggression, aggression and counter-aggression, aggression and retaliation are some of the terms used in the literature for denoting exchanges of taking. To avoid confusion we shall use the term *deprivation* to indicate the proaction, thus stressing the fact that the object of the proaction is deprived of some resource; the reaction —in which the deprived object becomes the actor—will be denoted by the term *retaliation*. This terminology implies that the interactive sequence is being considered from the viewpoint of the retaliator, as this is often the case in the studies we shall examine. When no ambiguity is involved the term *aggression* will also be used to indicate either proaction or reaction.

The two studies to which we now turn, dealing with cognition and overt behavior, were designed to test hypotheses about the relationship between the resource of proaction and that of reaction, in taking away exchange (Foa, E. B., Turner, and Foa, 1972). Specifically, the following hypotheses were tested:

1. *Direct retaliation hypothesis:* Given the freedom to choose from among different classes of retaliatory behaviors, victims of prior deprivation will show a preference for the return of injuries corresponding in kind to the harm received. Thus, the most preferred form of retaliation will be within the same resource class as antecedent aggression.
2. *Generalization hypothesis:* Preference for different forms of retaliatory behavior will decrease progressively the more distal, in the structure, that type of action is from the most preferred response, as specified in Hypothesis 1.
3. *Substitution hypothesis:* If victims prefer to retaliate within the same response class as prior aggression (Hypothesis 1), and if there is an ordered preference reflecting response similarity (Hypothesis 2), it follows that: when denied the possibility to retaliate in kind, victims will choose from available resources the one most similar to direct retaliation. Should the relationship between the resources of proaction and reaction prove different

from the one predicted in the first hypothesis, then the substitution hypothesis will have to be modified according to the most preferred response actually found. On the other hand, rejection of the generalization hypothesis will, *ipso facto,* result in denial of the substitution hypothesis as well.

Questionnaire Responses

Fifty-eight introductory sociology students at the University of Missouri, Columbia, were given the "Social Interaction Inventory" for negative behaviors (see Appendix D). In this inventory the subject is presented with six hypothetical situations, in each of which he has just been deprived of a particular resource. Loss of the various resources was described as follows. Love: "A person conveys to you that he dislikes you. He is unfriendly and avoids your company." Status: "A person degrades or belittles you. He lets you understand that you are worthless and that you don't do things well." Information: "A person gives you false or distorted information. His deceit leads you to make bad decisions in matters which are important to you." Money: "A person cheats you by taking or withholding money which belongs to you." Services: "A person injures you or gives you bad services. His behavior results in inconvenience or damage to you."

Following the same format as the inventory for exchange of giving, each situation is followed by fifteen pairs of items, where each item in the pair belongs to a different resource class. Since there are six classes of resources, the fifteen pairs allow for the combination of each class with every other one. In each instance the aggressive act is represented by a differently worded item, so that there are five representative items for each class. The subject was instructed to choose from each pair the item which he preferred for retaliation. Some of the items are as follows. Taking away love: "You let the person feel that you dislike him." "You convey to the person that you do not want to associate with him." Taking away status: "You belittle the person." "You let the person feel that you don't respect his abilities." Taking away information: "You deceive the person regarding information he requests from you." "You tell the person things that will lead him to the wrong decision." Taking away money: "You make the person lose some money." "You manage to gain possession of some money belonging to the person." Taking away goods: "You would confiscate goods belonging to the other person." "You help yourself to some of the other person's belongings." Taking away services: "You physically harm the person." "You withhold aid causing hardship to the person."

To balance sequential effects both the order of presentation of the situations across subjects, and the order of pairs within each situation, were randomized. The frequency of the preference for each response class was then calculated for each of the six stimulus situations.

Table 30 presents the mean frequency of choice for each class of retaliatory action contingent on each type of prior aggression. Since for each deprivation any given class of retaliation appeared five times in the fifteen paired alternatives, the range for the mean is from zero to five.

Table 30
MEAN CHOICES OF RESOURCES OF RETALIATION CONTINGENT
UPON RESOURCE OF DEPRIVATION

Resource of Deprivation	Resource of Retaliation						Row Variance
	Love	Status	Info.	Money	Goods	Services	
Love	4.71	3.71	2.81	.76	.88	2.10	2.42
Status	4.09	3.86	2.98	.78	1.47	1.83	1.82
Information	4.33	3.60	3.38	1.48	.86	1.45	2.03
Money	3.38	3.33	2.07	2.55	1.69	1.98	.52
Goods	3.69	3.64	2.36	2.14	1.47	1.71	.91
Services	4.17	3.67	2.38	1.55	.66	2.60	1.70
All Resources	4.06	3.64	2.66	1.54	1.17	1.95	

The "direct aggression" hypothesis predicts that subjects victimized by a given form of deprivation will prefer to retaliate within the resource class of previous aggression, so that the highest mean in each row of Table 30 should appear in the main diagonal cell. This prediction was not confirmed; no matter what deprivation preceded it, taking away love was always the most frequently chosen form of retaliation. Also relevant to the direct retaliation hypothesis is inspection of the columns of Table 30. Each column shows the frequency of choosing a given resource of retaliation in reaction to the various resources of deprivation. Again, according to the hypothesis, we shall expect the highest entries to be in the diagonal cells. This prediction was supported, except for taking away goods, where it deviated one step from the diagonal cell. Thus, if a given resource is chosen for retaliation, this choice is most likely to follow loss of a resource from the same class. The results indicate that while taking away love is the most preferred form of retaliation irrespective of the type of deprivation, the probability of choosing a given form of reprisal is highest when aggression in the same resource class preceded it.

The generalization hypothesis predicts that, given the most frequent response to a certain type of retaliation, the choice of other retributive acts will follow the cognitive structure of resources. This hypothesis is well supported by the data shown in Table 30. In the first row, where prior aggression involved disaffection, taking away love is also the preferred type of retaliation. Moving from left to right on the first row, the frequency of choice decreases, reaching the lowest point for money, then increases again for goods and more so for services. Thus, starting from the act with the highest frequency the pattern shows a decrease and then an increase, as the most preferred retaliation is approached from the other side of the circular order. The same pattern is also found in the other rows of the table, with one interesting exception: the frequency of taking away money, in retaliation for loss of it, is higher than predicted by the generalization hypothesis, although lower, as previously noted, than expected according to the hypothesis of direct retaliation. Although the columns reveal four deviations, the order is essentially the same as in the rows; the use of a given resource class is highest in retaliation for deprivation of the same class and tends to decrease gradually for more distal types of resources. The right-most column of Table 30 gives the variance of the entries in each row, and will be discussed later.

Experimental Results

In the second study observation of overt behavior constitutes the dependent variable. The subjects were 90 males, recruited from introductory psychology classes at the University of Missouri. Each subject was randomly assigned to one of six experimental groups, so that in each group there were 15 subjects. Each of the six groups was initially exposed to deprivation in one of the six resource classes: loss of love; status; information; money; goods; services. After being so victimized each subject was given a choice between two types of retaliation. The alternatives made available always consisted of one act belonging to the class most distal from prior aggression and one taken from the most proximal class. Since in a circular order each class has two neighbors, the selection of the proximal alternative was based on a previous finding (see Table 10) that one of the two neighbors of each class is usually perceived as more similar. Thus the two types of retaliation made available depended on the class of previous aggression and differed for each group. In this study each subject was presented with *only one* pair of retribution alternatives following his *actual* loss of *one* given resource. In the first study, on the other hand, the *full set* of 15 pairs of alternative retaliations was used in conjunction with each one of the *six hypothetical* deprivations.

Subjects were introduced to a confederate, who was presented as another subject, and were told that the experiment was designed to study the effects of stress conditions on learning after previous communication between the "stress giver" and the "subject." These two roles for the learning task were assigned by a loaded lottery which always designated the subject as the stress provider. The first part of the experiment consisted of having subject and confederate build a model brick house, ostensibly to provide them with an opportunity for communication. In fact, the joint task gave the confederate an occasion for aggressing against the subject. Upon completion of the construction task the confederate was removed under the pretext of instructing him regarding the learning task to follow. The subject was then provided with a sheet of paper on which two stress conditions were indicated. He was asked to choose the stress he would be delivering and was left alone to make this choice. In the alleged learning condition the confederate pretended to memorize the place of geometrical figures while the subject provided the form of stress he had chosen.

For taking away "goods" and "services" the first part of the cover story was modified to provide a suitable occasion for depriving the subject of these resources. The experiment was presented to subjects in these groups as a study of the effect of various types of stress conditions on learning; the subject (apparently chosen by a pre-arranged

Table 31

DEPRIVATION MANIPULATIONS AND THEIR RESPECTIVE
RETALIATION ALTERNATIVES

Deprivation	Retaliation Alternatives
1. *Loss of love:* Confederate says to the subjects: "Did anybody ever tell you that you are a very difficult person to work with?" In addition, the subject gets to see a questionnaire filled out by the confederate in which dislike is expressed.	*Loss of money:* You make your partner lose the money he expects to get for his participation in the experiment. *Loss of status:* You convey to your partner that he is unable to cope with this task, which is above his abilities.
2. *Loss of status:* Confederate says to the subject: "If you had been less clumsy we could have finished long ago." In addition, the subject gets to see a questionnaire filled out by the confederate in which his performance is rated low.	*Loss of love:* You convey to your partner that he is unpleasant to work with, that he is disliked and unappealing. *Loss of goods:* You make your partner lose some objects that he had been promised for his participation in this experiment.
3. *Loss of information:* Confederate gives the subject wrong plans for building. Later accuses him of refusal to build the correct model.	*Loss of services:* You administer noxious noise, through earphones, to your partner. *Loss of status:* You convey to your partner that he is unable to cope with his task, which is above his abilities.
4. *Loss of money:* Each of the partner is supposed to be paid two dollars, but confederate takes $3.20 for himself.	*Loss of goods:* You make your partner lose some objects. *Loss of love:* You convey to your partner that he is unpleasant to work with, that he is disliked and unappealing.
5. *Loss of goods:* Confederate sets up time limits on the subjects and does not allow him to gain a gift certificate.	*Loss of status:* You convey to your partner that he is unable to cope with the task, which is above his abilities. *Loss of money:* You make it impossible for your partner to gain the money.
6. *Loss of services:* Confederate deliberately chooses to deliver very intense shocks to the subjects.	*Loss of information:* You give misleading directions to your partner with regard to the way he should pursue his task. *Loss of love:* You convey to your partner that he is unpleasant to work with, that he is disliked and unappealing.

lottery) performed an intellectual task while the confederate arbitrarily delivered high intensity shock (services) or denied him the opportunity to win a prize (goods). The second part was the same as previously described. The deprivations used in the six groups and their respective retaliatory alternatives are given in Table 31.

The substitution hypothesis predicts that subjects will choose from the two available alternatives for retaliation the one most similar to the antecedent aggression they had experienced. This prediction assumes, of course, that the direct retaliation hypothesis will also hold true. The number of times each one of the two retaliatory alternatives was chosen in every one of the six deprivation conditions is shown in Table 32.

Table 32

FREQUENCY OF CHOICE BETWEEN TWO RESOURCES OF
AGGRESSION FOR EACH GIVEN RESOURCE OF FRUSTRATION

Resource Administered in Frustration	Number of Subjects Choosing Resource of Aggression				Total Subjects	Significance
	According to Hypothesis		Against Hypothesis			
Love	Status	11	Money	4	15	.018
Status	Love	11	Goods	4	15	.018
Information	Status	12	Services	3	15	.004
Money	Goods	13	Love	2	15	.000
Goods	Money	13	Status	2	15	.000
Services	Love	4	Info.	11	15	.941

Note: One-tailed significance of choice distribution computed by binomial test.

The results supported the hypothesis for all types of deprivation except for the last one. Subjects who were personally rejected by the confederate chose to derogate him rather than make him lose money. Those who were derogated chose to retaliate by expressions of dislike, more than by making their partner lose goods. The subjects exposed to cheating chose to derogate their frustrator rather than inflicting him physical discomfort. Those who were deprived of their money chose to make their aggressor lose the promised goods, and the ones who lost goods chose to retaliate by inflicting loss of money. Contrary to the substitution hypothesis, however, subjects who were exposed to electrical shock chose to give misleading instructions rather than to take away love.

The second hypothesis was also tested in this experiment. This hypothesis states that given the most preferred act of retaliation, preference for other resources will follow the order: resources proximal to the most preferred one will be chosen more than the remote ones. In order to test this hypothesis the frequency distribution of choice for each resource, over all six groups, was computed. This frequency was divided by the number of times the resource was offered for choice. The results are summarized in Table 33.

Table 33

MEAN NUMBER OF CHOICES FOR EACH RESOURCE
OF RETALIATION

Resource	Frequency of Choice	Number of Times the Resource Was Presented for Choice	Mean Number of Choices of Resource for Each Presentation
Love	17	3	6
Status	25	3	8
Information	11	1	11
Money	17	2	8
Goods	17	2	8
Services	3	1	3

The hypothesis is again supported by the results. Giving misleading directions (information) was most preferred; the least preferred retaliation, physical discomfort (services), is the one most removed from information. The remaining retributions occupy intermediate positions with respect to frequency of choice.

In summary, both Hypotheses 2 and 3, tested in this experiment, were supported, with one exception: subjects administered shock chose to retaliate by giving misleading information rather than by expressing dislike. The possibility that this result indicates that services and information are proximal in the order is discounted by the fact that misled subjects *did not* choose to retaliate by causing physical pain, but rather preferred to derogate the aggressor. Moreover this explanation does not fit the overall choice frequency of types of retaliation irrespective of deprivation (Table 33), nor previous results supporting the proposed order. An alternative, more situation-specific, explanation emerged from debriefing interviews: the shock received was seen as part of the experiment rather than being due to the initiative of the confederate, possibly because shock is so often administered in experimental situations of this type. Lack of arbitrariness may have reduced the feeling of loss so that misleading information could have been chosen more as a function of task relevance (i.e., disrupting learning) than of retributive hostility.

Comparison of Verbal and Overt Behavior

Results of both studies are consistent with the theoretical structure obtained by arranging the six classes of aggressive behavior on two dimensions, thus indicating that the order reflects associative ties among response classes which therefore are valid for negative as well as for positive exchanges.

The two studies, however, differ in the frequency distribution of the various resource classes. In the first study expression of dislike is the most preferred retaliation (bottom row of Table 30), with a gradual decrease for other classes, following the order. In the second study (right column of Table 33) the order is again preserved, but the most frequently chosen retribution shifts to information. Once again a change of frequency distribution leaves the order undisturbed.

The hypothesis that retaliation will be in the same class as previous deprivation is only partially supported in the first study; while it is true that a given class is preferred most in retaliation for aggression in the same class, taking away love remains the most preferred form of retaliation, irrespective of the preceding loss. The second study does not provide an explicit test of the direct retaliation hypothesis. The fact, however, that in this study the response most proximal to direct retaliation was usually preferred supports this hypothesis indirectly.

In summary, the major difference between the results of the two studies is that the overall preference for causing loss of love is stronger, in the questionnaire study, than predicted by the hypothesis of direct retaliation. This partial disparity in results may be clarified by considering difference in the design of the two investigations. As already noted, in the first study each subject was presented with all possible pairs of retaliatory alternatives to each one of the six deprivations, while in the second study only one pair of alternative retaliations was made available following each specific aggression. Separate analysis of only those contingencies common to both studies did not support the possibility that the selective sample of stimuli and responses employed in the experimental study would account for the dissimilar results. We therefore turn to discuss two other features in which the two studies differ: degree of arousal and expectation of immunity from further attack.

In the questionnaire study the subject was requested to indicate his preferences for retaliating against an hypothetical aggressor and the possible further consequences of retaliation were left unspecified. In the experimental investigation the subject was actually deprived and then permitted to retaliate in the relative safety and legitimacy of a psychological experiment. The hypothetical loss presented in the questionnaire seems unlikely to have aroused the respondent, while experimental subjects were noticeably upset by the behavior of the confederate. Emotional arousal and relative immunity may well have reduced the effect of inhibition in subjects participating in the experiment. The finding that inhibition produced switching to less direct forms of aggression has been reported by Bandura and Walters (1959, pp. 138–140) and Dinwiddie (1955). In contrast, social norms appear likely to be more salient when responding verbally to hypothetical situations, which provided neither arousal nor immunity. Further, these norms are more severe for certain resources than for certain others. Taking away money and goods even in small amounts usually constitutes a crime punishable by law. A similar but sometimes lower degree of legal protection is provided against bodily harm (loss of services). Giving false information or causing loss of status are not considered crimes, except in very particular circumstances. There are practically no legal restraints against expressing dislike for a person (loss of love), and this form of aggression appears to be the most socially acceptable. This norm is reflected in the preference for causing loss of love expressed by questionnaire respondents.

When deprivation involves love there is no conflict between the tendency for direct retaliation and the social norm, but this conflict is bound to increase as the resource of deprivation moves away from love toward its opposite in the order, money. The extent of such conflict is roughly indicated by the variance of the entries in each row (shown in the right-most column of Table 30). Where a conflict among alternative responses exists, retaliatory preferences should be less clear-cut, resulting in similarities among the various choice frequencies in the same row (some choosing by one criterion, some by the other and some compromising between the two), thus the variance is smaller. As conflict decreases, the entries of a particular row should be less similar (some resources being definitely preferred over others) and the variance consequently larger. This is precisely what happened; the variance was highest for deprivation involving love, lowest for money and tended to be ordered between these two extremes for the other resource classes.

The two studies presented suggest that while the frequency of emission of a particular class of aggressive responses varies with the situation, response classes contiguous in the order tend to have similar frequencies. The fact that the same order also occurs for exchanges of giving lends support to the proposition that the frustration-aggression sequence can be seen as a particular kind of interpersonal exchange where resources are mutually taken away rather than given. This approach is further developed in the next chapter.

When social norms (or some other obstacle) conflict with the tendency for direct retaliation, the frustrated individual may resort to indirect retaliation, which is likely to yield less satisfaction and to have a weakened cathartic effect. If so, the degree of catharsis will be inversely related to the distance in the structure between the resource class of deprivation and that of retaliation. This distance may also influence the intensity of the retaliatory response; the larger the distance the more intense the response. To the empirical test of these hypotheses we now turn.

EFFECTS OF INAPPROPRIATE RETALIATION

We have proposed that the dissimilarity (or distance in the structure) between the resource class used in deprivation and the class available to the victim for retaliation will affect both the strength of retaliation and the amount of residual hostility. A *larger* distance between the resources of deprivation and of retaliation will result in *higher* intensity of retaliation as well as in *more* residual hostility. The aggressive act deprives the victim of a certain resource; if he is then able to retaliate by taking away from the aggressor the same or a similar resource some equilibrium will be reestablished and less residual hostility will be left after the exchange has terminated. If, on the other hand, the resource available to the victim is different from the one of which he was deprived, then retaliation will not be effective in restoring equilibrium and more residual hostility will remain even if retaliation was quite intense.

These two hypotheses were tested in an experiment done by Gregory Donnenwerth (1971). Similar to the experiment discussed previously, subjects were first deprived by a confederate of one resource. Unlike the other study, however, they were not permitted to choose the resource of retaliation but were to choose the intensity of retaliation in the sole resource which was available to them.

Subjects were 140 female students recruited from introductory psychology classes at the University of Missouri, Columbia. Six types of deprivation were employed in the experiment, one for each experimental group. Some subjects were deprived of love; others of status, information, money, goods, or services. One hundred twenty subjects were assigned randomly to the six manipulations, twenty subjects to each group. The confederate's behavior in each experimental group is outlined in Table 34. Twenty additional subjects served as a control group. They were not deprived of any resource.

Half of the subjects in each group were then given the opportunity to retaliate against the confederate by subjecting her to expressions of dislike (taking away love); for the other ten subjects in each group the available retaliation involved money. The opportunity to retaliate with love was given under the guise of helping the experimenter to run an experiment investigating "behavior in conditions of deprivation." The subject was asked to set the intensity of an apparatus from which the confederate was to receive negative statements about herself. In money retaliation the confederate was supposed to play

Table 34

BEHAVIOR OF CONFEDERATE FOR DEPRIVING THE SUBJECTS

Resource of Deprivation	Behavior
Love	After the subject had disclosed herself, the confederate refuses to reciprocate self-disclosure by saying; "It seems to me that if you are the kind of person I think you are, I certainly don't want to reveal anything about myself to you."
Status	After completing a short form "I.Q." test ahead of subject, the confederate comments sarcastically, "Do you need some help." Further derogatory statements such as "That's not right, don't you know what _____ means" or "How did you ever get admitted to this university," were made.
Information	The confederate persuades the subject to agree with him on how to play a game so that both will win. The confederate then deceives the subject and thus wins five times as much. The amount of money involved in this situation was just a few pennies, so to stress deception rather than monetary loss.
Money	The confederate takes for himself three out of four dollars she and the subject jointly gained by participating in an experiment. On a previous trial the subject had control of the money and split it equally with the confederate.
Goods	Confederate takes a valuable pen, gives a plain wood pencil to the subject instead of a valued pen. (In a previous trial the subject had split equally between them the writing tablets obtained.)
Services	The subject and the confederate were asked to compute a set of scores, each was to complete twenty scores. The subject helped the confederate to finish her pile; then the confederate refused to reciprocate by helping the subject, telling her she did not feel like doing this job any more and that the subject could do her own computations by herself.

against the machine and to lose money. The amount of loss was determined by the subject. In the love retaliation the confederate would feed into the machine statements regarding her own behavior in an hypothetical group situation; the subject could then cause the machine to deliver negative responses to the confederate. These responses differed in intensity depending on the setting chosen by the subject. The intensity of retaliation set by the subject was recorded automatically by an Esterline-Angus event recorder.

Intensity of Retaliation

The mean strength of retaliation for each group is given in Table 35. The first row contains the means of intensity for each type of depriva-

Table 35

MEAN INTENSITY OF RETALIATION IN MONEY OR LOVE

Resource of Retaliation	Love	Status	Resource of Deprivation Information	Money	Goods	Services	No Deprivation (Control)
Money	28.3	21.8	15.3	16.7	18.8	20.5	9.3
Love	27.0	31.9	32.3	38.3	34.1	29.9	15.2

tion and for the control group, when retaliation was done by inflicting loss of money. The highest intensity occurred when subjects were deprived of love, the class most distal from money in the circular structure of resources; it decreased progressively as one moves away from the class of "love." According to the hypothesis we would have expected that the lowest intensity would occur when money was taken from the subject; instead, the intensity of retaliation was lowest when subjects were exposed to loss of information, a neighboring class to "money." The picture is completely reversed in the second row, when subjects retaliated by inflicting loss of love: here the strongest retaliation occurred when money was the resource of deprivation and the lowest intensity was found in the group which was deprived of personal liking. For the other classes of deprivation the strength of retaliation increased regularly the nearer they were to money. These results confirm the hypothesis that strength of retaliation is directly related to the distance between resource of deprivation and resource of retaliation. The subjects who were not exposed to any form of deprivation exhibited the lowest intensity of retaliation. Although not surprising, this result indicates that for any type of deprivation, deprived subjects tend to be more aggressive than those who have not suffered deprivation.

To summarize, the structural model of interpersonal resources and the assumption that people strive for restoration of equilibrium have led us to predict the relative strength of retaliation for each pair of deprivation-retaliation. The larger the cognitive distance between class of deprivation and class of retaliation, the higher will be the intensity. Specifically we have predicted that the peak will be found in the groups where the classes of deprivation and retaliation are most distal, i.e., "love-money" and "money-love." The lowest intensity will occur in the two groups where deprivation and retaliation involve the same resource, i.e., "love-love" and "money-money." The intensity of other groups will decline as to create a gradient from both sides of the peak. Except for the lowest point of the money retaliation, which shifted from "money-money" to "information-money," all other predictions were confirmed. Both analysis of variance and test for quadratic trend indicated high statistical significance for these results.

Resources of Residual Aggression

Residual aggression may be conceived as a potential for taking away behavior left in the subject after terminating the deprivation-retaliation exchange; as such, residual aggression demands specification of the resource for which a potential taking away exists. Hence, there are six kinds of residual aggression which should be considered, one for each resource class. Likewise, there are six resources of deprivation and six for retaliation, of which only two were investigated in this experiment. Altogether there are $6 \times 6 \times 2 = 72$ combinations of resources in the deprivation-retaliation-residual aggression paradigm of our experiment. Such a large body of data requires some general rules for prediction; to them we now turn.

Let us consider a case in which person A was deprived of love by person B; it can be expected that no matter how he retaliated the residual aggression will be stronger in love, the resource of deprivation, than in a distal resource such as money. After all why should a person inflict a loss of money on the one who had expressed personal dislike towards him? Thus the following hypothesis regarding the relationship between resource of deprivation and resource of residual aggression is proposed: *Residual aggression will be stronger in resources which are less distant from* (or more similar to) *the resource of deprivation.*

Suppose now that our person who was deprived of love had already retaliated by expressing dislike towards his depriver; his residual aggression will be lower in love than in a resource more remote from the one involved in retaliation. Thus, *residual aggression will be stronger in resources which are more distant from the resource of retaliation.*

To complete the picture let us remember our previous suggestion that the intensity of residual aggression is related to the distance between resource of deprivation and resource of retaliation. Hence, we shall consider again an hypothesis already familiar to us: *Residual aggression will be stronger the greater the distance between resource of deprivation and resource of retaliation.*

The three hypotheses combined suggest that there are three cognitive distances between resources to be considered when predicting the strength of residual aggression. This strength is directly related to the retaliation-deprivation and retaliation-residual aggression distances, and is inversely related to the deprivation-residual aggression distance.

Concrete examples may clarify this complicated relationship: one will maintain a high residual in a resource of which he had been deprived when his retaliation involved a dissimilar resource; conversely one will have a low residual in a resource distal from the one of which he had been deprived when having retaliated with a resource similar to that of which he was deprived.[1]

Partial data for testing these three hypotheses are provided by Don-

---

[1] The relationship among the three resources is further simplified by the fact that given two of the distances the third one is determined. Distance means simply the number of steps necessary to move from one resource to the other. In the circular order of six resource classes the maximal distance is three: three steps are, for example, required for going from love to money. The

nenwerth's experiment. After the subjects had completed their retaliation, they were asked to help test a new piece of equipment which detects whether a person expresses his true feelings or not. The subject was acquainted with the gadget and shown how a steep line appeared on a screen following an obvious lie, and a flat line followed a truthful statement. The subject was then connected to the "detective machine" through electrodes that were attached to his hands and head. He was instructed to rate a series of statements regarding his aggressive feelings toward the confederate in each one of the six resource classes. Let us consider these ratings.

Table 36

MEAN RESIDUAL AGGRESSION IN EACH RESOURCE, FOR EACH RESOURCE
OF DEPRIVATION, WHEN RETALIATORY ACT INVOLVED MONEY

Resource of Residual Aggression	Resource of Deprivation						Row Variance	No Deprivation (Control)
	Love	Status	Info.	Money	Goods	Services		
Love	17.9	13.0	14.1	10.5	11.9	12.9	5.3	3.4
Status	14.8	15.6	7.0	8.4	7.9	11.9	11.8	2.7
Information	7.0	6.6	12.0	7.6	3.7	4.9	6.8	2.4
Money	7.0	4.0	6.6	8.9	6.9	6.3	2.1	2.0
Goods	7.9	8.4	8.0	8.2	11.2	9.3	1.3	2.9
Services	13.8	8.9	10.1	7.1	7.4	14.2	8.5	3.0

Table 37

MEAN RESIDUAL AGGRESSION IN EACH RESOURCE, FOR EACH RESOURCE
OF DEPRIVATION, WHEN RETALIATORY ACT INVOLVED LOVE

Resource of Residual Aggression	Resource of Deprivation						Row Variance	No Deprivation (Control)
	Money	Goods	Services	Love	Status	Info.		
Money	12.4	7.5	5.9	2.4	6.3	9.2	9.4	1.4
Goods	8.9	8.5	7.6	4.9	6.7	8.8	2.0	1.8
Services	8.9	7.8	11.0	7.4	10.0	9.0	1.7	4.9
Love	15.0	11.6	11.7	10.3	11.6	14.2	2.7	5.4
Status	8.0	6.8	7.9	6.3	12.2	9.0	3.7	2.7
Information	7.2	7.5	6.5	5.3	5.9	14.4	9.3	2.0

The data of Table 36 pertain to the subjects who retaliated in money; they give the mean residual aggression in each resource for each resource of deprivation. Comparable means for subjects who retaliate in love are given in Table 37. Each row in these tables indicates the mean residual aggression in a particular resource. The resource of deprivation is given at the top of each column. The reader will notice

---

minimal distance is, of course, zero. Let us indicate the three distances among all the possible pairs formed by three classes by d_1, d_2, d_3. Then the following equality will hold:

$$\bar{d_3} = 3 - \overline{d_1 + d_2 - 3}$$

The bars indicate that the difference between 3 and the sum of d_1 and d_2 should always be taken with a positive sign. We are indebted to Paul K. Blackwell for pointing out this relationship among triads of resource classes.

that the first row and column of Table 36 indicate the means for "love" while in Table 37 "money" occupies this first column and row. The rest of the resources in both tables are given according to their sequence in the cognitive structure. The first row and column of each table represent the resource most remote from the one involved in retaliation. Table 36 gives the means for retaliation in "money," therefore it begins with "love;" Table 37 gives the means for retaliation in "love" and thus begins with "money."

In each row the cognitive distance between resource of retaliation and resource of deprivation decreases as one moves from left to right, reaches bottom in the fourth column and then increases again as we approach the first column from the other side of the circular structure. According to our original hypothesis we expect residual aggression to decrease when the deprivation-retaliation distance becomes smaller; thus its intensity will reach a peak in the first columns, decrease toward the fourth column and then increase again. The hypothesis relating the resource of loss and of residual leads, however, to a different prediction: residual aggression should be highest in the resource of loss and then decrease gradually in the usual manner. In consequence, the highest residual should be in the diagonal cell of each row, the cell where the resource of residual aggression and that of deprivation are alike; the lowest intensity is expected in the cell three steps removed from the diagonal; intensity should then increase again as we approach the diagonal cell from the other side of the circular structure.

It is only in the first row of both tables, where the diagonal cell is in the left-most column, that the two hypotheses lead to the same prediction, which was supported: the highest residual is in the first cell to the left, the lowest in the one three-step removed from it, while the other residuals decrease and then increase regularly between these two extremes, except for one deviation in Table 36. These results were found highly significant for overall differences and for quadratic trend.

In examining the other rows of Tables 36 and 37, where the two hypotheses lead to different predictions, the following procedure was adopted. First we checked whether the last hypotheses (highest residual in the diagonal cell and a gradual decrease on both its sides) was supported. When a deviation was found we noted whether it was in the direction predicted by the other hypothesis. For example: in the second row of Table 36 which gives the means for residual aggression in status, there is one deviation; subjects who were deprived of information indicate lower residual aggression than those deprived of money; this result is contrary to prediction since information is nearer to status than money. This deviation cannot be accounted for by the other hypothesis; according to it subjects deprived of money should show less residual than those deprived of information since in their case both deprivation and retaliation involved money. This instance of departure from both predictions is however not typical: out of 18 deviations (in both tables), from the prediction of gradual decrease on both sides of the diagonal, 15 are in the direction predicted by the distance between deprivation and retaliation.

It should be clear that these two hypotheses (deprivation-retaliation and deprivation-residual distances) are not alternatives from which to choose, but rather two different factors which determine the intensity of residual aggression, both contributing to it. The manner in which these two factors interact varies for the different rows. In the first row of both tables there is complete convergence in the effects of the two factors; indeed, out of 12 means (6 for each table) there is only one deviation in the prediction of the *relative* intensity of residual aggression. The effect of the two factors become most divergent as one moves toward the fourth row, resulting in more deviations from either hypothesis. If divergence between the two hypotheses increases towards the fourth row and then decreases, we should expect the variance of the entries to be smallest in the fourth row and to increase toward the extremes. In the fourth row, when one hypothesis predicts a high score, the opposite prediction is suggested by the other hypothesis. Thus, to the extent that the entries of this row are determined by these two hypotheses, they will tend to be similar to one another, being neither very high nor very low, and their variance will be small. On the other hand, in rows at the top and at the bottom of both tables the two hypotheses tend to agree on which entries should be high and which should be low; thus, here the variance should be higher than in the middle row of the tables. These variances are given in the farthest column, to the right, of Tables 36 and 37; although not exactly as predicted, these variances exhibit a tendency to decrease progressively toward the middle row of each table following the structural pattern of the resource classes.

We have discussed the combined effects of two hypotheses by considering each row separately. To examine the effect of the third hypothesis, concerning the distance between retaliation and residual aggression, we will have to compare different rows. We are uncertain, however, whether residuals in different resources are comparable. We shall therefore limit ourselves to note that entries on the main diagonal tend to decrease toward the middle of each table, indicating that residual aggression becomes less intense for resources which are similar to those employed in retaliation.

DEPRIVATION DELAYS HELPING BEHAVIOR

Donnenwerth's experiment suggests that behavior of taking is more likely to occur after deprivation had been experienced. Contrarywise positive behavior may be *less* likely to occur subsequent to deprivation. A positive behavior which has attracted considerable attention is helping in an emergency situation where the helper provides services to the victim and is reciprocated with expressions of gratitude (love). If the helping act involves danger or requires particular skill the helper may also be rewarded with status given to him by the victim and bystanders. Rarely, other resources such as monetary reward may also be involved.

Since helping is a behavior of giving we can expect that a person previously exposed to loss of resources will be more reluctant to extend assistance than will a non-deprived one. However, the act of helping provides the helper with the possibility of receiving love; for those who had been deprived of love this means an opportunity for restoration of their internal balance. Therefore, reluctance to help is expected to be least prominent for those who had been deprived of love and to increase gradually the less similar to love is the resource of deprivation. These considerations lead to the prediction that delay in proffering help will be longer for deprived individuals and the more so for those who had been deprived of non-particularistic resources. Such results were indeed obtained by Handfinger (1973), who had his subjects deprived of a given resource and then exposed to an emergency situation. Subjects were 80 undergraduates, randomly assigned to eight groups, ten subjects to each group. Each subject was deprived of a given resource while performing a joint task with a confederate. The resource of deprivation differed for each group; two groups were deprived of status, each in a different way. In one group no deprivation was employed; subjects in this group served as controls. After being deprived the subject was left alone in a waiting room; shortly thereafter he heard a sound of a crash and somebody falling in the next room. The time interval between the first crash and the subject opening the door to help constituted the dependent variable.

Deprivation Procedure

Each subject was met by the experimenter who began to explain to him the "study," when the confederate entered and asked if he was in the right room. The experimenter answered positively and invited him in; he then told subject and confederate that the "study" was not yet ready to begin, and asked them to sit and wait. This waiting period was used by the confederate for one of the resource deprivations described below.

Love: The subject and the confederate were told that the experimenter's dissertation committee felt it was necessary for the two participating in the study to become acquainted. Therefore, they had constructed a list of 20 self-disclosure statements that the subject and confederate were supposed to ask each other. The confederate asked the subject the first 10 questions. As the subject then began to ask the second 10 questions the confederate remarked "After hearing your answers, I don't feel you are the type of person who I would like to know anything about myself."

Status (Personality): The confederate asked the experimenter's permission to try on the subject a test which required the subject to assign personality characteristics to geometric figures. After completion, the confederate told the subject that his personality traits make him an undesirable person.

Status (Academic): The confederate asked the experimenter if he could administer a test he was working on in another class. The experimenter agreed and the confederate gave the subject 20 Miller Analogy Test questions. After completion of the test, the confederate looked at the answers and said ". . . don't you know the meaning of this? You have a very limited vocabulary . . . You really messed this test up."

Information: The experimenter told the pair about a new game he had devised consisting of pushing red and green buttons. If both pushed red buttons they each received 2 points. If one pushed red and the other green they received 1 and 3 points respectively. If they both pushed green buttons, neither got any points. After the experimenter left the room, the confederate convinced the subject that for the best possible result they should both push red. After 10 trials the experimenter told them that the confederate gained 30 points and the subject received 10 points.

Money: The experimenter asked the pair to participate in another study which had them work together on two sets of math problems. There were monetary rewards for accuracy to be divided by the subject in the first set and by the confederate in the second set (a phony random selection). After the first set the pair received two dollars, which the subject divided equally with confederate. After the second set the pair received 4 dollars which the confederate divided unequally (3 dollars for himself—1 dollar for the subject).

Goods: Same procedure as for money except that in the first set the reward was 6 notebooks which were divided equally by the subject. In the second set, 6 pens were given but the confederate took 5 and gave 1 to the subject.

Services: The experimenter asked if the pair would do some computations for him. They were given two sets of computations to make, and they decided to work on the confederate's set first. After they completed the confederate's set, he refused to help the subject. The subject then completed the set by himself as requested by the experimenter.

Following the deprivation episode the experimenter sent the confederate to the laboratory down the hall and he went into his office next door ostensibly to get the questionnaire for the subject and begin the study. The subject, who was now alone, heard the following conversation in the next room (actually a tape recording): "(Knock on door) Hi Bruce. How is the study going? Ok. I'm ready to begin but I can't find questionnaire number 5. Do you remember where I put it? No, but I'll help you look for it. Thanks! You look here while I go to the Conwell Office and look there. Look on the top shelves . . . but if you are going to stand on the chair be careful because it is shaky. (There is a 3 minute lull with only the sound of rustling papers. Then there is the sound of the chair being dragged across the room . . . the man standing on the chair and then falling off the chair with books and papers falling.)

The lapse of time between the first crash and the subject's entrance to the office was recorded. Subjects who failed to open the door after three minutes were considered as "no response."

Reaction Time

The mean reaction time, in seconds, for each group is shown in Table 38. Two computations of means were made: one includes all subjects with those who did not respond being assigned the maximum waiting time of 180 seconds; this set of means is given in the left-most column of the table; the next column shows the means for only those subjects who responded; the frequency of "no-response" is given in the right-most column. As predicted, the mean delay of response was lower for non-deprived subjects than for any of the experimental groups. Among deprived subjects, reaction time was lowest for those deprived

Table 38

MEAN REACTION TIME FOR HELPING BEHAVIOR
BY RESOURCE OF PREVIOUS DEPRIVATION

Resource of deprivation	Reaction Time (in seconds) All subjects	Responding Ss only	No. of no-response
None (control)	62.0	62.0	0
Love	92.7	92.7	0
Status (personality)	100.0	100.0	0
Status (academic)	111.0	103.3	1
Information	133.5	128.4	1
Money	140.0	130.0	2
Goods	123.5	117.2	1
Services	102.0	102.0	0

of love and increased gradually along to the structure of resources reaching the highest value for money, the resource class most remote from love. This order is maintained for both sets of means. Furthermore, the frequency of no-responses also followed the structure of resource classes in the same way as did the means. Finally the data indicated that deprivation of personality status was closer to love than that of academic status, thus supporting the notion that each resource class has its own inner structure in which certain types of behavior are placed nearer to one neighboring class than to the other (see page 82). The results were significant according to analysis of variance on the eight groups, for both sets of means; so was the test for quadratic trend.

The data show that deprivation creates resistance to enter subsequent positive exchange. Less reluctance occurs, however, when the resource expected to be gained is similar to the one of which the subject had been deprived. The latter finding raises an interesting question about the relationship between the two ways in which internal balance is re-established—retaliation and restoration (see Ch. 7). If retaliation prevails then the subjects who had suffered a loss of services are most likely to deny help. On the other hand, if restoration prevails the most reluctant subjects should be those deprived of money, the resource least similar to the expected one (love); conversely love-deprived subjects should be the most eager to help.

The results of this experiment supported the restitution alternative. It is thus possible that the presence of an opportunity for recuperating the lost resource may reduce the tendency for retaliatory behavior; this conclusion, if supported by further research, would be of considerable value in devising means for the reduction of violence. It should be noted, however, that in this experiment the victim of the "accident" or the potential source of love was neither the confederate nor the experimenter, but an unknown third individual, who had no part in the previous interaction. It is quite possible that the preference for restoration over retaliation may be stronger when the next interaction is with a new person, rather than with the depriver.

EFFECTS OF INAPPROPRIATE RECIPROCATION

We have examined some effects of deprivation; one of them is that when a person is deprived of a certain resource and then is able to retaliate by using an inappropriate resource, which he would not have chosen in a free situation, equilibrium is not re-established and residual aggression remains quite intense. Would an inappropriate exchange of giving produce a similar effect? We already know that people have definite preferences for exchanges of giving as much as they do for exchanges of taking away; this suggests that when reciprocation does not provide the preferred resource, a state of unbalance and dissatisfaction will be created. A real life episode which occurred in our laboratory illustrates the effects of such dissatisfying reciprocation. One of our graduate students came to the laboratory upset and angry. What happened? A young professor, with whom he maintained a close relationship, had just moved to another house and our student helped him in packing his belongings. After they had completed the moving the professor insisted on paying him for his help. He could not explain why this offer of monetary reward upset him so much. We thanked him profusely for bringing some evidence from the field for our ideas, and explained to him that it was the offer of the wrong resource, money instead of love, which upset him.

While this episode happened another student of ours, Meir Teichman, was busy at generating more systematic evidence on the same hypothesis. Teichman (1971c) wanted to know how a person feels when, after providing a certain resource to another person, he is reciprocated by him in a more or less appropriate manner. The first problem to be solved was how to induce a subject to provide a resource to another person, a confederate of the experimenter. Obviously having the experimenter instruct him to do so would have introduced into the situation an exchange between the subject and the experimenter: the subject, doing a service to the experimenter, would expect to get status from him (McGuire, 1969b).

Having decided that the experimenter could spoil the show, Teichman arranged for his subjects to meet the confederate, ostensibly another subject, in the waiting room. While they were waiting the stooge created a situation which would induce the subject to give him a specific resource. Six situations were devised, one for each resource class. Let us briefly describe them.

BIDDING FOR RESOURCES. To elicit *love* the stooge told the subject that she had just arrived on campus, she did not know anybody, missed her friends back home and felt lonely. Most of the subjects exposed to this situation invited the stooge to visit them and expressed the intention of establishing a closer relationship with her.

For getting *status* the confederate arrived in the waiting room with a folder of paintings, all with an "A" grade well visible. She showed the subject her paintings and told her that she was taking a course in painting at the local Art League. She wanted very much to become a painter but had no confidence in her abilities and therefore did not dare to major in art at the University.

Bidding for *information*, the confederate introduced herself as a transfer student from a small town; she inquired about shopping, administrative arrangements at the University, student activities, etc.

To obtain *services* from the subject, the stooge arrived with a package of questionnaires and optical scanning sheets. She asked the subject to help her by reading aloud the scores on the questionnaires so that she could be faster at marking them on the scanning sheets. She explained that this task was part of her job at the laboratory and, since it had to be completed by the next day, she thought of doing some of it while they waited for the experiment.

No credible waiting room situation was found for *money* and *goods*. A bogus experiment proved more suitable. The experiment was presented as a study of different reinforcers, money and school supplies, on performance. The two participants, subject and confederate, were told that their role in the study would be determined by a lottery; one of them will be the "experimenter" and the other one the "learner." The need for an additional experimenter was justified as a device to avoid the possibility that the real experimenter, knowing the hypotheses, would influence the results. In the lottery the subject was always designated as the "experimenter." Both the subject and the confederate were promised a payment of $1.50 or an equivalent amount of supplies. But while the "experimenter" (i.e., the subject) gets this amount for participation, the payment to the "learner" (i.e., confederate) is contingent upon completing her tasks. The "experimenter" was instructed to provide the "learner" with 25 cents (or one item of school supplies) for every successful trial, up to the sum of $1.50 or the equivalent in supplies. A time limit of three minutes was scheduled for the series of trials. However, the subject was told that she might shorten or prolong the time, thus increasing or decreasing the confederate's chances to get money or school supplies. During the three minutes, the confederate gained $1.50 (or 5 items). When the time was over, the confederate pleaded for additional time so she would gain more money (or items). Since the total amount of money given to both participants was fixed to $3.00, an additional gain for the confederate meant a decrease of the amount left for the subject. Thus, when the subject extended the time limit, she in fact gave part of her own money (or supplies) to the confederate.

Immediately after this stage of the experiment was terminated, the subjects were given a questionaire in which they were asked *what* they had just given. The results indicated that these biddings proved successful as the subjects perceived themselves giving the predetermined resource.

RECIPROCATION AND MEASUREMENTS OF SATISFACTION. Twenty subjects were exposed to each one of the six situations. Within each group, ten subjects later received money from the confederate, while the other ten received love. Both reciprocations were presented as spontaneous behavior of the confederate unrelated to the "experiment." In the money reciprocation the confederate, upon leaving the room, gave 75¢ to the subject telling her that she wanted to share her money. In the love reciprocation the confederate expressed affectionate feelings of warmth and friendship for the subject.

Following the exchange of resources between subject and stooge the residual satisfaction of the subject was measured by a procedure adapted from Aronson (Jones, Bell and Aronson, 1972). The subject was told that the "real" experiment would now begin and that its first step was to find out how accurately the subjects (i.e., the real subject and the stooge) were able to gauge their feeling toward each other, a variable of great importance for the experiment. For this purpose they were told their self-reports would be compared with the data supplied by an instrument capable of accurately measuring interpersonal feeling, a new invention of revolutionary importance in psychological research. After this explanation they were "wired" to the machine. Questions about the subject's feeling toward the stooge appeared on a memory drum that was connected to the dummy apparatus. The subjects were requested to guess how the apparatus would record their feelings by making appropriate marks on a six-point rating scale.

The following questions appeared in succession of the drum: (1) How satisfactory was your interaction with the other subject? (2) How fair was she with you? (3) How concerned were you with your partner's behavior? (4) How unjust was she with you? (5) How impartial was your partner with you? (6) How did you find her as a person? The ratings of these questions were combined into a satisfaction score. Successively the subjects were asked to indicate their expectations regarding the behavior of the other subject (the stooge) and then were debriefed.

Subjects were 120 female undergraduate students enrolled in a general experimental psychology class at the University of Missouri, Columbia. The subjects volunteered and received academic credit for their participation. Data from 11 other subjects were not included in this analysis: seven of them stated that they gave to the confederate a resource other than the one they were expected to give; the remaining four were dropped because of previous acquaintance with the confederate. Subjects were, of course, assigned randomly to each one of the 12 experimental conditions. The confederate, also a female, was the same for all subjects; she was naive about the hypotheses of the study.

Satisfaction with the Different Exchanges

We expected that satisfaction will be higher when the resource received by the subject was an appropriate exchange for the resource he had given. "Appropriate" means an exchange preferred in a free-choice situation. Table 28 indicates the outcomes of such a free situation. Let us have a second look at the *columns* of this table; considering columns rather than rows enables us to offset the strong effect, at the verbal level, of the love resource. In the first three columns of the table, which refer to situations where the subject had given love, status and information, reciprocation with love is preferred over reciprocation with money. This preference is reversed when money, goods and services had been given (see the last three columns on the right side of Table 28).

We suggest that the exchange will be more satisfactory when it follows the subject's preference than when it does not. More specifically satisfaction will be higher when a giving of love, status or information is reciprocated by love than when it is exchanged with money. The reverse will occur for the situations where money, goods and services were given.

Assuming again that resource classes closer in the structure are more similar, it is further expected that the degree of satisfaction will follow the structural pattern, being more similar for neighboring resources and more different for distal ones. Let us first consider the data relevant to this last hypothesis.

Table 39
POST-INTERACTION MEAN SATISFACTION SCORE

Resource Received in Reciprocation	Resource given by Subject					
	Love	Status	Info.	Money	Goods	Services
Money	25.5	26.3	27.4	27.8	29.9	26.3
Love	27.6	26.8	29.5	23.4	28.3	28.5
Love: Low Involvement	29.4	27.0	28.5	22.6	27.5	27.3
Love: High Involvement	25.8	26.3	31.0	25.3	30.2	30.2
Difference (third row less first row)	3.9	0.7	1.1	−5.2	−2.4	1.0

MONEY RECIPROCATION. The first row of Table 39 shows the mean satisfaction score of the subjects who received money in reciprocation for the resource they gave to the stooge. The resource given by the subjects is indicated at the top of each column in the Table. Among all the subjects who received reciprocation in money, the most satisfied were those who previously gave goods to the confederate. The least satisfied were those who traded love for money. Between these two extremes the satisfaction scores changed regularly following the order of classes.

LOVE RECIPROCATION. Let us now turn to the degree of satisfaction indicated of those who were reciprocated with love (second row of Table 39). As expected, the lowest satisfaction was reported by those who received love in exchange for the money they had given. Moving away from this bottom score satisfaction increased as predicted; then, *unexpectedly*, dropped again for love and status. We could also say that satisfaction for love and status were not too low, but rather that satisfaction with information was too high. This alternative would preserve the order but still leave unexplained why those who gave service were more satisfied than those who gave status or love. If we accept the first alternative that the givers of love and status were relatively unsatisfied then we should start looking for reasons explaining their unexpected low degree of satisfaction.

DEVALUATION EFFECT. Let us recall that the subject was induced to give a specific resource to the confederate by the latter's behavior. We speculate that by bidding for love or status the stooge devalued herself in the eye of the subject as a potential source of these particularistic resources: receiving love from a person who herself needs this resource so much is not particularly satisfactory. If this is true, one should expect that the devaluation effect will be stronger for subjects who became involved with the situation than for those who did not care so much. To test this possibility the subjects who received love reciprocation were separated into two groups: those who felt they gave above the median and also expected to receive above the median constituted one group which was labeled "high involvement." The remaining subjects were included in the "low involvement" group. The mean satisfaction scores for the "low involvement" group appear in the third row of Table 39; the means for the "high involvement" group are given in the fourth row. As expected, the "low involvement" subjects were more satisfied with the exchange of love and status for love than the "high involvement" subjects; the reverse occurred for the other resources. These results suggest that for particularistic resources, such as love and status, the value of what is received depends on *who* is giving them. The love of a person fishing for compliments is apparently not very appreciated. This effect was weaker for the "low involvement" subjects, since they related to the situation in a less particularistic manner.

DIFFERENTIAL SATISFACTION. We turn to the hypothesis on the relationship between amount of satisfaction and the resources involved in the exchange. According to this hypothesis, reciprocation with love should be more satisfactory than reciprocation with money when love, status and information were previously given. The contrary should occur when the resources previously given were money, goods and information.

To test this proposition the mean satisfaction of each group which received money was subtracted from the mean of the corresponding group (in terms of resource which had been given by the subject) that was reciprocated with love. We have excluded from this analysis the "high involvement" subjects, since their degree of satisfaction was effected by the extraneous factor of devaluation. Thus the scores of the first row in Table 39 (money reciprocation) were subtracted from the corresponding score on the third row—love reciprocation, low involvement. The differences between all pairs of groups appear in the last row of Table 39. A plus sign indicates that love reciprocation was more satisfactory than money reciprocation; a minus sign indicates higher satisfaction when reciprocation involved money. Confirming our prediction these differences were positive for the three columns on the left side: love reciprocation resulted in higher degree of satisfaction than money reciprocation, when subjects had previously given love, status or information. Conversely, money was more satisfactory as reciprocation for money and goods. Contrary to our prediction, however, subjects who previously provided services were more satisfied when reciprocated with love than with money. Nevertheless, the differences in degree of satisfaction tended to follow the structure of resources. The largest negative difference was found in the groups who gave money; love is indeed a poor reciprocation for money. The largest positive difference occurred in the groups who had given love; here reciprocation with money resulted in low degree of satisfaction. The differences for other resources are ordered between these two extremes; the only deviation involves those who gave status, they were less satisfied with love reciprocation (or more satisfied with money) than expected.

APPROPRIATENESS IN RETALIATION AND RECIPROCATION

The last two experiments were both designed to investigate the effect of inappropriate matching between the resource of reaction and the resource of proaction; the first experiment involved exchanges of taking while in the second, exchanges of giving were studied. Both investigations show that inappropriate resources of reaction leave an unbalanced state: strong residual aggression or low degree of satisfaction, respectively. In aggressive exchanges this effect was not offset by the higher intensity of inappropriate retaliation.

These results were obtained in a laboratory situation, where manipulations of high intensity are not feasible because of ethical considerations. Outside the laboratory stronger effect can be expected for at least three reasons: (a) Ethical considerations may not always prevail or it may not be considered unethical to reciprocate inappropriately or to deprive those who cannot retaliate in kind: a worker who seeks status and information may be given an increase in salary; parents who cannot provide love may buy many toys for their child; welfare recipients, patients, students may be deprived of status and unable to retaliate in the same resource.

(b) In real life the involvement of the partners in the exchange is likely to be stronger than in a laboratory situation.

(c) In real life the inappropriateness of the reaction is unlikely to be limited to a single exchange; more often these situations tend to repeat themselves again and again increasing unbalance at each round.

Another factor which may increase unbalance is reluctance to express a need for particularistic resources. Moreover, those who do express such needs are likely to be penalized by being devaluated as partners of particularistic exchanges; it did happen to the confederate in Teichman's experiment. Such inhibition may result in appropriate reciprocation: a child who does not communicate his want for love may present his parents with endless requests of "buy me something," only to become disinterested in the gift as soon as he receives it. Teichman's experiment indicates that more satisfactory results would be obtained by giving the child love or, if the parents are unable to do so, by providing him with personal services and status, two resources nearer to love than goods.

Knowledge about the effects of the relationship between proaction and reaction appears applicable to many other problems in real life. Let us mention two illustrative examples.

Much of the frustration felt by black Americans probably involves status deprivation. Yet until recently it was almost impossible for blacks to retaliate in kind for the insult and humiliation they have experienced. Destruction of property in riots, although less direct, was a more accessible reaction. As blacks acquire more status and become better able to take it away from whites, their retaliation becomes more appropriate. Consequently the intensity of retaliation as well as residual aggression should decrease, with less probability of indirect and more intense violence through riots.

Similarly the study of labor disputes suggests that nonmonetary grievances may culminate in strikes for higher wages; a demand for increase in pay is more institutionally appropriate and easier to express than negotiating for such resources as information or status. Yet, when higher wages constitute inappropriate reciprocation, one can expect dissatisfaction to continue even after a big increase in money; after all, the real needs still exist.

THE CHOICE OF A PARTNER FOR EXCHANGE

In the previous sections we have discussed some of the problems involved in the resources exchanged. Yet, an exchange situation involves not only resources but also the particular persons who are involved in the exchange. In a free situation, both the partner and the resource are chosen when an exchange is planned. Our resources are not boundless; consequently, we have to decide to whom we shall give our love, money, esteem, etc. Likewise, even among the most endowed of us, the capacity to hate is limited. It seems appropriate to conclude this chapter with considering some aspects of the process by which both the resource and the partner are chosen.

Some insight into the way in which preference patterns for the partner and the resource are combined is provided in an experiment conducted by Jim L. Turner (1971). In the first stage of the experiment subjects were exposed to successive interactions with two partners: with one they exchanged love, with the other—money. The subjects were then asked to choose, for a further interaction, one of the two previous resources and one of the two previous partners. Turner investigated how these subsequent choices of partner and resource are influenced by the following two factors: (a) The *mode* of initial exchange—giving vs. taking away; half of the subjects were given love and money while the other half were deprived of these resources. (b) The *feedback* level (high vs. low) provided to the subjects regarding the outcome of the initial exchange. Thus four experimental conditions were set up: giving with high feedback; giving with low feedback; taking with high feedback; taking with low feedback.

Successively the subjects were asked to choose one of the two partners and one of the two resources. Thus they had four alternatives from which to choose: love transaction with previous love partner; money transaction with love partner; love transaction with the money partner; money transaction with the money partner.

Subjects who were previously deprived were asked to retaliate; those who were given were asked to reciprocate.

The subjects were 80 female undergraduates at the University of Missouri, assigned randomly to the four experimental conditions, 20 subjects to each condition. All were volunteers from introductory psychology classes who received "credits" for participating in experiments. Four undergraduate males were hired to serve as confederates.

Assignment of confederate to condition was counter-balanced so that each played a given role approximately the same number of times.

The Initial Exchange

Half of the subjects were exposed to a sequence of episodes in which two confederates each provided her with a distinct resource. "Love" was given (or taken away) under the disguise of a study on self-disclosure and romantic attraction. The subject and the confederate were given a list of personal questions which they were to ask each other, but those to be asked to the subject were more intimate and revealing. Both participants were then requested to state their degree of affection and friendship toward each other. Before the subject had completed his assessment, the confederate's comments and statements were presented to her. In the giving condition the confederate rated her as sincere, sensitive and warm, "a rare combination of qualities that I personally find extremely attractive." In the taking condition, the comments emphasized that the subject was cold, insensitive and vain, "not the kind of person I personally find attractive or enjoy being with."

The *money* transaction was done under the guise of a study on social cooperation. Each participant was provided with a deck of 20 cards. The experimenter left the room for a few minutes, during which the confederate sought to convince the subject to work out a strategy by which they both would gain the same amount of money. All subjects agreed. This agreement was not kept by the confederate who, in the giving condition, let the subject gain $3.60 out of a total of $4.00 for them both. In the taking condition the subject was able to obtain only 40 cents with the remainder going to the confederate. When the money was actually paid the confederate was asked about the strategy he had followed in the game. His answer revealed that the outcome of the game was not a result of chance or error, but had been deliberately planned by the confederate.

MANIPULATION OF FEEDBACK. The above description pertained to high level of feedback. As noted earlier, half of the subjects were given ambiguous information regarding outcomes of their encounters with the affect-relevant and money-relevant targets. These "non-explicit" treatment conditions were identical to those described above in every respect with the following exceptions. After the interview session the accomplice was removed and the experimenter returned in the apparent process of examining his comments about the subject. After noting that her ratings of him were not relevant to the study she was told: "It is necessary in order to keep the experiment standardized that you not see this just yet. If you like you can take a look at it before you leave today." As an apparent afterthought the experimenter then noted: "I can see one thing, he's certainly not indifferent toward you." The only cue provided was that the experimenter delivered this latter comment either brightly (i.e., implying that the comments were favorable) or very seriously (i.e., implying that the comments were negative). Similarly, upon conclusion of the money game, the confederate was removed and subjects were told: "You'll be given the money you earned before you leave today. It's possible that he either let you take most of the money or that he tried to get most of it for himself, but given the card decks you both had available it's impossible that you could have split the money very evenly." At this point, the experimenter briefly glanced at the outcome sheet and noted either: "Looks like he treated you very well" or "looks like he didn't treat you very well," depending on treatment condition.

SUBJECT'S OPPORTUNITY FOR RECIPROCATION. Upon conclusion of the two initial episodes, the subject was removed to a conference room and led to believe that she had fulfilled her experimental obligation. The experimenter then left for a few moments and returned to ask if she would mind taking just a few minutes to help "Dr. Rucker, an industrial psychologist here at the Center." It was further explained that his research assistant had called in sick and that he needed a female assistant for the first ten minutes of his experiment. After agreeing to help, subjects were given brief instructions regarding the purpose of "Dr. Rucker's study" and their role as an experimental assistant. They were told that for this experiment only one subject was needed and the other was to participate in another experiment. The subject was told that in order to avoid experimental bias she was to choose one of the two "subjects" with whom she had previously interacted, and she will deliver "incentives" to him. It was further noted that the study was concerned with comparing "social" and "material" incentives so that she could choose the type she preferred to administer to the "subject."

Subjects in the giving conditions were given the following instructions: "Dr. Rucker will be interviewing you and asking you to make certain judgments with regard to his male subjects. Now the subject concerned is going to "accidently" overhear part of this interview over an elaborate intercom system that Dr. Rucker has hooked up in his experimental rooms. If the guy is going to get a material incentive, for example, he will, supposedly by accident, overhear you telling Dr. Rucker that he's your choice to receive $3.00 in payment for experimental participation. If the guy is going to get a social incentive, however, he'll overhear you telling Dr. Rucker that you have an affectionate attitude toward him." It was then explained that the interview with

Dr. Rucker would involve reading a prepared script, but that, whichever incentive she chose, she would be required to act very spontaneously as the subject receiving that incentive must be entirely convinced that she was personally responsible for what was going to happen to him.

Subjects deprived of love and money were told that they would be administering negative incentives in the same manner. Thus they could either choose the person "who will definitely not be paid the $3.00 he was promised for being in the experiment," or "he'll overhear you telling Dr. Rucker that you find him obnoxious and unattractive as a person."

After familiarizing the subject with her alternatives the experimenter gave her "one of Dr. Rucker's forms" on which to indicate the "subject" and the resource chosen by her.

Effect of Initial Interaction

Irrespective of the experimental manipulations (level of feedback and mode) subjects showed a marked tendency to react with the same resource that was previously exchanged with the partner they had chosen: 38 percent decided to deliver affective messages to the partner with whom they had initially exchanged "love"; 26 percent opted for money when the money partner was chosen; yet, 20 percent chose to deliver love to the money partner and 16 percent preferred to give or deny money to love partners. Thus 64 percent of the subjects preferred to stick to the same resource that they had previously exchanged with the particular person with whom they decided to interact.

Effects of Mode and Level of Feedback

When the effect of the experimental conditions on the choice of partner and resource was considered, an interesting picture emerged: each manipulation affected one of the two choices, but not the other. The *mode* influenced the choice of *partner:* the group which got positive affection and gained 90 percent of the total amount of money, chose the love-partner three times as much as the money-partner, while nearly two-thirds of those deprived of love and money preferred the money-partner. The mode, however, did not affect significantly the resource preference: subjects in both the giving and taking away conditions showed a slight preference for love.

By contrast, *feedback level* had a marked influence on the choice of *resource:* 78 percent of the subjects who received explicit information about the outcome of the initial interaction chose to react with love; 63 percent of those who were left uncertain about the outcome, preferred to react with money. Feedback level did not influence the choice of partner: low and high feedback subjects chose both partners with nearly the same frequency.

In summary, in exchanges of taking, one is more likely to choose a less particularistic partner, while for a positive exchange, a more particularistic partner is chosen. However, the resource of reaction is not affected by its mode. Furthermore, in conditions of uncertainty as to the outcome of proaction, one prefers a less particularistic resource but shows no preference for a particularistic partner.

Combining these two differential effects of mode and feedback level, we can predict the relative frequency of each choice in every experimental condition: preference for a particularistic partner *and* resource will be highest when the mode is giving and the feedback high, and lowest when the mode is taking and the feedback low. In the two other conditions (giving with low feedback and taking with high feedback) the frequency of the most particularistic choice shall be intermediate. Likewise the frequncy of choosing a particularistic partner and a non-particularistic resource should be highest in the giving mode with low feedback, and lowest in the taking mode with high feedback.

Table 40

PERCENTAGE FREQUENCY OF CHOICES ACROSS
TREATMENT CONDITIONS

Partner Chosen	Resource Chosen	Conditions				All Conditions
		Giving Mode		Taking Mode		
		High Feedback	Low Feedback	Low Feedback	High Feedback	
Love	Love	43	30	7	20	100% (30)
Love	Money	15	38.5	38.5	8	100% (13)
Money	Money	10	28	43	19	100% (21)
Money	Love	19	0	25	56	100% (16)

The relevant data for testing these predictions are given in Table 40. In this table, the frequencies of each row are presented in percentage form to eliminate the effect, already noted, of preference for certain alternatives, irrespective of the treatment. This transformation to percentages presents the results as if each alternative had been chosen equally overall. The absolute frequency of each row appears in brackets in the right-most column. For both rows and columns of this table the highest frequencies appear in the diagonal cell and the lowest in the cell two steps removed from the diagonal. The frequency of the other cells falls between these two extremes. This perfect order derives from the results examined previously: in the diagonal cell both treatment conditions facilitate the occurrence of the given outcome; in the cell two steps removed neither condition is favorable and in the remaining cells only one facilitating condition is present. Consider, for example, the first row: choice of love partner is more likely in the mode of giving, while choice of love resource is facilitated by high feedbak; both of these conditions occur in the first column and indeed the frequency is highest here; neither condition is found in the third column and the frequency is lowest in this cell; in the two remaining cells of the first row only one condition is favorable for choosing this alternative and the frequency assumes an intermediate value.

We can also analyze the frequency of choosing each of the four alternatives under every experimental condition by examining the columns of Table 40. Subjects who benefited from the initial interaction and had full knowledge of the outcome (first column to the left) preferred mostly the particularistic partner and the particularistic resource, while their least preference went to the non-particularistic partner and resource. In the second column, subjects who benefited, but did not know how much, preferred to give money to the partner who previously gave them love; in this condition the least preferred alternative was to give love to the one who previously gave them money. The two remaining alternatives for both groups show intermediate frequencies. In the third column the conditions are opposite to those of the first column (subjects were deprived but did not know how much); the frequencies also reveal a reverse pattern: here the highest frequency was in choosing a non-particularistic partner and resource and the least preferred alternative was the choice of particularistic partner and resource. Finally the frequency distribution of the rightmost column is a mirror image of the second one; indeed the experimental conditions in columns two and four are opposite.

In conclusion, the results of this experiment show that previous interactive experiences have a systematic influence on the choice of partner and resource for a further exchange. This study also provides an example of an experimental approach in which complex relationships among multiple independent variables are investigated in terms of underlying structural units.

SUMMARY

An exchange unit is composed of a proaction and reaction. A given resource is either given to or taken away from person A by person B; person A, in turn, reacts by either depriving or providing a given resource to the previous actor, person B. Certainly we expect the reaction to be influenced by the proaction. To determine some basic relationship between these two stages of the exchange unit and their after effects, several experiments were conducted.

If an exchange contains two actions, then it can be defined by the elements involved in the proaction and reaction. Since there are two actors (self or other) two objects (self or other), two modes (giving or taking) and six resources, there are many types of exchanges. Our studies have been confined to some of the most common:

1. Person A *gives* a certain resource to person B who, in turn, reciprocates by providing person A with the same or another resource.
2. Person A deprives (*takes away*) person B of a certain resource, and person B retaliates by taking away the same or a different resource from person A. The more rare, unbalanced exchanges in which one participant takes away and then is met with a giving action, or vice versa when he gives and then is deprived, are not dealt with here.

The issue under investigation was the relationship between the resources of proaction and reaction in "giving" and "taking away" exchanges. First we investigated the following questions: if A gives a certain resource to B, what resource would be preferred most in exchange, what would be his second choice, his third choice, etc.?

A questionnaire study was conducted in which subjects were presented with six hypothetical situations where they had given a resource to an unspecified person. Each situation was followed by 15 pairs of resources from which they were to choose the most preferred ones. The results indicated that the pattern preference follows the structure of resources. Given the most preferred resource, the preference for the remaining resources will follow the structure. The more similar the resource is to the most preferred one, the higher will be the preference for it. It was also found that the most preferred resource changes from one institution to the other, but the structure of preference remains invariant. The same pattern was found for negative actions, i.e., for deprivation-retaliation exchange. But while in both questionnaire studies of positive and negative exchanges the most preferred resource was love, an experimental investigation on negative exchange revealed a direct relationship between the resources of reaction and proaction. Subjects preferred to retaliate with a resource which is closer in the structure to the one of which they had been deprived.

We have established the fact that there are definite preferences concerning the resource involved in the reaction. We have also seen that on the behavioral level, this preference is influenced by the resource of proaction. What happens when one is reciprocated by, or retaliates with, an unpreferred resource? The answer is given by two experiments, one for deprivation-retaliation exchange and one for exchange of "giving." Subjects who were requested to retaliate with a resource distal from the one of which they had been deprived revealed higher intensity of reaction than those retaliating with the resource of proaction. Moreover, their residual aggression, after the exchange had terminated, was also higher the more dissimilar the resources of deprivation and retaliation. Again the structure of resources predicted the intensity of reaction: the smaller the cognitive distance between the resources of proaction and reaction, the lower the intensity of retaliation and residual aggression.

A slightly different question was asked for exchange of giving. Here we were interested in the amount of satisfaction derived from a preferred and an unpreferred reciprocation. Subjects were induced into a situation where they found themselves giving a certain resource to an accomplice of the experimenter; some were reciprocated with expressions of friendliness while others received money. It was predicted that the closer the cognitive distance between the resource given by the subject and the resource he later received, the higher his satisfaction with the interaction. This prediction was confirmed by subjects who were reciprocated with money. Those who gave money and later received money were the most satisfied. The degree of satisfaction declined gradually for both sides of the peak, being lowest for those subjects who gave love and received money. For subjects who received love, only those who were not very involved in the experimental situation confirmed the prediction. Those who gave love and received love were the most satisfied and those who received money for their love were the least satisfied; the rest were in between, following the structure of resources. Thus, again, the degree of satisfaction from the exchange could be predicted from the cognitive distance between the resources of proaction and reaction. The larger the distance, the lower the satisfaction. Those subjects who were highly involved in the situation, i.e., perceived themselves as giving a lot and expected high intensity of reciprocation, were not satisfied when giving love and receiving love. Our confederate was bidding for love by presenting herself as miserable and lonely. It could be that receiving love form a miserable person is not highly appreciated and not very satisfactory, especially for those who are emotionally involved in the exchange.

The effect of an exchange on successive behavior was further investigated in an experiment in which the resource of previous deprivation was related to willingness to help in an emergency situation. As expected, deprived subjects hesitated to help more than did nondeprived ones; hesitation was, however, reduced when the resource of deprivation was more similar to love, which was the resource expected in return for helping.

When one plans an exchange, not only the resources are chosen, but also the partner with whom the exchange will take place. Some insight into the factors involved in choosing a partner and resource was gained again by experimental study. Subjects received (or were deprived of) money from one person and love from another. Some were notified about what they gained or lost; others only knew that they received or were deprived, but did not have information on the exact outcome. Each subject was asked to choose one of the two previous partners and one of the two previous resources for further interaction. It was found that *mode* (receiving vs. being deprived) influenced the choice of *partner:* those who received money and love tended to choose the love-partner, while subjects who were previously deprived chose the money partner. The mode did not affect the choice of *resource,* which was however influenced by the *level of feedback.* Subjects who received explicit information about the outcome of the initial interaction chose to reciprocate with love, those receiving low feedback chose reciprocation with money. Thus preference for a particularistic partner and resource is highest for positive exchange with feedback, and lowest for negative exchange with low feedback.

The study of inappropriate exchanges has broad application for critical situations in everyday life. Workers striving for a sense of belongingness are often offered increased salaries and still reveal dissatisfaction; blacks deprived of status retaliate by burning shops, yet are left with high residual aggression. Investigation of the relationship between proaction and reaction in a dyad may also help in planning appropriate and satisfactory exchanges for larger groups and communities.

CHAPTER 7

SOME AREAS OF SOCIO-PSYCHOLOGICAL RESEARCH IN THE LIGHT OF THE RESOURCE EXCHANGE PARADIGM

Overview

THE THEORETICAL concepts developed in the previous chapters constitute a framework for describing and understanding interpersonal behavior. As such, they should bear relevance to practical and theoretical notions which have been widely discussed in the literature of social psychology and personality. In the present chapter, we shall attempt to demonstrate what additional insight could be gained by applying the resource exchange paradigm to issues such as the frustration-aggression hypothesis, complementarity of needs, interpersonal attraction, conformity, distributive justice (and cognate notions of reciprocity and legitimacy of exchange), and various strategies for obtaining resources, such as Machiavellism and ingratiation. We shall start with the frustration-aggression hypothesis, which clearly belongs to exchanges of taking away, and proceed through the other topics which pertain to exchanges of giving.

FRUSTRATION-AGGRESSION AS EXCHANGE OF TAKING

In the previous chapter, we have examined several studies on negative exchanges, where A deprived B of a certain resource and B, in return, retaliated by depriving A. We have also compared these studies with those involving positive exchanges, where A gave to B a certain resource and in turn is reciprocated by B.

Taking away (negative) behavior has rarely been considered from an exchange viewpoint, although some authors (e.g., Berscheid, Boye and Walster, 1968) came close to this formulation. More often, a theoretical framework for the study of negative behavior has been provided by the frustration-aggression hypothesis. Since it was first proposed some thirty years ago (Dollard, Doob, Miller, Mowrer and Sears, 1939),

220

the hypothesis that frustration instigates aggression has generated an impressive amount of empirical work, leading, in turn, to a re-examination of its theoretical foundations (e.g., Berkowitz, 1962, 1965 and 1969 b; Buss, 1961; Yates, 1962). By conceptualizing the frustration-aggression sequence as a type of exchange, we incorporate an enormous amount of research into the resource exchange framework and, hopefully, throw some new light on the rich data this research provided. To begin, let us examine similarities and differences between the frustration-aggression and the exchange formulations.

The Notion of Frustration

Two types of definition have been proposed for frustration. One type is exemplified by the classic definition of Dollard, et al. (1939), "an interference with the occurrence of an instigated goal response at its proper time in the behavior sequence" (p. 7). For these authors, as well as for Berkowitz (1965, p. 308) *thwarting* of a goal oriented response is a central element of the frustrating event. While sharing the same view about frustration, Buss (1961) considered the delivery of noxious stimuli as an additional antecedent of aggression. Later on (Buss, 1966), he suggested that attack is a more potent antecedent than thwarting; furthermore, he specified that only interference of a response "that has in the past led to a reinforcer" would create frustration. With this qualification of thwarting, Buss approaches the second type of definition, which centers on the *worsening of the reinforcement situation*. Representative of this approach are Bandura and Walters (1963, pp. 115–116), who define frustration as "delay of reinforcement."

The discrepancy between these two types of definitions is not as big as it seems: as noted by Buss, thwarting results in frustration only when the interfered activity is actually or potentially rewarding. Interference with the interminable chattering of a boring visitor will hardly lead to frustration. Thus, both types of definition suggest that a frustrating event consists of depriving the object-person of an expected resource. Indeed, in experimental manipulations, both actual and potential taking away of resources has been employed to create a state of frustration.

RESOURCES IN FRUSTRATION-AGGRESSION STUDIES. There is hardly a resource class which was not used in frustration-aggression studies. Yet, the fact that no explicit taxonomy of resource was available to the investigators had some undesirable consequences: (1) Resources belonging to two or more classes were often used jointly to create frustration, thus barring the study of their differential effects. (2) Some resource classes, such as services (e.g., electric shocks) and status, were exhaustively studied while other resources were neglected.

Mosher, Mortimer and Grebel (1968), for example, combined goods and status in creating frustration by making the loss of goods contingent upon losing a game. Geen and Berkowitz (1966) combined services and status by having their confederate express evaluation of the subject's performance through the administration of electric shock. The only study which employed deceiving as a source of frustration had it combined with loss of money (Conn and Crowne, 1964). The combination of resources is especially noticeable in the notion of "derogation," which includes loss of both love and status.

Since the resource involved in frustration or aggression was not considered a theoretically important variable, investigators preferred those resources which could easily be manipulated in an experimental setting. Thus, several manipulations were developed to induce loss of status. A common form is *ego threat*, which consists of creating a threat of failure or negative evaluation of the subject's performance. In some experiments, the subject is not allowed to finish an important task, or his performance is hindered, resulting in negative evaluation (Buss, 1963). In other experiments, competition is used to produce a threat of failure (Epstein and Taylor, 1967; Mosher and Proenza, 1968). In all these manipulations, a potential (future) loss of status is created. An actual loss of status is obtained by insult and failure, when the subject's performance or abilities are negatively evaluated (Feshbach, 1955; Geen and Berkowitz, 1966). Many studies had combined a potential loss of status with an actual one (e.g., the "insult-failure" technique proposed by Worchel, 1957, 1958, 1961). A second class of resources often used is services, mainly in the form of administering electric shock. A large number of studies utilized shock to measure aggression (Berkowitz, Lepinski and Angulo, 1969; Buss, 1961, 1963; Mallick and McCandless, 1966; Walters and Thomas, 1963). Epstein and Taylor (1967), as well as Taylor (1967), manipulated a potential and an actual loss of services as a source of frustration by informing subjects of the intensity of shock their opponents intended to administer them, as well as by actually administering shock.

In conclusion, the resources most frequently used in frustration-aggression studies were services, love and status, while information, money and goods have been rather neglected.

DEPRIVATION, NEED AND REACTION. This brief review of theoretical viewpoints and experimental practice suggests that both actual and potential deprivation of specific resources may lead to frustration. Some results (Geen and Berkowitz, 1967; Geen, 1968; Mallick and McCandless, 1966) support Buss' suggestion (1966) that actual deprivation produces more powerful effects than does potential deprivation, as measured by the strength of reaction. Yet the effects of both actual attack and interference are in the same direction, both are likely to induce frustration.

A substantial amount of research was directed towards exploring the conditions under which actual or potential deprivation will result in frustration. If frustration is defined as deprivation, obviously there is no place for such investigation. Yet current conceptualizations of frustration cover not only the taking away behavior of the frustrator but also, with various degrees of explicitness, the internal state or drive situation of the victim (see, e.g., Dollard, et al., 1939, p. 11). Thus the issue can be stated in terms of the conditions under which deprivation will result in a state of internal imbalance. Such imbalance will depend not only on the act of deprivation, but also on the previous state of the victim in terms of resource accumulation: an individual who had plenty of a given resource will be less affected by the deprivation than he who had little of it. Support for this suggestion is provided by Rosenbaum and deCharms (1960) who exposed high and low self-esteem subjects to insult. Some subjects were then given an opportunity to retaliate either directly or vicariously. The residual aggression of each subject was finally measured. High self-esteem subjects were not irritated by the insult as much as the low self-esteem ones. Moreover, their residual aggression after retaliation did not decrease as much as for low self-esteem subjects.

This experiment illustrates the general problem of how to measure the degree of frustration (in terms of internal imbalance). Usually the intensity of the following aggression is taken to measure the degree of frustration. It is reasonable to assume that when frustration is low, retaliation will be milder. However, the reverse may not be true: aggression may be inhibited and its expression mild in spite of a high level of internal imbalance. It has been found, for example, that anticipation of punishment reduces the expression of aggression (Berkowitz, 1962, pp. 75–79); there is no reason to assume that such anticipation reduces the level of imbalance. In some situations, however, a decrease in expressed aggression may well reflect a reduction in drive level. Kregarman and Worchel (1961), for example, found that subjects who expected interference in task completion were less aggressive than those who expected to complete their task. Apparently, the first group expected the task to be less rewarding and thus the interference created a lower level of imbalance. Some conditions may influence both the drive level and the degree of inhibition to aggress. It has been repeatedly reported that less aggression is expressed when the frustrating action is non-arbitrary (Allison and Hunt, 1959; Cohen, 1955; Pastore, 1952). Later results indicated that this reduction of aggression is partly due to inhibition, possibly because aggressive reaction to legitimate deprivation would result in social disapproval, i.e., loss of status. Rothaus and Worchel (1960) repeated the Pastore study, but asked subjects to indicate the reaction of another imaginary person, in addition to their own. The result that in the non-arbitrary conditions more hostility was attributed to the other person than to the self, was taken to indicate inhibition of aggressive tendencies. While these results were based on questionnaire responses, subsequent experimental findings essentially supported them (Burnstein and Worchel, 1962).

There is an additional aspect differentiating between arbitrary and non-arbitrary frustrations which has not been noted by previous investigators, probably because of the scarce attention paid to the resources involved: an arbitrary deprivation produces the loss of more resources, often love and/or status, in addition to those lost in a comparable but non-arbitrary situation. If the bus failed to stop because it was on its way to the garage, one was deprived of a service; if, however, the driver did not care to stop to pick him up, a person lost not only service, but also status. This difference is bound to reflect on the resulting state of need since a broader range of resources is involved when deprivation is arbitrary. Hence, arbitrariness appears to affect not only the inhibition of aggressive response, but also the need state.

In summary, the notion of frustration, as treated in current theory and practice, embraces two elements: one is a taking away behavior which deprives the object-person of some resources; the other is the state of need created in the object-person who has been so deprived. In an individual who possesses a large amount of a given resource, deprivation of moderate strength may not create a need, and therefore no retaliation is required. But even when deprivation does reduce the residual amount below minimum, the deprived individual may not attempt to re-establish it by retaliatory action. Such aggressive reaction tends to be inhibited when it is likely to result in a further loss of resources.

The Notion of Aggression

We have already noted that several studies operationalized aggression by employing loss of resources. Proposed definitions of this notion, although differing in details, show considerable congruence with the operations employed. For Dollard, et al. (1939, p. 9), aggression is a sequence of behavior "the goal-response to which is the injury of the person toward whom it is directed." Buss (1961, p. 1) defines aggression as a response that delivers noxious stimuli to another organism. Walters (1964) adds that aggression is usually characterized by responses of high magnitude. There is substantial agreement among the various definitions that aggressive behavior is injurious to the recipient. The injury may be directed towards the belongings of the recipient, or towards his person. In the latter case, it can take physical and symbolic forms, or it may worsen the individual's information state, when deception or misleading is employed. Each of these various types of injury damages the recipient in a particular resource. It appears, therefore, that aggression is *a behavior which deprives the recipient of one or more resources*. Once again, deprivation may pertain to an *actual* loss of a resource already possessed by the victim, or it may consist of depriving him of a resource he expects to obtain in the future.

It has been suggested that mere deprivation is not sufficient to characterize aggression (e.g., Bandura and Walters, 1959; Sears, Maccoby and Levin, 1957). An *intention* to harm is an essential element of its definition; another qualification which has been widely accepted (e.g., Walters, 1964) is the *absence of social approval*. Thus, the motorist who unintentionally hurts a person in a traffic accident, and the judge who legitimately imposes a fine on the defendant, would not be considered aggressive, although both events result in loss of resources. These qualifications may be important, yet we believe it is preferable to consider them as conditions impinging on the *perception* of aggression, rather than as elements of its definition. At least we should recognize that frustrative behavior and aggression are both forms of taking away resources, although they may have additional characteristics which differentiate them from other forms of taking.

Experiments in social exchange often include taking away behaviors which are basically similar to those employed in frustration-aggression studies (e.g., Blumstein and Weinstein, 1969; Leventhal and Bergman, 1969; Pepitone, Maderna, Caporicci, Tiberi, Iacono, Di Maio, Perfetto, Asprea, Villone, Fua and Tonucci, 1970; Weinstein, Beckhouse, Blumstein, and Stein, 1968). Yet the use of a different terminology hindered an exploration of the relationship between the investigations of equity in social exchanges and studies on antecedents of aggression. By pointing to the similarities between these two theoretical approaches, studies in one tradition may be used to develop the other.

Classification

In recognizing frustration and aggression as forms of taking away behaviors, we are immediately provided with a classification of their types according to the resources involved. Moreover, we are able to re-analyze various phenomena in this area, as well as forming and testing new hypotheses, by considering the structure of resources which has already been established.

Previous attempts at classification are not altogether remote from the present one. Rosenzweig (1944) realized that frustration involves unsatisfied needs, but faced difficulties in using needs as a criterion for classifying frustration: "It is not possible," he states, "in the present state of psychology to provide an adequate classification of needs —perhaps because the criteria for such a classification have not yet been discovered . . . ." (p. 38). The beginning of a classification based on needs or resources has been provided by Maslow (1941). For him, need deprivation will be followed by frustration only when it involves a threat to personality. In essence, Maslow suggests that frustration should involve a perceived loss of love or status. A child deprived of an ice cream cone is not frustrated unless he perceived this act as denial of love by his mother. According to Maslow, no frustration will occur when deprivation of ice cream is perceived as intended to avoid a belly-ache.

Buss' (1961) classification of aggression, although stated in instrumental terms, bears relevance to various resources; indeed the specific behaviors involved in deprivation may differ for different resources. Buss differentiates between two major types of aggression according to the body's organs involved: physical and verbal aggression. The former is an assault against an organism by means of the attacker's teeth, limbs or by weapons; the latter is delivered by speech. In both types, noxious stimuli are delivered: in physical aggression, they consist of pain and injury, while noxious stimuli delivered by verbal aggression are rejection and threat. Rejection includes negative affective reaction as well as criticism and derogation. Buss is aware of the shortcomings stemming from the use of the organ system as a criterion for classification: rejection, for example, may be conveyed by nonverbal as well as by verbal means. Nevertheless, in most cases, insult and emotional rejection are likely to be verbal.

While Buss (1963) did use his classification to investigate the reactive effects of different types of frustration, most other investigators paid little attention to the resources involved in their experiments; moreover, some (e.g., Berkowitz, 1962, p. 49) argued against any differentiation in terms other than intensity. Consequently, the vast majority of the studies on frustration-aggression do not bear upon the findings reported in the previous chapter: preference to react with a resource similar to the one involved in the proaction, and higher intensity of reaction, as well as of residual aggression (particularly in the resource of proaction), found when proaction and reaction differ in their resources. Some studies which are relevant to these issues, although somewhat indirectly, will be considered next.

Resource Reciprocity

Graham, Charwat, Honig and Weltz (1951) presented subjects, through a questionnaire, with a variety of frustrating situations, differing in intensity. They found that each intensity of frustration tended to elicit aggression of a similar intensity. Since, in this study, different intensities were represented by different resources (physical aggression, i.e., services, represented the highest intensity), the results indicate a preference for retaliation in kind.

Relevant to the hypothesis that aggressive reaction is more intense when retaliation is not appropriate, is Buss' study (1963) which was already mentioned. Three different procedures to induce frustration were used, one for each group of subjects: two procedures involved status (task failure and thwarting the obtaining of a good grade) and one involved money. All three experimental groups were only slightly higher than controls in the intensity of the shock they delivered to the frustrator. These results appear to contradict Donnenwerth's findings (1971 and Ch. 6): since shock (services) is rather distal in the structure from both resources of frustration (status and money), one would have expected a higher intensity of reaction. Moreover, in another study, when subjects were told that by administering shock to the other they would increase their chance of succeeding in their task (gaining status), they gave more shocks than controls (Buss, 1966).

Experiments in which residual aggression is measured usually support Donnenwerth's finding that residual aggression is lower when proaction and reaction involve similar resources. Baker and Schaie (1969) created frustration by interfering with the subject's task, thus depriving him of the resource (probably status) expected from successful completion. Each subject was then provided with an opportunity to aggress: some could take status, some employed services and still others took away information. Blood pressure after aggression was lowest for those who aggressed by taking away status, the resource which was also involved in their frustration. Geen and Berkowitz (1966) frustrated subjects by shock (service) and communication of failure (status). Subjects were then enabled to reciprocate in kind, and finally expressed their liking (love) for the frustrator by filling a questionnaire. Frustrated subjects were more aggressive than controls, but no differences were found in the amount of disliking expressed. It seems that retaliation in kind was effective in reducing residual aggression. In another experiment (Mallick and McCandless, 1966), subjects were deprived of status and money; after an intervening activity, which varied for each group, they were given an opportunity to retaliate against the frustrator by depriving him of services (shock) and love. The least aggressive were those for whom the intervening activity consisted of talking about the frustrator with the experimenter who depicted him as penniless, sleepy and upset, suggesting that he would have behaved better had the subject shared with him some of the money he had received. The two other activities consisted of target shooting and of an irrelevant social talk with the experimenter. The intervening activity which succeeded in lowering aggression is, admittedly, a complex one; in our interpretation it involves lowering the status of the frustrator. Since status was one of the resources involved in frustration, the effectiveness of the intervening activity in reducing aggression may be due to this common resource.

The Object and the Actor in the Frustration-Aggression Sequence

We have been concerned so far with the relationship between resource of frustration and that of subsequent aggression. In particular, we suggested that the preference for a certain type of aggression is determined by the type of frustration previously experienced, and that the amount of residual hostility is affected by the structural relationship between the two resources. The resource employed, however, is only one element of a social event; other essential elements are the person emitting the response (the actor) and the one towards whom it is emitted (the object). The classical exchange paradigm of frustration-aggression involves two individuals, A and B, and two stages—frustration and aggression. In the first stage, the frustrator, A, is the actor, while the victim, B, is the object or the recipient of A's aggression. The roles are reversed in the aggression stage: the previous object (B) becomes the actor of aggression, while the previous actor (A) becomes the object. As in any dyadic exchange, here too, the two participants alternate in being actors and recipients of the action.

Yet, isolated dyads are found mainly in the laboratory; in everyday life, the relationship between two individuals often affects a third person. An individual who was refused recognition by his boss may berate his subordinate; an older child may protect his younger brother by aggressing against the latter's frustrator. In the first example, B was frustrated by A, but the object of retaliation is not the previous frustrator; this phenomenon of directing retaliation towards a third individual is denoted as displacement. The second example is a case of vicarious aggression, when B is frustrated by A, and C, a third individual, retaliates against A; here the actor of retaliation is not the previous victim.

We shall discuss these three paradigms—direct retaliation, displacement and vicarious aggression—with respect to the two issues considered before: the effects on residual aggression and preferences, this time not among resources, but among various available "third persons." The differential effects of resources have been usually considered as generalization of the aggressive response; the choice and effects of the participants is known as *stimulus* generalization. While this terminology is not particularly suitable to the present theoretical approach, it is desirable to recognize the relationship of topics discussed here with the research and theoretical approaches advanced by other authors.

DIRECT RETALIATION. The effectiveness of direct retaliation in restoring internal balance is often estimated from the amount of residual aggression left after retaliation had taken place. The findings usually suggest that direct retaliation results in a decrease of subsequent aggression. Berkowitz and Holmes (1960) found that college girls who were frustrated by a confederate, as well as by a peer, expressed more favorable judgments on their peer's fairness after administering shock to him. Pepitone and Reichling (1955) found that those who expressed the strongest hostility tended to give the most favorable ratings later on. Berkowitz (1966) reported that subjects who expected to retaliate and were permitted to do so were less aggressive than those who were not permitted to retaliate. We have noted earlier that Rosenbaum and deCharms (1960) found a decrease in hostility after communicating with the frustrator as compared to non-communication groups, but only for low self-esteem subjects. For high self-esteem subjects, who had more status to begin with, deprivation was probably not strong enough to reduce the level below the optimal range, so that they did not feel imbalance. Hokanson (1961) frustrated subjects by insult, permitted them to aggress physically and then measured residual hostility in love and status. He found that the more the subjects aggressed physically, the less hostile they were afterwards. Reduction in aggression expressed in attitude scale was found by Worchel (1957), whose subjects were insulted and then given an opportunity to criticize the frustrator in his absence. Lower residual hostility following aggression is also reported by Berkowitz, Green and Macaulay (1962) and Thibaut and Coules (1952).

In these studies, at least two out of the three resources involved were identical or close in the structure. Rosenbaum and deCharms (1960) used status and love for the frustration, retaliation and residual aggression stages. Worchel (1957) used status for all three stages. Berkowitz, et al. (1962), used status and services both for frustration and retaliation while measuring the residual aggression for love, a neighbor of both status and services in the proposed structure.

DISPLACEMENT. Three types of displacement, i.e., change of object, have been discussed in the literature: displacement towards a third individual, towards self and towards an inanimate object. Let us consider each briefly.

Displacement towards a third person. Laboratory and field studies have indicated that displacement of aggression to a third individual or group occurs when either of the following conditions exists: (a) the original object is not within reach, or (b) the original object is perceived as powerful in that he can deprive the subject of important resources if retaliated against.

Who is likely to become a target of displaced aggression? Berkowitz (1962, p. 139) aptly noted that the choice of displaced object is influenced by the conditions which had led to displacement. When the original target is not available, aggression will be directed toward a target most similar to the original one. The choice of object under such conditions is parallel to the choice of substitute resource; in both, preference is based on the similarity between the new event and the original but unavailable one. However, when aggression against the primary target is inhibited by fear of retaliation, the choice of a substitute target will be governed by two conflicting tendencies: the tendency to choose a target similar to the original one, and the tendency to reduce the chances of a punitive reaction by choosing a target less powerful than the original one. The resultant, suggests Berkowitz, will be to choose an individual with an intermediate similarity. It should be noted that the conflict between the two tendencies refers only to the power dimension and not to other dimensions of similarity. Thus, when the primary target is too powerful to be attacked, the displaced target will be less powerful than the original, but similar to him in other aspects.

At this point it is appropriate to recall the dimensions of role differentiation, sex, power and resources, which may prove to be relevant criteria for object similarity. It was suggested earlier that the target of displacement will differ from the original one on the power dimension. If, however, the six types of power are considered, one for each resource class, we may be able to make more precise predictions: We suggest that the target of displacement will be less powerful than the original one with respect to that specific resource which the actor fears to lose. For example, if one is inhibited to aggress against an individual powerful in love, he will displace aggression to a person less powerful in this resource; the displaced target, however, may not be less powerful than the original one in other resources, to which no fear of loss is attached.

Roles are also characterized by specific resources, so that not every resource may be employed in a given role. From previous work on resource substitution (see Ch. 6), we know that people prefer to retaliate with the resource previously involved in their frustration. Since not every resource may be employed in a given role, the preference for a specific reaction constitutes a restriction on displacement. The substitute target will be chosen from a role similar to that of the original target, so that it will be appropriate to employ the resource previously used by the frustrator. This hypothesis is reflected in notions such as "father figure." A child may tend to displace aggression from an authoritarian father to the teacher—in both, status is a prominent resource, but the father is more powerful in it.

Another dimension of roles to be considered is sex. In Chapter 2 we have suggested that the earlier the differentiation, the less permeable are its boundaries. Sex is the first role dimension to be differentiated; therefore, diffusion of aggression across sexes is least likely. Resources are differentiated last and their boundaries more permeable, thus they are more likely to be substituted one for another. Differentiation by power, which occupies an intermediate position with regard to developmental sequence, will also occupy an intermediate position with respect to generalization facilitation. There is little in the literature which is relevant to these hypotheses, but they are definitely testable.

Some indication that instigation to aggression—as distinct from its actual expression—may be reduced by aggressing against a third individual, is provided by the work of Gambaro and Rabin (1969). Their subjects were insulted and then permitted to shock the experimenter, who was not the previous frustrator. Diastolic blood pressure decreased after aggression in low-guilt subjects, but no change was found in high-guilt subjects. These results may indicate that displacement does not affect instigation to aggression in high-guilt individuals; a feasible alternative explanation, however, is that aggression against an innocent target has increased their guilt and subsequently emotional arousal remained high, although instigation to aggression may have been reduced.

Work on displacement of aggression involved the three most particularistic resources: services (Hovland and Sears, 1940; Janis, 1951; Miller, N.E., 1948, 1959; Miller and Bugelsky, 1948); love (Pepitone and Reichling, 1955); and status (Burnstein and Worchel, 1962; Gambaro and Rabin, 1969; Mosher and Proenza, 1968; Thibaut and Coules, 1952). We were unable to find evidence of displacement for the remaining three resource classes: goods, money and information. Since, as already noted, investigators of aggression, in general, employed particularistic resources more than non-particularistic ones, this preference may be reflected in displacement studies as well. An alternative explanation to be considered is that displacement occurs mainly for particularistic resources. This explanation, however, contradicts the notion of particularism, which means that the particular partner with whom the exchange takes place is an important determinant. If particularism is a relevant dimension in displacement, a change of target is more likely to occur when the exchange involves non-particularistic rather than particularistic resources.

SELF-AGGRESSION. There is evidence indicating that frustrated subjects may direct aggression toward themselves. Burnstein and Worchel (1962) found that frustrated subjects evaluated themselves more negatively than non-frustrated ones, especially when frustration was non-arbitrary. A somewhat related finding is reported by Rothaus and Worchel (1960) who showed that frustrated subjects with high self-ideal discrepancy reported significantly higher self-hostility than those with low self-ideal discrepancy: for the former groups of subjects, self-hostility was indeed consonant, while being dissonant for the latter group.

Opinions differ as to the conditions inducing self-aggression. Dollard, et al. (1939), believe that it occurs when there are barriers to expressing aggression toward the other, while Berkowitz (1962) states that self aggression results from perceiving the self as the source of frustration. A third alternative is suggested here: self-aggression is the product of response generalization, or spread of effect from the other to the self, and stems from perceived proximity between self and other. This proximity, in turn, depends partly on the resource involved in aggression and its position in the structure: it will be highly positive for love, and will decrease and become negative as one moves around the circle from love to money. For the latter resource, the relationship will be high and negative.

There is indeed evidence indicating that the relationship between taking away from other and from self is more positive for love than for status. Correlations between taking from self and from other for the resources of love and status are given in Table 41. These correlations were obtained from the administration of the Role Behavior Test (see Appendix A) and refer to various groups of normal subjects, in different roles, varying in culture, sex and age. In all cases, except the Greek

Table 41

CORRELATION BETWEEN TAKING AWAY FROM SELF
AND FROM OTHER FOR LOVE AND STATUS

Population	Role	Sample Size	Correlation for Love	Status
Israel, male adults	Husband to Wife	633	.28	.18
Israel, female adults	Wife to Husband	633	.34	.24
Missouri, boys	Son to Father	46	.53	.08
Missouri, boys	Son to Mother	50	.54	.36
Missouri, girls	Daughter to Mother	51	.30	.24
Missouri, girls	Daughter to Father	47	.42	.37
Senegal, male adults	Son to Mother	50	−.07	−.09
Senegal, female adults	Daughter to Father	50	.58	.15
Greece, adults	Spouse	29	.35	.37
India, male adults	Son to Father	46	.30	−.01
India, male adults	Son to Mother	49	.65	−.02
India, male adults	Husband to Wife	38	.53	.31
India, female adults	Daughter to Mother	54	.44	.19
India, female adults	Daughter to Father	51	.44	.15
India, female adults	Wife to Husband	39	.63	.10

sample, the correlation between taking from self and from other is more positive for love than for status. These results suggest that generalization of aggression to self is stronger for love than for status. However, the data presented here refer to in-group roles, more precisely, to family roles. Whether the results will be maintained for out-group roles, such as a foe and a stranger, is a question which has been briefly considered previously (see Ch. 5).

In moving along the structure of resources from love and status toward money, the two neighboring resources are information on one side of the circular order and services on the other side. For services, one may expect a slight positive relationship: a physical attack on the other may result in a minor damage to the body of the attacker, particularly if no weapon is used. No relationship appears likely to occur for information: misleading or cheating the other will neither increase nor decrease the amount of information possessed by the cheater, except perhaps for the additional information that the victim has fallen into the trap. Finally, taking away goods and money from the other will usually increase the amount possessed by self, so that for these resources, the relationship between taking away from other and taking away from self will be negative—more so for money than for goods, as some of the latter may be damaged or destroyed in the process of taking them away.

The data and the theoretical considerations discussed above suggest that displacement to self will occur when the frustration involves particularistic resources and when the aggression expressed is particularistic. One would not tend to inflict loss of money on himself while intending the other to lose it, whereas he may direct resentment and disrespect towards himself and even damage his own body (e.g., commit suicide).

SYMBOLIC DISPLACEMENT. A change of object occurs also in symbolic displacement, where the object of aggression is inanimate, such as dolls, shooting at a target, T.A.T. stories, etc. (Bandura, 1965; Feshbach, 1956; Hokanson and Burgess, 1962; Mallick and McCandless, 1966). In the literature, fantasy aggression (Feshbach, 1955) is often considered a form of symbolic displacement. While both phenomena have in common the characteristic of not requiring an actual interpersonal situation (in neither case aggression is communicated to a human being), displacement to another object does not necessarily happen in fantasy aggression. The object can be, and is likely to be, the frustrator himself.

In most of the studies dealing with the effect of displacement on aggression, retaliation was directed toward an inanimate object while residual aggression was observed with respect to the original frustrator. No difference in residual aggression was reported by Mallick and

McCandless (1966) in three experiments where money was taken away from subjects, who then either shot a target with figures of boys and girls or did not aggress. All frustrated groups were more hostile than the non-frustrated ones, no matter whether they displaced aggression or did not aggress at all. Likewise, Feshbach (1956) did not find change in classroom aggressive behavior before and after letting the children aggress in play sessions. In several experiments, T.A.T. cards were used for expression of aggression. Feshbach (1955) found a decrease in hostility toward the frustrator following T.A.T. stories. Hornberger (1959) attempted to replicate the Feshbach experiment, but failed to get differences among the various groups except an *increase* of hostility for the group who hammered nails.

Vicarious Aggression: Generalization of Actor

Displacement has been defined as a change in object while the actor is the previously frustrated individual. Vicarious aggression, on the other hand, occurs when the actor of the aggression is a third person but the victim is the original frustrator (deCharms and Wilkins, 1963; Rosenbaum and deCharms, 1960). While some investigators used the term "vicarious" to convey change of both actor and object (Bandura, 1965; Feshbach, 1955), there is an agreement that this term involves a change of *actor*. In most of the studies on the effect of vicarious experience on subsequent behavior, a movie is shown to the subject. In those movies, the aggressor and his victim are usually different individuals from those involved in the previous frustration (Berkowitz, 1965; Berkowitz and Geen, 1966; Feshbach, 1955; Geen and Berkowitz, 1966). Sometimes when the object is inanimate, only the actor may differ (Bandura, 1962). Very often the resource in the movie is the same as in the aggressive act, mainly services (e.g., Berkowitz and Geen, 1966; Geen and Berkowitz, 1966), but sometimes the resource also changes, being service in the movie and love and status in the measurement of aggression (Feshbach, 1956).

There are not many studies on residual aggression where only the actor changed. Rosenbaum and deCharms (1960) let the subject hear, but not see, a vicarious aggressor berate their frustrator. They found a decrease in residual hostility for low self-esteem subjects, but no change for high self-esteem ones. Indirect support for a cathartic effect of vicarious aggression is suggested by Baker and Schaie (1969), who found no difference in systolic blood pressure and other physiological indications of arousal, between those who aggressed directly and those who did it vicariously. On the other hand, deCharms and Wilkins (1963) reported an increase in aggression following vicarious retaliation. The subjects who witnessed another person aggressing toward their frustrator were the most aggressive. Similar results were obtained by Piroj-nikoff (1958) in a study combining direct with vicarious aggression, but probably with a prevalence of the latter. This investigator allowed insulted subjects to complain and insult the experimenter in a group discussion. He found that subjects performed worse on tasks after this group interaction had taken place than before, possibly as a result of increased anger. Since in group discussion, each participant spends more time in listening to the attacks of others (vicarious) than in talking (direct aggression), the increased anger may be seen mainly as an effect of vicarious retaliation.

Most studies on the effects of watching an aggressive movie showed an increase in subsequent aggression (Albert, 1957; Berkowitz, 1966; Hartman, 1969; Lovaas, 1961). Similarly, watching an aggressive game such as football also results in increased hostility, while no such increase is evident after observing a gymnastic meet (Goldstein and Arms, 1971). Although Feshbach (1955, 1961) did find a decrease in aggression following a violent movie, there is a considerable agreement that exposure to violent behavior increases subsequent aggression. The previous review on displacement indicates that a mere change of object does not increase residual aggression, therefore it seems justified to ascribe the increment of aggression following a movie to change of actor.

It seems reasonable that similarity between the original and the vicarious actor is a relevant variable in predicting the magnitude of subsequent aggression. The more similar the actors are, the more incre-ment in aggression will occur. Moreover, the role dimensions, dis-cussed in reference to third person displacement may prove relevant as well, to similarity among actors. There appears to be no work which bears upon similarity between actors, but there is evidence that increased aggression in the frustrated individual is a function of similar-ity between the object of vicarious aggression and the original frustrator, who is the object of retaliation.

For theoretical and practical purposes, it seems important to study systematically the differential effects of direct retaliation, displacement and vicarious aggression. The available data tend to suggest that direct retaliation yields a decrease in residual aggression, displacement does not affect it, and vicarious aggression results in an increase of sub-sequent aggression. This suggestion, however, is only tentative, since the data came from many studies differing in methodology as well as in types of frustration and aggression. Keeping all relevant variables constant while changing only the *paradigms* would yield a purer test of their differential effects on residual aggression. It seems that pro-grams for controlling aggression of individuals as well as groups, may benefit from such research.

Up to now we have examined the consequences of changing resources, objects and actors in aggressive interaction. To complete the discussion, we shall turn to the remaining behavioral dimension—the mode or direction of the action.

Change of Mode: Restitution

The aggressive sequences considered so far were characterized by a change of object and/or actor from proaction to reaction. In direct retaliation the two participants just alternate positions: the previous actor becomes an object, while the former object becomes the actor. In displacement and vicarious aggression a third individual becomes, respectively, object or actor. All three paradigms were perceived as ways for restoring the victim's internal balance, which had been disrupted by the frustrative act (see Ch. 5). If indeed frustration does impair the internal balance of resources by being an act of deprivation, then an obvious means by which it can be reestablished, and residual aggression reduced, is *restoration*. In this paradigm neither the actor nor the object changes, only the mode alters: the same actor who had emitted the frustrative act now provides the victim with one or more resources.

Surprisingly, the restoration paradigm has been barely explored. The scarce research that has been done on it is mostly within the framework of dissonance and exchange studies rather than in reference to aggression: "the possibility for compensation is eliminated from experimental designs so consistently that experimenters sometimes forget that this reaction to harming a victim exists," noted Berscheid and Walster (1967).

The first question to be asked is whether, indeed, restoration reduces the instigation to aggression after frustration has taken place. Worchel (1961) clearly showed that hostility induced by taking away status is subsequently reduced by status restoration. Even more cogent evidence for the effect of restitution is implicit in the results of an experiment on attraction by Aronson and Linder (1965). In their investigation subjects in one group received only positive evaluations; in a second group evaluation was always negative; evaluation changed from positive to negative in a third group and from negative to positive in a fourth one. Subjects in this last group were thus deprived of status in the early stage of the experiment and then obtained restitution. These subjects liked the person who evaluated them much more than subjects who were deprived but did not experience restitution; in fact liking for the evaluator was highest in this group. This cathartic effect of restoration cannot be easily explained by interpreting frustration to thwarting. Restoration does not undo thwarting as would resumption of the interrupted activity; it does, however, counteract the resource deprivation experienced in frustration, thus reducing or eliminating the need to reestablish balance by retaliation. The conceptualization of frustration-aggression sequence as an exchange which is directed toward maintaining an internal balance provides, therefore, a straightforward explanation for the effects of restoration. This explanation is further supported by some experimental work. Walster, Walster, Abrahams and Brown (1966) found that subjects who had expressed unjustified hostility towards an individual, later on expressed more liking than did controls; those who had expressed unjustified liking, subsequently tended to give less favorable ratings than did controls. One might say that the amount of liking expressed in the second evaluation was guided by the perception of what constitutes a proper balance.

Why do people tend to restore what they have taken away? Carlsmith and Gross (1969) suggested that guilt rather than sympathy was the critical variable. Those subjects who had shocked the confederate were later significantly more likely to comply with his request to run an errand for him (i.e., make some telephone calls), than did those subjects who only witnessed the confederate being shocked by a third person. The authors reasoned that hurting another individual results in guilt feelings which are then decreased by helping him. In our terminology, the actor of aggression takes away love from himself (feels unworthy) and consequently, his internal balance is disrupted; the act of restitution, while restoring the victim's internal balance, also restores the actor's own balance—he is again a worthy person. Another reason for restitution is probably the fear of retaliation; by restoring the victim's internal balance, one assures that his own balance will not be disrupted by a retaliatory act. As far as we know, no data are available regarding this last hypothesis.

Another question to be asked is what constitutes a proper restitution? We know that the probability of emitting a restorative act increases as one can give back exactly what he had taken away (Berscheid and Walster, 1967); indeed, both deprivation and restitution usually involve the same resource class in studies of restoration. What happens when the resource of deprivation differs from that of restoration? It seems reasonable to suggest that the more the two resources are removed in the structure, the higher will be the amount of restitution needed for reestablishing the victim's internal balance. Thus, if deprivation involves love, and restitution is done by giving money, a larger amount of the latter resource is needed for reestablishing balance than if love was restored. Moreover, the victim may never feel that the harm was undone when restitution involved an improper resource: The German government spent enormous sums of money to compensate those who had suffered under the Nazis, yet it is doubtful that this restitution allayed hostile feeling.

In everyday life, restoration is often offered by a third individual rather than by the previous frustrator. A child may be rejected by his peer and then comforted by his parents. Would such restoration, by a third individual, be effective in reestablishing the disrupted balance? The theoretical considerations on displacement and vicarious aggression may apply also here. The more similarity there is between the original frustrator and the actor of restoration, the less residual aggression will be left. Again, similarity may involve the role dimensions of sex, power and resources. The boy who was rejected by his male-peers will feel less frustrated if restoration is carried on by his father, than if it is done by his mother; the former is more similar to peers, having the same sex and in using the same resource (status). This hypothesis, like some other questions we have previously raised in discussing restitution, must await further research.

Investigation of the cathartic effects of restitution is important not only because of its significance in clarifying the conceptualization of frustration, but also in view of its practical relevance: restitution has the obvious advantage over counter-aggression (direct, displaced or vicarious) that it may reduce residual hostility while avoiding further taking away behavior.

With these considerations on restitution, our review of the frustration-aggression sequence comes to a close. Two main points emerge from our reanalysis of the research literature on this problem: (1) The frustration-aggression sequence is an exchange of taking away which may differ from other such exchanges by some specific conditions. (2) The previously developed notions of interpersonal exchange provide a framework suitable for classifying earlier investigations in this area and for suggesting new, more specific hypotheses.

In the studies discussed so far in this chapter, behaviors of taking were prominent; giving appeared only in the proaction of the restitution paradigm. We now turn our attention to investigations dealing with problems in exchanges of giving.

NEEDS OF EXCHANGE PARTNERS: SIMILAR OR DISSIMILAR?

A good deal of controversy has developed around the issue of what need combination is most suitable to exchange partners. In particular, it was debated whether similarity of needs leads to more stable relations than does dissimilarity. Winch (1958) proposed that a person will tend to choose a spouse whose needs are different than his own rather than one having similar needs. Later on, when faced with seemingly contradictory results, Winch (1967) introduced the congruence between role demands and needs as an additional element in predicting the stability of exchange relationship. The more congruence there is between role demands and the participants' needs, the more stable will be the relationship. Instability will occur, for example, when a dominant person occupies a role which is culturally defined as submissive (e.g., employee), or vice versa, when a dominant role (e.g., boss) is occupied by a submissive person. Having noted earlier (see p. 152) that institutional norms may conflict with individual needs, we find ourselves in full agreement with Winch's statement. However, this amplification has little to do with the original problem, as it does not predict if and when stability is associated with similarity of needs between exchange partners.

In a later study, Centers and Granville (1971) reported disconfirmation of Winch's hypothesis, but aptly noted that "applying the principle to those need variables where it was seen as logically and theoretically appropriate resulted in a distinctly more supportive picture for it". A more specific prediction of when complementarity will or will not provide better conditions for partnership is provided by two of the resource properties already encountered in Chapter 5: the relationship between self and other as objects, and the exchange in kind. It will be recalled that the more a resource is particularistic, the stronger the relationship between giving (or taking from) to self and to other and the higher the likelihood for exchange in kind. Love is most often exchanged with love and by giving love to the other one also gives love to himself; thus in an exchange of love one gains not only what he receives, but also by giving to himself. In consequence, when two persons need love they can hardly do any better than exchanging love with one another; here similarity of needs contributes to the stability of the relationship. The contrary happens for money; if two persons need money, they are unlikely to enter into a transaction: money is rarely exchanged with money; furthermore, the amount of it given to the other is lost to self. Therefore, if one is in need of money, he will probably refer to somebody willing to buy his services, his goods or his information; here dissimilarity of needs is advantageous.

In general, it is proposed that dissimilarity of needs will become more desirable the less particularistic the resources needed are. Yet, it has been suggested (see, e.g., Carson, 1969, p. 153) that in a resource as close to love as status, complementarity will result in a better outcome than similarity: a dominant individual will be more satisfied with a submissive partner. The simplicity of this formulation is convincing, but deceptive. Being dominant means giving status to self and taking it from the other. Contrariwise, the submissive person gives status to the other and takes it from himself. If, indeed, such need combination is frequent, we would expect a negative correlation between giving status to self and to other. Yet, we have seen (Ch. 3) that empirical data point in the opposite direction; giving status to self and to other are positively related, at least in the family roles of normal individuals.

It follows that mutual exchanges of status are more common than the situations where one always takes while the other always gives. Furthermore, the failure to take into account all the exchanges which take place between two individuals may hinder our understanding of this problem.

Usually, complementarity implies that while one partner has the need to receive a certain resource, the other has the need to give it. If we limit our observation to one resource, we may conclude that this is a general pattern of exchange for a given pair of persons. But when all resources are observed, we probably will find that while one is willing to give one resource, he expects the other to reciprocate with another resource. For example, when one partner is dominant with respect to status, the other may dominate in information. Consequently, the total exchange pattern will tend to approach balance rather than being a flow of resources only in one direction. Whether the resources exchanged are identical or different will depend, at least in part, on their location in the structure: the more particularistic they are, the more they will be exchanged in kind.

If need combination determines the stability of an exchange, it can be suggested that partners who are matched in their respective needs will find one another attractive. This leads us to the more general topic of interpersonal attraction.

INTERPERSONAL ATTRACTION

The attraction one individual feels for another, and particularly romantic attraction, has always been a focus of interest and speculation, and an ever recurring theme in the literature. However, it became subjected to scientific investigation only in the last two decades. The research work on attraction has mainly concentrated on conditions which enhance attraction and on personality variables of the attractive person. In discussing this area of research we shall be mainly concerned with the additional insight which may be contributed by the resource exchange paradigm, rather than attempting an exhaustive review of the literature. The reader interested in a comprehensive survey may wish to consult Marlowe and Gergen (1969, pp. 621–637) or the work of Berscheid and Walster (1969). These latter authors organized their presentation of attraction around the proposition that we are attracted by those who can provide rewards for us, a position rather close to the one advanced here.

We have repeatedly suggested that social interaction constitutes an opportunity for resource exchange; in keeping with this approach, we propose that a person will be found attractive to the extent that he is considered as a potential partner for the transaction of resources. Attractiveness, so defined, rests essentially on two factors: (a) the extent to which the other is a potential provider of resources we need, and (b) the extent to which we are in a position to satisfy some of his needs. The second factor plays a larger role as a determinant of attraction when the probability of an actual interaction with the other is perceived to be high. One may be attracted to a movie star or to a charismatic statesman even when he has nothing to offer; since the likelihood of actual interaction with such a figure is very low, one can be attracted without worrying about his part in the exchange. Such "abstract" attraction is mainly influenced by the resources the figure possesses.

When an actual exchange appears within the realm of possibilities, one estimates the probability of its success. We all know that in order to have a satisfactory relationship, some balance of giving and receiving should be maintained. Consequently, we take in account what the other can offer to us as well as what we can offer to him in return. A superior individual is not an ideal partner for exchange; while he has a great deal to offer, there is not much that he needs. When, however, this individual shows some weakness, he becomes potentially a better exchange partner, as the possibility of benefiting him, if only through sympathy, is brightened. This is precisely what Aronson, Willerman and Floyd (1966) demonstrated. Their subjects listened to a tape of a stimulus person answering a quiz. Half of them were exposed to the performance of a superior person, while for the other half, the individual on tape showed only average ability; each group was further subdivided into two conditions: half of the subjects heard the stimulus person spilling a cup of coffee on his suit and making apologetic remarks; this episode was omitted in the performance heard by the other subjects.

The superior person who spilled the coffee was liked more than one without pratfall; the contrary was found for the average person: he was liked less when spilling the coffee. The experiment was replicated by Helmreich, Aronson and LeFan (1970) with one addition which proved important: subjects were classified into low, average and high self-esteem, prior to being randomly assigned to the four experimental conditions. The previous findings were supported only by the subjects of average self-esteem; they indeed liked the less-than-perfect superior most. However, high and low self-esteem subjects expressed more liking for the "perfect superior". How can these results be interpreted? We suggest that the amount of liking experienced by subjects with moderate degree of self-esteem was influenced by the two factors —their own potential to give as well as the other's potential. However, for low and high self-esteem, attractiveness was determined mainly by what the other person had to offer and, therefore, they liked more the perfect superior. The effect of the second factor—what they could offer to the other was weakened in these subjects, although for different reasons. High self-esteem subjects, having high regards for themselves, could hardly doubt their capacity to give, thus they become more tuned to the resources the other could bring to the exchange. Low self-esteem subjects, on the other hand, view themselves as having little to offer even to the less-than-perfect superior; both superiors were not perceived as serious potential partners for exchange, and therefore the question of what the subjects could offer had little relevance.

If this explanation is valid, we should expect people with low self-esteem to be attracted by highly endowed individuals. Yet, the contrary was reported in the following experiments. Sara Kiesler and Roberta Baral (1970) manipulated the self-esteem of male subjects by telling them that they had done well or poorly on a bogus test predicting "success in life." During a following "break", the subject was introduced to a female confederate who was made up to be very attractive or unattractive. Subjects who believed they succeeded in the test directed more attention to the girl when she was beautiful, while those who "failed", were more attentive to her when she was sloppy. In a similar experiment (Sigall and Aronson, 1969), it was found that male subjects who had been positively evaluated by a female clinical psychologist liked her more when she was pretty than when she was ugly. Following negative evaluation, however, the ugly psychologist was liked slightly more than the beautiful one. The psychologist was again a confederate of the experimenter and, as in the previous experiment, her change in appearance was obtained by appropriate make-up and dressing.

Apparently in these two experiments, attractiveness was influenced not only by what the target person had to give, but also by what the subject could offer in exchange. How to account for the discrepancy between this finding and the ones obtained by Aronson (1970) and his associates? Some explanations can be suggested:

1. In the last two studies, self-esteem was manipulated by the single event of confronting the subject with information about his success or failure; it is possible that this manipulation was not strong enough to push self-esteem to extreme high or low values and the subjects remained within the mean range where consideration of their own ability to give is an effective determinant of attraction.

2. The latter experiments were more realistic, as the stimulus was a real person, rather than on tape; moreover, attraction was measured *after* an interaction had actually occurred, rather than

in respect to an hypothetical future interaction as done in the previous investigation. This difference may have enhanced the relevance of what one himself has to offer.

3. In the latter experiments, subjects were males and the stimulus person was a female, whereas in the other study both the subjects and the stimulus person were males. In a relationship between males, non-particularistic resources may be more prevalent, while an heterosexual relationship is dominated by exchange of love. Since love requires need-similarity (see p. 239), one is inclined to be attracted by a partner who is similar to him in the need to be loved; similarity, on the other hand, becomes less appropriate when the resources are less particularistic.

In general, it is suggested here that persons are attracted by those who are potential partners for exchange of the *particular* resource they need. It follows that attraction is not a unitary concept; those who need money will be attracted to the rich, while those who seek status would be attracted by "important" persons. A long time ago, Moreno (1934) insisted that a sociometric investigation should refer to a specific situation since a person chosen as a partner for a given purpose will not necessarily be preferred in a different situation; indeed, the resources involved in the two situations may be different. An attractive business partner does not *ipso facto* constitute an attractive love partner. Studies supporting this view have been reviewed by Marlowe and Gergen (1969, p. 633). The structure of resources suggests, however, that a person will be similarly attractive for resources proximal in the order: an important individual may be a potential source not only of status, but also of information. In Teichman's study of expectations in a task group (see Ch. 5), we would predict that members will be attracted to the person who is expected to give more information, as the task consisted of preparing a joint paper. It was indeed found that the most and least attractive partners differed most in the amount of information expected from them; the difference for status was lower than that of information, but higher than the difference for love, which is more remote from information than status in the structure of resources.

In conclusion: we are attracted by persons whom we consider to be potential partners for exchange because they are perceived as able to give some resource we need and appear to need some resource we possess. Thus, attraction is resource-specific, yet it generalizes to resources proximal in the order. Attraction is essentially a condition which precedes the exchange, although it may be influenced by past experiences of exchange situations with the same or different partners. We now turn to discuss studies which attempt to predict the outcome of the exchange.

FAIRNESS IN EXCHANGE

The intuitive notion that an exchange of resources may be more or less equitable appears often and prominently in the discussion of human affairs. One may hear the argument that it is unfair to pay migrant agricultural workers subsistence wages for their labor, or that depriving a child of his preferred toy because he had disrespected his parents constitutes excessive punishment. Thus, the notion of fairness is applied to exchanges of giving as in the migrant workers example, as well as to exchanges of taking away, as in the case of the rebellious child. This notion is also used when resources are apportioned among individuals or groups by a third party: it is unjust for a mother to allocate unequal amounts of love to her children; it is unfair to pay different wages to people doing the same job or to punish one person more severely than another for the same violation.

There have been many attempts to spell out, in more precise terms, the intuitive notion of fairness. Social philosophers and reformers, concerned mainly with the distribution of wealth, have proposed rules such as: the same to everybody; a guaranteed minimum income to everybody; to each one according to his needs, his efforts, or abilities. Industrial psychologists dealing with job evaluation have struggled with the problems of determining fair wages for jobs differing in skills, danger, effort or unpleasantness. They too were concerned with economic resources.

Attempts to incorporate particularistic resources within the notion of equity were pursued by a relatively small group of social psychologists. Two issues are prominent in their work: (a) definition of a fair or just exchange; and (b) predicting the consequences of an unjust exchange.

Theoretical Formulations

RECIPROCITY. Gouldner (1960) postulated a norm of reciprocity which he considered to be universal and applicable to every human society, although varying in its specific manifestation by time and place; the norm consists essentially in the obligation we have to help those who had helped us and not to injure them. The amount reciprocated would be commensurate to the amount and value of the reward previously received.

DISTRIBUTIVE JUSTICE. A formulation which takes into account reciprocal rewards as well as reciprocal costs was proposed by Homans (1961, p. 75). Distributive justice occurs when the ratio of profit to investment is the same for each participant. Profit, in turn, is defined as the difference between reward and cost. According to this formulation, just exchange will occur when, for example, A's reward is valued 14, his cost 6 and his investment 20, while the respective values for B are 10, 8 and 5. Then A's profit is $14 - 6 = 8$ and B's profit is $10 - 8 = 2$. The ratio between profit and investment is the same for both participants, being 2/5 in each case. It appears realistic to assume, as this example does, that the reward of each participant will be higher than the cost incurred by the other; if indeed, each participant gives what he has in relative abundance and receives what is scarce to him, then the marginal utility of the receiver is higher than the one of the giver. Indeed, we tend to value more what is scarce than what we have in abundance.

Of particular interest to us is Homans' suggestion that a person who cannot repay in kind might reestablish justice by giving status to the other, e.g., by expressing gratitude, esteem or indebtedness. Here is the beginning of a differentiation among various resources with the consequent notion that when the appropriate resource is not available, another can be substituted for it. Testing this proposition, Blumstein and Weinstein (1969) found that indeed, subjects who received more than their fair share from their partner expressed more esteem for him. Another study (Weinstein, DeVaughan and Wiley, 1969) showed, however, that status is not the sole substitute resource: when the other person was a friend, subjects who previously benefited beyond fairness gave him status by openly expressing gratitude, by thanking him for his superior performance and by inviting him to assume leadership in a second joint task; when, however, the partner was a stranger to the subject, he preferred to reestablish reciprocity by giving services.

For distributive justice to be established, the previous recipient should reciprocate appropriately. A proper reciprocation may be defined in terms of the relationship between the amount of the resource one had received and the amount he can give. When more than one resource is involved, proper reciprocation may also be defined in terms of the appropriateness of a given resource as an exchange for that which was previously received; for example, there is considerable agreement that money is not an appropriate resource for love. What happens when a recipient finds himself unable to reciprocate appropriately? In the exchange paradigm of aggression-restoration, Berscheid, Boye and Walster (1968) reported that when the proper channels for restoration are not open to the harm-doer, he usually justifies his act by derogating his victim. Generalizing from these results to the present paradigm of positive reciprocation, one would predict that the recipient of resources, who is not in a position to reciprocate appropriately (in terms of the amount and/or the class of resource available to him), he will feel scarce attraction for the giver. This prediction was indeed confirmed in an experiment done by Gergen and his associates (Gergen,

1969, pp. 77-80). Players who were made to lose in a game, received an unexpected amount of chips from an anonymous source. Attached to the chips was a note prepared in three different ways: one version stated that the subjects could keep the chips without incurring any obligation; another version requested them to return the same amount of chips; the third one demanded payment of interest and some other unspecified favors. The highest attraction for the unknown giver was expressed by those requested to return the same amount of chips. These findings had an international flavor in more than one sense. First of all they were replicated in three different countries (United States, Japan, and Sweden). Secondly, as noted by Gergen, they have broad implications for foreign aid. In this practical situation, the negative effect of inappropriate exchange is likely to be stronger than in the experiment just described since the donor is not anonymous and there are actual contacts between the receivers and the givers, who usually send technicians, experts, and missions. When an "undeveloped" country gets aid, it is usually expected that they will reciprocate with status. From Teichman's and Donnenwerth's experiments (see Ch. 6), we would predict that if reciprocation involves a resource which is remote in the structure from the one previously given, the amount of the latter will be larger than when the resource reciprocated with is closer to the one given. Status is more remote from goods and money than from information. Consequently, it is less suitable for reciprocation when the aid consists of goods and money than when it provides training and instruction. Indeed, countries providing economic aid appear to be more disliked than countries providing training. It has been noted (Laufer, 1967, esp. p. 207) that Israel's modest program of foreign aid has been particularly attractive to recipients. Perhaps this success is related to the fact that the program, very much like the U. S. Peace Corps, provides information rather than goods and money. Futhermore, when the giver is a small country which sorely needs support, there are more opportunities for the recipient to reciprocate than when the giver is a superpower.

EQUITY. The formulation suggested by Adams (1965) appears rather close to the one proposed by Homans, although the terminology is different: instead of distributive justice, the term "equity" is used; input takes the place of investment; positive outcome replaces reward, and negative outcome might be somewhat similar to cost. Equity is then defined as a situation where the ratio of outcome to input is constant for various individuals or groups; in this formula the term "outcome" is presumably used to indicate the difference between positive and negative outcomes, thus perhaps corresponding to Homans' "profit." Adams' major contribution is a systematic treatment of the ways for reducing inequity and relating some of them to dissonance reduction; we have already noted (see Ch. 5) that several dissonance experiments involve exchange situations in which the perceived inequity is reduced by modifying the value of the resources involved; for example, a subject who was paid little for presenting a view he opposes will reduce his "input" by accepting the view as his own.

PAY-OFF MATRIX. The conception of equity emerging from the social exchange theory of Thibaut and Kelley (1959) is more flexible than the ones examined so far. Like other students of social exchange, they assume that each participant in the transaction receives rewards and incurs costs; both reward and cost depend not only on the course of action chosen by the individual but also on the behavior of the other partner. This notion finds expression in the pay-off matrix, which is simply a tabular arrangement where rows indicate the various alternatives open to one participant and columns represent the options available to the other partner. Each cell, at the intersection of a given row with a given column, contains two entries which are the outcomes for each of the two participants when one of them chooses the alternative indicated by the row and the other chooses the option shown in the column. Thus, certain combinations of proaction and reaction may result in a loss for both participants, others may result in a gain for one of them or for both. The tendency of each participant to choose alternatives which maximize his gains is moderated by the fact that the outcome depends also on what the other is going to do, as well as by the possibility that the other may leave the exchange, finding it unattractive. The decision to terminate the exchange or to continue it depends on the reward obtained as well as on the availability of alternative exchanges for satisfying the same needs; for example, a worker may not be happy with his job, but he is unlikely to leave it unless he found another, more attractive place.

These constraints in the choice of alternative actions result in a process of accommodation between the exchange partners, which does not rest on a rigid definition of fairness, but rather on what they both find agreeable and profitable. It should be noted, however, that even in more formal definitions of equity, considerable flexibility is provided by recognition that the value of rewards, costs and investment depends in part on the subjective evaluations of the individuals concerned. Indeed, it was shown by Pruitt (1968) that the amount of money a subject reciprocated to the confederate depended not only on the amount given to him by the confederate, but also on the quantity of resource the confederate was thought to possess; since the marginal utility of money decreases for successive increments, the same amount had more value when given by a poor confederate than when allocated by a rich one. The same effect has been found for particularistic resources. In a series of studies Aronson and his associates (Aronson, 1970, pp. 150–159) have shown that when a confederate first expressed dislike towards the subject and then evaluated him positively, he was liked more than the one who was positive all the way.

The various theoretical formulations of exchange, although differing in details and, even more so, in terminology, have a common core in the notion that the amount given or taken by an individual is positively related to the amount which was previously given to or taken from him. There is indeed considerable empirical evidence in favor of this proposition.

Evidence for the Tendency Toward Equity

In view of the noted similarity among the major theoretical formulations, it seems unnecessary to present separately the empirical work of the various schools; instead we shall follow the example set by Adams (1965) who, in reviewing the reduction of inequity, quotes works of Homans and of Thibaut as well as those closer to his own formulation. It is, however, desirable to discuss separately those studies in which equity is maintained by the subject as opposed to investigations in which the subject acts to reduce a pre-existing inequity. Let us begin with the maintenance of equity.

Pruitt (1968), in the experiment already mentioned, found that the amount of money the subject provided to the confederate was positively related to the amount the latter had previously made available to him. Investigating exchange of particularistic resources, S.C. Jones (1966) arranged groups of four subjects, continually exchanging evaluations of one another's artistic opinions. He found that subjects tended to reciprocate the evaluations they had received. It has also been shown that a person who received help is more likely than the one who was refused assistance, to offer help to his benefactor (Goranson and Berkowitz, 1966) as well as to a third individual (Berkowitz and Daniels, 1964). In these studies, the same resource is involved in each stage of the exchange; keeping the resource constant while varying its amounts enhances the manifestation of reciprocity, since, as we have seen in the previous chapter, a change of resource modifies the effects of its amount. The effect of introducing an additional resource, although not explicitly, is well exemplified in a study by Leventhal and Bergman (1969). About 37 percent of the subjects who were grossly under-rewarded money-wise as well as derogated by the confederate, when having the opportunity to modify their share, chose to decrease it rather than increase equity. The evidence presented by the investigators suggests that this behavior served to *increase* the status of the subjects;

thus, having to decide between establishing equity in status or in money, they chose the former. Indeed, only 22 percent of those who were deprived of money but not of status chose to decrease their share.

In this last experiment, the subject's reaction to inequity was studied. In several other investigations of this type, it was generally found that when subjects had been over- or under-rewarded, their behavior in a subsequent interaction tended to compensate for the "error" and was directed toward reestablishment of justice (Blumstein and Weinstein, 1969; Leventhal, Allen and Kemelgor, 1969; Pepitone, 1971; Walster, Walster, Abrahams and Brown, 1966). It was predicted that this tendency to restore equity will be stronger for the victims who were under-rewarded, than for those who received above their fair share. While this prediction was confirmed for preschool children (Leventhal and Anderson, 1970), adults' behavior did not support it (Leventhal and Lane, 1970). In spite of the scarce empirical support, there is theoretical justification to expect that victims will attempt to redress injustice more than beneficiaries. When the subject is a victim, he faces both a dissonant situation due to a discrepancy between his efforts and his reward (Alexander and Simpson, 1964; Aronson, 1961), and a loss of resources; perceptual modification of the event takes care of dissonance, but not of the resource loss. On the other hand, when it is the other who received too little, it is possible to reduce dissonance by underestimating his contribution, without experiencing any actual loss. Of course, one could also reduce dissonance by allocating more to the other, but then at the cost of depriving himself. Consequently, perceptual modification appears more likely to occur with respect to the other than in regard to the self. Some support for this proposition is provided by Leventhal and Michaels (1969).

Other studies dealing with the reduction of inequity were reviewed by Adams (1965) who classified them according to the method by which inequity was reduced. Some of these studies show that workers paid above or below what they considered a fair wage tended to modify the amount and/or quality of their performance to make it commensurate with their wage. Adams devotes considerable attention to the problem of which method for inequity reduction will be preferred in a given situation. We have already proposed that perceptual modification is more likely to be chosen for the behavior of the other than for the behavior of self; this proposition is shared by Adams, although on a somewhat different theoretical ground.

Earlier (Ch. 5) we have proposed that symbolic resources may be more amenable to perceptual modification than concrete ones: it might be easier to modify perception regarding the amount of information and status received or given, than to do so for goods and services. In summary, there is considerable evidence that individuals tend to behave in a manner consistent with maintaining or restoring a ratio between what they receive and what they give, but the order of preferences among various ways of restoring equity is only partially understood.

Resources and Equity

How different is this line of research from the theoretical and experimental work on resource exchange presented in Chapter 6? There are at least two points which deserve to be noted: one is the notion of cost, the other is the specification of the resources involved in the exchange.

Most formulations of exchange theory, borrowing from economics, assume that a partner in an exchange must incur certain costs in order to obtain rewards, so that in every exchange there are losses as well as gains. This is perfectly plain in economic exchanges: one has to give money to obtain goods and thus, after the exchange had terminated, he will have more goods but less money; likewise, one has to work and expend efforts to obtain money; thus his profit, as Homans suggested, is the difference between the value of what he received and the value of what he gave. In the arithmetics of economic exchanges, costs are a value to be subtracted, a value with a negative sign; indeed, in these exchanges there is a negative relationship between what remains to self and what is given to other (see Ch. 5). This relationship, however, becomes less negative and then positive as one moves, in the structure of resources, toward the particularist ones; hence the cost becomes smaller and then positive and turns into a reward. The property of resources regarding the relationship between self and other can be re-formulated as follows: the more particularistic the resource, the less negative the cost of giving it. To illustrate this point, let us consider two lovers, or perhaps a married couple, having sexual relations: each is giving a great deal of pleasure to the other, but where is the "cost"? Giving pleasure to the other *adds* rather than *subtracts* to one's own enjoyment; the cost is positive. Although this may be most evident in love making, the same considerations apply to other particularistic exchanges as well. One might experience a certain difficulty to associate the term "cost" with a positive value; words are tyrannical and rarely neutral; the term cost has intuitively a strong negative connotation. Yet it is not uncommon for a person, thanked for a favor done, to answer "Nothing at all," meaning "My cost was zero"; in French more than in English, one may also answer "It was my pleasure" which we interpret to indicate that he did it for love, so that his cost was positive as he derived pleasure from doing the favor.

These considerations lead us to the second point of our discussion—the relevance of the resources involved in the exchange. In the theoretical formulations just examined and in the related empirical work, the resources exchanged do not play an explicit role; they are all covered by the notion of amount of (positive or negative) reinforcement. We have seen, however, in Chapter 6, that quantity and quality interact: in Teichman's experiment the same amount of resource reciprocated had different effects on satisfaction depending on its appropriateness to the proaction; Donnenwerth's investigation further showed that a larger amount of an unappropriate resource was reciprocated. These and other studies reviewed show that resources are not equivalent; therefore it is not sufficient to state "how much," one should specify "how much of what."

It may be suggested that the more appropriate the resource is the smaller the amount of it required in order to establish equity and satisfaction. Appropriateness, in turn, depends on the need of the recipient and on the institutional setting; in our imperfect world these two do not always go together: one may need a given resource, which is not suitable for exchange in a particular institution. In such conflictual situations, giving precedence to individual needs over institutional requirements is likely to backfire, according to some experimental results. In a study by Schopler and Thompson (1968) female subjects who had received a small gift (a flower) from the confederate were later more responsive to his request of testing the handwashing of a blouse, than were those who received no flower. These results were, however, obtained only when the situation was described as informal, and were reversed in formal situation: here, those who received no favor were more willing to help than those who got a flower, possibly because the small gift was inappropriate in this setting.

Such interaction between the situation and personal needs was also reported by Brehm and Cole (1966) in an entirely different setting. Subjects were assigned to a task of rating a confederate. Half of them were told that the task was highly important; for the remaining subjects, the task was presented as of low importance. Within each condition, half the subjects received a soft drink by the confederate who bought himself a coke from a vending machine and "thoughtfully" brought one back for the subject as well. The other half did not receive a drink. Later on, the confederate was requested to stack sheets of paper for the experimenter. When the rating was presented as unimportant, most subjects who had received the drink reciprocated by helping the confederate; they did not offer help when the task was important. Willingness to help was about the same in the two conditions of importance, for subjects who did not receive the drink. Givers of favor were not rated differently, on the average, than those who did not offer the drink. Unwillingness to help drink-providers when the rating was seen as important may be due to their favor being considered inappropriate to such a situation—sort of "bribe."

These two studies suggest that initiation of an exchange which is institutionally inappropriate may well leave the proactor disappointed. Chances of success in obtaining the resource desired, in spite of it being contrary to institutional norms, will be presumably better when the proactor pretends to propose a different, institutionally appropriate, exchange, without revealing his real purpose. To these manipulatory techniques we now turn.

MANIPULATIVE TECHNIQUES

When a person finds himself in a situation which does not permit an exchange of the very resource he needs, he may still attempt to achieve it within the same setting through manipulative techniques. There are several such non-conventional exchanges, of which two—ingratiation and Machiavellism—have been studied intensively, although with different research strategies. Ingratiation experiments typically consist of placing the subject in a situation where he is dependent on the other for certain resources, but cannot obtain them by proposing a straightforward exchange; his behavior in this situation is then observed. Studies of Machiavellism on the other hand, focus on differences regarding the exchange behavior of individuals who had been previously rated high or low on a scale of "Machiavellism." Although this difference in research strategy does not facilitate a comparison between ingratiators and Machiavellians, they appear to have at least one element in common: concealing from the other what resource they strive to obtain from him.

Ingratiation

A most comprehensive and penetrating study of ingratiation has been provided by E.E. Jones (1964), who devoted considerable attention to the tactics and goals of the ingratiator. We shall refer to his work with only minimal changes in terminology; tactics denote the behavior of the ingratiator toward the other while goals are the behaviors that the ingratiator attempts to elicit in the other. Some of the tactics described by Jones pertain to the self presentation of the ingratiator, or behavior toward self; Jones aptly notes that presentation of self may include various combinations of self enhancement (giving status to self) and self effacement (taking status from self) depending on the circumstances. We have noted earlier, in discussing interpersonal attraction, that giving status to self signals to the other that the ingratiator is a valuable exchange partner as he possesses large amounts of a valuable resource. On the other hand, taking away status from self is functionally equivalent to spilling coffee on the suit, in Aronson's experiment: it signals that although our person has much to give there is something he needs as well. Other tactics, also described by Jones, consist of providing the other with status, goods and services, and perhaps some other resources which may be needed by him. Ostensibly the other will be expected to reciprocate this giving with love. We have indeed seen (Table 28) that in the institution of friendship, it is appropriate to reciprocate with love most of the resources received. Once a relation of friendship has been established, an attempt to achieve the hidden goals becomes feasible. Experimental results previously mentioned have indicated that the initiator of an illicit exchange runs the risk of being disliked by the other. Building a strong friendship first may offset this expected reduction in liking, making safer for the ingratiator to bid for his goals.

The goals of ingratiation considered by Jones are essentially of two types: (a) Receiving from the other specific resources which are controlled by him and cannot be easily obtained elsewhere; (b) Preventing the other from taking away the resources which are more valuable to the ingratiator than those he is willing to give. The resources which constitute the ingratiator's goal are unlikely to be the ones which characterize the friendship institution, i.e., love and, to a lesser extent, status and services. If, indeed, these resources would constitute his goal, there would be no need for ingratiation and for deception; in friendship it is well within the norms to expect particularistic resources. Therefore it is more likely that the ingratiator is after less particularistic resources, the very ones which are not usually exchanged among friends. Likewise when the ingratiator offers friendship to avoid a loss, it seems that the resources he is attempting to preserve are the less particularistic ones.

Another variation of ingratiation occurs when the goal is to receive status or avoid losing it in reference to a third individual or group. One may, for example, cultivate the friendship of a high-status person in order to receive status (and possibly other resources as well) from his peers by virtue of his highly placed relationship. Conversely, one may attempt to ingratiate an individual who can damage the ingratiator's standing in the community by revealing some unsavory details of his life and activities (e.g., that he is an ex-convict). Here again, resources less particularistic than status, such as the salary obtained from a job, may be protected by ingratiation. When the ingratiator protects himself by giving money rather than love, blackmail is the appropriate term for his behavior.

In the experiments described by E.E. Jones (1964) the subject is often asked to strive for a resource (a job, a travel fellowship) which is controlled by the other and which may be obtained by winning the other's approval (Jones, p. 158). In discussing the behaviors used by subjects to obtain this approval, Jones (p. 193) notes that the strategy for obtaining love will differ from the one used for status. When attempting to obtain a positive rating for task performance, the subject will tend to describe himself as "competent and respectworthy" rather than "friendly and affable". The latter presentation is more likely when "the goal is to be judged a congenial or compatible partner". Love and status do not, however, constitute goals but rather mediate toward the achievement of other, less personalistic resources. Another interesting finding is that low status subjects are more likely to use self-enhancement, to agree with the other on important items, and perhaps also to use other-enhancement as a technique of ingratiation. High status subjects, on the other hand, are more likely to present themselves as modest, to agree on non-important items and to avoid other-enhancement. Thus each type of ingratiator tends to stress the condition for exchange which is less evident on him: the low status ingratiator implies possession of resources; the high status one indicates his willingness to receive. These general trends are modified, Jones shows, by the need to maintain credibility.

Conformity

One of the tactics used by ingratiators is conformity, where they change their beliefs and behavior in order to become more similar to another person or group. In ingratiation, conformity will succeed only to the extent that the ingratiator is able to conceal his ulterior goal (Jones and Gerard, 1967, p. 586). Conformity also occurs outside the ingratiation situation, when there is no concealed purpose and as such, it has been widely studied (see Kiesler and Kiesler, 1969 for a review), particularly in the context of group pressure and attitude change. The terms compliance persuasion, influence, diffusion of innovation, which have been used in this line of investigation, have a good deal in common with the notion of conformity, although they differ in details and in emphasis. The basic unity of these phenomena in social influence has been put in evidence by Nord (1969) who suggests that individuals conform in order to obtain approval, love and status in our terminology. Seen in this light, conformity becomes a proaction in an exchange of resources: in accepting the values or behavior of the other (or of the group) the conformer implies high regard for him and expects to receive love and status in return, in the guise of approval. It has been found, indeed, that persons tend to like those who are similar to them; by conforming one becomes more similar to the other, therefore increasing his chances of being liked.

The tendency to conform was demonstrated in the pioneer work of Sherif (1935a), Asch (1951) and Festinger, Schachter and Back (1950, Chs. 5 and 6). Once this fact was established, subsequesnt research was directed at clarifying who is more likely to conform, and under which conditions conformity is more likely to occur. Some of the findings obtained fit remarkably the exchange interpretation of conformity.

If conforming is a bid for status and love, it can be expected that persons who have a stronger need for these resources will be more likely to conform; yet the act of conforming implies giving these very resources to the other, thus it requires a previous possession of them by the conformer; in consequence, persons who are more likely to conform will possess a moderate amount of status and love: they should have enough to make the initial investment, but not so much to disregard the opportunity to receive more of these resources. Individuals who are very rich or very poor in love and status will be less likely to conform, although for different reasons: the former do not need to receive, while the latter do not possess enough to make the initial investment, particularly if it requires a large amount, as for example when there was a previous public committment to a different position (Lana, 1969); furthermore, as noted earlier (see Ch. 5), the expectation of receiving status will be dissonant to persons who feel they do not deserve it; therefore they will be more reluctant to invest toward a goal which will create a dissonant situation. These considerations suggest that when there are few "poor" individuals in the population studied, or when the amount required for investment is moderate, the relationship between conformity and the amount possessed will be negative: the more a person possesses love and status the less is the probability that he will conform. Conversely, a positive relationship is expected when the initial investment is high and/or when there are many resource-poor persons in the population. Finally, when the population includes both very "rich" and very "poor" persons and the initial investment is moderate, the relationship between the amount possessed and conformity will be curvilinear, with those possessing moderate amounts conforming most. This analysis of conformity as a proaction of an exchange may provide an explanation for the contrasting results reported in the literature regarding the relationship between influenceability and self-esteem (i.e., the amount of status possessed by the person). Indeed, McGuire (1969a, pp. 250–251), in summarizing research in this area, notes that while many studies reported a negative relationship between self-esteem and influenceability, many others provided evidence for a positive or curvilinear relationship. A curvilinear relationship has also been reported between conformity and affiliation need: subjects with a moderate need conform more than those at the extremes (Byrne, 1962; Hardy, 1957). This need covers a range of resources, including the one involved in self-esteem, status; this common resource may explain the similarity of findings.

McGuire's attempt to account for this complex relationship between self-esteem and conformity is far less parsimonious than ours as it postulates five genotypical principles as well as differential interactions between personality and situational variables (McGuire, 1969a, pp. 243–247). In any event, neither his reasoning nor ours explains the strong negative relationship between conformity and non-manipulated self-esteem found in a population of hospitalized mental patients (Janis and Rife, 1959). Presumably self-esteem is low in such a population, so that we would have expected to find in them a positive, rather than a negative relationship between this variable and conformity. Our second proposition, that powerful persons who possess a large amount of status are less likely to conform, is reflected in Hollander's notion of idiosyncrasy credit (1958); indeed, the degree of deviation from norms permitted to an individual by the group before sanctions are applied, constitutes an indication for the amount of status and love he possesses.

There is a certain similarity in the relationship of self-esteem to conformity, just considered, and to attraction, which was examined earlier in this chapter: in both cases high and low self-esteem subjects are alike while differing from subjects of moderate self-esteem. This parallelism is not pure coincidence: both attraction and conformity involve consideration of what one needs to receive and of what he can give in the exchange, but attraction refers to expectations regarding a future exchange, while conformity is a first step in an exchange that has already begun; both involve love and status although love may be a more prominent resource in attraction while status is more prominent in conformity. The closeness of the two notions of attraction and conformity was noted by Festinger (1953) when he suggested that full acceptance of conformity, as distinct from mere compliance, occurs only when the conformer is attracted by the person to whom he conforms. Yet, experiments on dissonance, reviewed in Chapter 5, suggest that compliance will increase attractiveness when nonparticularistic reciprocation is scarce or absent: girls who complied with the demands of severe initiation found the bogus and boring sex discussion group most attractive. Research dealing more directly with the relationship between conformity and attraction was, however, mainly concerned with the effects of the latter on the former. It appears that one is more likely to conform to a group which he considers attractive (Marlowe and Gergen, 1969, pp. 615–616); in other words, the first actual step in an exchange (conforming) is more likely to be taken when an exchange seems to be feasible (attraction). Indeed, group variables which have been found to increase conformity are permanence of the group, the extent of interaction within it, and the existence of an achievable common goal (Tajfel, 1969, p. 336); all these factors appear to enhance the possibility of resource exchange within the group (Blake and Mouton, 1961).

After this digression on conformity, which may or may not be a manipulative tactic (depending on the resource expected to be gained), we return to the main topic with a discussion of Machiavellism.

Machiavellism

Since five centuries ago when Machiavelli wrote "Il Principe," a book of cynical advice to the ruler, the name of this Florentine writer has become synonymous with manipulative behavior. In the last several years there has been a surge of interest in the scientific study of this interpersonal behavior.

As noted earlier, studies of Machiavellism have followed a paradigm quite different from those of ingratiation. Jones' work has been mainly concerned with studying the differential behavior patterns of subjects more or less dependent on the approval of the other. Research on Machiavellism, on the other hand, has particularly focused on the identification of situational characteristics for which individuals scoring high on a Machiavellism scale out-perform low scorers (Christie and Geis, 1970). The Machiavellian was found to win more often when there is face to face interaction, when he can devise his response rather than having to choose it among predetermined alternatives, and when the situation has emotion-arousal connotations (which he usually disregards).

High Machiavellians are characterized as being less persuasible, less affected by social pressure or by inconsistencies in their attitudes or behavior, less likely to be emotionally involved, while more attentive to the informative aspects of the situation. "In general, high Machs appear to have as little defensive investment in their own beliefs as they have in others or in interpersonal relations"(Christie and Geis, 1970, p. 313). Thus, highly Machiavellic individuals seem to be less in need to receive love (and perhaps also status) than less Machiavellic ones. Consequently, particularistic transactions do not constitute for them a goal in itself, but merely stepping stones to the acquisition of less particularistic resources which they value more. Their typical way to handle a competitive situation will be to maximize their share of non-particularistic resources while letting the other have the particularistic ones he cherishes. "The best way to handle people is to tell them what they want to hear" (i.e., to give them love and status), runs an item of the Machiavellism scale (Christie, 1970). As for the Machiavellian himself "it hurts more to lose money than to lose a friend" (scale version for children, Christie and Geis, 1970, p. 327).

This interpretation of Machiavellism in terms of resource preference for dispensation and achievement explains why Machiavellians do better in situations which permit the transaction of particularistic resources in addition to the non-particularistic ones (chips, money) explicitly played for. In a face to face interaction and in a less structured situation, Machiavellians can give particularistic resources or "irrelevant affects" (Christie and Geis, 1970, p. 288) in exchange for the non-particularistic ones. These affects are irrelevant to the high Machiavellic, but quite valuable to the low one.

There is also some evidence, albeit not conclusive, suggesting that the superiority of the Machiavellist is stronger when the experimental situation is more realistic. Indeed, only in a realistic situation are there non-particularistic resources to be gained, while lack of realism does not preclude, and may even enhance, the exchange of particularistic resources; when the chips are "worthless" they provide status for the winner, but no money. A person who values money but does not care for status is unlikely to take a great interest in such a game.

Machiavellians agree less with others and are less self-consistent. Agreeing with the other is a tactic for receiving love and status; it has been shown indeed (see, e.g., Byrne, Ervin and Lamberth, 1970) that one is more likely to feel esteem for a person who holds attitudes similar to his own. Maintenance of self-consistency is also related to self-esteem. Since the Machiavellian is after less particularistic resources, he does not indulge in behaviors which will provide him with status (such as agreeing or being consistent), yet, he can be persuaded by "more factual" information which relates to resources he values. Agreement to the viewpoint of the other is, thus, likely to occur in the Machiavellian when winning his approval is necessary for obtaining resources controlled by him. This situation is often found in Jones' experiments on ingratiation, and explains the apparent discrepancy between the high persuasibility of the ingratiator and the weak effect of social pressure on the Machiavellic individual. In those situations where approval results in obtaining only status, Machiavellians will not be persuasible; when, however, the other's approval mediates access to less particularistic resources, they will yield to social pressure. Indeed, when nothing but status was to be gained by winning the other's approval, Machiavellic subjects were found to engage less in ingratiation than did subjects low on Machiavellism (Jones, Gergen and Davis, 1962).

If Machiavellic persons are usually rich in love and status, being charming individuals who are not particularly concerned with obtaining status or being approved by others, and willing to trade these resources for less particularistic ones, it can be expected that they will score low on approval need (Crowne and Marlowe, 1960), while being high on the need for non-particularistic resources. Non-Machiavellic individuals, on the other hand, may or may not be high on need approval. Some support for this hypothesis is found in work done by Donnenwerth, who administered both the Crowne and Marlowe approval scale and the Mach IV scale to 140 female subjects. Both score distributions were then dichotomized at about the respective means for national norms, i.e., score 15 for the approval scale (Crowne and Marlowe, 1964, p. 211) and score 88 for Mach IV (Christie and Geis, 1970, p. 79). The joint distribution thus obtained is given in Table 42. Subjects low in Machiavellism are divided almost evenly with regard to their need for approval, 59 percent showing a low need and 41 percent a high need score. On the other hand, the large majority of Machiavellians (82%) are low in need approval.

Table 42

JOINT DISTRIBUTION OF 140 FEMALE SUBJECTS
ON NEED APPROVAL AND MACH IV SCALES

Mach IV	Need Approval		
	Below Mean	Above Mean	Total
Below mean	59%	41%	100% (123)
Above mean	82%	18%	100% (17)
Total	(86)	(54)	(140)

Persons with a high Machiavellism score are found more often among young people, among those raised in a large city and among those belonging to a less traditional culture (Christie and Geis, 1970, pp. 315–321). Modern society, and particularly its urban subculture, appears to favor nonparticularistic exchanges over particularistic ones (see Ch. 5). It seems therefore, that Machiavellic individuals are particularly adjusted to the exchange conditions of modern urban culture, having low need for particularistic resources and high need for non-particularistic ones. At the same time, they thrive on the need of others for particularistic resources in a culture scarce of them.

There are no legitimate institutional avenues for exchanging money with love (see Ch. 5) and only a few for trading it with status, such as mecenatism (support of the arts and sciences) and philanthropy (support of the needy), where status is given to the donor by a third party rather than by the recipients of financial support. In absence of an institutional setting where he can give love and status and receive money, the manipulator will have to dissimulate his real exchange intentions and to begin by offering what the other needs.

A more extreme variety of the Machiavellic pattern is the confidence plot, where the victim entrusts his material resources (usually money) for an empty promise such as high returns. As implied by the name, the plot may succeed only after the trust of the intended victim has been secured. As trust is a characteristic of particularistic resources (see Ch. 5), here again, the victim is given love and status and finally deprived of money or goods. Other illicit exchange patterns may be found in practice, although they have not attracted the same amount of investigation as ingratiation and Machiavellism. We have already mentioned, *in passim,* black-mail, where the victim is offered a choice between losing particularistic resources (status and sometimes also love) or losing money to the blackmailer.

In a study described earlier (see Ch. 5), Staub and Sherk (1970) reported that children high in need for approval were likely to renounce a less particularistic resource (candy), presumably in a bid for approval. Similar results were obtained by Blumstein and Weinstein (1969). By manipulating both the share of a stooge in a joint task and his claim to a share of the reward, these authors created conditions in which the confederate's claim was above, below or commensurate to his actual contribution to the task. Dependent variables were the subject's claim on a second interaction with the same stooge and his evaluation of the confederate. Subjects high on need for approval were reluctant to claim a major share for themselves, even when previously victimized, possibly to avoid disapproval. Machiavellic subjects, on the other hand, tended to claim more when the stooge's demands had been modest. The different behavior of these two types of subjects illustrates once more the influence of the individual's needs: each person strives for the resource he values most.

Another illicit pattern of exchange is illustrated by the behavior of impostors, who are individuals posing at being richer in money, more learned or skilled than they really are in order to offer these imaginary resources in exchange for actual status. Their tragedy is that when they are discovered, they are likely to experience an almost total loss of status, the resource which they strived so hard to obtain.

The patterns described in this section have two characteristics in common: (a) They do not conform to exchanges which are typical of any social institution; and (b) they meet the need for specific resources in the individual who initiated them. In other words, these exchanges are unorthodox, and usually illicit patterns of achieving need satisfaction.

Licit but Roundabout Patterns

Other behavioral patterns for obtaining a resource which is not directly available through appropriate institutional exchange, do not involve deception but may look peculiar to the outsider. We have already noted (see Ch. 5) the case of a person going to the doctor in order to receive sympathy and affection rather than medical services (Shuval, 1970). Other examples of the longer and devious routes taken to achieve a needed resource are found among American blacks. Let us consider the following behavior patterns which have been ascribed to some of them: (a) preference for conspicuous consumption items like flashy cars and clothes, rather than purchasing more "solid" items; (b) demanding integrated facilities where there is separation and separate ones where there is integration; (c) enrolling in black studies programs which do not provide training for specific future jobs. There seems to be little in common among these behaviors except that none of them appears oriented toward long-range goals. A meaningful picture emerges, however, when they are seen as different paths of achieving status, the resource of which black people have been most deprived. Conspicuous consumption goods are exchangeable with status. Refusal of social contact, by insisting on separate facilities, means taking away status from the rejected ones, and thus the real issue is not integration versus separation but who is taking away status from whom. The information gained in black studies may not be useful on the job, but it is a means to a needed increase in self pride.

The comparison of these latter patterns with Machiavellism provides an interesting contrast. The manipulator uses particularistic resources to gain non-particularistic ones. In the other examples of exchange, the reverse often occurs: particularistic resources are sought through the mediation of less particularistic ones. A person high in particularistic needs and low in non-particularistic ones is, indeed, the ideal partner for a sucker.

With an attempt to integrate several aspects of interpersonal relations within the framework of resource exchange, we have concluded the second part of this volume, dealing with the dynamics of interpersonal behavior. A basic requirement of efficient communication is that a message will have the same meaning for the receiver as for the sender; if one communicates love to the other, the latter should perceive that he received love and react accordingly. Sharing meanings of behavior requires a similarity between the cognitive structures of the participants; in the study of resource exchange, we have assumed the existence of such structural similarity. We shall now abandon this assumption and turn to a comparison of cognitive structures, noting the effects of their similarities and differences on interpersonal communication and adjustment: this is the topic of the third and last part of our book.

SUMMARY

Interpersonal behavior has been conceptualized in this book as a mechanism enabling individuals to maintain their optimal level of resources. If indeed any social interaction consists of an exchange of resources, then the notion of exchange should provide a framework for interpreting many socio-psychological phenomena. Thus in the present chapter, some of the issues in social psychology which generated theoretical and empirical work have been reanalyzed in terms of the resource exchange paradigm. We have discussed the frustration-aggression sequence, complementarity of needs for exchange partners, interpersonal attraction, equity or justice in resource transactions, ingratiation, conformity, and Machiavellism.

The frustration-aggression sequence is a negative exchange where person A (the frustrator) causes a deficiency in person B (the victim) and is "reciprocated" with the latter attempting to deprive him of one or more resources. By considering definitions of frustration as well as the actual manipulations used in studies of frustration-aggression, it becomes clear that actual or potential (future) deprivation of resources is a necessary component of the frustrating event; a second component is the need state of the object-person. When deprivation results in producing a need, the victim will tend to re-establish balance by retaliation. It follows that an individual possessing a large amount of the resource of which he was deprived will be less likely than a "poor" person to experience a deficit, and therefore, to be aggressively aroused.

Often the degree of frustration has been inferred from the intensity of the following aggression; it is indeed reasonable to assume that when frustration is low, retaliation will be milder, but the reverse is not necessarily true; aggression may be inhibited and its expression mild in spite of a high level of internal arousal. Thus, the intensity of retaliation is a function of two factors—the drive level and the degree of inhibition to aggress. In general, retaliation serves to re-establish the optimal level which was upset. However, when a victim foresees a high probability that retaliation will bring a further loss of resources, he will refrain from retaliation.

Examination of the notion of aggression has led us to define it as a behavior which deprives the recipient of one or more resources. Thus, frustration and aggression are both events in which resources are taken away although they may differ as to the conditions producing them and the way they are perceived by the participants of the interaction.

By considering the frustration-aggression sequence as a case of negative resource exchange, we are immediately provided with a classification of both frustration and aggression in terms of the six resource classes. Then, we can explore the relationship between the class of frustration and that of aggression and study its effects on the restoration of internal balance, as measured by residual hostility. It is suggested that the preference for a certain class of aggression is determined by the class of frustration previously experienced, and that the amount of residual aggression is affected by the structural relationship between the two resources. There is a preference to retaliate in kind or with a resource similar to the one involved in the frustrating event. When preferred retaliation is feasible, residual aggression is lower than when a remote resource is employed.

Other factors which influence restoration of the internal balance are the actor and the object in the frustration-aggression sequence. Three paradigms of exchange have been studied with different degrees of intensity: (1) Direct retaliation, where the previous actor (the frustrator) becomes the object of retaliation and the previous object (the victim) becomes the actor of retaliation; (2) Displacement, where the object of retaliation is not the previous frustrator but a third individual although retaliation is carried out by the previous victim; (3) Vicarious aggression, in which the object of retaliation is the original frustrator but retaliation is carried out by a third individual rather than by the previous victim. The available data tend to suggest that direct retaliation yields a decrease in residual aggression, displacement does not affect it, and vicarious aggression results in an increase of subsequent aggression. This suggestion, however, is only tentative since the data originated in many studies differing in methodology as well as in the resources of frustration and aggression.

Direct, displaced and vicarious retaliation have been investigated for their possible effectiveness in restoring the victim's internal balance, which had been disrupted by the frustrative act. If indeed frustration impairs the internal balance of resources by being an act of deprivation, then a straightforward means by which it can be re-established is restoration. In this paradigm, neither the actor nor the object changes, only the mode alters: the same actor who had emitted the frustrative act now provides the victim with one or more resources. The few data available on restoration point to its effectiveness in reducing residual aggression. Unless frustration is viewed as deprivation, this cathartic effect of restoration cannot be explained. Further research is needed in this area as to the differential effect of restoration and retaliation on residual hostility. Beside the theoretical interest, the study of restitution has practical relevance: restoration has the obvious advantage over counter-aggression that it may reduce residual hostility with positive rather than negative activities.

Turning to positive exchanges, the first issue examined was what need combination provides for a successful exchange partnership. While some data indicate that similarity of needs leads to more stable relations, other studies indicate the reverse. The dilemma can be solved by considering two exchange properties (see Ch. 5) of resources: the relationship between self and other and the exchange in kind. The more particularistic a resource is, the stronger the relationship between giving it to self and to other and the higher the likelihood for an exchange in kind. Consequently, similarity of needs is advantageous for particularistic resources, while complementarity is desirable for non-particularistic ones.

If need combination determines the stability of a given relationship, it can be suggested that "matched" partners will find one another attractive. Attractiveness, then, is a perceived potential for a successful exchange. Thus defined, attraction rests on two factors: (a) the extent to which the other is a potential provider of resources we need, and (b) the extent to which we are in a position to satisfy some of his needs. When an actual exchange is considered, one estimates the probability of its success. We all know that a satisfactory relationship requires some balance of giving and receiving. A superior individual as well as an inferior one are not ideal partners for exchange. While the first has a lot to offer, there is not much he needs; the reverse is true for the inferior individual. It is further suggested that persons are attracted to those who are potential partners for exchange of the particular resource they need. Thus, attraction is resource-specific, yet it may generalize to resources proximal in the structure. Attraction is essentially a condition which precedes the exchange, it is an estimate of the feasibility of a particular exchange.

This definition of attraction suggests that people have fairly clear ideas about what constitutes a successful transaction. There have been various attempts to spell out this intuitive notion of fair exchange, among them is Homans' formulation of distributive justice, Adams' notion of equity and Thibaut and Kelly's pay-off matrix. Common to these formulations is the idea that every social transaction involves certain rewards and certain costs. This is perfectly true for economic transactions concerning money and goods, as in these exchanges there is a negative relationship between what remains to self and what is given to other. This relation, however, becomes positive for the particularistic resources, hence the "costs" become positive; in an exchange of love, each participant gives a pleasure to the other, but where is the "cost"? Giving pleasure to the other *adds* to one's own enjoyment, rather than subtracts from it. Another important variable in determining equity is the relationship between the resources exchanged. When the same resource is involved in proaction and reaction, the amount given and received determines the equity. But when two different resources are exchanged, the appropriateness of the exchange determines the amount necessary for establishing equity. The more appropriate the resource received is, the smaller the amount of it required for establishing equity. Appropriateness, in turn, depends on the need of the recipient and on the institutional setting.

What happens when a person finds himself in a situation which does not permit an exchange of the very resource he needs? This person may resort to a non-conventional exchange in which he gives a resource appropriate to the institution, but aims at obtaining a non-appropriate one; he may, e.g., pretend to be friendly with a rich person with the hope of gaining financial help. Two such exchange strategies—ingratiation and Machiavellism—have been studied intensively; both have the common element of the initiator concealing from the other what resource he strives to obtain from him. Most often the ingratiator is willing to exchange particularistic resources for non-particularistic ones. One of the tactics used by ingratiators is conformity, acceptance of the beliefs and behaviors of the other. Conformity is also used by non-ingratiators, but with the distinct difference that they are aiming at receiving, in exchange for giving status, particularistic resources, while the ingratiator reaches for non-particularistic ones.

The preference for non-particularistic resources over particularistic ones appears to characterize individuals who score high in Machiavellism. Indeed, they were found to engage less in ingratiation when the situation offers only a gain of status. The modern urban environment is 'rich in non-particularistic resources and poor in the particularistic ones. It seems, therefore, that Machiavellic individuals are particularly adjusted the exchange conditions of this subculture.

Another behavioral pattern is the use of non-particularistic resources for obtaining particularistic ones. The preference of some American blacks for conspicuous consumption items like flashy cars and clothes may be a path of achieving status, the resource of which black people have been most deprived. Sometimes the motivation behind charity is the same: giving money to gain status. In general, people prefer to give what they have in abundance and to receive what is scarce to them. It is only when the situation does not permit such exchange that one may resort to manipulative techniques, to satisfy his needs in spite of institutional barriers.

This reinterpretation of some of the main topics of concern to socio-psychological research in terms of resource exchange concludes the second part of our book.

PART III:

DIFFERENTIAL

CHAPTER 8

COGNITIVE MATCHING AND MISMATCHING IN INTERPERSONAL COMMUNICATION

Overview

O UR DISCUSSION ON the development of cognitive structures and their relevance to interpersonal behavior has tacitly assumed that structural characteristics are invariant within and across cultures. Yet individual and cultural differences do exist and their identification is important for understanding and predicting outcomes of interpersonal situations. Therefore, the third and last part of this volume is devoted to the comparison of cognitive structures and to the analysis of their similarities and differences. We shall begin, in the present chapter, by considering the effects of cognitive differences on communication and performance; Chapter 9 will deal with comparisons across cultures, while deviations from the normal cultural pattern will be examined in Chapter 10.

Investigations of interpersonal behavior often assume cognitive similarity and successful communication among participants; in dissonance experiments, for example, the investigator relies on his own cognition in contriving a dissonant event and assumes that such event will also be perceived as dissonant by his subjects. The manipulation checking, reported in many experiments, has essentially the purpose of showing whether the subjects perceived behavior directed toward them in the same way as intended by the experimenter.

Knowing that miscommunication may occur makes it appropriate to inquire into the conditions which facilitate and hinder the process of interpersonal communication. We propose that cognitive differences constitute a major obstacle to effective communication while cognitive similarity facilitates it. This proposition is supported by several studies which will be discussed here. Furthermore, cognitive similarity among members of a task group facilitates performance although some moderate degree of dissimilarity may enhance group creativity.

269

The relationship between cognition and performance is further pursued in the second section of this chapter with a discussion on the problem of matching the group leader to the situation; a leader seems to be more effective when his cognition matches the problem presented by the task situation. Moreover, knowledge about the leader's cognitive structure may increase the accuracy of predicting what type of behavior he will emit while under stress and whether his performance following training and experience will improve or deteriorate.

In the last part of this chapter we shall discuss the relationship between the type of communication transmitted by the parents and the child's cognitive growth. Parent-child communication is perceived here as a mechanism which has the dual function of providing the child with resources and with the cognitive information needed for his structural development. Communication which is inappropriate with regard to one or both functions will impair the cognitive development of the child, leaving him as a deviant within his own culture. When child-parents communication is appropriate but the parents belong to a minority subculture, the cognition they transmit to the child may be at variance with the prevailing culture although consonant with his immediate social environment. The first type of cognitive deviation is discussed in Chapter 10; the second type is directly related to cross-cultural differences which constitute the topic of Chapter 9. Thus, a discussion of child-parents communication provides an introduction to the following two chapters.

COGNITIVE SIMILARITY AND EFFICACY OF COMMUNICATION

Imagine yourself crossing the path of a friend who waves his hand in greeting. You may respond by waving back, by saying "Hi" or by smiling. Behaviorally, these three responses are dissimilar as they involve different neuro-muscular systems. Their equivalence and interchangeability is due to their shared meaning, i.e., they belong to the same cognitive class. Thus it is the meaning which is attached to a behavioral event, rather than the behavior itself, that bears relevance to interpersonal communication. Indeed, it is well known that the same behavior may have a different meaning in various cultures and accordingly will lead to different responses.

Assigning the Stimulus to a Class

This process of mapping stimuli into prior cognitive representations has been proposed as the essence of perception in general. In summarizing the matching-response model, Rodgers and Ziegler (1967) note that "Several theorists have postulated that a central cognitive representation is generated which is then compared to sensory input from the periphery. MacKay (1963), for example, posits a 'matching-response' model of psychophysical judgment, and uses it to account for Stevens' psychophysical power functions. G.A. Miller, Galanter and Pribram (1960) suggest a TOTE theory to account for behavior and, presumably, for the perceptions that underlie behavior. According to them the initial 'test' phase of every behavioral act is a comparison of sensory data about the state of the world to a cognitive model about the desired state. This is followed by 'operations' to eliminate mismatches between model and sensory data, until subsequent 'tests' indicate the desired goal has been reached. 'Exit,' which may mean a perception that the desired condition exists, follows lack of detectable mismatch between cognitive model and comparison sensory or proprioceptive data. Just so, perception in MacKay's model of psychophysical judgment is an internally generated psychic function that is not detectably mismatched by comparison sensory data. Chomsky (1963) presents a highly similar theory of perception of language, in which he posits that the hearer generates a message unit according to internal language rules and then 'hears' the internally generated message if it is not contradicted by the sensory input from the speaker" (pp. 161–162).

Common to all these models is the proposition that perception involves the mapping of stimuli into classes. Morin, Hoving and Konick (1970) set up an experiment to test whether stimuli are compared directly or whether they are first mapped into cognitive classes so that the classes rather than the stimuli themselves are compared. Their subjects were presented with two line drawings projected on a milkglass screen. They were asked to indicate, as fast as possible, whether the two stimuli belonged to the same set. These sets of figures which had been previously shown to the subjects, consisted of two or four stimuli: in some sets all the stimuli belonged to a given class (e.g., figures of animals); the objects of other sets were arbitrary collections of objects belonging to different classes. The dependent variable was the time lapse between presentation of the stimuli and the subject's decision as to whether they belonged to the same or to different sets. The investigators reasoned that if the stimuli presented are mapped into classes before comparison is made, the number of objects in each original set would not influence the speed of decision; each object is mapped into its class, then the two classes are compared to see whether they are alike or different; the number of objects, previously shown, belonging to each set is irrelevant in this process. However, if comparison is not mediated by mapping into classes but rather by recalling each object of the previously seen sets, then the larger the number of items in a set, the longer will be the time required for reaching a decision.

The results obtained strongly suggest that items are first assigned to their classes which are then compared. Obviously, this process is possible only when appropriate classes exist in the cognitive structure of the subject; otherwise, the only alternative left is comparison by items. Indeed, the authors found that when the compared objects originated from class-homogeneous sets, response time was not related to the number of items in the set. On the other hand, when original sets were composed of items from different classes, a longer time was required to respond for sets of larger size, than for smaller sets. This difference between homogeneous and heterogeneous sets was less pronounced for kindergarten children, who tended to be influenced by set size even when the set was homogeneous. This last result may indicate that at least some of the cognitive classes involved in the task were not yet differentiated in the structure of these children; thus, for them, there was not much difference between the two types of sets. Altogether, this line of experimentation, further pursued by Egeth, Marcus and Bevan (1972), indicates that when the relevant classes are available, stimuli are mapped into them before further cognitive processing takes place; it also shows that this pattern increases efficiency of performance: comparison by classes was in general faster than by items, particularly when the sets were larger.

The realization that a perceived stimulus is first mapped into a cognitive class uncovers the "mystery" of results such as those reported by Maltzman, Langdon and Feeney (1970), showing that prior conditioning is not necessary for obtaining semantic generalization. Subjects were instructed to perform a motor response when hearing the word "light." They were then exposed to a list of words which did *not* include this word; nevertheless, when they heard a related word, "lamp," they manifested an autonomic response (GSR) similar to the one of those subjects who had been previously trained to respond motorically to the word "light." Training at the behavioral level seemed superfluous because the appropriate cognitive classes were already available. Had the relevant class not been in existence, generalization could not be expected, as shown by some experiments described in Chapter 2 (pp. 27–28). It should be remembered, however, that the acquisition of classes results from prior learning, partially through a conditioning process.

In interpersonal communication, the stimulus or the message perceived by the receiver, originates from the cognitive structure of the sender, through a process which is analogous but reversed to the stimulus-mapping of the recipient. Thus, interpersonal communica-

tion involves matching between the cognitive structures of the participants.

The Communication Process: Encoding and Decoding

Schematically we can describe the process of interpersonal communication by the following sequence of steps:

1. One or more cognitive classes in the sender's structure are
   activated; the sender intends to emit a given message, specified
   by the activated classes.
2. The message is encoded in a behavioral pattern (speech, gestures,
   facial expression, giving an object, performing an activity) which,
   according to the mapping rule, belongs to the activated classes.
3. The behavioral pattern is perceived by the receiver and decoded
   (i.e., recognized as belonging to a given class or classes) according
   to the mapping rule, thus acquiring its meaning for the receiver.
   This sequence is depicted in Figure 13.

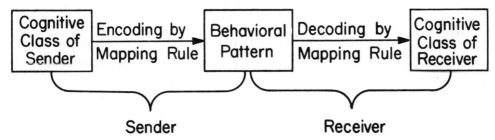

Figure 13. A schematic view of the interpersonal communication process.

In examining Figure 13 it is apparent that the meaning of the message
received will correspond to the sender's intention, when the cognitive
class from which the message originated matches the one to which
it was finally assigned. This process of cognitive matching was studied
in two experiments to which we now turn.

CLASSES OF ENCODING AND DECODING. In Donnenwerth's experiment
which was summarized in Chapter 6, a confederate was instructed
to deprive the subjects of resources belonging to a specific class. The
experimenter wanted to find out whether the confederate's behavior
was perceived by the subjects as intended. Thus, each subject was
asked to describe this behavior on a checklist of 24 adjectives, with
4 adjectives for each resource class. Specifically, subjects were
requested to indicate, on a ten-point scale, the extent to which each
adjective described adequately the confederate's behavior toward
them. Because of the interrelationship among resource classes, it was
expected that the behavior would be encoded into more than one class.

However, if there is correspondence between the receiver and the sender, the highest score should be assigned to that resource class from which the confederate's behavior was encoded. The data presented in Table 43 indicate precisely this pattern for each intended resource class. Remember that in this experiment, each group of subjects was deprived of one resource; thus, there were six types of behavior, one for each resource class. Each row in Table 43 pertains to a different type of confederate's behavior.

Table 43
INTENDED AND PERCEIVED RESOURCE OF LOSS

Intended Resource (Encoding)	Perceived Resource (Decoding)					
	Love	Status	Information	Money	Goods	Services
Love	34.53	33.20	17.27	17.57	23.40	26.13
Status	25.33	31.60	18.07	16.47	19.80	26.87
Information	20.13	22.50	34.57	22.50	22.62	20.50
Money	18.86	20.00	20.14	28.50	23.44	16.57
Goods	23.92	25.00	18.83	21.38	31.69	16.25
Services	28.09	27.34	16.89	17.05	19.81	32.18

Examination of the data given in Table 43 reveals a consistent pattern: in each row the highest mean score is always in the diagonal cell, where the class of decoding corresponds to that of encoding. The mean score tends to become progressively lower as one moves away from the diagonal in both directions. Thus a loss in a given class tends to generalize to neighboring classes and less so to more remote ones. There are only four deviations from this structural pattern.

Similar results were obtained by Teichman (1971c): in his experiment (see Ch. 6, pp. 204–209) the confederate bidded for a specific resource to be provided by the subject. The experimenter checked whether the bidding proved effective by presenting the subjects with a questionnaire containing six statements, one for each resource class. Subjects were to indicate, on a five-point scale, the degree to which their behavior toward the confederate was similar to the one described in each statement. The mean scores are presented in Table 44.

Table 44
RESOURCE REQUESTED AND GIVEN

Resource bidded for by confederate	Mean amount of resource given by subject					
	Love	Status	Info.	Money	Goods	Services
Love	4.8	4.0	3.0	1.8	2.3	3.3
Status	3.2	4.7	3.5	2.3	2.4	2.9
Information	3.7	3.6	4.8	2.0	2.1	3.3
Money	2.9	2.9	2.8	4.4	3.0	3.1
Goods	3.1	3.3	3.0	3.0	4.5	3.4
Services	3.5	3.1	3.2	2.3	2.6	4.8

The pattern of results is identical with the one obtained by Donnenwerth: in each row, the highest mean score is always in the diagonal cell where the bidded resource is identical to the one given. This score then tends to become progressively lower as one moves away from the diagonal in both directions.

The results of these two studies indicate that although communication between confederate and subject was generally effective, some miscommunication occurred.

Types of Communication Failure

The communication model schematized in Figure 13 combined with our conceptualization of cognitive structures suggest at least two types of miscommunication:

1. MISMAPPING. The mapping rule used by the sender to encode the message may be different from the one used by the receiver in decoding it. In other words, a specific event may be categorized into different classes by different individuals. Consider, for example, an American who intends to express friendship to a Thai; he may encode the intended message —"giving love"—in the behavioral pattern of pat on the back. Unfortunately, the Thai mapping rule for this behavior is different and the Thai who receives it will decode it as an insult, or "taking away status." Thus the message intended will be quite different from the one received. We denote this type of communication failure by the term mismapping. Mismapping occurs mostly in cross-cultural encounters; yet even within the same culture certain persons may use mapping rules which are not shared by others, thus causing misunderstanding. Indeed, some individuals are better communicators than others(Foa, 1958b).

2. MISMATCHING. The degree of differentiation among classes may differ for the sender and the receiver. If the sender differentiates more than the receiver, he activates only one or a few classes for a given message, while in the receiver's cognition more neighboring classes will be activated as well. The differentiation between love and status, for example, is stronger in the American culture than in more traditional ones such as the Arab culture. Consequently, criticism of performance does not imply personal dislike for an American as it does for an Arab by whom the message "you can do a better job" is decoded as "I dislike you and your work." Schizophrenics seem to differentiate less than normals between self and other as objects; the message "I am very tired," sent to a schizophrenic by another person, could be decoded as "you should go to bed" and may upset him considerably when he himself happens to be widely awake. This type of communication

failure, due to different degrees of differentiation, is called mis-matching.

As the previous examples may have shown, mismatching occurs when the two participants differ in their respective distances among classes, although the sequence of proximity of classes may be the same for both: even if love and status are more similar for an Arab than for an American, they still remain contiguous resources in both cultures. Another source of mismatching stems from differences in the cognitive structure. Suppose that in the sender's cognition, classes A and B are neighbors while class C is farther away from A than from B. On the other hand, in the receiver's cognition, class C is closer to A than to B. These two individuals will differ not in the relative degree of differentiation, but on the structural arrangement. What will happen when they communicate? Let us consider, for example, an encounter between high self esteem and low self esteem persons.

The confident individual perceives the notion of self as more related to success than to events of failure; the opposite is true for the low self esteem individual. Now, suppose that the confident person detects some uneasiness in his friend's behavior; naturally he will send him messages of encouragement such as "you are doing very well," "you have succeeded." The receiver will find himself in a dissonant position—he "cannot" succeed as for him the notion of self is remote from the class of successful events; obviously his uneasiness will increase, leaving his confident friend puzzled. In examining dissonance (Ch. 5, pp. 140–150), we have focused on the discrepancy between the message and the receiver's cognitive structure. In the present con-text we realize that the message is congruent with the sender's cognitive structure while incongruent with the receiver's one; thus, ultimately, the incongruence is between the participants' cognitions.

Extreme incongruence occurs when the environment is random so that no organized cognition could possibly match with it. Seligman (1969) has pointed out the disruptive effects of random environment on the behavior of laboratory animals. Bresnahan and Blum (1971) exposed children to a brief sequence of random reinforcements and observed its effect on performance. Subjects were 60 first-grade children, 30 belonged to families of high socio-economic status and 30 came from low status families. The children were presented with a triangle and a circle on either red or green background. Two stimuli were projected simultaneously on a screen, the various combinations of shape and color appearing with equal frequency in random order. Subjects were told that if they chose the correct figure, they would be rewarded with a penny. One third of the subjects were reinforced each time they chose the triangle. The remaining subjects were randomly reinforced for 6 and 12 trials before the triangle was consistently reinforced. When reinforcement was the same from the beginning, high status children performed much better than low status ones. The introduction of random reinforcement in the initial stage of the experiment resulted in lower performance for the high status group, while no marked effects of random reinforcement were found for low status children. Consequently, following twelve random reinforcements, the two groups performed at about the same low level. The authors suggest that poor performance in general, may result from previous chaotic reinforcement. While interpretation of the results is somewhat open to question, this work has the merit of relating cognitive processes to performance and to early behavioral experiences, two topics which will be discussed later in this chapter.

Effect of Cognitive Similarity on Communication

Among the various studies relating communication effectiveness to cognitive similarity, those of Triandis (1959; 1960 a and b) are of particular interest. In one experiment (1960a); each of 40 subjects was shown 12 sets of three pictures each, depicting faces with various emotional expressions. They were asked to indicate which picture was most different from the other two and in which way it was different. The responses of each possible pair of subjects were scored according to their similarity. Subjects were then paired at random for the communication stage of the experiment, which consisted of six games. Each member of the dyad was provided with two out of the three pictures previously presented; one picture was identical for both partners. Players were to find out which was the common picture; obviously they were not allowed to see the pictures held by the other, but they could exchange messages indicating the extent to which given traits (e.g., intelligent—unintelligent) were expressed in a picture. The degree of success in identifying the common picture on the basis of the information exchanged was taken as a measure of communication effectiveness. While no clear cut differences in performance appeared for subjects of medium or high similarity, communication was less effective for the most dissimilar pairs. Moreover, subjects with similar cognition exchanged fewer messages than did less similar ones. Thus, similarity not only made communication more effective, but more parsimonious as well.

The same problem was investigated in another study (Triandis, 1959) which was carried out in the natural situation of an industrial plant, rather than in the laboratory. Subjects were 155 workers and their supervisors. As in the previous study, they were presented with three stimuli and asked to indicate which of the three was most different from the other two, and in which way. This time, however, the triads were made up either of jobs or of people working in the plant. In addition, each participant rated the same jobs and people on semantic differential scales. Two measures of cognitive similarity were thus obtained for each possible pair of subjects. Neither of them is identical with the types of similarity that we have proposed, but the one based on semantic differential is closer to our notion of degree of differentiation. An attitude scale was used to assess communication effectiveness, a less direct and less convincing method than the one employed in the previous study. The degree of liking for the other was also recorded by an attitude scale. The results essentially supported the findings of the previous study, that cognitive similarity results in better communication; they also provided some refinements. Different measures of similarity were not equally effective in predicting communication: the best predictor was similarity in semantic differential rating of jobs, particularly for subjects in management positions. The effectiveness of cognitive similarity, measured by the semantic differential, in improving communication was further supported by another study (Triandis, 1960b).

Ayer (1968b) set up groups of triads who again differed in the degree of their cognitive matching. This time effectiveness of communication was not observed directly, but rather as a function of the time required to perform the task and of the subjective feelings of group members. Cognitive characteristics of the subjects were assessed by presenting them with all the possible combinations of 30 interpersonal verbs with 30 adverbs. They were instructed to rate each verb-adverb combination as to whether it was fitting (e.g., attack violently), permissible (e.g., attack quickly) or anomalous (e.g., attack meekly); (for details on the theoretical background of this procedure, see Osgood, 1970). On the basis of these ratings, subjects were sorted into types, obtained by inverse factor analysis. These types served to set up three kinds of groups: homogeneous with all members belonging to the same type; heterogeneous with each member being different from the two others, but moderately so; and odd-man group, where one member differed sharply from the two others, who belonged to the same type.

Each group then played a semantic game; they were provided with a board having a series of concentric circles, in the manner of a target, the verb "confuse" appearing in the center; they were also given 39 interpersonal verbs, constituting a balanced sample of these verbs in the English language. Their task was to place the verbs on the board in such a way that words perceived as similar would be near to each other, while those considered different would be farther apart. Thus, the task seems to involve the same cognition that served as a basis for composing the group in the previous stage of the experiment. Placement of each word on the board could be done only after the three group members had reached consensus on the position appropriate to it. A total of 12 groups was studied, four of each type.

The results indicated that the time to complete the game was longer for the odd-man groups than for the other ones; the game was enjoyed most by members of homogeneous groups and least by those in odd-man groups; involvement in the play was also highest in the homogeneous groups, but lowest in the heterogeneous ones. It was also noted that these last groups produced the richest, most semantically refined solutions. The fact that the moderately heterogeneous group worked well, fast and with some enjoyment of the task appears to suggest that a modest degree of cognitive differences among group members may facilitate creativity without producing disruption in the group. However, when these differences become too large, the advantage gained in creativity is probably offset by the resulting communication difficulties.

Triandis' work has shown that cognitive similarity facilitates communication. The Osgood-Ayer experiment has provided some insight on the relationship between cognitive similarity and certain aspects of performance, albeit in a rather unusual task. There is also evidence that certain communication networks lead to better performance than certain others (Leavitt, 1968). Before embarking on a more detailed analysis of the effects of cognition on performance, it seems appropriate to note that similarity of cognitive structure alone does not guarantee effective transmission of messages. We already know that processing of a communicative input requires time and that more time is needed the more particularistic is the resource transmitted (Ch. 5, p. 166). Consequently, particularistic communications suffer most in a large group where inputs are abundant. When the group is fairly large, competition of inputs does not occur only among resources, with a decrease in the particularistic ones, but also among communicators; if some participants command a great deal of attention, communication with the other members may suffer. It was found, for example, that when a foreman is busy with management, his workers are less able to predict his responses (Foa, 1960). Furthermore, the attention of the leader is unlikely to be evenly divided among group members, particularly in a larger group. It was thus noted (Foa, 1954) that a leader concerned with the task performance of the group is likely to focus his attention on members with highly satisfactory or a mildly dissatisfactory performance; on the other hand, when the leader is concerned with group members as individuals, as, e.g., in a training group, he will attend more to those who are mildly satisfactory or highly unsatisfactory. This study is just one of the many showing that different situations call for different types of leadership: a person who is an effective leader in a given situation does not necessarily remain so when the situation changes.

Katz, Blau, Brown and Strodtbeck (1967) have found that a leader is more likely to lose his position when the new task is imposed on the group by external circumstances rather than chosen freely; the contrary, however, happens when the original task was chosen by the leader but rejected by the group.

When the leader cannot be demoted his suitableness to the situation is reflected in workers' satisfaction. A study by Foa (1963) indicates that although some workers are happier with a permissive leader, some others do not mind a disciplinarian boss. The problem of how to match leader and situation to maximize performance has been intensively studied by Fiedler (1967). Since his work provides further understanding of the relationship between cognition and performance, it seems appropriate to discuss it somewhat extensively at this point.

THE LEADER'S COGNITION AND GROUP PERFORMANCE

In his extensive study on leadership effectiveness, Fiedler (1967) has provided us with a classification of situations and types of leaders, demonstrating that specific combinations of situation and leader result in better performance than do other combinations. To reach an optimal level of performance, matching between the situation and the leader is thus required.

In Fiedler's theory, situations are classified in terms of their favorableness for the leader; a number of variables have been used to determine favorableness, but the original classification of situations rests on the following ones: (a) leader-member relations; (b) structure of the task; and (c) leader-position power (Fiedler, 1964).

The classification of leaders is based upon the leader's perception of his least preferred co-worker. The leader is asked to think about all the persons with whom he has ever worked and to describe on bi-polar adjective scales the person with whom he has had most difficulty working, i.e., his least preferred co-worker (LPC). The more favorable is the leader's rating of this co-worker, the higher his LPC score. A very large number of laboratory and field studies conducted by Fiedler (1967) and his associates have shown that situations of moderate favorableness call for high LPC leaders while in highly favorable or unfavorable situations the best performance is provided by low LPC leaders, i.e., persons who describe their least preferred co-worker in negative, rejecting terms.

Earlier interpretations of the least preferred co-worker score have been primarily in motivational terms. The high LPC leader has been described as someone whose major need gratification is derived from good interpersonal relations with others. The low LPC person has been described as someone who seeks need gratification from performance and achievement on the task itself. It follows that the two types of leader differ in the resources they need: the high LPC is characterized by the predominance of particularistic needs, while for the low LPC, non-particularistic needs are more prominent.

Recently, there has been interest in conceptualizing the LPC from a cognitive viewpoint (Mitchell, 1970; Schroder, Driver and Streufert, 1967, p. 134; Shima, 1968). More specifically, it has been proposed that high LPC leaders differentiate more than low LPC's between the task and the interpersonal aspects of a situation (Foa, Mitchell and Fiedler, 1971). Since the task involves less particularistic resources than do interpersonal relations, we might say high LPC leaders differentiate more along the particularistic dimension of interpersonal resources. One may wonder whether the motivational and cognitive interpretations of the LPC constitute alternative or complementary explanations.

Motivational and Cognitive Aspects of the LPC

It is appropriate to begin an analysis of the relationship between motivational and differential aspects of the LPC by taking a close look at this instrument; it consists essentially of a series of bi-polar scales (e.g., efficient-inefficient, friendly-unfriendly). The subject is requested to use these scales for describing "the person with whom you had the most difficulty in getting a job done," viz., the least preferred co-worker. The more positive the description of the least preferred co-worker, the higher the LPC score of the subject. Some of the LPC items refer to aspects of task performance such as efficiency and cooperativeness; most items, however, pertain to the interpersonal aspects of the relationship (e.g., warmth, friendliness, acceptance); thus the LPC score indicates the degree to which the co-worker who created most difficulty in doing the job is perceived as an attractive individual. When the least preferred co-worker is perceived as personally attractive (high LPC) the subject is said to be mainly interested in interpersonal relations and/or to differentiate highly between them and task performance. On the other hand, low LPC subjects are described as more interested in doing a good job and/or as differentiating rather poorly between task and interpersonal aspects of the situation. It is thus suggested that: (a) Low differentiation will be found in task-oriented individuals rather than in those who are mainly concerned with relations; and (b) high differentiation will go together with interpersonal orientation more than with interest in task performance.

To clarify the proposed relationship between differentiation and needs, it is useful to consider the institutional setting and the resource exchanges typical to it. Clearly the social framework of leader-worker exchanges is the institution of work: the group is to perform a task by providing services (labor) and, sometimes, information in return for monetary or some other compensation. Thus, the typical resources of this institution are non-particularistic, although, as any interpersonal encounter, it also offers an opportunity for particularistic exchanges; these latter may be either ancillary to task performance or enjoy a fairly independent status. At any rate institutional norms indicate that the "least preferred co-worker" is a person who does not perform well on his task, rather than a person who cannot maintain a positive interpersonal relationship.

A leader whose main concern is getting the job done will be likely to consider interpersonal relations merely a component of the task situation: a worker is a nice person when he performs well and a poor worker can hardly be an object of friendship; for this type of leader, efficiency and friendliness go together, he is a low differentiator. Since the person referred to in the LPC instrument is a poor worker, this type of leader will rate him low in personal traits as well, he will thus be a low LPC leader.

The leader who values interpersonal relations as an independent entity of the situation is also required, by the institutional norms implicit in the LPC instructions, to refer to a worker who performs poorly in his job. If this leader is able to differentiate between particularistic and non-particularistic aspects of the situation, he can then recognize that an ineffective worker may still be quite attractive as an individual; in this case his LPC score will tend to be rather high. When, however, the least preferred co-worker happens to be not only a poor performer, but also an unpleasant individual, then the LPC score will be low, in spite of the high differentiation and of the interpersonal orientation of the leader.

To complete the picture, there are two additional types of leader to be considered: those who are relations-oriented and have low differentiation, and high differentiators with task motivation. As we have already suggested, these two types are likely to be rather infrequent, at least in Western culture. A relations-oriented low differentiator will tend to consider performance as subordinate to interpersonal rapport: regardless of the quality of performance, somebody who is warm and friendly is perceived as a good worker and the person who is cold and hostile is also seen as a poor performer. This type of leader will thus tend to have a low LPC score. An individual presenting this motivational-cognitive combination is, in effect, attempting to turn the work situation, characterized by non-particularistic exchanges, into an institution providing him with the particularistic resources he needs. This position, deviating from the prevailing institutional norms, is probably quite infrequent.

Another anomalous combination occurs when a high differentiator is task-motivated. If interpersonal relations are of secondary interest to him, what is the point of separating them from his main source of motivation, the task, in an institutional setting which fits his motivational preferences? High differentiation would be nonfunctional here, and it seems unlikely that this combination will occur in sizeable frequency. If a leader who neither pays attention to the personal attributes of his workers, nor infers them from their task performance does indeed exist, he will probably experience difficulties in rating his least preferred co-worker.

In summary, high differentiation is functional only when the main need occurs for resources which are not typical of the institution in which the exchange takes place. It appears, therefore, that in most cases, a low LPC leader will be a low differentiator and task-oriented, while a high LPC leader will tend to be a high differentiator and to value more interpersonal relations. The measurement of the motivational and structural states provided by the LPC instrument is somewhat indirect. A more direct and separate observation of the hierarchy of needs and of the degree of the differentiation among them is, however, desirable in order to open the problem of their interrelationship to empirical investigation. Nevertheless, there has been accumulating evidence regarding the relationship between the LPC measure and the degree of differentiation, to which we now turn.

LPC as a Measure of Differentiation

If subjects with high LPC scores do differentiate more between task and interpersonal attributes, one should expect that the correlation between task and interpersonal items of the LPC instrument will be lower for high LPC respondents than for low LPC ones, as high correlation indicates low differentiation. This hypothesis was tested on 167 subjects, dichotomized at the median, so that 85 had low LPC and 82 high LPC scores (Mitchell, 1970). For each subject, a separate score was computed for task items, interpersonal items, and for a residual class of items which were somewhere between the first two classes. The sum of these three scores is, of course, the original LPC score. Two items were found to be task-relevant: efficient-inefficient and helpful-frustrating. Three items were classified as mixed: cooperative-uncooperative; supportive-hostile; and self-assured-hesitant. The remaining 12 items were considered interpersonal. Some examples are: friendly-unfriendly; tense-relaxed; cold-warm; open-guarded. The correlations between the scores on the three types of items, computed separately for low and high LPC, are given in Table 45.

Table 45

INTERCORRELATION AMONG SCORES FOR THREE TYPES OF
LPC ITEMS FOR HIGH AND LOW LPC SUBJECTS

Type of Items	High LPC			Low LPC		
	Task	Mixed	Inter-per-sonal	Task	Mixed	Inter-per-sonal
Task	—	40	−05	—	54	20
Mixed	40	—	23	54	—	26
Interpersonal	−05	23	—	20	26	—

Note: Decimal point omitted.

First let us note that, for both low and high LPC, the correlation between task and interpersonal scores is lower than the correlation of either of these scores with the mixed score; thus the mixed variable occupies an intermediate position between the two others. This lends some support to our classification of items into three types. More directly relevant to our hypothesis is the fact that each correlation for the group of low LPC subjects is higher than the corresponding one for the high LPC subjects, as predicted. The probability of obtaining these differences under random conditions is $p < .01$. The statistical test used here and in some of the analyses that follow determines the probability of two matrices being from the same population (Cooley and Lohnes, 1962). Even for the low LPC subjects, however, the correlation between task and interpersonal variables is quite low: although they differentiate less than the high LPC subjects, they still employ some differentiation between the two types of items.

The internal analysis of the LPC instrument cannot be regarded as conclusive. In fact, if the LPC score is related to differentiation between interpersonal relations and the task, difference in complexity should be reflected not only by responses on the LPC scale, but also by other behavioral variables where these classes appear. A more stringent test of the hypothesis is provided by the results of another study with different subjects and including variables other than LPC (Mitchell and Foa, 1969).

After completing an experimental group task, 32 leaders rated their groups on the following five scales: Task performance of the group; the leaders' own task performance; the leaders' behavior toward the group as a whole; the leader's behavior toward individual group members, and behavior of the group toward the group (e.g., the group atmosphere was pleasant). The intercorrelation among the five scales for the 16 high and 16 low LPC leaders is given in Table 46. High intercorrelations indicate an undifferentiated perception of the situation, while low intercorrelations indicate more differentiation. According to our hypothesis, correlations should be higher for the low LPC leaders. With the exception of only one case, the correlation between any two given variables is indeed lower for the high LPC leader than for the low LPC leader. For example, the correlation between the leader's ratings describing his behavior toward the task and those describing his behavior toward a member is .44 for the high LPC leader and .72 for the low LPC leader. The difference between the two correlation matrices is significant at the $p < .01$ level. Since a lower correlation coefficient indicates more differentiation, the results support the idea that the high LPC leader differentiates more than the low LPC leader between task and interpersonal behavior, as well as between his own behavior and group behavior.

Table 46

INTERCORRELATION AMONG RATING SCALES FOR
HIGH AND LOW LPC LEADERS

Leader Rating of:	High LPC					Low LPC				
	GT	LT	LG	LM	GG	GT	LT	LG	LM	GG
Performance of Group Task (GT)	—	47	41	16	69	—	65	79	63	46
Performance of Leader Task (LT)	47	—	72	44	36	65	—	75	72	46
Leader Behavior to Group (LG)	41	72	—	80	47	79	75	—	93	57
Leader's Behavior to Group Members (LM)	16	44	80	—	32	63	72	93	—	57
Group Behavior to Group (GG)	69	36	47	32	—	46	46	57	57	—

SOME CORRELATES OF THE LPC SCORE. Further, but indirect support for the cognitive interpretation of the LPC score is provided by its relationship to a number of other complexity and interpersonal variables. If differentiation may be specific to a given dimension, as suggested by Scott (1963) and Vannoy (1965), the relationship between the LPC score and general measures of differentiation cannot be considered decisive with regard to the present interpretation of LPC. Yet some relations have been found, but not consistently. A sample of 100 University of Illinois students completed two of Scott's (1962) sorting tasks. They were asked to arrange a list of objects (nations, groups, etc.) into categories which "belong together" and to indicate what they thought the objects had in common. Thus, Italy, Greece, and Spain might be classified as peninsulas; Spain, Yugoslavia and others as dictatorships, etc. The score indicates the number of different dimensions used by the subject in sorting a set of objects like groups or nations. The LPC score of these subject correlated .51 with the group domain and .28 with the nations domain of Scott's sorting task. The correlation between these two sorting tasks was .57. Lower correlations, but in the same order, were obtained for female subjects who, on the average, tended to have considerably less previous experience in work groups. This result has been replicated (Mitchell, 1970) with a sample of 49 males yielding a correlation of .49 ($p < .05$). A later replication (Larson and Rowland, 1972a), however, did not show any significant relationship.

The theoretical considerations and the results reviewed so far lend support to the hypothesis that the LPC score, which constitutes the basis for classifying leaders, provides some indication of the extent to which the subject differentiates between the particularistic resources exchanged in interpersonal relations and the less particularistic ones involved in the performance of the task. Let us now turn to analyze the group situation, i.e., the social event confronting the leader.

Resource Differentiation in Task Situation

The contingency model postulates three dichotomized variables (leader-member relations, task structure, and the leader's power position) which were originally used by Fiedler (1967) for ordering task situations according to the degree of difficulty faced by the group leader. The first variable, leader-member relations, refers to the degree of difficulty in the interpersonal area. The situation is assumed to be less difficult when these are good than when they are poor. The second variable, task structure, refers to difficulty in the task area: A structured task is less difficult for the leader than an unstructured one since it provides the leader with greater influence and control. Position power is also a task variable as its usefulness for the leader appears to be inversely related to task structure. Fiedler (1967, p. 144) notes that the degree of formal leadership power is less important when the task is highly structured. More power will, therefore, be needed in an unstructured task than in a structured one to retain the same degree of control over task performance. A situation with an unstructured task will be easier for the leader when he has high power. Task structure and position power thus appear to be in some respects interchangeable aspects of the task situation, both affecting the leader's control of task-oriented behavior.

The first variable, leader-member relations, refers to particularistic exchanges of love and, to a lesser extent, of status, between leader and members. The two task variables—structure and formal power—involve less particularistic resources. Formal power is usually meant to indicate that the leader has control over the promotion, demotion, transfer of members and the monetary rewards; contrary to our definition of power (Ch. 5), the current usage of the term "powerful" does not apply to a leader who has to rely on the liking and respect of group members: "The leader with low position power . . . . must be continually aware that his hold on his group members is tenuous and dependent on his personal relations with the individuals in his group" (Fiedler, 1967, p. 25). Thus the term "position power" indicates whether or not the leader is able to modify the amount of non-particularistic resources received by group members.

Both in structured and unstructured tasks, the group is required to provide non-particularistic resources; yet the resources appropriate to a structured task appear likely to differ from those of an unstructured one along the second dimension of the structure of resources—concreteness. In a structured task, members will be expected to perform concrete activities, i.e., to provide services; in an unstructured task, the exchange of information, a more symbolic resource, is likely to be prominent. Workers on an assembly line (a typical structured task) will have scarce need to exchange information; their job is to perform a concrete operation on a given good and to move it forward to the next man in the line. The situation, as Fiedler notes (1967, p. 27), is quite different in a committee planning policy; here a great deal of information will be exchanged among group participants.

The analysis of types of leaders and situations in terms of resources indicates that a more precise specification of the resource involved in each situation and of the degree to which the leader differentiates among resources appears desirable in future research on the optimal match between leaders and situations; the data presently available, however, do permit consideration of the gross distinction between the more particularistic resources involved in the leader-member relations, and the less particularistic ones necessary for the task execution.

When the situation is either very easy or very difficult, the interpersonal and task aspects will tend to be equally favorable or equally unfavorable to the leader, so that no differentiation will be required between them. However, this is not the case in situations of intermediate favorableness. Here, a particular aspect, say, leader-member relations, may be favorable, while another one, e.g., task structure, is unfavorable. Thus, a situation of medium favorableness is likely to be more differentiated than a situation in which leader-member relations as well as position power and task structure are very favorable or unfavorable. When group situations are ordered from least to most favorable, the differentiation among the various aspects of the situation, according to level of favorableness, will necessarily be minimal at the extremes (all good or all bad) and it will increase toward the midpoint of the situational favorableness continuum (some good and some bad). It should be expected, then, that a leader who differentiates (high LPC) will find it easier to perform in a situation presenting difficulties in either interpersonal relations or task, thus requiring differentiation between them. A low LPC leader, on the other hand, will find it easier to perform when both or neither the task and the interpersonal relations present difficulties, so that a differentiation between them is unnecessary. A leader making a differentiation not required by the situation will tend to focus attention on a given aspect rather than on the total situation, so that he will be less effective.

Cognitive and Situational Differentiation Compared

To test whether the contingency model can be reinterpreted in cognitive terms, the results of a large number of studies reported by Fiedler and his associates (Fiedler, 1967) were re-analysed (Foa et al., 1971), together with some more recent data (Chemers and Skrzypek, 1972; Rice and Chemers, 1973). These studies give the correlation between the LPC score of the leader and measure of task performance, under various conditions of situational favorableness. In the reanalysis, situations were classified according to whether they presented difficulties in either the interpersonal or task aspects, in neither aspect, or in both. According to our hypothesis, the high LPC leader should perform more effectively when only one aspect of the situation is difficult, so that the correlation between LPC and performance should be positive in this case. The low LPC leader, on the other hand, should be more effective in situations which are difficult in both aspects or in neither aspect, so that these correlations should be negative.

Table 47 gives the frequency distribution of 80 correlation coefficients between performance and LPC score according to the sign of the correlation and to the favorableness of the situation in the task and interpersonal areas. The correlation is negative when the two areas are undifferentiated; the low LPC leader is more effective in this situation. When the two areas differ in favorableness, the high LPC leader obtains better performance; the correlations are positive. In Octants 3 and 7, unstructured task and strong position, the task situation has been labeled as favorable, in keeping with the notion that strong power will reduce the difficulty posed by the unstructured task. The results in these two octants are not clear-cut as in the other octants but still support the proposed effect of high position power: most coefficients have the predicted sign, negative in octant 3 and positive in octant 7. The appearance of some coefficients deviating from prediction in these two octants suggests that strong position power and an unstructured task do not produce a task situation as favorable as the one with a structured task.

Table 47

SIGN OF CORRELATION BETWEEN PERFORMANCE AND LPC SCORES
AS RELATED TO THE SITUATION

Octant	Leader-Member Relations	Task Structure	Leader's Position Power	Favorableness of the situation with respect to Interpersonal Relations	Task	Frequency of positive and negative correlations between leader LPC and group performance Positive	Negative
1	Good	Structured	Strong	High	High	—	10
2	Good	Structured	Weak	High	High	—	6
3	Good	Unstructured	Strong	High	High	4	10
4	Good	Unstructured	Weak	High	Low	11	1
5	Poor	Structured	Strong	Low	High	7	—
6	Poor	Structured	Weak	Low	High	2	—
7	Poor	Unstructured	Strong	Low	High	10	4
8	Poor	Unstructured	Weak	Low	Low	1	14

Further evidence pointing in the same direction is provided by other investigators. Michaelsen (1971) found that the correlation between leader's score on interpersonal orientation and group performance was positive in situations of intermediate difficulty and negative when the situation was either very favorable or very difficult. These results are of particular interest since they indirectly support the proposition that high LPC leaders tend to be relations-oriented. The other side of the coin—relationship between LPC score and cognitive differentiation—was further explored in two studies by Mitchell (1970). In both studies subjects were asked to make judgments about situations which included information about the structure of the task and the interpersonal relations. The results indicated that the high LPC subjects used more varied information and used it in a more differentiated way than did the low LPC subjects. It appears, therefore, that the effect of differentiation matching between situation and leader has been fairly well clarified.

The matching notion has been supported under other conditions as well. Using measures of differentiation of a different type, Tuckman (1967) was able to show that high differentiators perform significantly better than low differentiators in an abstract and unstructured group task. However, in this study low differentiators were not found superior to higher ones in a more routine and structured task. Tuckman hypothesized that matching of performers to task is only one of the conditions leading to success; another variable is the degree of matching among group members. It is not clear from Tuckman's data whether superior performance occurs when all group members have the same level of complexity or when there is some variance among them in this respect. His findings would have been easier to interpret had he restricted his manipulation to complexity matching, instead of combining it with degree of dominance. Previous studies by Tuckman

(1964) and by Schroder, Driver, and Streufert (1967) have shown that groups composed of abstract members (complex) perform better on complex tasks than groups composed of concrete members.

Behavior of Low and High LPC Leaders Under Stress

We have seen that leaders who are high differentiators and motivated towards interpersonal relations do better in a differentiated situation, while leaders with lower differentiation and with task-orientation are more effective when the situation does not call for differentiation. These results suggest behavioral differences between high and low LPC leaders and raise the possibility that within each type of leader, behavior may vary under different conditions. A number of studies dealing with behavioral differences have been conducted; in these studies, the leader's behavior is usually classified into two classes, behavior pertinent to relations with group members and behavior directly relevant to performance of the task. The frequency of each class is then compared between the two types of leaders, for situations which are more or less stressful to him. Thus, in essence, these investigations are concerned with the frequency of emitting particularistic and non-particularistic resources by the various types of leaders under various types of stresses. Within this general outline, there are considerable variations in the design of the various studies, so that we should be cautious in the comparison of their results. In one study, for example (Fiedler, Meuwese and Oonk, 1961), the behavior of the group, rather than the behavior of the leader constitutes the dependent variable. Techniques for classifying the leader's behavior also vary widely both in terms of the categories used and the method of observation. In one study (Fiedler, 1966) the data were obtained from post-experiment rating of the leader by group members, in other studies, direct observation was employed. When this latter method was used, there is a strong possibility that non-verbal interpersonal messages (tone of voice, gestures, etc.) may have escaped the attention of the observer, particularly when these messages are emitted concurrently with a verbal communication pertaining to the task; this eventuality will result in reducing the recorded frequency of communications pertaining to group relations. Finally, in some of the investigations the type of stress is ambiguous: stress results in increased difficulty in the situation. We have seen previously that some difficulties refer to group relations while others pertain to the performance of the task. It seems, therefore, desirable to classify stresses according to the type of difficulty they produce and to use types of stress which are clearly related to either performance or interpersonal relations, rather than stresses which are open to varying interpretations. We shall return to this point when discussing the results of these investigations.

Several of these studies have been reviewed by Fiedler (1971, a) who reached the conclusion that under stress, each type of leader increases the emission of behavior in the area where his need is greatest; thus, Fiedler proposes, the low LPC leader, being task motivated, puts more efforts in task performance when the situation is stressful; in the same situation, the relations-motivated high LPC leader increases his relations-oriented behavior.

There is a clear parallel between this formulation and behavior in disaster situations (Killian, 1952); when one cannot satisfy more than one goal, he will tend to choose the one most important to him. This element of mutually exclusive choices is not, however, clearly apparent in the stress situations devised for studying the behavior of the leader; in none of them was the leader faced with a sharp alternative between relations and performance.

Although the theoretical explanation proposed by Fiedler has not yet been entirely proved, there is clear evidence that, under stress, the low LPC leader decreases his emission of relations-oriented behavior and increases behavior bearing on task performance. The response of the high LPC leader is, however, less consistent: sometimes his behavioral change is indeed opposite to that of the low LPC leader; yet in some other studies, the behavioral patterns of the two types of leaders appear quite similar.

Before examining the relevant evidence, let us introduce some theoretical considerations. If indeed the low LPC leader does not differentiate much between task and interpersonal aspects of the situation, then he should notice that the situation is difficult without attempting to analyze whether the difficulty lies in group relations or in the task; for him, group relations are subordinated to, and depending on, the task so that any difficulty stems from the task: this leader will therefore increase his task oriented behavior when under *any kind* of stress. Consequently, he will do poorly when the stress is restricted to relations, but do well when it is mainly related to the task.

The high LPC leader, on the other hand, does differentiate between performance and relations so that he is expected to intensify his behavior in the area where stress occurs. If the difficulty is group relations, he will send more messages in this area, thus behaving contrarily to the low LPC leader in the same situation. When, however, stress is task related, he will behave just like the low LPC leader and intensify task relevant behavior. In consequence, the high LPC leader will be more effective when the difficulties are either related to the task or to interpersonal aspects; his differentiation will become a hindrance when both difficulties are prominent.

In summary, it is predicted that when stress is higher, the low LPC

Table 48

PERCENTAGE FREQUENCY OF RELATIONS- AND TASK-RELEVANT BEHAVIOR OF HIGH AND LOW LPC LEADERS BY TYPE AND INTENSITY OF STRESS

Study	Stress Type	Intensity	Low LPC Relations	Low LPC Task	High LPC Relations	High LPC Task	Remarks
Dutch, Fiedler, 1967 p. 187	Relations	Low: homogenous group, appointed leader	33	66	24	75	Behavior of whole group, not leader only.
		Medium: homogeneous group, elected leader or heterogeneous group, appointed leader	33	67	33	67	
		High: heterogeneous group, elected leader	24	76	30	62	
ROTC, Fiedler, 1967 p. 190	Relations	Low: good group atmosphere, by leader rating	40	55	21	73	Groups without external stress only. Relations include: group participation and democratic leadership; Task: new ideas and integrating ideas.
		High: medium or poor group atmosphere	28	65	33	60	
Study I, Larson & Rowland, 1972,b.	Relations	Low: subject requested to help in improving test	54	46	27	73	
		High: test to probe progress made at management course	12	88	69	21	
Study II, Larson & Rowland, 1972,b.	Same	Low: as above	56	44	33	67	
		High: as above	24	76	68	32	
ROTC, Fiedler, 1967 p. 190	Task(?)	Low: no superior officer present	32	61	29	65	For different levels of group atmosphere combined
		High: presence of rating senior officer	27	66	27	66	
Ayer, 1968, a	Task(?)	Low: no superior officer present	23	77	22	78	As summarized in Fiedler, 1971, a
		Medium: presence of approving senior officer	12	88	18	82	
		High: presence of disapproving senior officer	14	86	18	82	

leader will increase the frequency of task relevant behavior, irrespective of the type of stress, while the high LPC leader will increase the behavior which is relevant to the specific stress. To test these hypotheses the data available from several studies have been reanalyzed; they are presented in Table 48. The results are given in percentage form irrespective of the form they were presented in the original study; often the original classification of behaviors involved more classes than those presented here, so that the percentage of task-oriented and of relations-relevant behaviors does not always add up to 100 percent. For this as well as for reasons previously noted, the data cannot be compared across studies, but only within each one of them.

To the original presentations, we have added a classification of stresses into relation- and task-pertinent. In the first two studies on top of Table 48, stress clearly involved particularistic resources. In the two sets of Larson's data, essentially a replication of the same experiment, stress was produced by telling the subjects, who were officials participating in a management training program, that their results would be used to measure what they had learned, with implicit possibility that this could affect their future career in the agency, and thus the stress seems to be task-related. However, in view of the fact that the seminar focused on human relation problems, the stress may be interpreted as pertinent to interpersonal relations. In the last two batches of data in Table 48, the stress consisted of having a senior officer watching the performance of the group; once more, this kind of stress is open to different interpretations; since, however, the members were to perform on their job, it seems reasonable to assume that the senior officer was perceived by the subjects as an evaluator of the job done, rather than supervising the relations among group members. Thus, in these two last studies, stress was classified as task-relevant.

Let us now discuss the results. In all stress situations, irrespective of type, the low LPC leader decreases the emission of relations-oriented behavior and increases the behavior relevant to the task; this pattern is repeated, without exception, in all the six sets of data. An opposite pattern of change is found in the high LPC leader when stress refers to relations; relations-related behavior increases in frequency, with a corresponding decrease in task-related behavior. In the two last studies in Table 48, where stress refers to task performance, the picture presented by the high LPC leader is identical with the one given by the low LPC: relations-oriented behavior decreases, while task-oriented behavior increases.

An experiment investigating the effect of both relations- and task-stress was done by Barron (1967); subjects were senior R.O.T.C. cadets from the Army and the Navy, assigned to 54 three-man teams, 18 teams to each stress condition. For the low stress groups, cadets wore civilian clothes and were assured that the results would not become part of their record. In the relations-stress condition, conflict was created in the team by various devices including mixing Navy and Army cadets, all in uniform, and appointing the lowest in rank as leader. In the task-stress a high ranking Army officer watched the task performance and expressed dissatisfaction with it. All teams were given two tasks in succession: the first one consisted of formulating a proposal for equalizing financial benefits in the R.O.T.C. program; teams were then asked to compose a short story, suitable for elementary school children, on national defense problems. Team activity was recorded and leader behavior was noted from the typescript.

Table 49

LEADER'S BEHAVIOR IN DIFFERENT STRESS CONDITIONS

Stress	Behavior			
	Low LPC		*High LPC*	
	Relations	Task	Relations	Task
Low	49	51	40	60
High in Relations	44	56	49	51
High in Task	42	58	38	62

To test our hypothesis the data were re-analyzed: the results for the "story" task are given in Table 49. Changes in leader's behavior for the various types of stress are small but in the predicted direction: under either type of stress low LPC leader increased the relative frequency of task-oriented behavior; high LPC leaders, on the other hand, increased the type of behavior which is relevant to the type of stress. In the other task, preparation of proposal, both types of leader increased, however, task oriented behavior when under stress. The results reviewed tend to support the hypothesis that under stress the high LPC person will "gear" his behavior to the type of stress, while the low LPC individual will indiscriminately increase focus on the task. Some uncertainty remains regarding the classification of stress situations. In any event, it is quite clear that the low LPC leader exhibits consistent behavioral changes when under stress, while the high LPC leader may either increase or decrease his relations-oriented behavior. Some further research, where the type of stress is systematically varied, is required before the relationship between degree of differentiation and change in behavior can be clearly demonstrated.

Irrespective of the situation and the type of leader, the frequency of task-oriented behavior is usually higher; as previously noted, this result may be artifactual: relations-oriented behavior is often non-verbal and thus more difficult to observe and to record. In Larson's experiment, there was no possibility of sending non-verbal messages, since all communication was in writing; it is perhaps not by chance that the only cases in which task-oriented behavior is lower than relations-oriented appear precisely in this study. Even after controlling for this possible artifact of observation, we can still expect that the frequency of task-oriented behavior will be high; after all, this behavior involves non-particularistic resources which are typical of the institutional setting within which the studies took place.

Effects of Leader's Training and Experience on Performance

We have seen that when the leader's degree of differentiation between task and relations matches the degree required by the situation, better performance is obtained. These findings suggest that any manipulation which increases matching will improve performance, while a manipulation decreasing matching will impair it. Training and experience appear to be manipulations which affect matching in either direction.

In his careful review of the literature, Fiedler (1971b) has shown that trained or experienced leaders do not, on the average, perform better or worse than do untrained or inexperienced ones. In one study, for example, the performance of groups led by petty officers of the Belgian Navy was compared to the performance of groups led by a recruit (Fiedler, 1966). The petty officers had two years of formal training and an average of ten years of experience; the recruits had, of course, neither training nor experience; the two types of leader were matched on intelligence and LPC score. The experimental tasks were fairly similar to those performed by petty officers in the regular course of their duties. In all the tasks, mean performance scores for groups led by petty officers were about the same as for those groups which had a recruit as leader.

The evidence mustered by Fiedler on the ineffectiveness of training and experience may appear startling: it certainly runs against the common belief that an experienced or well-trained individual will do a better job. We have seen, however, that higher quality of performance is obtained when the leader's degree of differentiation between task and relations matches the degree required by the situation. It seems therefore appropriate to inquire about the effects of training and experience on such matching: when training or experience increase matching, performance will improve; when they result in more mismatching, the quality of performance will be impaired. Averaging these contrasting effects over several groups may then show that training and experience have no influence on performance.

There are two possible ways in which matching may be affected: modification of the leader's style or change in the situation. Fiedler (1971b) has proposed that training and experience make the situation easier for the leader: if training is in human relations, it may help the leader improve his relationship to group members; if it is technical, it will tend to make the task more structured; experience may have similar effects. In both cases, Fiedler suggests, the situation will become less difficult. It was found that low LPC leaders perform better in extreme situations, while high LPC leaders are more successful in situations of intermediate difficulty. Suppose now that, as a result of training or experience, a very difficult situation becomes one of intermediate difficulty: this change in difficulty will improve the performance of the high LPC leader, while impairing that of the low LPC leader who does better in a situation of extreme difficulty. If on the other hand, a moderately difficult situation becomes an easy one following training, opposite results will be expected: now the low LPC leader will improve while the performance of the high LPC will be impaired. In both cases, the average effect of training on performance will be negligible if both types of leaders are nearly equally represented in the population of trainees.

The results provided by Fiedler do not directly test his hypothesis that training or experience make the situation easier. They rather show that experience (or training) is positively related to performance when the situation is extreme and the leader's LPC score is low, or when the difficulty is intermediate and the leader's LPC score is high. Under the remaining conditions, the relation between training and performance is negative. In other words, when the leader is matched to the situation, experience (or training) is useful, while being deleterious in an unmatched situation. It should be noted that the situation considered is the one existing *after* training. If we assume, with Fiedler, that *before* training the situation was more difficult than following it, then these results can be explained by the proposed effect of training on the degree of situational difficulty.

The suggestion that training modifies the situation raises some theoretical and practical problems: if the degree of situational difficulty is relative to a specific leader, it cannot be assessed independently, apart from the leader's ability. In consequence, the process of assigning an appropriate leader to a given situation becomes much more complex. Suppose, for example, that the situation is considered as being of intermediate difficulty; according to the previous findings we shall assign a high LPC leader to this group. Having found such a leader, we may discover that *for him* the situation presents no difficulty. Should we then conclude that the situation is easy and thus requires a low LPC leader?

These problems are avoided by the alternative possibility that training influences matching by affecting the leader's style rather than the situational difficulty. After all, it is the leader and not the situation who has been trained or has acquired experience. The notions of assimilation and contrast in attitude change (Triandis, 1971, pp. 194–198) may provide some guidance in conceptualizing the possible effects of training on the LPC score. Suppose a leader is exposed to human relations training, where the importance of paying attention to the interpersonal relationship with the workers is stressed: if the trainee is fairly high in LPC, exposure to such training will increase his LPC by a process of assimilation; if, however, the trainee is rather low in LPC, a contrasting effect will take place, causing him to become even lower. Task oriented training may operate along the same lines, but in the opposite direction: by assimilating effect, those low on LPC will become even lower, while high LPC will become higher, through the contrast effect. Thus, training, and possibly also experience, may result in more extreme LPC scores.

How will this proposed change in the LPC affect performance? Consider, for example, a leader with a moderately high LPC who performs rather well in a mixed situation; if his LPC increases following training, his performance will improve; thus, for this combination of type of leader and situation, the relationship between performance and training will be positive. A moderately low LPC leader, on the other hand, will do rather poorly in the same situation; if after training, his LPC decreases, performance will be even worse; hence a negative relationship is expected here between performance and training. In general, when the situation and the leader are matched, a more extreme LPC score following training, will result in improving performance; training and performance will be positively related. When there is mismatching between leader and situation, training will increase this mismatch through producing a more extreme LPC score, thus decreasing efficiency of performance; here the relationship between training and performance will be negative.

These predictions are quite consistent with the results obtained by Fiedler (1971b). Yet there is no evidence about the proposition that training or experience will modify the LPC score in the specific way we suggested; there is however some support for the more general notion that this score is affected by environmental factors: Muller (1970) randomly assigned leaders to experimental task groups; these groups differed in closeness of supervision and thus, presumably, in the frequency of interaction between leader and members; in half of the teams a report on performance was required from the leader every five minutes and in the other half only every 15 minutes. The LPC form was administered at the end of the task which lasted 50 minutes. Leaders who reported more often had a significantly higher LPC score than those who reported at longer intervals.

Although this finding suggests that the LPC score is changeable, a decision as to whether training modifies matching by changing the situation or by changing the leader's cognition must await further investigations. What appears clear so far is that training and experience have either positive or negative effects on performance, depending on the type of leader and on the type of situation.

The research on leadership just reviewed has provided an abundance of data for exploring the effects of cognitive matching as well as the relationship between cognition and behavior. We have seen that performance is improved when the leader's differentiation is matched to the situation and that highly differentiating leaders are more flexible in their behavior; this degree of differentiation may be modified by environmental factors such as training and experience.

More generally it has been argued here that cognitive matching is a necessary condition for effective interpersonal communication and therefore is vital for the exchange of resources: resources are, indeed, given and taken via social communication. Interpersonal communication contains not only specific resources but structural information as well: the structure of the message reflects the cognitive structure of its sender and may or may not fit the structure of the receiver. This structural aspect of communication acquires special significance when its recipient is an infant. While communication among adults serves mainly as a channel for provision of resources, for a child it has the dual purpose of supplying resources as well as the structural information necessary for his cognitive growth. Let us turn to describe the manner in which parent-infant communication affects cognitive development.

PARENT-INFANT COMMUNICATION

In Chapter 2 (pp. 47–48) we have briefly discussed the relationship between the parents' behavior and the degree of differentiation acquired by the infant. The very fact that a given message or encounter is consistently contingent upon certain environmental conditions and/or the infant's behavior, reflects an association among events, i.e., a structural pattern. Moreover, messages often contain more than one resource; these resources are not randomly paired but again reflect the structure of the sender: resources proximal in his structure will appear jointly more often than remote ones. While, as we said, adults utilize mainly the content of the message, infants process both the structural and the substantive aspects of it. The content supplies the resources he needs while the structure provides information for his cognitive development.

Two consequences stem from these considerations:

1. When the cognitive structure of the parent is at variance with the prevailing culture, the child is likely to develop a similarly deviant structure.

2. Early deprivation has more long-lasting effects than deprivation which occurs later in life, since it impairs cognitive development.

The first consequence was discussed briefly in Chapter 2. Here we would like to share with the reader some thoughts regarding the effect of early deprivation on cognitive development.

Cognitive Deprivation

The term cognitive deprivation is used in the psychological literature to denote several different conditions (Cole and Bruner, 1971; Jessor and Richardson, 1968, p. 2). The most common usage refers to situations where a resource is not provided in sufficient amounts. In the same way that a child who is not fed enough is deprived of food, the one who has few encounters with adults or met with indifference is deprived of love and possibly services. An extreme instance of this condition is represented by those experiments in which animals are raised in isolation.

Another use of the term deprivation refers to situations where a resource is often taken away. Here the number of parent-child exchanges may be as high as for a non-deprived child; but the total amount of "taking away" a particular resource will exceed the amount of "giving," so that the receiver can still be considered a deprived individual. This latter usage of the notion deprivation is mostly applied to particularistic resources, especially to services, love and status, a condition also indicated by terms such as parental rejection.

Empirical evidence suggests three main consequences of early deprivation:

1. A narrower optimal range in the resource involved.
2. Isolation or low frequency of exchanges does not provide enough opportunity for the development of cognitive structures.
3. Rejection leads to different mapping rules and deviant degrees of differentiation.

THE OPTIMAL RANGE. There is evidence that an insufficient amount of a given resource in early life narrows its optimal range (see Ch. 5, pp. 127–130) by lowering its upper limit; thus the actual need becomes smaller, although the potential need may be quite high. A limited range reduces the ability to receive the resource, and leads to withdrawal from contacts in which this resource may be received. Results supporting this proposition with regard to love were reported by Harlow and Suomi (1970). One baby monkey was raised with a warm surrogate mother for one month, then with a cold surrogate for one week and again with the warm mother for another week. The opposite sequence was adopted for the second baby monkey, so that he spent the first four weeks with a cold mother, one week with a warm one then he was switched again to the cold surrogate. The authors describe the results so clearly that we could not do any better than quote them: "This infant (the second one) became anything but attached to the cold surrogate during the initial four-week period, spending most of his time huddling in the corner of his cage. . . . In succeeding weeks, even with the warm surrogate, he failed to approach the levels of contact exhibited by the other infant to the cold surrogate. Apparently, being raised with a cold mother had chilled him to mothers in general, even those bearing warmth and comfort" (p. 167).

A complete withdrawal from love exchanges was practiced by "Joey: A Mechanical Boy" (Bettelheim, 1959). Again it was not an excessive amount of punishment that brought Joey to such withdrawal but rather extreme indifference on the parts of his parents. "We were struck especially by her (the mother's) total indifference as she talked about Joey," ". . . Joey's existence never registered with his mother," notices Bettelheim. As a result of these experiences Joey was not able to process any love relationship. Mirsky (1968) in summarizing the effects of early isolation states "that the (isolated) animals manifested only minimal social interactions, and those that did occur were of an increasingly aggressive nature" (p. 133).

With regard to deprivation of another resource, information, Hunt (1961) provided an exhaustive review of findings in animals and humans and concluded thus: "It is fairly clear from the evidence surveyed in these chapters that impoverishment of experience during the early months can slow up the development of intelligence" (p. 346).

In these studies deprivation was mainly due to lack of giving. Rosen and D'Andrade (1959), however, investigated the effects of actual taking and found that dominating fathers (i.e., fathers who take away status) tended to have sons who were low on need for achievement. Once more, early deprivation resulted in lowering the *actual* need, this time the need for status.

DEFICIENT COGNITIVE DEVELOPMENT. Isolation, or a low amount of social stimulation not only deprives the young individual of resources, thus narrowing his optimal range, but denies him the structural information required for his cognitive development. Mason (1968) observed that rhesus monkeys raised in isolation later exhibited deficiencies in social communication. Thus for example, sexual cues coming from a female would initiate a non-sexual play (a clear case of mis-mapping) or be ignored altogether. Mirsky (1968) demonstrated the absence of mapping rules in his "cooperative-conditioning" experiment. Monkeys were conditioned to press a lever upon exposure to a visual stimulus in order to avoid shock. When animals had acquired the avoidance response they were paired in an experiment in which one monkey received the conditioned stimulus but did not have access to the lever. The second monkey in the pair did not receive the conditioned stimulus but could reach the lever. The latter animal was, however, able to watch the facial expression of his partner. Wild-born animals were successful in encoding and decoding this facial expression, so that when the one who was exposed to the conditioned stimulus showed signs of distress the other monkey pressed the lever. By contrast, animals raised in isolation were incapable of sending the appropriate message or of interpreting the message sent to them, even after three years of social experience. Interestingly, these monkeys learned the avoidance task just as well as those who were not isolated in infancy: it seems, therefore, that social isolation interfered mostly with the learning of the appropriate mapping rules for facial expressions.

Structural deprivation occurs also when the individual is raised in an inconsistent environment which, like isolation, does not allow for the formation of distinct classes and for the development of mapping rules. Indeed the hyperexcitability of previously isolated monkeys resembles the unorganized behavioral patterns of monkeys who were faced with a random schedule after being taught an elaborate signal for obtaining food and avoiding shock (Masserman, 1970).

There is, however, an important difference between isolation or scarce stimulation and disorganized environment: the former deprives the young organism of both resources and structural information; the latter is deficient in structural information, but does not necessarily involve resource deprivation. On the contrary, inconsistency usually implies the administration of both reward and punishment, although in an unorganized manner; consequently the optimal range may be quite normal in this condition. It is not surprising therefore, that while isolation results in withdrawal, inconsistent socialization leads to over-dependency: difficulties in cognitive development interfere with the achievement of autonomy; at the same time a normal range allows for social contacts. Fisher (cited by Higgins, 1968) exposed dog puppies to a 13 weeks socialization period. One group received petting and fondling whenever they approached the experimenter. The other group received the same treatment with the addition of an equal number of sessions in which they were handled roughly or shocked whenever they approached the experimenter. The "inconsistent-environment" group was found more dependent as measured by the amount of time the animal spent near a quietly sitting person. This group appeared also more fearful of humans than was the group raised under consistent conditions.

COGNITIVE DEVIANCE. The proposition that a certain amount of deprivation or frustration is necessary for cognitive development was discussed in Chapter 2 and seems to have gained considerable acceptance; Jessor and Richardson (1968), for example, suggested that the development of high self-exteem requires a combination of acceptance and limiting rules (i.e., frustration). Some supportive evidence was provided by Mason (1968) who found that monkeys raised with moving rather than stationary dummies were less fearful, more active, moved more in the cage and were quicker to interact with people. The author explained these differences on the basis of the occasional frustration imposed on the infants by the moving dummy.

When rejection becomes predominant, different consequences are likely to happen: the most obvious one is narrowing of the optimal range as a result of resource deprivation. There are also some indications of possible cognitive deviation. Harsh punishment administered by the parents was found to be an antecedent of low self-esteem (Coopersmith, 1967); in an individual lacking self-esteem the differentiation between actual and ideal level is likely to be stronger than in individuals having a higher self-esteem. Consequently the experience of success will be perceived as a dissonant event by the low self-esteem individual and in order to preserve his deviant structure, he will tend to interpret success as "I was lucky" or "it was not a real success."

The overpunished child is also likely to classify as "bad" events which were associated with punishment, thus adopting a mapping rule deviating from the one prevailing in the culture at large. Thus, rejection may lead to deviance in structure as well as in mapping rules, in addition to narrowing the optimal range.

In summary, social isolation and rejection both produce resource deprivation and a consequent narrower optimal range; rejection may also result in cognitive deviances while isolation and inconsistent reinforcement lead to structural deprivation. Since all three conditions affect differentiation and mapping rules, they are likely to cause some communication difficulty later in life. Another factor impinging on the communication process—cross-cultural differences in cognitive structures, will be examined in the next chapter.

SUMMARY

The present chapter is an introduction to the study of cognitive differences and similarities within and across cultures. Its main goal was to demonstrate the relevance of cognitive comparisons to the understanding and prediction of interpersonal behavior.

Along with other investigators we have proposed that perceived stimuli are assigned, by the perceiver, to classes of meaning before further processes, including overt behavior, take place. In interpersonal communication, the stimulus, or the message perceived, originates from the cognitive structure of the sender through a process which is analogous, but reversed, to the stimulus-mapping of the receiver. It follows that interpersonal communication involves matching between the cognitive classes of the participants, mediated by the encoding of outgoing messages and decoding of incoming ones. The meaning of the message received will correspond to the sender's intention when the cognitive class from which it originated matches the one to which it is finally assigned. Experimental data on the encoding-decoding process in confederate-subject communication indicate that although a given event tends to be mapped into the same class by both participants, some miscommunication did occur.

There are at least two types of miscommunication:
1. *Mismapping*, where the mapping rule used by the sender to encode the message is different from the one used by the receiver in decoding it. 2. *Mismatching*, where the degree of differentiation among classes differs for the sender and the receiver. Mismapping will result in each participant assigning a different meaning to the same event. On the other hand, in mismatching the event is assigned into the same class by both sender and receiver, yet one of the two activates more classes than the other in the mapping process. Mismatching occurs either when the degree of differentiation between neighboring classes is dissimilar in the cognition of the participants, or when they differ regarding the order of the classes. The latter type of mismatching is experienced by the receiver as dissonance: a sender may transmit a message containing elements which seem congruent to him. If, however, the receiver carries a different structure, where these elements are remote, the message will create dissonance for him. A message may be congruent with the sender's cognitive structure while incongruent with the receiver's one; thus, ultimately, incongruency is between the participants' cognitions.

Experiments employing different procedures and measurements have all indicated that communication between individuals, dissimilar in their cognitions, was less effective and less parsimonious. However it seems that some degree of cognitive difference may facilitate creativity without disrupting communication. It is important to note that similarity of cognitive structures alone does not guarantee effective transmission of messages. We have already noted that communication involving particularistic resources requires more time and a smaller group. Thus, the nature of the situation as well as the cognitive structures of the participants contribute to the efficacy of communication and to the level of group performance.

Fiedler's work on leadership has provided considerable insight into the relationship between cognition and performance. It is suggested that leaders who value interpersonal relations in work situations are high differentiators between particularistic and non-particularistic resources; those who value more the task aspects will be low differentiators along the particularistic dimension. High differentiators perform best when confronted with situations which require such differentiation; conversely, low differentiators are better leaders in situations where the particularistic and non-particularistic aspects are not differentiated. Thus, the best group performance is achieved when the leader's cognition is matched with the requirements of the situation.

The two types of leaders differ in their behavior under stress conditions. The low differentiator decreases his emission of relations-oriented behavior and increases behavior bearing on task performance. The high differentiator's behavior depends, however, on the type of stress he is faced with: when the stress is related to the task aspect he will increase task-oriented behavior; when the stress involves interpersonal relations he will increase relations-oriented behavior.

How is matching between situational requirements and degree of cognitive differentiation affected by training and experience? Fiedler has suggested that the situation becomes less difficult for the leader as a result of training and/or experience. However, the alternative possibility that the leader's cognition is modified by training seems more plausible and avoids theoretical and practical problems which arise from Fiedler's suggestion. In essence, it is proposed here that training will *increase* differentiation of high-differentiators and *decrease* differentiation of low differentiators, thus making the leader's style more extreme. This cognitive change will improve performance when the situation and the leader's cognition are matched. When there is mismatching between leader and situation training will increase mismatching, thus decreasing efficiency of performance.

The investigations discussed in this chapter suggest that cognitive matching is a necessary condition for effective interpersonal communication and therefore for the exchange of resources. Interpersonal communication carries not only specific resources but structural information as well. While communication among adults serves mainly for resource provision, its structural aspect becomes of great significance when the recipient is an infant; receiving this information is a necessary condition for the infant's cognitive growth. What happens when the amount of adult-infant communication is not sufficient, or when it is of such a nature that the infant is deprived of his basic needs for resources and structural information?

Empirical evidence suggests that insufficient resource provision results in narrowing the optimal range and consequently, in reduced ability to absorb, later on in life, the resource even when it is available. Structural deprivation, on the other hand impairs the encoding-decoding process. Three types of deviant socialization conditions were discussed: isolation, inconsistency and rejection. Social isolation and rejection produce resource deprivation with consequent narrowing of the optimal range; isolation and inconsistency lead to structural deprivation and thus to lack of appropriate mapping rules; rejection may also result in cognitive deviance. All three conditions are likely to cause communication difficulties and resource shortage later in life.

Chapter 9

CROSS-CULTURAL: INTERPERSONAL STRUCTURES IN DIFFERENT SOCIETIES

Overview

THOSE WHO HAVE experienced interaction with members of a different culture know that although special efforts are required in order to avoid miscommunication, cross-cultural transactions are often carried out successfully. In the previous chapter we suggested that cognitive similarities facilitate communication while dissimilarities hinder it. It seems reasonable to assume then that cross-cultural difficulties stem from cognitive differences; at the same time, some aspects of interpersonal cognition are invariant across cultures, thus providing a common ground for cross-cultural interaction. We shall consider here the nature of these similarities and differences.

In the first part of the book we have presented several cognitive structures; in each structure variables are arranged in a specific pattern such that some are next to each other while others are more remote. Is this pattern specific to each culture or does it remain invariant across cultures? There is considerable evidence that it does not change much from one culture to another. An invariant structure does not mean, however, that its dimensions are equally differentiated in various cultures; it is quite possible that the degree of differentiation will vary from one culture to another, leaving the structural pattern unchanged. For example, the resources of love and status are more differentiated—along the particularistic dimension—in modern Western culture than in some traditional ones; yet, in both cases love will be closer to status than to information, if the structural pattern remains invariant. It follows that cultures can be classified according to their relative degree of differentiation on various dimensions. In comparing different cultures, three types of differentiation will be considered:

306

1. Differentiation among social institutions or more precisely, among corresponding roles (e.g., father-to-son and boss-to-worker) in different institutions. We have already noted (see Ch. 5) that institutions differ in the resources exchanged within their context; these institutional differences can be stronger in one culture than in another. In a given society, for example, the boss may assume a father-role toward his workers, while behaviors in these two corresponding roles may be quite dirreren-tiated in another society.
2. Differentiation among roles belonging to the *same* social institution, such as father-to-son and son-to-father; behaviors in reciprocal roles are expected to be more similar in egalitarian society than in a patriarchal one.
3. Differentiation *within* each role; societies may vary, for example, in the degree to which behavior toward self is differenti-ated from behavior toward other in any given role.

The manner in which these differentiations are modified in response to certain events may also vary across cultures. Such modifications are exemplified in a comparative study of Americans and Far Easterners under conditions of success and failure. Here again, however, we shall find that the structural pattern is the same in both cultures and is not modified by the external event. The comparison of modern Western culture with more traditional ones suggests that the highly differen-tiated social institutions of our society provide fewer avenues for par-ticularistic exchange, thus contributing to the scarcity of particularistic resources in this culture. Adopting the behavioral patterns of traditional cultures through training may enable members of modern society to increase their particularistic exchanges. A more immediate goal of such training programs is to improve communication among members of different cultures: if cultures do indeed vary on the degree of differen-tiation of certain dimensions, cross-cultural communication will be impaired as suggested in the previous chapter. Training procedures for reducing difficulties in cross-cultural communication will be dis-cussed in the last portion of this chapter and their effects will be considered; as we shall see, training reduces cognitive differences and improves relations among members of different cultures engaged in a joint task.

STRUCTURAL INVARIANCE

Cross-cultural comparison is not an entirely new topic to the reader; in presenting evidence for the structures of interpersonal behavior (Ch. 3) and family roles (Ch. 4), we have provided supporting data drawn from different cultures. The fact that the same structural pattern was found in several cultures reflects an invariant aspect of cognition which may well be common to the human race in general.

The existence of invariant features is proposed by the hypothesis of "psychic unity of mankind," which has been critically reviewed by Wallace (1961). This hypothesis may sound as a romantic idea, spurred by irrational and moral motivation rather than by scientific considerations; yet it contains important implications for empirical research. Paradoxically the investigation of cross-cultural differences requires a framework which is constant across cultures. Whiting and Child (1953), for example, were able to compare weaning, toilet and independence training, control of sex and aggression in different cultures only after reaching the conclusion that these problems of child training exist in every society, although their solution may differ from one culture to another. Since in all cultures children are toilet trained, it was possible to compare the effects of earlier vs. later training on personality. The proposition that the problems of child training chosen for investigation by Whiting and Child are universal is quite tenable. Until we find a culture where adults are fed from the nipple or newborns are spoonfed, we are justified in considering weaning as a pancultural occurrence; it then becomes possible to inquire whether it is gradual or abrupt and at which age it begins. Many cross-cultural investigations simply assume that the variables studied will be found in each culture, while their values will, of course, vary from one culture to the other. This assumption is quite realistic. R.W. Brown (1956, p. 307) has noted that although a word for indicating a particular notion may not exist in a given language, it is usually possible to denote it by a combination of words. In English, for example, the word "aunt" is used to denote both father's and mother's sister; but if one needs to be more specific, he can always use the father's sister and mother's sister circumlocutions. Cross-cultural similarity may be even stronger at the non-verbal aspects of communication. Indeed Ekman (1972) has shown that certain facial expressions of emotions are common to different cultures.

In pursuing the exploration of cross-cultural invariance it is important to inquire whether the structural patterns of interpersonal variables are the same in various societies. In essence, it is proposed that the *order* among basic cognitive classes of social events will be the same in different cultures. We have seen that giving status to other is more related to giving love to other than to giving love to self (p. 68); we have also found that husband's behavior toward his wife is more similar to son's behavior toward his mother, than to son's behavior toward his father (p. 103). The hypothesis of structural invariance proposes that these relationships will remain constant across different cultures.

It has been suggested that the cognitive structure of the adult results from the developmental sequence by which differentiations were acquired in childhood. If this is true then pancultural invariance of structures indicates that the development sequence of differentiation is also universal. This hypothesis appears particularly plausible with regard to the earliest and most basic differentiations which constitute the foundation of interpersonal relations. Thus developmental sequences regarding interactions with members of the family seem to be pancultural. On the other hand, with regard to relationships outside the family, each culture will give priority to those differentiations which are most relevant to it; consequently the temporal sequence in which these later differentiations are acquired and their resulting structures will differ in various societies. Indeed the work of Levi-Strauss (1966) revealing the manner in which the environment is conceptualized by the "savage mind" may be interpreted to indicate that certain dimensions of conceptualization differ from one culture to another. The proposition that cross-cultural invariance is more likely to be found in earlier differentiations is indirectly supported by comparing linguistic and paralinguistic communication. It is reasonable to assume that facial expressions precede the development of language (Andrew, 1965) both ontogenetically and philo-genetically. It is hardly necessary to note that different languages are used in various societies so that verbal communication is not cross-culturally invariant, even if, as proposed by Chomsky (1962), it might rest on a cognitive substratum of linguistic universals. On the other hand, evidence has been presented (Ekman, 1969 and 1972) regarding the existence of pancultural elements in the facial display of emotions. This contrast between paralanguage and language supports the notion that cross-cultural invariance is more likely to be found in structures which develop earlier, such as those described in the first part of this book. The evidence available so far indicates that the structures of behavior and of family roles (see Chs. 3 and 4) are invariant cross-culturally. Similar findings regarding interpersonal behavior were reported by Longabaugh and Whiting (1963), Longabaugh (1966), and Triandis (1972, pp. 72–74, and 282). The latter author investigated interpersonal behavior in many roles and found several common factors in Greece, India, Japan, Peru, Taiwan and the United States. Jordan (1971) reported cross-cultural invariance in the structure of interpersonal attitudes. Similarly, work on the semantic differential (e.g., Jakobovitz, 1966; Osgood, 1964; Tanaka, 1967) indicates that the dimensions of evaluation, potency and activity are used, in most cultures, for the categorization of concepts. Because of its primary nature, we expect that the structure of resources will also be invariant across cultures; unfortunately such data have not yet been collected.

Structural invariance does not require that the *degree* of differentiation should be the same in diverse cultures. For example, we have seen that in the cultures examined, the behaviors directed toward a wife are more similar to behaviors directed toward a mother than to those emitted toward father. Yet, in a culture where sex differentiation is strong and power differentiation weak, behaviors toward wife and mother will be very similar, while both these roles will be quite dissimilar from behavior emitted toward father. In a culture where power is more sharply differentiated than sex, there will be little difference in the way people behave towards their mother and father, while behavior toward wife will differ considerably from both. In these two cultures, however, behavior toward wife will still be more similar to behavior toward mother than to that toward father. Thus the structure of family roles remains invariant, although similarity between given pairs of roles may not be identical. The fact that, within a common structural framework, degrees of differentiation vary cross-culturally suggests a basis for comparison and classification of cultures. Obviously, this is not the only possible approach to the classification of cultures; traditionally anthropologists have focused mainly on characteristics which are readily observable, such as food-producing activities, exogamy, size of household and polygyny; however, some differentiations—e.g., father-uncle, sibling-cousin—have also been the objects of their attention (Murdock, 1957; Sawyer and Levine, 1966). The relationship between these more traditional criteria of classification and the approach adopted here remains largely to be explored; it may be hypothesized, for example, that when certain practices hinder the development of a given differentiation, the culture will adopt other practices which will facilitate its acquisition. Whiting (1964), for example, found that cultures with a long post partum sex taboo and common sleeping arrangements for mother and child are more likely to have severe male initiation rituals; the first two variables seem to hinder role differentiation by sex, which is then facilitated by severe initiation. Prolonged prohibition of sexual relations between father and mother, suggests Whiting, permits, in turn, longer lactation, thus securing for the child an adequate supply of proteins in cultures where diet is protein scarce. A similar line of reasoning may perhaps explain the correlation of .31, reported by Sawyer and Levine (1966), between presence of father-uncle differentiation and absence or unimportance of agriculture. In any event, the emphasis on differentiation we have adopted here is directly relevant to the problems of interpersonal communication across cultures which will be discussed later in this chapter.

COMPARISON AND CLASSIFICATION OF SOCIETIES

A society is a system of institutions—religious, political, ecomomic, educational, etc. Each institution, in turn, is characterized by the resources which are typically exchanged within it: money and goods are exchanged in trade; money and services in work; information in education; services, love and status in the family. Other resources, besides the typical ones, can be exchanged in a given institution, but usually only in adjunct to the essential ones. In each institution there are different roles which can be specified by indicating both the actor and the object of each. Son-to-father and son-to-mother are examples of family roles; in other social institutions we find roles such as: foreman-to-worker and worker-to-worker (work), sales person-to-customer (trade), student-to-student (education); minister-to-member of congregation (religion).

A role within a particular institution specifies which of the resources typical to the institution is given by the actor to the object or taken away from him. An instructor gives information to the student; a mother gives love and care to her infant; a customer, money to the sales person; a judge fines a defendant. The ability to provide indicates that the actor possesses some power regarding a specific resource; thus each role is characterized by the amount of power in specific resources that the actor possesses with respect to the object; in some roles this power tends to be nearly equal as in the wife-to-husband role; in other roles, such as instructor-to-student, foreman-to-worker and father-to-son, the actor has more power than the object. Still in other roles the actor possesses less power than the object (e.g., daughter-to-mother, defendant-to-judge, student-to-dean).

This conceptualization of society, which has already been introduced in Chapters 4 and 5, provides a basis for comparing and classifying societies. The broadest level of comparison is the institution. We can enquire whether the institutions of a certain society are more resource-specialized than those of another one. It has been noted, for example, that in modern Western society the range of resources exchanged in the family has shrunk in comparison to more traditional societies; several needs that were previously satisfied in the family are now in the province of other institutions. We shall see later that the tendency of modern society to restrict the range of resources exchanged in a given institution is not limited to the family. Thus resource specialization of institutions emerges as a criterion for classifying cultures. Institutional comparison can be done by considering interpersonal behavior in corresponding roles, i.e., roles having a similar power relationship between actor and object, but belonging to different institutions. We can compare roles in which the actor has less power than the object, such as son-to-father, worker-to-boss, pupil-to-teacher; likewise roles in which actor and object have similar power, such as brother-to-brother, worker-to-worker, friend-to-friend could be considered. If the resources exchanged in these corresponding roles overlap in culture A more than in culture B, we may conclude that the latter culture is more specialized than the former one.

Other criteria for the classification of societies emerge from the comparison of roles belonging to the same institution. We can establish, for example, the degree of similarity between reciprocal roles such as worker-to-boss and boss-to-worker. High degree of similarity would indicate that the culture is egalitarian; conversely, in a culture where authority figures are highly respected, reciprocal roles will tend to be different. In an egalitarian society there is little diversity between the behavior of father-to-son and that of son-to-father, or between the behavior of a foreman toward a worker and of a worker toward a foreman. On the other hand, a slave's behavior toward his master is quite different from his master's behavior toward him. This is probably the most extreme example of inequality between reciprocal roles. Thus similarity of behavior in reciprocal roles reflects the egalitarianism of society. The extent to which a culture shows a generation gap can be gauged by comparing roles where the same person is an object of one and the actor of the other; for example we can compare the interaction between son and father when the son in one role is, in turn, the father in the other role; if people behave toward their sons in the same way that their fathers behaved toward them, we might conclude that there is continuity between generations in this particular society. On the other hand, in a society where social changes are rapid we will expect that behavior in the same role will vary considerably across generations.

Additional information can be obtained by comparison among the various roles of the self or of the other. Hsu (1961, p. 405) has suggested that a culture is characterized by a predominant family role pair: the husband-wife roles are predominant in the Western culture, the son-mother roles in the Indian culture, the father-son roles in the Chinese culture, and the brother-brother roles in the cultures of black Africa. These dominant roles are expected to be more specialized, more differentiated, less similar and, thus, less correlated with the other roles of self or of other. This interpretation of Hsu's hypothesis suggests, in essence, that each culture stimulates and rewards differentiation of a given role pair at the expense of others. If this hypothesis is correct, the predominant role (of self or of other) should be less related to the remaining family roles. Thus, for example, the husband-to-wife role should be less similar to other roles in Western culture, where it is predominant, than in Chinese society, where it is not. Hsu further proposes that a society where the same individual can assume in succession both roles of the predominant pair will tend to have more intergenerational continuity and stability; a son can become in due time a father, but a husband does not become a wife. Thus Chinese society, with the dominant father-son relationship, will tend to be more stable than Western society where the husband-wife pair dominates. This notion assumes that the intergenerational continuity, established in family relations, will extend to other institutions as well. Thus it rests on both the criteria of continuity and specialization which we have proposed for classifying cultures.

Finally, societies can be compared according to their degree of differentiation in the dimensions of each role. Some cultures are more tolerant than others to the co-existence of aggressive exchanges with transactions of giving. Very little tolerance is found in Far Eastern cultures where even a moderate expression of anger such as shouting is considered an unpardonable breach of etiquette. By contrast, in the Eastern Mediterranean, an exchange of harsh words does not destroy a friendship. Societies may also differ in the degree to which self, as an object, is differentiated from other; in the relationship between actual and ideal level; and in the ability of their members to take the viewpoint of the other.

In summary, societies can be classified on the following criteria: specialization of their institutions; equality of reciprocal roles; role continuity across generations; predominance of a specific role-pair within an institution; and within-role differentiations. We turn now to consider some illustrative examples of these cross-cultural comparisons starting from the last and most specific one, comparison within role.

Differentiation Within Roles

The degree of differentiation within roles was studied on a sample of 633 married couples from Jerusalem, Israel (Foa, 1964). Spouse roles were compared between the two cultural groups included in the sample; one originating from Europe and the other from the Middle East. The instrument used was the Role Behavior Test described in Appendix A. The husband and wife of each couple were interviewed separately and simultaneously in their residence by two field workers. Each subject was also asked to state the community to which he belonged. A separate analysis of results was made for subjects who belonged to the Ashkenazi community and those belonging to the Sephardi or Oriental communities. Ashkenazi Jews who originate from Eastern and Central Europe, will be called "Western." Sephardi and Oriental Jews who came from the Mediterranean and the Middle Eastern countries will be called "Middle Easterns." The cultural distribution of the sample is shown in Table 50.

Table 50
CULTURAL DISTRIBUTION OF SAMPLE

Cultural Group	Husband	Wife
Western (Ashkenazi)	267	259
Middle Eastern	365	366
(Sephardi and Oriental)		
Not Known	1	8
Total	633	633

Hypotheses on intrarole differences between these two cultural groups were derived from the broad notion that the degree of differentiation in each stage of the development sequence (see Ch. 3) will be influenced by the degree to which such a differentiation is required by the needs and values of the culture. Indeed societies do differ in the degree of distinguishing a given concept from similar others and in the development of appropriate linguistic tools for indicating such distinction. The Wintu, for example, make a living by raising cattle: they differentiate among many kinds of cows and have different words for indicating them. The fine distinctions of the Wintu would make little sense to a city dweller for whom all cows are alike. Consequently, his responses to different types of cows will be more similar or less independent than those of the Wintu cattleman.

The application of these considerations to the specific dimensions of behavioral classes leads to the following hypotheses:

1. The culture of our Middle Eastern group is more permissive with regard to aggressive behavior than Western culture. In this group wife and children beating is still an accepted practice and is not interpreted as lack of affection. On the other hand, in Western culture, the presence of taking behavior tends to exclude the presence of giving behavior. For the Middle Easterns giving and taking tend to be *more* independent than for the Westerns; therefore the correlation between classes of behavior, which have a different mode (giving and taking) but are alike on other dimensions, will be *lower* (in absolute value) for the Middle Eastern than for the Western group.

2. Unpublished data collected in this study indicated that the number of tasks in housekeeping and child care which are considered as shared by husband and wife is smaller in the Middle Eastern than in the Western group. It is therefore expected that the correlation between classes of behavior which have different objects (self and spouse), but are alike in other dimensions will be *lower* for the Middle Eastern than for the Western group.

3. In the Middle Eastern culture, status tends to be ascribed, whereas in Western culture status is achieved. Behaviors *indicating* the status of a person are found in both cultures, but the types of behavior designed to *change* the status of a person are less relevant to the Middlle

Eastern culture, where status is ascribed, than to the status-achieving Western culture. In the Middle Eastern culture the manipulation of status is *less* independent from the manipulation of other aspects of the interpersonal relation, such as love, than in Western culture. It is therefore expected that the correlation between status-manipulating behavior and the corresponding love-manipulating behavior will be *higher* for the Middle Eastern than for the Western group.

The coefficients of correlation between behavioral classes which differ in one dimension only were computed separately for the two cultures in the following areas: behavior of the husband as reported by himself, behavior of the husband as reported by the wife, behavior of the wife as reported by the husband, behavior of the wife as reported by herself. The results are given in Table 51.

Table 51

COEFFICIENTS OF CORRELATION BETWEEN BEHAVIOR TYPES
DIFFERING IN ONE DIMENSION ONLY FOR THE
WESTERN AND MIDDLE EASTERN CULTURAL GROUPS

Differing dimension and correlated types of behavior	Correlation coefficients for behavior of: Wife as perceived by					
	Wife			Husband		
	W	ME	d	W	ME	d
Mode						
Giving status to and taking from spouse	.54	.41	.13	.84	.52	.32
Giving love to and taking from spouse	.46	.35	.11	.56	.57	−.01
Giving love to and taking from self	.20	.14	.06	.16	.22	−.06
Giving status to and taking from self	.41	.27	.14	.35	.27	.08
Object						
Giving status to self and spouse	.23	.22	.01	.19	.18	.01
Giving love to self and spouse	.31	.24	.07	.19	.16	.03
Taking status from self and spouse	.27	.24	.03	.16	.15	.01
Taking love from self and spouse	.34	.36	−.02	.22	.21	.01
Resource						
Giving love and status to spouse	.61	.70	−.09	.72	.74	−.02
Giving love and status to self	.63	.45	.18	.61	.64	−.03
Taking love and status from self	.37	.37	.00	.45	.47	−.02
Taking love and status from spouse	.58	.61	−.03	.65	.73	−.08
	Husband as perceived by					
	Husband			Wife		
	W	ME	d	W	ME	d
Mode						
Giving status to and taking from spouse	.42	.54	−.12	.35	.57	−.22
Giving love to and taking from spouse	.31	.26	.05	.35	.46	−.11
Giving love to and taking from self	.21	.15	.06	.17	.14	.03
Giving status to and taking from self	.38	.14	.24	.34	.22	.12
Object						
Giving status to self and spouse	.32	.28	.04	.39	.24	.15
Giving love to self and spouse	.39	.32	.07	.23	.30	−.07
Taking status from self and spouse	.21	.17	.04	.29	.26	.03
Taking love from self and spouse	.32	.25	.07	.24	.27	−.03
Resource						
Giving love and status to spouse	.64	.63	.01	.66	.76	−.10
Giving love and status to self	.57	.58	−.01	.56	.55	.01
Taking love and status from self	.30	.42	−.12	.28	.55	−.27
Taking love and status from spouse	.59	.61	−.02	.67	.71	−.04

Note.—d = difference W−ME.

The first group of data (rows 1–4) compares the degree of differentiation between giving and taking away the same resource from the same object. The second group (rows 5–8) compares the degree of differentiation between self and spouse when the resource and the behavioral mode (direction) are kept constant. In the last group of data (rows 9–12), the degree of differentiation between love and status is compared; while, again, the remaining two dimensions, object and mode, are kept constant. We have predicted that the Middle Easterns differentiate *more* than the Westerns between giving and taking and between self and spouse; on the other hand, they differentiate *less* than Westerns between status and love High differentiation implies high degree of independence and therefore will result in lower coefficients.

Let us now examine the results given in Table 51. The first row and first column pertains to the Western wife's report regarding the frequency of her giving status to her husband and the frequency of her taking status from him. The correlation between these two behaviors, .54, is higher than the corresponding coefficient for the Middle Eastern group (.41), given in the second column of the first row. The difference, .13, is given in the third column. Since Middle Easterns differentiate more between giving and taking, all their coefficients in the first four rows should be *lower* than the corresponding ones for Westerns. This hypothesis was confirmed for 11 out of the 16 coefficients. With regard to the next four rows of the table, where coefficients between behavioral classes differing in object are given, it was again hypothesized that Middle Easterns will differentiate more between self and spouse and therefore will have lower coefficients. There are three deviations from this prediction.

The last four rows pertain to differentiation between love and status. It was predicted that here Westerns would show higher degree of differentiation and therefore lower coefficients. There are three deviations from this prediction and one case of no difference between the groups.

The sign test (Siegel, 1956, pp. 68–69, 250) was used to compute the probability of obtaining a number of deviations not larger than the one actually found, if the two cultural groups are random samples of the same population. The results of the test are summarized in Table 52. The sign pattern is significantly different from randomness in the last two groups of data (object and resources).

The results support the hypotheses that the differentiation between behavior toward the self and corresponding behavior toward the spouse is higher for the Middle Easterns than for the Westerns, while the differentiation between love and status is lower in the Middle Eastern

Table 52
SIGN TEST OF THE HYPOTHESES

Dimension	Hypothesis	In favor	Against	Equal	Total less Equal	p
Mode	Western higher	11	5	—	16	.105
Object	Western higher	13	3	—	16	.011
Resource	Western lower	12	3	1	15	.018

than in the Western group. It seems, therefore, that concepts developed at a given stage may become more differentiated or independent when a corresponding differentiation is found in the cultural value system. The culture of our Middle Eastern group differentiates more than Western culture between behavior objects and less than Western culture with regard to achieved status. These cultural differences are reflected in interpersonal behavior: Middle Easterns tend to differentiate more than Westerners between behavior toward the self and toward the spouse and less than Westerners between behaviors indicating love and status. A differentiation required by the culture seems more likely to be rewarded. Learning to differentiate among various kinds of snow may be more rewarding for an Eskimo child than for a Western child. Learning to differentiate between the manipulation of love and the manipulation of status may be more rewarding for a Western than for a Middle Eastern child. Yet the development stage at which such a diffentiation is made seems to be the same in different cultures as suggested by structural invariance.

This type of analysis regarding cross-cultural differences within roles is, of course, more interesting and rewarding when its findings tend to remain the same across different roles. It is then possible to make statements such as "differentiation between the resources of love and status is stronger in Western than in Middle Eastern society." If we had to specify that these results hold only for a given role but not for others, then our attempt to classify cultures on the basis of these differences would founder in a maze of details. The developmental considerations which have been presented earlier (see Ch. 2) suggest constancy across roles; differentiations within roles begin in specific roles, primarily child-parents roles, and are later applied to other roles as well. The results just examined involved only two roles: husband-to-wife and wife-to-husband as perceived by both spouses. The fact that there is consistency across these four sets of data suggests such generality, but their range is too limited to justify the statement that within-role differentiations are invariant across roles. Furthermore the differences found between the two cultural groups, although systematic, are quite small; these, however, may be accounted by the fact that Western and Middle Eastern Jews live side by side in the city of Jerusalem and a good deal of mutual acculturation had probably taken place.

Scarce differentiation between resources as well as between positive and negative behavior, which characterize our Middle Eastern group, were also found in another Eastern Mediterranean culture. Triandis (1967a) reported that in Greece, differentiation among resources is lower than in the United States; Vasso Vassiliou, a Greek psychologist quoted by Triandis (1972), noted that a Greek mother may change swiftly from an intense expression of love for her child, to a threat of killing him for some misbehavior.

Differentiation Among Roles of the Same Institution

Differentiation among the roles of a social institution seems to vary from one society to another. In examining examples of such differences we shall begin by considering first reciprocal roles in the family, and then devote some attention to non-reciprocal roles; finally we shall consider the possible extension of these findings to other social institutions.

Data for family roles were obtained with the Role Behavior Test (see Appendix A) in Greece, India, Israel, Senegal and U.S.A. The Greek study was carried out by Dr. Vasso Vassiliou and Dr. Kymissis, the Indian by Professor Chatterjee and the Senegales project by Professor Collomb and Dr. de Preneuf. The role-pairs studied, as well as the number of subjects, varied from one country to another and are summarized in Table 53. In each role pair the first element indicates the subject; thus the notation husband-wife means that these results were obtained by administering the test to the husband. All subjects were adults, except for those from the U.S.A. (Missouri) who were juveniles.

Table 53

NUMBER OF SUBJECTS IN EACH ROLE-PAIR AND CULTURE

Role-Pair	Culture				
	Greece	India	Israel	Senegal	U.S.A.
Husband-wife	29	38	633	—	—
Wife-husband	29	39	633	—	—
Son-father	—	46	—	—	46
Son-mother	—	49	—	50	50
Daughter-father	—	51	—	50	47
Daughter-mother	—	54	—	—	51

RECIPROCAL ROLES IN THE FAMILY. As noted earlier, similarity in behavior of reciprocal roles can be taken as an indication of the degree to which the culture is egalitarian; the behavior of father to son will be more similar to the behavior son to father in an egalitarian society than in one in which the parent occupies a position of authority. To provide data for this comparison, each of the four behavioral classes (giving love and status, taking love and status) toward the other was correlated with the corresponding class in the reciprocal role; a mean of these four coefficients was then computed for each role-pair and culture. The results are given in Table 54.

Table 54

MEAN CORRELATIONS BETWEEN ACTUAL BEHAVIORS TOWARD
OTHER IN RECIPROCAL ROLES

Role-Pair	Greece	India	Israel	Senegal	U.S.A.
Husband-wife (by husband)	.36	.29	.56	—	—
Wife-husband (by wife)	.38	.34	.51	—	—
Son-mother	—	.49	—	.38	.64
Son-father	—	.33	—	—	.60
Daughter-father	—	.44	—	.09	.59
Daughter-mother	—	.38	—	—	.50

A high coefficient of correlation is interpreted as an indication of close similarity in the reciprocal roles of each pair, and thus, of a more egalitarian society. With regard to the spouse roles, the highest correlation was found for Israel, followed in decreasing order by Greece and India. Even sharper is the indication of egalitarism provided by the parent-child role pairs, because of the difference in power position within each pair. Here the highest correlation was found in the U.S.A., followed by India and then Senegal. Thus, from this analysis, U.S.A. and Israel emerge as the most egalitarian with respect to family relations; India and Senegal are the least egalitarian and Greece occupies an intermediate position.

NON-RECIPROCAL ROLES. The data available permitted a comparison of non-reciprocal family roles only between India and the U.S.A. with respect to roles differing in sex: behavior of father and mother toward son (or daughter) and behavior of son (or daughter) toward each parent.

An interesting hypothesis regarding these role relationships has been proposed by Hsu (1961), who suggested that the son-mother role-pair is the most prominent in the Indian family. One will then expect that in this culture, the mother's behavior toward son will be very different from father's behavior towards son; the son likewise will behave differently toward his father and his mother. In the American culture, on the other hand, where neither of these role-pairs is pivotal, the behavior of the two parents, as well as the behavior toward them, will be more similar. Furthermore, it is expected that in the Indian culture the son will differentiate more between parental roles than does the daughter, while no such difference will be found in the American culture. None of these expectations was supported by the data: these two cultures failed to reveal any systematic difference in the relationship between parental roles; to the extent that there was a difference between daughter and son, it was against the hypothesis: for Indians, even more than for Americans, differentiation was somewhat higher for daughters than for sons. It is possible, of course, that these results were due to age difference between the two culture groups: sex differentiation tends to decrease after childhood (Emmerich, et al., 1971), so that Indian subjects may in fact differentiate more than Americans of comparable age.

While no between-culture difference emerged when different behaviors were averaged, an interesting tendency was revealed by considering each class of behavior separately. For the behavior of giving, and particularly giving status, the differentiation between parental roles was stronger in the Indian than in the American group; for taking behaviors the contrary happened. These results appear to suggest that Indian parents differ more when they reward, while American parents are more different when they punish.

RECIPROCAL ROLES IN OTHER INSTITUTIONS. We have seen that reciprocal roles of the family tend to be more similar in modern societies than in more traditional ones: relations in the modern family are rather egalitarian; its members treat each other more as peers than as superior or inferior. If family relations provide a point of departure for the cognitive development of roles in other institutions, then it can be expected that the same cross-cultural difference will hold for non-family institutions as well. Some information on this point is provided by the analysis of cross-cultural episodes involving interaction between Americans and people from several other cultures, which were collected as part of a *Culture Assimilator* program for training Americans to interact with foreigners (Fiedler, Mitchell and Triandis, 1971). The technique of critical incidents developed by Flanagan (1949) for investigating job training requirements was adapted in this study. Individuals with cross-cultural experience (military, businessmen, exchange students), were asked to describe episodes which had changed for better or worse their perception of the other culture, by leading to tension between the two cultural groups or to a better understanding of members of one group with respect to the culture of the other one.

Most of the episodes thus collected dealt with situations at school, work, the military and friendship, i.e., with institutions where cross-cultural contacts are most likely to occur. Other episodes were extracted and adapted from relevant anthropological literature. The procedure for training subjects with the culture assimilator and its effects will be discussed later in this chapter. At this stage we are interested in whether the analysis of the incidents will provide support for the hypothesis that reciprocal roles are less differentiated in modern culture than in traditional ones, in other social institutions besides the family. A set of these episodes deals with interaction between Americans and Arabs. Most incidents occur in a heterocultural setting, but in a few cases the contrast is obtained by comparing similar incidents in a different cultural setting. One American episode, for example, runs as follows: An American professor was 20 minutes late for an appointment that he had made with two of his graduate students. The students were looking at their watches when the professor finally came into the room. The professor said, "I am terribly sorry I am late." The two graduate students jokingly replied, "Better late than never." The professor laughed and after a few more informal exchanges of conversation the group enthusiastically got down to the business that the appointment had been scheduled for.

In the assimilator, the following was asked: Judging from the behavior exhibited in this incident, which one of the following do you see as the most accurate description of what that behavior mainly signifies?

A. The students do not have the proper respect for their professor.

B. No Americans like to be kept waiting 20 minutes for an appointment, regardless of what the status of the person who is late may be.

C. The professor is asserting his status and authority over the students by making them wait until it is convenient for him to meet with them.

D. The professor felt that the students were impertinent in their manner and remarks.

E. The students were flattered to have a special appointment with their professor.

According to the hypothesis, there should be no large difference between the behavior of the professor toward the students and the behavior of the students toward him. The American professor recognizes, indeed, the nearly equal-status-norm by apologizing for being late. Being late is a denial of status to the students; apologizing means restoring status to the students. The professor thus suggests that the equilibrium is re-established. The students' joking comment contains a mild taking of status from the professor and acceptance of the equilibrium thus established. Through these status-manipulating behaviors, the two sides reconcile the situation to the culturally approved position of nearly equal status from which it had deviated due to the status-taking behavior of the professor (being late). Thus, the correct explanation for the American culture, according to the hypothesis is B. This is also the correct alternative indicated by the assimilator, on the basis of empirical evidence. In the Middle Eastern version of the same situation, the superior does not apologize and the subordinates behave toward him in the usual deferent manner. In the Arab culture, indeed, the subordinate is expected to give status to the superior even when the latter denies status to him. The correct explanation of this story, as given by the assimilator, is "In Arab countries, subordinates are required to be polite to their superiors, no matter what happens, or what their rank may be." That is, the differentiation between the behavior of the higher status person and the behavior of the lower status person is stronger in the Middle Eastern culture than in the American one. Thus, again, the Culture Assimilator supports our hypothesis.

A more formal analysis of the Arab culture assimilator (Foa and Chemers, 1967) showed that it contained 22 episodes involving reciprocal roles in institutions other than the family. Only two episodes did not support the hypothesis; both were derived from the literature rather than from real life. Among the 13 obtained from interviews, none deviated from the hypothesis.

Considered in conjunction with the previous data on family roles, these results suggest that differentiation between reciprocal roles is weaker in modern cultures than in traditional ones and that this difference holds across various institutions of the societies compared.

Comparison Across Institutions

As already noted, family roles can be considered as prototypes for the roles of other institutions: thus, the role of son-to-father may serve as a model for such roles as pupil-to-teacher, worker-to-foreman and worshipper-to-priest. The degree to which corresponding roles in different institutions become differentiated from one another may be higher in modern culture than in traditional ones. More specifically we propose that in traditional societies there is less differentiation between the resources exchanged in one institution and those transacted in another one, so that in these cultures, behavior in different institutions tends to be more similar than in modern society. To make this proposition more concrete let us consider some other episodes of the Arab assimilator; this time we shall present incidents involving more than one institution. The following episode illustrates low institutional differentiation between school and friendship in an Arab subject:

Haluk, an Arab exchange student, was working on a class project with several American students. At a meeting of the project staff, the Arab student was asked to give his suggestions concerning the way the project should be carried out. Immediately after he finished talking, Jim, one of the American associates, raised his hand and said in a clear voice that he disagreed with Haluk's proposals. Then he pointed out a number of specific difficulties that Haluk's approach would incur for the project as a whole and its staff. After the meeting, Haluk told Jim and another student on the project that he would not be able to go to the movies with them as they had planned because he had just remembered that he had to get a book out of the library to prepare for a class the next day. When the two boys expressed disappointment and suggested that they could go the next evening, Haluk politely told them that he already had another appointment for the next evening.

Assume that you were the other student who had planned to go to the movies with Jim and Haluk after the meeting. Which of the following thoughts would you regard as most likely to be a correct analysis of the situation as you went off to the movies with Jim?

A. Haluk was certainly a more serious student than you and Jim.
B. Haluk was offended because Jim had disagreed with his ideas in front of others.
C. Jim really should have listened more carefully while Haluk was talking.
D. Jim always talked loud, but this shouting in the meeting had been unnecessary.
E. You should have gone to the library with Haluk.

In this story, Haluk is denied status by Jim in the school institution. Haluk transfers this denial to the leisure institution, in terms of affect, i.e., Haluk feels: "If Jim denies me status at work, this means he also denies me affect, so I must not give affect (go to the movies) to him." The correct explanation for the Middle Eastern culture, as suggested by our hypothesis is, indeed, B. The American, Jim, differentiates more than his Arab friend between affect and status as well as between work and leisure, so for him the relationship between denial of status in work and denial of affect in leisure is not as strong as for Haluk.

The following episode involves differentiation between the resources exchanged in hospitality (love and status) and those exchanged in business (money, goods and services). Once again the Arabs differentiate less than the Americans.

Three American military emissaries were sent to a Middle Eastern country. Their job was to establish a favorable working relationship with the natives of a particular rural area where an American military base was to be located in the near future. The high military officials of the foreign country suggested that the Americans go into the rural areas and talk to the villagers. When the Americans arrived in the village with their native interpreter and native liaison officer, they were immediately invited to dinner and conversation with the headman of the village after they had presented their credentials to him. They readily accepted the invitation and were pleased with their progress. During dinner, the conversation drifted to the plans for the new base and the possibility of the villagers helping in the construction of the necessary buildings. The head villager made several suggestions concerning the recruitment of the native laborers. However, the ranking American officer disagreed with him and said that his suggestions could not be accepted because they would be in violation of the policies set for and followed by the American armed forces. The village headman made no further suggestions and, for the remainder of the dinner, conversation consisted of general questions about the area, its people, and the nationally famous pottery which the villagers make. As the three Americans were taking leave at the end of the evening, one of the women of the headman's house appeared and handed the host several beautiful and apparently expensive plates and vases made by local potters. The headman offered them to the Americans as a gift of welcome, but the Americans made several excuses for refusing them, and they left without the ceramic ware. The village members proved to be somewhat hostile to the personnel of the new base when it was being built and after it began operations. It was often difficult for the Americans to find villagers to work on the base in the jobs that were available, and it was necessary to raise the local employee payroll to the maximum that the military scale permitted for each of the job classifications filled by native personnel.

In view of the sequence of events described in this incident, which interpretation of the villagers' reluctance to work with and for the American military is the most accurate?

A. They did not help the American military because to do so would jeopardize their loyalty to their own country.
B. They did not help the American military staff because they had realized that if the three American military envoys wouldn't accept bribes then they would be impossible to "work" with.
C. If the Americans would not accept the village headman's suggestions, which he made as an authority on village affairs, then he would not cooperate, and neither would his people.
D. The villagers felt that the Americans were disrespectful of the village headman and that they did not like the village as a whole either.

The conflict situation results from cross-cultural diversities in the differentiation of exchanges between the primary institution of hospitality and the secondary institution of business. The two institutions are more related for the Arabs than for the Americans; thus the villagers are angered by the American intention of keeping the two situations separated. The last explanation is, therefore, the best one.

The relatively low differentiation, in the Arab culture, between the commercial catering institution and hospitality is well exemplified in the following incident:

An Arab graduate student asked his co-workers on his lab assistant-ship if they wanted to go to lunch with him at the Student Union. They agreed, adding that it was time to eat, and they all chatted as they went to the Union where they got in line at the cafeteria. When they reached the cashier's station, the Arab student who was first in line, paid for all of them. When the group got to their table, his two co-workers insisted on giving the Arab student the money for their lunches. The Arab refused it, but the Americans insisted, and the one sitting beside him swept the money off the table and dumped it into the foreign student's jacket pocket. Later, the Americans commented that the Arab student had been unusually quiet and reserved while he ate his lunch.

This episode was followed by these alternative explanations:

A. The Arab student must have had an upset stomach.
B. It is the Arab custom not to talk during meals.
C. The Arab student had wanted to pay for their lunches and he was hurt that they wouldn't let him.
D. The Arab student felt the Americans thought he was too poor to pay.
E. When he was away from the lab, the Arab had nothing to make conversation about.

The correct explanation is, of course, C. The Arab student wanted to pay because in his definition of the situation, he was the host.

In the Arab assimilator, 21 episodes were found to involve more than one institution. In every one, the comparison of the correct explanation, provided by a panel of Arabs, coincided with the explanation proposed by the hypothesis that Arabs differentiate less between institutions than do Americans, although, as we have previously seen, they differentiate more within institutions.

THAI AND AMERICAN CULTURES. A similar picture is presented by critical incidents between Americans and Thais (Mitchell and Foa, 1969). The tension present in these incidents often stems from cultural differences about the resource appropriate to a particular institution, usually work. The resources which seemed appropriate to the American did not match the expectation of the Thai. Frequently the Thai expected to receive status and sometimes also love in institutional contexts where other resources were more relevant, according to American culture. To illustrate this point, two episodes will be presented. In the first one, the Thai's expectation of receiving status, in addition to infor-mation, is not met. Colonel Samuel Holden and three other American staff officers arrived at a conference to talk with the Thai Army staff in developing the defensive fortifications of Thailand. One of the Thai staff officers, Lt. Col. Bancha, who a few weeks earlier had been in a short training course conducted by Col. Holden, came up to say hello and exchange pleasantries. The American said hello, but remarked that he had little time at the moment and wished to get the meeting started. During the meeting, Col. Holden introduced many U.S. proposals for helping the defensive build-up, and the conversation between the Thais and the Americans flowed freely. Only Colonel Bancha failed to participate.

In the second episode the Thai expects to receive love, but his expectation is not fulfilled: he receives only money. The Thai Government had given an American construction company a contract to enlarge and remodel the national railroad station in Thorburi. Charles Adams was appointed manager to handle the company's business in Bangkok, and Charles recruited a staff of about 40 local personnel to handle bookkeeping, records, etc. From the time these employees began their work with the company, Charles found himself having to listen to and advise them on their family affairs and health problems. This took so much of Charles' time that he found it necessary to tell them to stop seeing him about personal affairs that were not the company's business. Soon Charles felt that his employees were not as friendly to him as before, and he noticed that they often went to talk to his Thai assistant.

All these episodes reflect events which actually occurred. Only names and a few other irrelevant details were changed to prevent identification. A sample of subjects from the target culture was asked to choose the "correct" explanation among the various alternatives proposed, or to suggest a new alternative. This stage of the work was carried out by an experimenter who was unaware of our hypotheses regarding the correct explanation. The choices made by native subjects firmly supported the hypothesis, that in some traditional cultures the process of institutional differentiation is less pronounced than in modern society. Thus, in these cultures, exchange of particularistic resources occurs in a larger number of institutions.

Love Poverty in Modern Culture

Non-family institutions in a traditional culture have retained similarity to the family by allowing particularistic exchanges to take place in their settings. On the other hand, there is some evidence that a process of assimilation in reverse may have started in the American cultures so that in the family as well as in other institutions, non-particularistic resources have become more prominent. The practice of paying a child for services he renders (baby sitting to younger siblings, mowing a lawn) is quite common. Bronfenbrenner (interview in *Time,* December 28, 1970, p. 37) notes that parents give things to children instead of giving themselves, i.e., the particularistic resources, whose transmission require face-to-face contacts. He quotes the case of a shoemaker who took a second job as cab driver for the purpose of buying expensive gifts for his children with the extra money thus made. Because of the extra work, the children would see little of him for several weeks; indeed, they received more goods but less love and status. A side-effect of this stress on material things is that children tend to have less opportunity of interaction with their parents and they increase exchanges with peers. This state of affairs seems as a sure recipe for increasing the generation gap: the less opportunity children have to interact with parents, the less likelihood there is that they will learn their roles by modeling on those of their elders.

We have noted earlier (Ch. 5) that particularistic exchanges are also hindered by the high population density of the urban environment. Through the combined effect of institutional specialization and urban concentration, modern society may well have reached a point where the amount available of the most particularistic resource, love, is below what is required for the normal functioning of an individual as a member of society. Love is somewhat like air: it cannot be stored inside the body in large amounts and for a long time; an easy access to supply is needed to avoid reaching the lower bound of tolerance. Where points of replenishment are scarce, particularly in areas where many individuals are concentrated, shortages will occur frequently in many individuals.

Some readily observable symptoms reinforce this suspicion. Modern society is widely accused of being materialistic, dehumanizing, leading to a mad race for more goods and to a feeling of emptiness and inner dissatisfaction. In the best-seller "The Greening of America," Reich (1971) asks "What have we all lost? What aspects of the human experience are either missing altogether from our lives or present only in feeble imitation of their real quality?" (p. 165). And later he adds "The most powerful, the loudest, and the most persistent command in our society is the command to buy, to consume, to make material progress, to 'grow' " (p. 179). Such books, which describe the predicament of modern society and propose remedies, even if unrealistic, are avidly bought, read and discussed. Criticism of modern culture has been characterized by anti-intellectualism, i.e., by lack of trust that man's rational facilities are capable of providing an answer to the problems of present-day society. This attitude may well reflect the intuitive feeling that the logic and arithmetics of money do not apply to love (see Ch. 5, p. 161). In exchanges of love, unlike those of money, two and two equals more than four, since by giving to the other one also gives to self. Love, however, is not unlogical; it just follows different logical rules.

Another significant modern trend is the proliferation of institutional settings which specialize in the exchanges of particularistic resources at the exclusion, almost completely, of other exchanges. Their names vary (sensitivity training, encounter, marathon) with some of their features, but one thing is common to all: the provision of a setting for the exchange of emotional feelings. In this way the shortage of love created by institutional specialization is remedied by further specialization: the provision of institutions which specialize in love. On the other hand, urban and rural communes, which seem to be increasing in number in the U.S.A., run against the specialization trend; they provide a setting for a wider range of resources, very much as the traditional extended family.

The shortage of particularistic resources in modern society has been particularly hard on its poor: while they do not share in the prevailing abundance of material things, they have also been hit by the common shortage of particularistic resources. We interpret O. Lewis' (1966) notion of "culture of poverty" to indicate poverty in both particularistic and non-particularistic resources; simple poverty, which is still prevalent in many countries in earlier stages of economic and technological development, implies shortage of economic resources only.

DIFFERENTIAL EFFECTS OF FAILURE AND SUCCESS

The comparison of the ways in which the social environment is conceptualized in various societies indicates that, while the structural pattern tends to remain invariant, cultures vary in the degree to which their common and basic dimensions are differentiated. In each culture, the degree of differentiation does not necessarily remain the same over time; it has been shown, indeed (Emmerich et al., 1971), that during development, certain differentiations increase up to a maximum and then decrease. We have further noted (Ch. 5) that although a single dissonant event may not be sufficient to modify the degree of differentiation, a consistent series of such events will probably result in such modification. These changes may again vary in different cultures. To illustrate this point we turn now to consider a study on changes in differentiation following an experience of success or failure in two cultural groups.

Americans and Far Easterners Compared

It has been noted that response to criticism differs in American and Far Eastern cultures; this difference results in miscommunication between members of these cultural groups. When an American criticizes a Far Eastern, i.e., takes away status from him, the latter's performance tends to deteriorate and tension is created, much to the surprise of the American who expected that criticism would result in an effort to improve, as often is the case in the U.S.A. (Mitchell and Foa, 1969). In the highly mobile Western society individuals are indeed continuously evaluated and their status increases or decreases according to their performance; in this society a moderate loss of status often leads to attempts to do better in order to regain it. In Far Eastern cultures, by contrast, taking away status is severely limited by social norms which protect the individual from "loss of face." Criticism, when uttered, results in deterioration of the relationship. Thus in these two cultures the same stimulus, taking away status, produces quite different responses. If, as repeatedly suggested in this volume, cognitive structures mediate between stimulus and response, then it becomes of interest to investigate differences between cultures in the cognitive changes following gain and loss of status.

Foa, Mitchell and Lekhyananda (1969) studied the effects of success and failure on American students at the University of Illinois; Far Eastern students (from Burma, China, Hong-Kong, Japan, Thailand, and Viet Nam) at the same university; Thai students from Thamsart and Kasetsart Universities in Bangkok. In each group, students were further subdivided into academic successes and failures according to the following criteria: undergraduates with a grade point average above B and no failing grades (Es) in the last semester, and graduate students with a grade point average above B and no failing grades (Cs) in the last semester, were defined as having been academically successful. Undergraduates with a grade point average below C and at least one E in the last semester were defined as failures, as were graduate students with a grade average below B and at least one C in the last semester. The frequency distribution of the six groups of subjects is given in Table 55.

Success and failure students were tested separately. At the beginning of the session a professor gave a brief talk about the academic standing

Table 55

FREQUENCY DISTRIBUTION OF SUBJECTS BY
CULTURE GROUP AND ACADEMIC PERFORMANCE

Academic Performance	Culture group			
	Americans	Far Easterners in U.S.A	Thais in Thailand	Total
Success	23	26	40	89
Failure	28	14	40	82
Total	51	40	80	171

of the students, stressing their respective success and failure. The professor was an American in the groups at Illinois, and a Thai in the groups tested in Bangkok. Following the talk, the subjects completed a semi-projective questionnaire which was translated into Thai for the Bangkok subjects. This questionnaire covered four variables, with four multiple-choice items for each variable. The variables were taken from the Role Behavior Test (See Appendix A) and modified to suit the roles of the situation being studied. All the variables dealt with the mode of taking; the resource, actor and object varied from one variable to another. A shortened illustrative example of items for each variable is given at the bottom of Table 56. The actual items were semi-projective, patterned on those of the Role Behavior Test.

Table 56
DESIGN OF THE VARIABLES

Variable	Mode	Resource	Actor	Object	Institution
1	Taking	of status	by other (instructor)	to other (student)	university
2	Taking	of status	by self (student)	to self	university
3	Taking	of status	by self	to self	generalized (person)
4	Taking	of love	by self	to self	generalized (person)

Shortened examples of items: Variable 1. Instructor says I am failure as a student
Variable 2. I am a failure as a student
Variable 3. I am a failure as a person
Variable 4. I dislike myself for being the sort of person I am

The order of the four variables, as given in the table, reflects the degree of similarity; neighboring variables are more similar in their respective elements than are remote variables. Indeed, only the actor and the object change from the first to the second variable; in the third variable there is a change in institution as well, as this variable pertains to the generalized person, whereas the previous two variables deal with the university setting. In the last variable there is a change in resource—the other three variables dealt with status while this one deals with love. Thus the closer, in the order, two variables are, the more similar are the elements composing them. The first variable is more similar to the second than to the third variable, and least similar to the fourth one. The second variable is more similar to the third than to the fourth one. Finally, the last variable is more similar to the third than to the second variable, and least similar to the first one.

This order among the variables is predicted to be invariant: irrespective of the cultural group and the condition (success and failure) the correlation between any two variables will be higher the more similar they are, i.e., the closer they appear in the order given in Table 56.

Cross-Cultural Similarity and Dissimilarity

The predicted order is well supported by the pattern of intercorrelations among the four variables given in Table 57. Except for a couple

Table 57

VARIABLES INTERCORRELATION IN SUCCESS AND FAILURE BY CULTURAL GROUP

Academic performance		American					Far Eastern					Thai			
		1	2	3	4		1	2	3	4		1	2	3	4
Success	1	—	54	52	25	1	—	36	34	05	1	—	61	46	29
	2	54	—	73	69	2	36	—	30	31	2	61	—	64	40
	3	52	73	—	71	3	34	30	—	62	3	46	64	—	53
	4	25	69	71	—	4	05	21	62	—	4	29	40	53	—
Failure	1	—	25	09	05	1	—	33	−04	−10	1	—	35	34	26
	2	25	—	64	63	2	33	—	56	51	2	35	—	71	47
	3	09	64	—	62	3	−04	56	—	86	3	34	71	—	61
	4	05	63	62	—	4	−10	51	86	—	4	26	47	61	—
Difference Suc.—Fail.	1	—	+29	+43	+20	1	—	+03	+38	+15	1	—	+26	+12	+03
	2		—	+09	+06	2		—	−26	−30	2		—	−07	−07
	3			—	+09	3			—	−24	3			—	−08
	4				—	4				—	4				—

of minor deviations, the first variable correlates higher with the second than with the third, and least with the fourth. The second variable is more related to the third than to the fourth; the third variable correlates higher with the second than with the first variable, and the fourth is related most to the third and least to the first. Thus, once again the structure remains invariant across cultures and even across success and failure conditions. On the other hand, the size of the correlations differs systematically for success and failure; the pattern of this difference varies with the cultural group. In the American group, the correlations obtained from successful students are always higher than the ones obtained from failing students; thus, the difference of success less failure, given in the lower part of Table 57, is always positive for the Americans. In both the Thai and Far Eastern groups, only the correlations of the first row are higher in successful students while the correlations in the remaining three rows are higher for the failing students. This pattern is again reflected in the lower part of Table 57; in the first row of the two Asiatic groups the differences are positive, whereas in the remaining rows all differences are negative. The first row refers to the relationship between the instructor's behavior toward the student and the latter's attitudes towards himself, as a student and as a person; the other rows pertain to the correlations among the various attitudes of the student towards himself. The Asiatic groups differ from the Americans in the way in which relationship among attitudes toward the self changes from success to failure; this relationship becomes weaker for the failing American and stronger for the failing Asians. Test for equality of co-variance matrices indicates that the difference between success and failure conditions in each cultural group is significant at least at the .01 level.

The possibility that these differences may depend on variations in the reliability of the instrument is discounted by the finding that the order of the coefficients is invariant across conditions and cultural groups. Changes in reliability should have been very systematic to maintain such an order. Another alternative to be considered is that the differences are not cultural in origin, but due to some factor associated with the degree of selectivity of the student population studied. The Thai students are probably more carefully selected than the Americans since the percentage of people attending universities is smaller in Thailand. Far Eastern students going abroad undergo an even stricter selection than those studying at home. The fact that the same reactive pattern was observed in Far Eastern students in the U.S. and in Thai students in Thailand, in spite of their difference in degree of selectivity, appears to rule out the possibility of explaining the results in non-cultural terms such as intellectual capacity and level of aspiration. For the same reason, the culture of the experimenter and the language of the instrument (different in the two Far Eastern groups) do not seem to have influenced the results.

While the data clearly indicate that differentiation in success and failure follows a dissimilar pattern in Western and Far Eastern cultures, they do not prove that the change is due to the experience of failure. Such proof could be achieved only by randomly assigning subjects to contrived situations of success and failure. The application of this procedure was discarded on suspicion that debriefing would not have proved sufficient to avoid lasting damage to Far Eastern subjects exposed to failure, precisely because they were less able to face it than were American subjects. The Far Eastern sensitivity to loss of face and the differential reaction to failure in the cultures tend, however, to support the view that the cognitive changes noted constitute a reaction to failure.

How can these differential effects of failure be explained? The smaller correlations in the failure condition, found in the American student, indicate an increase in the degree of differentiation among various aspects of the self, as well as between these aspects and the instructor's attitude. This higher degree of differentiation increases flexibility of the cognitive organization, thus weakening the diffusion of status deprivation. Indeed, the mean difference between success and failure decreases gradually and rapidly as one moves from the first to the fourth variable: 2.81, .81, .32, and .18. The change of condition affects the first variable most and the last one least. Furthermore, the mean difference between the first variable and the other variables is always smaller in success than in failure. The mean score difference between Variables 1 and 4, for example, is .48 for success and 3.11 for failure. These data show how the cognitive structure of Americans changes according to the nature of messages coming from the outside. It becomes more rigid (less differentiated) when communication is positive, thus facilitating the spread of its desirable effect.

When the message is negative, the structure becomes looser (more differentiated) thus reducing the diffusion of resource deprivation. This reaction of the American subjects to failure appears to be well-adjusted, since it preserves contact with the external social environment while maintaining an inner core of positive self-image—two necessary conditions for future attempts to improve performance. If pushed to the extremes, this reaction pattern may, however, result in personality disorganization, as the variables become too independent of each other.

The Far Eastern reaction to failure, on the other hand, consists in increasing differentiation between self and external source of negative communication, while decreasing differentiation among the various aspects of the self-image. This reaction is conducive to the behavioral response of leaving the field or losing interest in performance, which has been already noted. Its adjustive value depends, of course, on the culture. It can work well in a Far Eastern society, where criticism is rare and loss of face avoided. In the West, it would lead to a progressive withdrawal from the social environment. In both Americans and Asians, the degrees of differentiation found in failure appear appropriate to the requirements of their respective cultures; thus the proposition that a given degree of differentiation is adjustive when it matches the requirements of the social environment is again supported. A change in the environment, as was the case in our Far Eastern students in America, is likely to result in mismatching: the individual who is exposed to social events generated by the new environment and uses his old coping mechanisms will probably experience dissonance. This situation, which often arises in cross-cultural interaction can be reduced by cross-cultural training. To this topic we now turn.

CROSS-CULTURAL TRAINING

Differentiation varies across cultures and hinders inter-cultural communication; the aim of a cross-cultural training program can then be viewed in terms of providing the trainee with a cognitive map for the target culture. Such a map will enable him to decode the messages received by using the code of the sender, rather than the trainee's own code; it will also enable him to predict how his messages will be decoded by a member of the target culture. Consequently, communication will be improved and tension reduced.

Interpersonal contacts among members of different cultures have become increasingly frequent in the modern world, in a variety of political, economic and social situations, thus increasing the need for improving transcultural communication. It is not surprising, therefore, that several methods for solving this problem have been proposed. In an evaluative review of cross-cultural training programs, Brislin (1970, p. 58) notes that most of the research on the effectiveness of such training involved the method called "Cultural Assimilator." We have already become familiar with some episodes of the Arab and Thai assimilators when comparing these cultures with American society. We shall now turn to examine this training method in more detail.

The Cultural Assimilator

The assimilator is a set of episodes pertaining to cross-cultural interactions; each episode is followed by four alternative explanations of the incident. The trainee is instructed to choose the most "correct" alternative, using his own judgment. If his choice was correct, he is provided with verbal reinforcement regarding his good performance and with additional information about the nature of the cross-cultural difference embedded in the episode. He is then instructed to proceed with the next episode. If the trainee chooses the wrong explanation, he is instructed to read the episode again and make another choice. The "correct" explanation was determined by a panel of judges from the target culture. They also rated each episode in terms of its realism and relevance to the culture; these latter ratings provided criteria for deciding whether or not the episode should be included in the training program.

The episodes given in the assimilator usually include events which are dissonant to the American, i.e., they do not fit his cognition: often in these events the member of the target culture withdraws from interaction (keeps silent, refuses to meet or to participate in the discussion) following antecedent circumstances which, for an American, are unlikely to be associated with withdrawal. We know from dissonance experiments (see Ch. 5) that a person confronted with a dissonant event will tend to modify his perception of the event so that it will fit his cognition; indeed, some of the alternative explanations following each episode represent cognitive modifications of this type: the serious-minded Arab student preferred the library to the theater; another student had an upset stomach, and therefore kept silent; the villages were unwilling to cooperate with the foreign military because of loyalty to their country; these interpretations, which are consonant for the American trainee were labelled as erroneous because they were dissonant with the structure of the target culture. Thus, the alternatives given for each episode reflect conceptual differences between the two cultures, the trainee's culture and the one he learns to understand. The trainee is rewarded for choosing the alternative which is dissonant to his structure but consonant for members of the target culture. The same type of cultural difference recurs several times in the assimilator, usually through episodes involving different contexts and situations. This repetition reduces the possibility that the trainee will associate the correct response with irrelevant cues. It is expected that repeated exposure to the cognitive structure of the target culture will enable the trainee to encode and decode messages in a manner which is appropriate to such culture.

Training Effects

The effects of assimilator training on relations and performance in heterocultural situations has been the subject of several investigations; by contrast there are only scarce data on the cognitive changes induced by assimilator training. While the effect of training on cognitive differentiation is of great scientific interest, the practically-minded administrator wants to know whether the training succeeds in reducing tension and improving performance. Evidence regarding these latter variables has been obtained both in laboratory experiments and in field studies. We shall consider it first and then proceed to discuss the cognitive aspects.

In laboratory research experimental subjects were trained in the culture assimilator; proceeding at their own pace, these subjects read each episode, chose one the the four alternative explanations and read the relevant feedback. Control subjects were trained by the same procedure with a program which was identical in format to the culture assimilator but differing in content: the topic of the control training was the geography of the target country. Following training, each subject was assigned to lead a small team composed of natives of the target culture. Together they were to perform a given task. The group activity was evaluated with regard to both efficiency and interpersonal aspects. Groups with a culture-trained leader were then compared with those having a geography-trained leader (Stolurow, 1965). In one of these investigations (Chemers, Lekhyananda, Fiedler, and Stolurow, 1966), twelve American R.O.T.C. cadets were trained with an Arab assimilator. Twelve other cadets were trained with a control program on the geography of the Middle East. Each cadet was then assigned to a group composed of himself, as leader, and two Arab students.

Each group performed three tasks: a structured routing task, an unstructured cooperative task and a negotiation task. A variety of criterion variables was used, dealing with both evaluation of the task product and the group socio-emotional climate. For almost all of these variables, the difference between culture- and geography-trained groups was in the expected direction, and in two of the climate variables it reached statistical significance. These findings supported the notion that the culture assimilator succeeds in lessening the difficulties of a culturally heterogeneous task group, especially in the social emotional area.

Using the Thai assimilator, Mitchell and Foa (1969) conducted an experiment with thirty-two American R.O.T.C. cadets. Subjects were matched according to rank and randomly assigned to two groups. The experimental group was trained with the culture program and the control group studied the geography material. Sixteen pairs of foreign students from the Far East participated in the study. In fourteen pairs, one member was Thai. (No Thai subjects were available for the two other pairs). The distribution of non-Thai members was as follows: 13 Koreans, 3 Vietnamese and 2 Burmese. Thus, most of the groups were composed of one Thai and one Korean. Each pair of foreign students worked successively with a culture-trained and a geography-trained American. All the foreign students had the command of English required for the task. Two similar construction tasks were used: the Kenner Panel and Girder set, and the American Plastic Bricks set. They were chosen for several methodological reasons. First, after running a few pilot groups with different tasks it was found that this task produced more variance in interpersonal and task oriented behavior. Second, it did not require technical and elaborate discussions which might have been difficult for the foreign students. And third, it yielded obvious and easily obtainable measures of productivity.

Each pair of foreign students worked on both tasks with different leaders. Immediately before the group session, every American was given five minutes of training with the construction materials and was shown how the final product was to look. His job was to get the building constructed as quickly as possible and without mistakes. He was only to supervise his two-man team; he himself was not permitted to work on the task. The American gained technical superiority over the other team members not only by his five-minute pre-task training, but also by the fact that he alone was permitted to consult the construction plans during the task. This procedure was designed to approximate the real-life situation of a Western expert working in a developing country: the expert is usually better qualified technically than his co-workers, and is expected to give instructions and to supervise rather than doing the job himself.

The interaction was observed by trained Thais who recorded those behaviors of the American leader which would be considered inappropriate in the Thai cultures. Two Thai observers participated in the study, each observing one of the two sessions which were run concurrently. In summary, there were two tasks, two Thai observers, and two trials; the culture-trained American could be either the first or the second leader of a given group. Eight combinations are possible for these three variables; each appeared twice for the culture groups and twice for the geography groups, thus counter-balancing the design to avoid the possible effects of task, observer, and trial sequence.

At the end of each session, the observer, the American, and the two foreign students filled out a 31-item evaluation form. All the respondents except the American answered an additional rating form of 17 items, after the end of the second session, comparing the two American leaders. Since culture- and geography-trained Americans alternated in the sessions, this latter rating was essentially a comparison between the two kinds of training. The 48 rating items were scrambled in the forms, thus avoiding possible sequential contamination. However, in the analysis, items were grouped into classes according to whether the *actor* of the rated behavior was the leader or the group, and whether the *object* of this behavior was the task, the group or a member. Altogether there were five groups of items (variables) rated by four persons (leader, Thai member, non-Thai member, and observer), thus yielding 20 scores. The mean differences between groups with a culture-trained leader and those with a geography-trained leader are given in Table 58. These differences were converted to standard scores in order to permit comparison across variables. A positive difference means that the culture-trained groups were rated more positively (e.g., more efficient, pleasant, etc.), and thus indicates that the program was effective. A negative difference shows that the geography-trained leaders were rated as more effective on the particular variable, by the particular rater. Most differences were positive since, in general, the behaviors emitted in the groups led by a culture-trained leader were rated more positively by various raters. However, only four of the differences reached a significant level. The largest difference between experimental and control group was reported by the observer regarding the leader's behavior toward the group. The other differences tended to be smaller the more distal they were, in the Table, from the highest one. This order in the size of differences indicates a progressive weakening of the experimental effect (Rosnow, 1968; Rosnow and Robinson, 1967). This effect was stronger in the observer's ratings than in those of leader and of the Thai members, and is weakest for the non-Thai members. As to the different variables observed, the experimental effect was strongest for the leader's interpersonal behavior and is less effective for the leader's task performance and for the behavior of the group as a whole.

Table 58

MEAN DIFFERENCES BETWEEN RATINGS OBTAINED FOR
EXPERIMENTAL AND CONTROL GROUPS ACCORDING TO
BEHAVIOR RATED AND RATER

Variable	Rater			
	Leader	Observer	Thai member	Non-Thai member
Group to Task	.00	.17	−.02	−.14
Leader to Task	.20	.67	.12	−.06
Leader to Group	.50	1.38**	.65	.15
Leader to Member	.66*	1.31**	.28	.04
Group to Group	.27	1.02**	.25	.10

* p < .05
** p < .01

No significant differences between experimental and control groups were found in terms of the time required to complete the task and the number of mistakes made in construction. Experimental groups were slightly slower in completing the task and made more errors. On the other hand, the number of "mistakes" in the leader's interpersonal behavior, as recorded by the Thai observers, was significantly lower (p = .05) for the culture-trained leaders. Thus, the results indicate that cultural training was effective in improving the interpersonal relationship with members of the target culture—the Thai—but not with participants from other Far Eastern societies. Moreover, no evidence was obtained that performance improved following training. These results refer, however, to short-term performance; it is possible that in a long term task, performance would have been influenced by interpersonal relations, thus benefiting indirectly from the cultural training. Some results pointing in this direction were obtained from field studies to which we now turn.

FIELD STUDIES. Three studies assessing the effectiveness of the assimilator in field conditions have been reported for the cultures of Central America, Thailand and Greece. A culture assimilator for Honduras was administered to 119 teen-age volunteers who planned to spend the summer in Honduras and Guatemala helping villages in public health and community development work, under the sponsorship of *Los Amigos de las Americas* of Houston, Texas. Another 146 volunteers who went the same summer received the usual orientation program offered by the same sponsoring organization; this latter group did not receive the assimilator training. The activity of all these participants was rated by supervisors as well as by the volunteers themselves;

the latter ratings were compared for the first and third week of activity in the field. The analysis of these ratings indicated that trained volunteers improved their work performance and adjusted better than did control subjects. Moreover, the positive effects of the assimilator training were particularly strong for those volunteers who had already participated in the project during the previous summer. These latter results suggest that the structural information provided by the assimilator was effective in organizing previously acquired cross-cultural experience (Fiedler, Mitchell and Triandis, 1971).

The Thai and Greek studies involved a small number of U.S. military personnel stationed in these countries. In Thailand the control group was provided with a conventional essay on the country and its people; the control group in Greece received no training. A few months thereafter, participants filled self-rating forms. The results showed a trend in the expected direction: assimilator-trained personnel felt better adjusted, more productive, and more satisfied with their relations to local people. Perhaps the most important finding of these two studies is that differences were found some months after the training had taken place (Worchel and Mitchell, 1970).

The evidence provided by the laboratory and field investigations summarized here indicates that assimilator training improves relations among persons varying in cultural background and might also, in the long run, improve their performance in a joint task. Culture-trained leaders appear to behave differently, and more appropriately, than do untrained ones, although the training involves no overt interpersonal behavior. How does assimilator training affect behavior?

Cognitive Modifications

We have proposed earlier that these behavioral changes are mediated by cognitive modification. According to this view, cultural training modifies the degree of differentiation among interpersonal dimensions and provides mapping rules which fit the target culture. Provided with a more accurate mapping of the cognitive organization of interpersonal relations in the other culture, the trained individual improves his ability to communicate with the foreign partner both as a receiver and as a sender of messages. Does this mean that an American trained in the Thai assimilator will become more similar to a Thai? This possibility was explored by using data obtained in the Mitchell-Foa experiment previously described: the ratings of the Thai participants and observers were correlated with those of the trained and non-trained American leaders. If the assimilator made the Americans more similar to Thais, these correlations would be higher for the experimental than for the control group. The results were negative: corresponding correlation coefficients in the two sets of data were practically the same.

Failure to obtain any indirect evidence of cognitive change led to the proposal that training will influence the cognition *ascribed to the foreign partner*, rather than the trainee's own point of view. As Goodenough (1969) noted "people are able to learn more than one cultural order, just as they can learn more than one language." In evaluating the task group, the trainee gave his own viewpoint; therefore no effects of training were evident here (Mitchell and Foa, 1969). The cognitive effects might have been manifested had we asked the subject to respond as he thought a Thai would have responded. Such a procedure was used by Triandis and Mitchell (Foa, Mitchell and Fiedler, 1971). Five groups of American subjects participated in these experiments. One group was trained with a shortened version of the Thai assimilator; the second group was given a conventional essay on the same culture; the third and fourth group received respectively, assimilator or essay for Greece; finally a fifth group was trained in an irrelevant geography program and served as control. Before and after training, participants were administered the *Role Differential* (Triandis, 1967, b), an instrument which indicates what behaviors were considered by the subject as appropriate or inappropriate to a given role. Participants were instructed to respond as if they were members of the target culture. Using the scores obtained, interrole correlations were then computed separately for the first and the second administration of the role differential in each group of subjects.

Table 59 shows the correlations among three corresponding roles (i.e., roles differing in social institution but alike in power relationship and sex): nephew to uncle, citizen to policeman and university student to university administrator. A higher coefficient indicates more similarity of behavior between the correlated roles. Since the roles considered are similar in power and sex but differing in social institution, an increase in correlation following training indicates a reduced differentiation between the respective institutions. Conversely, a decrease in correlation signifies increase in such differentiation.

Subjects trained in the Thai culture showed an increase in correlations for all three role-pairs following training: apparently they had learned that in the Thai society there is less differentiation among institutions than in America. The pattern of change is different for subjects trained in the Greek culture: differentiation between the family and the two other institutions became stronger, as indicated by the decreases in correlation, while the relationship between non-family institutions remained the same. This result again fits a characteristic of the target culture. Indeed, Greeks differentiate very much between

Table 59

CHANGES IN CORRELATION AMONG BEHAVIORS IN DIFFERENT ROLES
FOLLOWING CULTURAL TRAINING

Correlated Roles	Type of Training	No. of Subjects	Correlation		Difference (After less before)
			Before Training	After Training	
Nephew to Uncle and Citizen to Policeman	Thai Assimilator	17	.38	.59	+.21
	Thai Essay	15	.44	.63	+.19
	Greek Assimilator	17	.25	-.14	-.39
	Greek Essay	21	.24	-.19	-.43
	Control	20	.35	.31	-.04
Nephew to Uncle and University Student to University Administrator	Thai Assimilator	17	.56	.70	+.14
	Thai Essay	15	.58	.73	+.15
	Greek Assimilator	17	.42	.19	-.23
	Greek Essay	21	.47	-.15	-.62
	Control	20	.30	.22	-.08
Citizen to Policeman and University Student to University Administrator	Thai Assimilator	17	.34	.69	+.35
	Thai Essay	15	.43	.55	+.12
	Greek Assimilator	17	.32	.32	.00
	Greek Essay	21	.55	.49	-.06
	Control	20	.50	.61	+.11

ingroup—mainly the family—and outgroup (Triandis and Vassiliou, 1972). In control subjects, trained in a geography program, correlations before and after training are practically identical: no change occurred for this group in the degree of differentiation among institutions.

These results provide evidence that assimilator training modifies the differentiation ascribed to the foreigner in a direction which actually corresponds to the characteristics of the target culture. Moreover, they may suggest an entirely new perspective for the cultural assimilator, as the prototype of a methodology for modifying cognitive differentiation. We have repeatedly noted the maladjustive effect of mismatching between the cognitive map of the individual and the one reflected in events of his social environment. The possibility of changing differentiation through training may be applicable well beyond the heterocultural situation: if, for example, mental patients differ from normals in their degree of differentiations, methods of modifying differentiation may have therapeutic value. These considerations will be developed in the next chapter where the problem of cognitive deviance in mental patients is discussed.

SUMMARY

Cross-cultural interaction involves more tension and higher probability of miscommunication than do intra-cultural encounters. Yet quite often people from different cultures communicate successfully. In the previous chapter we have suggested that communication is hindered by cognitive dissimilarity and is facilitated by similarity. It follows that cross-cultural difficulties stem from cognitive differences, but communication is still possible because of the pancultural aspects of interpersonal cognition. The nature of these similarities and differences is the topic of the present chapter.

The idea that some psychological features are invariant underlies many cross-cultural investigations which assume that the variables studied will be found in each culture, although their values may vary across cultures. This assumption was indeed supported by studies on habits as well as verbal and non-verbal communication. Our interest in the structure of interpersonal cognition has led us to investigate the structural similarity across cultures. It was found that the behavioral and family structures are invariant across the populations studied.

The cognitive structure of the adult is assumed to be determined by the sequence by which its dimensions were differentiated in childhood. Structural invariance, thus, reflects a pancultural developmental sequence. We should remember, however, that the two invariant structures, the behavioral and the family ones, are basic and develop early in life. It is expected that those structures which develop later in life will be specific to each culture rather than pancultural.

Structural invariance does not require that the *degree* of differentiation among elements should be the same in diverse cultures. The *order* of the classes may remain invariant even when their relative degree of similarity is specific to each culture. In traditional cultures love and status are less differentiated than in modern society; yet in both cultures love is more similar to status than to information. The fact that the degree of differentiation among cognitive classes is variant while their pattern of proximity is the same in each culture, provides a suitable ground for cross-cultural comparison.

Society is perceived here as a system of institutions, characterized by the resources exchanged within them. A role within a particular institution specifies which of the resources typical to the institution is given by the actor to the object, and the relative power of the actor, regarding his resource. This conceptualization provides a basis for comparing and classifying societies according to their degree of differentiation (a) among institutions, (b) among roles in the same institution, and (c) in the dimensions of each role.

In a study of intrarole differences, Israelis originating from Europe were compared with Israelis of Middle Eastern origin. Specifically, this study investigated the degree of differentiation in spouse roles between (a) positive and negative behaviors, (b) self and spouse as objects of behavior and (c) the resources of love and status. The results indicated that differentiation between self and spouse is higher for Middle Easterns, while differentiation between status and love is higher among Westerns. Differentiation between giving and taking tended to be lower in Middle Easterns but did not reach statistical significance. Scarce differentiation between resources as well as between positive and negative behavior, which characterized the more traditional Middle Eastern Jews, were also found in another Eastern Mediterranean culture—in Greece.

The second level of comparison among societies involves differentiations among roles belonging to the same institution. Of particular interest is the comparison between behaviors in reciprocal roles (e.g., father-son and son-father) as similarity between these roles indicates the extent to which egalitarism exists in the culture; the behavior of father to son will be more similar to that of son to father in an egalitarian society than in an authoritarian one. With regard to the spouse role, the highest similarity was found in Israel, followed in decreasing order, by Greece and India. The comparison of parent-child role pairs revealed highest similarity in the U.S.A., followed by India and Senegal. Thus, U.S.A. and Israel emerge as the most egalitarian and Greece occupies an intermediate position followed by India and then Senegal.

If reciprocal roles in the family are more differentiated in traditional cultures, it seems reasonable to suggest that such differentiation will be transferred to other institutions as well. An analysis of interpersonal situations between Americans and Arabs in institutions other than the family showed, indeed, support for this proposition: out of 22 episodes involving reciprocal roles only two episodes failed to indicate that in Arab society these roles are differentiated more than in the American culture. These results, in conjunction with the previous data on family roles, suggest that differentiation between reciprocal roles is weaker in modern cultures than in traditional ones, not only in the family, but in other institutions as well.

Another level of comparison among cultures pertains to differentiation among corresponding roles from different institutions. We have proposed that in traditional societies there is less differentiation between the resources exchanged in one institution and those transacted in another, so that in these cultures, behavior in different institutions tends to be more similar than in modern society. An analysis of episodes collected for the Arab assimilator supported this hypothesis. A similar picture is presented by Thai assimilator episodes. In particular, these episodes revealed the Thai's expectation to exchange particularistic resources in work situations, an expectation not shared by Americans for whom these exchanges seem inappropriate to work relationship.

Non-family institutions in a traditional culture have retained similarity to the family by allowing particularistic exchanges to take place in their setting. In American cultures a process of assimilation in reverse seems to take place such that in the family as well as in other institutions non-particularistic resources have been more prominent. Through the combined effect of institutional specialization and urban concentration (Ch.5), modern society may have reached a point where the amount of love available is below what is required for normal functioning. Along with increased criticism regarding the scarcity of love in modern culture, there is also a trend to develop institutions which specialize in the exchange of this resource (e.g., sensitivity groups). A different solution is suggested by urban and moral communes which run against the specialization trend by providing a setting for a wide range of resources, modeling on the traditional extended family.

Societies differ not only in their general degree of differentiation on a certain dimension, but also in the way their members react to external events. If cognitive structures mediate between stimulus and response, it becomes of interest to investigate the cultural differences in the cognitive changes which take place following an external event. American students, Far Eastern students in America, and Thai students in Thailand were exposed to communication regarding their failure or success as students. The attitudes ascribed to the communicator (a professor) as well as their attitudes toward themselves as students and as persons in general, were measured. In all groups, the *structure* among the variables was the same; it remained invariant across cultures as well as across success and failure conditions. However, the degree of differentiation among the variables differed systematically for success and failure; the pattern of this difference varied with the cultural group. In American students, all differentiations among the variables became stronger following failure. This higher degree of differentiation increases flexibility of the cognitive structure, thus weakening generalization of status deprivation. The structure becomes more rigid (less differentiated) when the communication is positive, thus facilitating its transmission to other classes and increasing the gain. The Far Eastern reaction to failure consists of *increasing* differentiation between the external source of failure and their reaction while *decreasing* differentiation among the various aspects of self-image. This cognitive reaction leads to leaving the field or losing interest in performance. These two differential mechanisms of coping with failure are appropriate to their respective cultures. However, the individual who is exposed to a new culture and uses his old coping mechanisms will probably experience mismatching and dissonance. Such mismatching can be reduced by cross-cultural training.

Most of the studies on cross-cultural training used the culture-assimilator. In this training, the trainee is provided with interpersonal episodes where some tension and misunderstanding was generated. He is given a set of alternative explanations to each episode and is asked to choose the correct one. Most of these studies investigated the effects of training on task performance and on group socio-emotional climate. It was usually found that training improves the interpersonal climate in an heterocultural task group. The effects of task performance are less clear in the experimental studies where short-term performance was investigated; it is possible that improvement in interpersonal relationship will enhance long-term performance. Field studies have indeed indicated that trained Americans who worked in Honduras improved their performance and adjusted better than did a control group. Similar results were obtained for trained U.S. military personnel in Thailand and Greece.

It is suggested that the behavioral effects of the assimilator program are mediated by cognitive modification. Cultural training modifies the degree of differentiation among interpersonal dimensions and provides mapping rules which fit the target culture. It was indeed found that trainees who were administered the Role Differential instrument and were instructed to answer as if they were members of the target culture changed the degree of differentiation among institutions in the direction appropriate in the target culture. This result seems to suggest that the assimilator may be viewed as a method of wider application for inducing cognitive changes.

CHAPTER 10

THE INTERPERSONAL COGNITION
OF DEVIANT INDIVIDUALS

Overview

IN THE PREVIOUS TWO chapters we have seen that cognitive differences lead to miscommunication, tension and ineffectiveness in task performance, which may be reduced by training. The evidence presented so far, from cross-cultural as well as from intracultural studies, pertained to normal populations. In Chapter 8 we discussed cognitive differences among normal individuals belonging to the same culture; in Chapter 9, the cognition of normal individuals from different cultures was compared. We now turn to examine cognitive differences between normals and deviant persons within the same culture and to consider the effects of psychotherapy in modifying the cognition of mental patients toward the normal cultural pattern.

Both laymen and experts are struck by the difficulty to communicate with mental patients. Indeed, some theoretical conceptualizations have explicitly viewed miscommunication as the core of psychopathology. The data presented so far suggest that communication failures with patients are caused by differences between their cognition and that of normals. These failures, in turn, reduce the patient's opportunity to obtain resources through interpersonal exchanges. Thus, cognitive deviation is seen as a cause of miscommunication, while resource deficit is the result of unsuccessful encounters.

We shall start by considering the communicative behavior of schizophrenics and then turn to compare certain aspects of their cognitive structure with those of neurotics and normal individuals. Next, we shall examine data which bear on the proposition that the supply of resources is more limited in mental patients. The conceptualization of psychotherapy in terms of cognitive deviance, communication difficulties and resource deficit, leads to enquire as to the effects of psychotherapy on these three aspects; it is suggested that therapeutic

346

procedures should focus on the attainment of specific cognitive modifications. The application of structural notions to techniques of behavior therapy is presented as an example of the way in which the knowledge of cognitive organization reported in this volume, may be integrated into current clinical practice.

In the last section of this chapter we shall consider the interpersonal cognition of three deviant groups, other than mental patients: juvenile delinquents, deaf and blind. The comparison of normals with persons deprived of auditory or visual cues may help us understand which differentiations rely mainly on auditory messages and which are the ones more related to visual cues.

MENTAL PATIENTS: CAUSES AND EFFECTS OF THEIR COMMUNICATION DIFFICULTIES

Schools of psychotherapy differ widely in their conceptualization of mental disorders; yet both experts and laymen share the observation that mental patients have difficulties in communicating with others and even with themselves. The layman is likely to use descriptive notions in reference to pathological behavior by labelling it as bizarre, unpredictable, inappropriate or unjustified. Indeed, the behavior of the socially isolated person who fears being contaminated by people and spends hours washing off this "dirt" is bizarre. The expert's conceptualization usually involves explanatory features: behaviorists may emphasize the reinforcement value attached to the act of washing, as it decreases the high level of anxiety aroused by the thought of being contaminated by people. Psychoanalysts may label this compulsive behavior as "anal-fixation" thus relating it to experiences in early childhood. The explanations may vary and so will the therapeutic technique, but at a purely phenomenological level, most schools focus on a common problematic core: the interpersonal behavior of the patient (Adams, 1964). The notion of impaired interpersonal communication becomes an explicit central construct in some conceptualizations of psychopathology (e.g., Carson, 1969; Jackson, 1969; Leary, 1957; Ruesch, 1957 and 1961; Sullivan, 1956); " . . . what we call social or psychological pathology is embedded in communicative behavior," proposes Ruesch (1961, xiii). A corollary of disturbed communication is scarcity of resources found in mental patients. Indeed, resources are obtained in interpersonal situations through communication; if communication is impaired, the opportunity to receive needed resources is reduced. Disturbed individuals often reveal self-resentment, low self-esteem and inability to process information or to earn a living; all these terms denote resource scarcity and/or difficulty in acquiring them through interpersonal exchange.

We have proposed in Chapter 8 that communication failures result from mismapping and mismatching. Mismapping occurs when individuals use different mapping rules in assigning behaviors to classes, so that each will assign the same behavior to a different class. Mismatching occurs when individuals differ in their degree of differentiation among certain classes. It is thus possible that miscommunication with mental patients is due to the fact that they use different mapping rules and/or that their structures differ from those of normal people.

A mismatching hypothesis has been advanced by Federn (1952) who proposed that inability to differentiate between self and non-self constitutes a fundamental disturbance in schizophrenics. The same notion of weak differentiation is conveyed by terms such as "weak ego boundaries" and "weak ego functioning." Indeed Bateson, Jackson, Haley and Weakland (1956) define ego function as "the process of discriminating communicational modes;" likewise the "double-bind" hypothesis of schizophrenia (Bateson et al., 1956) suggests that attempts to differentiate between giving and taking result in punishment, for the recipient of the "double bind" message. On the other hand, over-differentiation between actual-self and ideal-self has often been considered a characteristic of neurotic patients (e.g., Hillson and Worchel, 1957).

Akin to our notion of mismatching is the fit hypothesis (Wechsler and Pugh, 1967) proposing that "people with a particular personal characteristic who are living in communities where the characteristic is less common should have a higher rate of psychiatric hospitalization than people with the characteristic living in communities where it is more common." The two investigators studied 350 towns and cities in Massachusetts—excluding Boston—and were able to identify a number of characteristics for which their hypothesis was supported: younger or medium-aged persons, married individuals, people born in Massachusetts or in other states and persons in specific occupational groups were found to have a higher rate of psychiatric hospitalization in towns where their characteristics were found in low proportion of the population than in towns where a high proportion of persons possessed them. It seems plausible that these background traits are related to differences in cognition; therefore, interpersonal communication will be easier for individuals who are similar in these traits. Communication difficulties may, in turn, create high degrees of tension which may lead to hospitalization.

Following the pioneer work of Bleuler (1950), considerable attention has been given to the "thought disorders" of schizophrenics, also labeled as cognitive or conceptual disorganization and psychological deficit. Schizophrenics were found to differ from normals in the way they relate and classify concepts and objects (e.g., Hamlin and Lorr, 1971); most of this work does not provide a clear indication as to whether these differences are due to mismapping, mismatching or both. Schizophrenic mismapping has been, however, described by Arieti (1959, p. 479) as " . . . a change in the process of symbolizing, . . . which will permit the loss of the introjected symbols which originate from others and the replacement with more primitive ones." Another step forward in the classification of various types of cognitive deviance is provided by Wynne and Singer (1963) who distinguish between undifferentiated forms of thinking (amorphousness) and failure to relate classes (fragmentation). The authors aptly noted that these disturbances could be more precisely called "communicative disorders." Interpersonal communication of schizophrenics has been intensively studied by Longabaugh and his associates.

The Interaction of the Schizophrenic

In a brilliant series of studies, Longabaugh and his associates recorded interpersonal interactions which involved schizophrenic patients. The observations were done by trained observers and were sorted into classes provided by a previously developed classification system (Longabaugh, 1963). The main features of this classification of interpersonal exchanges are rather similar to those developed by us, a fact which will facilitate the presentation of Longabaugh's findings.

One of the populations studied (Eldred, Bell, Sherman and Longabaugh, 1964) was a hospital ward composed of 22 staff members and 18 females diagnosed as chronic schizophrenics who had been hospitalized continuously for at least six years.

The following main results were reported:

1. The frequency of resource exchanges was greatest between staff members, lowest between patients, with staff-patient exchanges occupying an intermediate position.

2. In staff-patient interactions, the staff member was more likely to be the provider of resources, while the patient was more likely to seek a resource from him. However, the likelihood of patients to seek a resource from the staff was equal to them seeking it from another patient.

The outcome of interactions involving schizophrenics was studied by Longabaugh, Eldred, Bell and Sherman (1966). The authors devised an index called "interaction efficiency" which is the ratio between success and failure in resource transactions; a success is said to occur when the resource given by the actor is received by the object; inability to obtain a sought resource or offering a resource which is not accepted by the object are defined as failure. Staff members were more efficient than patients, particularly when they interacted with other staff members rather than with patients; patients, on the other hand, were more efficient when dealing with staff members than when interacting with other patients. These results seem to indicate that instances of miscommunication were highest between patients, lower when one of the participants was a staff member and lowest in interactions involving only staff members. These results can be compared to those obtained for normal subject in Teichman's experiment (see Table 44, p. 274) where the bidded resource closely corresponded to the resource given, although some miscommunication did occur.

Was the communication failure of schizophrenics due to mismapping, mismatching or both? The study was not designed to answer this question. We should remember, however, that the ongoing interpersonal behavior was categorized by observers who presumably used the mapping rules of the prevailing culture for classifying the observed behavior. If schizophrenics used idiosyncratic mapping rules, rather than those prescribed by the culture, the observer's mapping rules would be at variance with theirs while being congruent with the ones used by the staff. Consequently, the results may reflect the extent to which the observer's mapping is different from the one employed by the various observed interactors. The fact that the observer ascribed to staff more success in resource exchange, indirectly suggests that some mismapping was involved in the communication failure of patients. Indeed, communication inefficiency was significantly related to various indices of severity of illness: communication was poorer for the more disturbed patients. On the other hand, neither the frequency of interaction nor the giving-seeking ratios were related to severity of illness.

The communication pattern of schizophrenics was further investigated in a later study (Longabaugh, 1971). Subjects were 45 female patients diagnosed as schizophrenics, who were admitted to a research ward; most of them came from the community and a few from other wards. Using the procedure of the previous study, interpersonal behavior involving a patient was systematically observed and recorded on a time sampling basis, until discharge or for a whole year, if the patient was not discharged earlier.

Schizophrenic behavior is often described as unpredictable; Longabaugh examined the proposition that unpredictability is directly related to severity of illness. Percentages of predictability were computed for patients as well as for staff members; they indicated the extent to which any given behavioral class could be predicted from the behavior which either preceeded or followed it. In some sequences the two adjacent behavior units were emitted by the same person, the patient or the staff member; in the other sequences, each act was emitted by a different person. In the same-person sequences, the predictability percentage indicates how much the person's act is predictable from *his own* adjacent behavior; in different-person sequences, the person's act is predicted from the *other's* adjacent behavior. Thus, while the scores of the second type reflect the effectiveness of interpersonal communication, the first type indicate the consistency of the observant's behavior.

Severity of illness was determined by a prognostic score based on items indicative of a "shut-in" personality (lack of heterosexual contacts, scarce or narrow interests, low energy tone). Previous research had shown that these items have better prognostic value than items related to "insidiousness" of the onset of disturbance (e.g., lack of precipitating condition).

Prognostic score, predictability percentages and frequency of occurrence of resource exchange were then intercorrelated. The hypotheses investigated were:

1. Seriousness of disturbance would be negatively related to certainty of communication and to its frequency.

2. Interaction would be more frequent when there is more certainty.

The results indicated that prediction of patient's reaction to staff member's proaction was more difficult for the more disturbed patients although the correlation was not large enough to reach statistical significance. Certainty of communication was not affected by seriousness of disturbance when the interaction sequence was initiated by the patient rather than by staff, and when the patients interacted with other patients. These findings may indicate that even a relatively mild degree of disturbance is sufficient to impair communication. Since there are no comparative data on interaction between normal individuals, this interpretation remains an open question.

More conclusive, although quite surprising, were the data on behavioral consistency: the more serious the patient's condition was, the less consistent was the behavior of staff members when relating to him. The relationship between the consistency of the patient's behavior toward staff or other patients, and the degree of his disturbance were in the predicted direction, but failed to reach statistical significance. Apparently, the more disturbed the patient, the less consistent is the behavior of others, particularly staff members, toward him. Seriously ill patients are also less consistent in their behavior; yet the degree of their disturbance influences their own behavior *less* than it does for those interacting with them.

The results may indicate that staff members, and possibly other individuals, are trained by the schizophrenic to become inconsistent when interacting with him, rather than training him to maintain consistency of communication. But why should the relationship between inconsistency and severity of disturbance be *stronger* for the staff than the patient himself? An alternative, and perhaps a more plausible explanation is that staff changed their behavior unsystematically in an effort to "hit" the correct class of the patient's cognition, attempting, thus, to overcome the difference in mapping. They behaved somewhat like a shooter who cannot see the target: if he spreads his fire rather than concentrating on a single point, he is more likely to hit the unseen target; the observer who knows where the target is will obviously perceive such behavior as inconsistent. Similarly, the observers in this study, using the prevailing mapping rules, placed the staff behaviors in different categories; the more disturbed the patient was the more categories were used by staff when interacting with him.

The same study also showed that the frequency of participating in exchanges was lower for patients who had greater difficulty in communication and were more seriously disturbed; this result stands in contrast with the one found in a previous study (Longabaugh et al., 1966). These studies, however, employed different indices of morbidity and were conducted on different populations. In the first study patients were chronically ill and had been hospitalized for a much longer period. Therefore their resource bankruptcy was chronic and extreme; even the "least disturbed" patient of this population was seriously ill.

The studies summarized here have provided evidence on the communication difficulties presented in interaction with schizophrenics; some aspects of these difficulties were found to be related to the seriousness of the disturbance. As interpreted by us, the data indicate that schizophrenics use mapping rules which are different from those prevailing in the culture. We now turn to consider the second type of miscommunication—mismatching, by discussing differences in degree of differentiation, between normals and mental patients.

Deviances in Degree of Differentiation

Using the Role Behavior Test (see Appendix A) for spouse roles, Edna Foa (1970) studied cognitive differentiations of mental patients. Each patient, who had not been hospitalized for at least six months prior to his admission, was administered the test within the first three days of hospitalization. The final analysis included thirty schizophrenics and thirty neurotics. The comparison between these two groups suggested several cognitive differences. Of particular interest is the finding that schizophrenics differentiate significantly less than neurotics between self and other as objects. This finding supports the long standing notion that schizophrenics have "weak ego boundaries," or that they underdifferentiate between self and other (Federn, 1952). Later on, the study was replicated with other patients and was extended to include additional family roles. At the same time, Professor Chatterjee collected data on normals and mildly disturbed individuals who applied for outpatient treatment in Benares, India; Professor Collomb and Dr. de Preneuf investigated normals, mildly disturbed patients and schizophrenics in Senegal. Translations of the Role Behavior Test were used in these latter studies, thus permitting a cross-cultural comparison.

SELF-OTHER DIFFERENTIATION. Table 60 summarizes the data on self-other differentiation in various roles and cultures for each group of subjects. The entries in this table are mean correlations for the actual behavior of the subject toward himself and toward the other; each mean was obtained by averaging the correlations for giving and taking away love and status. In the American samples, subjects labeled as "mildly disturbed" were diagnosed as neurotics; the data for normals in this culture were obtained from the previously mentioned study on juveniles; male roles were omitted since the number of patients was not large enough (see Table 62 for the number of cases).

In all cases, except one, the correlations between behavior toward self and behavior toward other are higher for schizophrenics than for either mildly disturbed or normals; since high correlation indicates low differentiation, these results support the view that schizophrenics underdifferentiate between behavior directed toward self and that directed to other. A similar but weaker trend can be noticed for mildly

Table 60

MEAN CORRELATION BETWEEN ACTUAL BEHAVIOR OF SUBJECT
TOWARD SELF AND TOWARD OTHER

Culture and role	Severity of disturbance		
	Normal	Mildly disturbed	Schizophrenic
India (Benares)			
Wife to husband	32	41	—
Daughter to father	33	40	—
Daughter to mother	27	28	—
Husband to wife	46	42	—
Son to father	28	41	—
Son to mother	33	50	—
Senegal			
Daughter to father	52	11	34
Son to mother	16	45	54
U.S.A. (Missouri)			
Wife to husband	—	25	56
Daughter to father	45	40	63
Daughter to mother	37	51	58
Spouse to spouse	—	32	64
Median (all cultures and roles)	33	40	57

Note: Decimal point omitted

disturbed individuals: they also differentiate less than normals, but not to the same extent as schizophrenics. The median correlation for all cultures and roles combined, appearing in the bottom row of the table, is lowest for normals and highest for schizophrenics; moreover, there is almost no overlapping between the values obtained in normals and those found for schizophrenics: only one correlation of these patients is lower than the highest one for normals. It seems therefore, that the schizophrenic characteristic of under differentiating between self and other as objects has gained some cross-cultural validity.

BETWEEN-ROLES DIFFERENTIATION. Using the previous sources of data, the degree of differentiation between roles was investigated in the various cultural groups; no systematic differences between normal and disturbed subjects were found except for the tendency of schizophrenics to underdifferentiate between reciprocal roles and to overdifferentiate between non-reciprocal ones. Overdifferentiation among non-reciprocal roles was also found by Teichman (1971a) in neurotics. Using a revision of Kelly's role construct test, Teichman asked ten normal students and ten students diagnosed as neurotics to describe various family members on bipolar scales. The results indicated that neurotics tended to describe family members as more dissimilar than did normals.

Bannister, Fransella and Agnew (1971) investigated the relationship among personal constructs (a notion akin to role) by using a simplified version of Kelly's procedure (Bannister and Fransella, 1966). They found that schizophrenics deviate from the normal pattern of interrelationship more than do other patients. The deviation was strongest for schizophrenics who were independently diagnosed as having thought disorders. Schizophrenics were also found to have stronger differentiation then do neurotics, especially those who were clinically diagnosed as thought disordered. This last result coincides with our finding that schizophrenics overdifferentiate among non-reciprocal roles.

If differentiation is the hallmark of cognitive development (see Ch. 2) why would it be more pronounced in patients whose thinking is severely disturbed? An indirect answer is provided by examining the pattern of intercorrelations among constructs, obtained in successive administrations of equivalent instruments.

CONSISTENCY AND DIFFERENTIATION. Schizophrenics, and more so the thought-disordered group, show low consistency between equivalent instruments (Bannister et al., 1971). This finding seems to indicate an erratic mapping: stimuli which would be assigned to the same class by normal individuals were categorized by schizophrenics into different classes, thus decreasing the relationship among classes and presenting an empirical picture of high differentiatiation. This effect is equivalent to low reliability of a testing instrument; it is well-known that a test with low reliability cannot have high validity. In the present case, however, low reliability is due not to the instrument, but to the subject. Consistency and interrelationship among constructs tend, indeed, to correlate highly in a psychiatric population while being more independent in normal subjects (Bannister and Fransella, 1966; Bannister et al., 1971). Consequently, low relationship among constructs indicates high differentiation when the population is normal; it merely reflects vagaries in mapping for psychiatric patients. Therefore, correlational evidence for strong differentiation in disturbed individuals should be treated with extreme caution. On the other hand, high correlations in mental patients can be taken safely as evidence for underdifferentiation; these correlations would probably be even higher had the counterproductive effect of low consistency been neutralized. Thus, the effect of inconsistency does not invalidate the finding, discussed earlier in this chapter, that schizophrenics underdifferentiate between self and other as objects.

STRUCTURAL PATTERN. The erratic mapping which characterizes psychiatric patients and schizophrenics in particular is expected to cause deviations in the structural pattern, as some correlations will be lower than predicted by their position in the matrix. Moreover, there should be more deviance in schizophrenics than in neurotics.

Table 61 presents the correlations among classes of interpersonal behavior in the spouse role for 30 schizophrenics and 30 neurotics who were residents of Mid-Missouri. The normal structural pattern is already familiar to the reader from Chapter 3 (see Table 4). The order of correlations found in normals is somewhat preserved here, even in the schizophrenic group; however, there are fifteen coefficients deviating from the normal pattern in schizophrenic patients, while only eight deviations are found in neurotics. In other samples of schizophrenics there were even more deviations and the structural pattern was hardly recognizable.

In summary, there is some support for the proposition that mental patients differ from normal individuals of their own culture both in the mapping rules they use for categorizing interpersonal stimuli into classes, and in their degree of differentiation among classes; of particular interest is the finding that the schizophrenic's underdifferentiation between self and other as objects appears to have cross-cultural validity. There is no solid evidence, as yet, that different diagnostic groups correspond to specific patterns of cognitive deviance. Exploration for such correspondence will require methods of observation and analysis which will clearly separate between the effects of mapping and those of dimensional differentiation, to avoid the spurious effect

Table 61

INTERCORRELATION AMONG TYPES OF ACTUAL BEHAVIOR OF SUBJECT,
FOR NEUROTICS AND SCHIZOPHRENICS

	Diagnosis															
	Schizophrenic								Neurotic							
Behavior type	1	2	3	4	5	6	7	8	1	2	3	4	5	6	7	8
1 Giving status to spouse	—	49	51	46	14	22	27	32	—	67	30	19	−09	−12	20	36
2 Giving love to spouse	49	—	63	49	40	55	64	48	67	—	17	−04	31	07	33	22
3 Giving love to self	51	63	—	71	40	54	60	46	30	17	—	54	05	32	08	04
4 Giving status to self	46	49	71	—	23	26	42	31	19	−04	54	—	36	37	15	11
5 (Not) Taking status from self	14	40	40	23	—	74	44	74	−09	31	05	36	—	54	20	40
6 (Not) Taking love from self	22	55	54	26	74	—	66	75	−12	07	32	37	54	—	51	31
7 (Not) Taking love from spouse	27	64	60	42	44	66	—	58	20	33	08	15	20	51	—	43
8 (Not) Taking status from spouse	32	48	46	31	74	75	58	—	36	22	04	11	40	31	43	—

Note: Decimal point omitted

of erratic mapping on the apparent degree of differentiation. Furthermore, it is questionable whether current classifications of mental diseases combine patients who have similar patterns of deviance and distinguish among those having different patterns. Further investigation of deviance in cognitive structures may lead to new ways of classifying psychiatric diseases, which will be directly related to treatment. We shall elaborate on this topic later in the chapter.

DO MENTAL PATIENTS CONSTITUTE A SUBCULTURE? We have just considered some evidence suggesting that mental patients differ from normal individuals belonging to the same culture with regard to degree of differentiation. Similar findings have been reported in Chapter 9 when we compared normal subjects across various cultures: there too, differences in differentiation degree were noted. Should we then infer that mental patients deviate from the prevailing culture in the same way as strangers do? Are patients, in other words, just like individuals from another culture?

A positive answer to this question would rule out the possibility of defining normality, other than in the statistical sense of being the situation prevailing in the majority of a given population. Another consequence would be to put a question mark on the ethics of psychotherapy: if patients are just different, what right do we have to make them similar to the majority; the alternative possibility to modify the majority to fit mental patients would be equally valid on a moral plane, although not so on a practical one.

If, on the other hand, the cognition of mental patients not only differ from normals' but is inadequate to secure interpersonal communication even with individual cognitively similar to them, then we shall be justified in rejecting the view that they constitute a minority culture. A sufficient degree of differentiation between self and other may be a necessary condition for relating to other individuals: we have seen (Table 60) that differentiation between self and other as objects is low in mental patients irrespective of their culture; on the other hand, the same table shows that normal individuals from different cultures tend to exhibit a similar degree of differentiation; thus we found in this dimension, a pronounced patient-normal difference and scarcely any cross-cultural difference. Contrarywise, dimensions on which cultures differ—discussed in Chapter 9—do not appear to differ between patient and normals. The only possible exception is that differentiation between objects was found to be lower among Israelis of European origin than among those from the Middle East; however, the former group still differentiate more than mental patients, particularly schizophrenics. The highest correlations between behavior toward self and toward other reported in Table 51 for Israelis of European background is .34; the corresponding correlations for schizophrenics, given in Table 60, are at least equal to this maximum value—in one case, or higher; in the mildly disturbed group, eight out of twelve coefficients are higher than .34.

Another requirement of effective communication is that mapping rules should be fairly constant: if the same individual uses different mapping rules at different times—as it seems to be the case with schizophrenics (see p. 354), then the task of learning which rule is used at a particular instance will become impossible for the other, with resulting communicative failure. Mapping rules also differ from one culture to another, but—among normals—they tend to be constant within the culture, so that the stranger gets a fair chance of learning what these rules are.

In conclusion, cognitive differences hinder communication across cultures as well as between normal and disturbed individuals; yet the deviations found in mental patients appear to be such as to impede communications even among individuals who do not differ cognitively: without a certain amount of differentiation in some basic dimensions the possibility of interpersonal communication appears quite problematic. Indeed the work of Longabaugh and his associates, reported earlier in this chapter (see p. 350), has shown that interaction efficiency is lower when a schizophrenic interacts with another patient than when he communicates with staff.

Scarcity of Resource Exchanges

We have considered some evidence suggesting that mental patients deviate from the mapping rules and the degree of differentiation found among normal individuals from the same culture. These deviations explain the communication difficulties of patients found by Long-abaugh and his associates; indeed cognitive similarity is a necessary condition for efficient interpersonal communication (see Ch. 8), and for successful exchange of resources. This line of reasoning leads to the proposition that giving and receiving resources will be less frequent. in psychiatric patients than in normal persons.

Data bearing on this hypothesis are given in Table 62. Once again we are comparing three types of population—normals, mildly disturbed and schizophrenics—within each culture and role. The source of data is the cross-cultural study described earlier in this chapter, in reference to Table 60. The entries of Table 62 are mean frequencies for giving love and status by the subject and to the subject, and taking these resources by him and from him. The highest possible score is 12, indicating that the behavior considered is extremely frequent; the lowest possible score is zero, signifying almost complete absence of the

Table 62

MEAN FREQUENCY OF RESOURCE EXCHANGE FOR LOVE AND STATUS COMBINED

Culture and role	Behavior												Number of Subjects		
	Subject to other						Other to subject								
	Giving			Taking			Giving			Taking					
	N	M	S	N	M	S	N	M	S	N	M	S	N	M	S
India (Benares)															
Wife to husband	9.5	6.1	—	1.1	3.8	—	8.8	4.9	—	2.4	4.4	—	39	9	—
Daughter to father	9.4	6.5	—	0.6	3.0	—	8.8	4.1	—	1.5	3.1	—	51	11	—
Daughter to mother	9.8	6.2	—	1.1	3.2	—	8.8	5.8	—	2.1	3.1	—	54	14	—
Husband to wife	8.4	8.2	—	1.4	2.5	—	10.3	7.3	—	0.8	2.5	—	38	18	—
Son to father	9.6	7.7	—	0.9	3.2	—	8.9	6.6	—	1.5	3.7	—	46	25	—
Son to mother	9.5	7.6	—	1.3	2.4	—	8.7	6.7	—	2.2	2.3	—	49	21	—
Senegal															
Daughter to father	9.0	9.2	8.5	0.5	0.7	1.9	8.7	8.1	8.6	1.4	1.5	2.4	50	21	20
Son to mother	9.5	9.8	9.2	0.4	1.0	1.1	9.2	9.2	8.9	1.2	1.8	2.2	50	30	31
U.S.A. (Missouri)															
Wife to husband	—	8.3	7.7	—	1.8	3.0	—	7.0	7.3	—	2.9	4.0	—	44	29
Daughter to father	7.4	7.0	6.9	1.4	1.1	1.8	8.1	6.4	7.2	1.2	1.5	1.8	47	20	24
Daughter to mother	7.3	8.6	8.1	1.4	0.8	2.5	7.3	8.3	8.1	1.4	1.7	2.7	51	23	19
Husband to wife	—	8.7	9.9	—	1.6	0.8	—	7.7	6.3	—	2.6	6.7	—	15	6
Son to father	8.2	7.3	5.3	1.1	2.6	3.3	8.8	7.3	5.4	1.2	2.3	3.4	46	7	9
Son to mother	8.3	7.3	6.0	0.9	2.1	1.4	8.5	7.7	7.2	1.1	1.8	1.8	50	14	20
Spouse to spouse	—	8.4	8.8	—	3.3	4.6	—	7.4	7.0	—	4.2	6.2	—	30	30

Note: N = Normal subject; M = Mildly disturbed subject; S = Schizophrenic subject.

described behavior. These scores were computed from the answers provided by the subject and therefore represent the frequency of participating in exchanges of love and status, as perceived by him. To simplify the presentation, scores for exchanges of love and status were averaged for each behavior. The number of subjects in each group, culture and role appears in the three rightmost columns of the table.

In most comparisons, normal subjects reported that they give more to the other and receive more from him. Furthermore, there is some tendency for schizophrenics to report lower frequency of exchanges than do mildly disturbed individuals; thus, on the whole, the frequency of positive exchanges appears to decrease the more disturbed the group is. The data thus support the proposition that mental illness reduces positive exchanges, at least for love and status. With regard to negative exchanges, the picture is completely reversed: the more disturbed the subject is, the higher his reported frequency of negative behavior, both as an actor and as an object. In general, the frequency of taking away behavior is highest for schizophrenics and lowest for normal individuals, with mildly disturbed patients being in between. The higher frequency in perceived negative exchanges reported by more severe patients, runs contrary to our original prediction that mental patients will show lower frequency of positive as well as negative encounters. This result, however, is consistent with the finding that cognitive differences produce tension and frustration. We can thus conclude that cognitive differences, cross-dultural as well as intracultural, reduce positive exchanges while increasing negative ones.

Some readers may be inclined to interpret these results in terms of social desirability. Social norms prescribe giving love and status to other members of the family, while disapproving acts of taking them away: less disturbed subjects are more likely to describe family relations in accordance with social precepts than would schizophrenics who may be less sensitive to these norms. The social desirability explanation is denied by Longabaugh's finding, previously reported, showing scarcity of exchanges in schizophrenics; his data were recorded by independent observers who presumably were not more socially sensitive when observing staff members than when recording patients' behavior. Moreover, if the relationship between severity of disturbance and frequency of positive and negative exchanges reflects differences in sensitivity to social norms, then it should not be found for behaviors which are neither approved nor disapproved. One such behavioral class is "giving love to self." Psychologists have recognized self-acceptance as an important ingredient of mental health, but at least in Western culture, there is no specific norm prescribing or forbidding it; the Biblical injunction "love thy neighbor as thyself" implicitly connotes that self-love does not constitute a moral problem.

Table 63

MEAN FREQUENCY OF "GIVING LOVE TO SELF"

Culture and role	Severity of disturbance		
	Normal	Mildly disturbed	Schizophrenic
India (Benares)			
Wife to husband	9.8	5.6	—
Daughter to father	9.6	6.3	—
Daughter to mother	9.3	5.9	—
Husband to wife	9.6	8.3	—
Son to father	8.9	7.0	—
Son to mother	9.0	7.6	—
Senegal			
Daughter to father	10.9	10.2	9.4
Son to mother	11.0	10.3	9.8
U.S.A. (Missouri)			
Wife to husband	—	6.4	6.3
Daughter to father	7.3	7.0	6.5
Daughter to mother	7.1	7.0	6.5
Husband to wife	—	8.5	7.8
Son to father	7.8	5.6	5.4
Son to mother	7.9	6.9	7.0
Spouse to spouse	—	5.3	6.6

Table 63 gives the mean frequency of "giving love to self" as reported by the subjects. The trend found in Table 62 for behavior toward other is even more pronounced here: the reported frequency of giving love to self was always highest in normal subjects, followed in decreasing order by mildly disturbed and then by schizophrenics; there were only two deviations where the frequency for schizophrenics was lower than for the mildly disturbed. The extent of giving love to self is thus inversely related to severity of disturbance. Apart from refuting the social desirability explanation, this result is of intrinsic interest as it suggests that the difficulties experienced by disturbed individuals in interpersonal exchanges exist also in intrapersonal ones.

We have considered three interrelated aspects of interpersonal rela-. tions in mental patients: difficulty of communication, cognitive deviance and scarcity of positive exchanges. We turn now to examine some eventual effects of psychiatric treatment on these three aspects.

PSYCHOTHERAPY AND COGNITIVE DEVIANCE

The conception of psychopathology proposed here—anomolous mapping rules and deviant degree of cognitive differentiation, resulting in communication difficulties and hence paucity of positive resource exchanges—suggests that treatment should aim at cognitive modification. An increase in the provision of resources may be a desirable short-term goal, particularly when it leads to cognitive changes; by itself, however, the non-contingent atmosphere of acceptance, provided in some therapeutic settings (see Ch. 5, pp. 153–155) is unlikely to produce long-lasting effects. If communication difficulties persist, the resource deficit will reappear. Yet, in the literature on effects of treatment, it is easier to find evidence for resource increase than for cognitive changes. This fact does not necessarily indicate that such changes do not occur: it may merely reflect the preference of the investigators or the relative difficulty of studying cognitive processes.

Increase in Resources

An attempt to study changes in cognition as well as in resource provision, following short-term hospitalization was made by Teichman, Bazzoui and Foa (in preparation). Every patient admitted to a ward of the Mid-Missouri Mental Health Center during a period of eight months was administered the Role Behavior Test (see Appendix A) within the first three days of hospitalization. Only those who were later diagnosed as neurotics or schizophrenics were retained in the present study and were retested with the same instrument one or two days before discharge. Subjects were 32 neurotics and 16 schizophrenics, all married females maintaining marital relationship with their husbands.

The diagnosis of schizophrenia was made only in the presence of unequivocal Bleulerian criteria. The schizophrenic group was composed of different categories with the exception of chronic schizophrenia. In the neurotic group, most forms of the common neuroses were represented. The Mid-Missouri Mental Health Center is oriented toward a short-term hospitalization and treatment (two months or less). During this period the patient receives individual, group, family and/or drug therapy, according to his needs. Only patients who may be treated in an open ward system are admitted.

In order to locate changes in the accumulation of love and status by the patient, mean scores for the various behavioral classes were compared before and after treatment. Significant improvements in resource accumulation were found for neurotics, but not for schizophrenics; in particular, neurotics increased the perceived frequency of giving love and status to themselves and decreased the frequency of self-rejection; their behavior toward their spouses followed the same trend but the change was less pronounced. Some tendency for change in the same direction, although smaller and less consistent, was also found in schizophrenics. All these changes referred to actual behavior; no significant influence of treatment was detected at the ideal level. Consequently, differentiation between actual and ideal levels was somewhat reduced for neurotics. No further evidence for cognitive changes following treatment was obtained in this study.

Findings bearing on resource improvement, following treatment, have been described by other investigators as well (e.g., Butler and Haigh, 1954; Harrow, Fox and Detre, 1969; Harrow, Fox, Markhus,

Stillman and Hallowell, 1968). Reduction in discrepancy between actual-self and ideal-self following therapy has also been reported (e.g., Varble and Landfield, 1969).

Reducing Mismatching and Mismapping

The penury of empirical evidence on the cognitive effects of psychotherapy does not negate the possibility that such changes do actually occur. A common result of treatment is a change in the frequency of emitting a given behavioral class toward or away from the frequency of another class; such change will alter the degree of differentiation between these two classes. If, for example, a patient behaves ambivalently toward his spouse, he can be trained to reduce the frequency of negative behaviors and to increase the frequency of giving behavior. This training should result in increased differentiation between giving and taking which, as noted in Chapter 9, is essential in Western culture for maintenance of interpersonal relationships. In general, when behavioral classes which tend to occur jointly are differentially reinforced, an increase in the differentiation between the two classes will be evident. Such treatment is fairly common in behavior modification techniques.

Similar changes may also occur in Rogerian treatment, although in a less direct manner: during treatment sessions the therapist emits only "giving" behaviors toward the client; this unconditional acceptance by the therapist is intended to help the client accept himself. If the patient increases the frequency of "giving love to self," in spite of the fact that he may still be rejected by significant others, differentiation between self and others as actors should increase. Thus, changes toward normalcy in the cognitive structure of patients may be obtained in existing schools of treatment, although their theoretical justification will usually differ from the one proposed here.

Concern with the twin problems of communication—mapping and differentiation matching—becomes more explicit when the therapeutic situation is conceptualized as an interpersonal relationship. Thus, Ruesch (1961, p. 460) clearly states that "therapeutic communication differs from ordinary communication in that the intention of one or more of the participants is clearly directed at bringing about a change in the system and manner of communication." A first step in this task is to learn the mapping rules of the patient: ". . . the psychiatrist has the task of ascertaining in each case how the individual uses words and what relation, if any, these have to action . . ." (Ruesch, 1961, p. 275). Then problems of anomalous differentiation can be attacked: "Separation of elements of behavior which in the course of events have become linked but which do not belong together is an essential therapeutic task." (Ruesch, 1961, pp. 260–261). The therapist's activity, when helping families with schizophrenic offspring in reaching shared mapping rules, is described by Mosher (1969) as follows: "Statements which were *inherently* unclear were questioned and probed until everyone clearly shared their meaning."

Another procedure which aims at changing mapping rules is Frankl's "paradoxical intention" (1962, pp. 125–129). In this technique the patient is invited to reclassify a non-desirable behavior into a desirable one, and he is instructed, humorously, to increase its frequency. For example, a patient who experiences difficulty in falling asleep is instructed to stay awake as long as possible. In the cognition of patients thus treated, ideal behavior is often negatively related to actual behavior: "I am unable to do what I ought to do;" in consequence, reclassifying the undesirable behavior as desirable results in its extinction.

Cognitive Similarity Between Patient and Therapist

The conceptualization of psychotherapy as an interpersonal encounter where communication is processed, led to investigate the effects of cognitive similarity between patient and therapist on the therapeutic outcomes. Landfield and Nawas (1964) found that treatment was more likely to succeed when patient and therapist shared a similar interpersonal cognition. Similarly, Carr (1970) reported that "differentiation compatibility of patient and therapist is essential to improve outcome as perceived by the patient and as evidenced by his reported symptom reduction." He also noted that when such compatibility in interpersonal differentiation was not present initially, it tended to increase during the early stage of treatment; a later stage, however, was characterized by an increase in the therapist's differentiation. It seems that initial convergence serves to facilitate communication through which the therapist, later on, transmits structural information to patient. This process bears similarity to parent-infant communication (see Chapter 8, p. 298); psychotherapy was indeed conceptualized as a form of socialization (Levine, 1969).

In both studies, the subjects were outpatient neurotics who presumably had come to treatment with a certain degree of differentiation and some constancy in mapping rules, which are necessary for communication. For these patients, initial cognitive similarity with the therapist may indeed be an advantage. However, when the patients lack these minimal requirements for communicating, as schizophrenics may do, strong similarity may well hinder treatment. In line with results reported by Carson and Heine (1962), extreme similarity as well as extreme dissimilarity are expected to be detrimental to treatment outcome with psychotics.

In these investigations as well as in similar studies relating cognitive matching of patient and therapist to treatment outcome, the therapist's responses referred to his own cognition rather than to the cognition he ascribed to his patient. Yet, the study of cross-cultural training (Chapter 9, pp. 339–342) has indicated that effective communication is achieved when one communicator learns the structure *ascribed* to the other; it follows that a successful therapist does not have to be cognitively similar to the patient, he should be able, however, to accurately assume his patient's viewpoint.

Changing Cognition Through Psychotherapy

In the present state of affairs, the ability of the therapist to predict the patient's viewpoint rests mainly on his intuition. Moreover, most of the cognitive changes produced through psychotherapy are induced either accidentally or unsystematically. Consequently, little attention has been paid to the use of communication in therapy; Mosher (1969) complains that he "was unable to find a recent article on family therapy which gave primary emphasis to the treatment of defective family communication processes." However, as we progress in discovering in what ways the cognition of specific types of patients deviates normalcy, it becomes increasingly possible to substitute intuition with systematic information. This knowledge will not only improve patient-therapist communication but, more important, will provide a clear goal for treatment in terms of modifying the cognitive deviance specific to each type of patient; in this way an organic link will be established between the diagnostic classification of cognitive deviances and the treatment required for their modification.

Changes in differentiation could be induced through the analysis and discussion of actual episodes, preferably supplied by the patient himself, where the maladjustive effects of "wrong" degree of differentiation are reflected. For example, the patient who is distressed because his spouse would not go to sleep when he is tired ascribes his needs to the other and thus shows lack of differentiation between objects. When such behavior is repeatedly analyzed and new forms of behavior introduced into the patient's behavioral repertoir, differentiation between self and other increases. As previously noted (Chapter 9, pp. 334–342), this technique of modifying structures has already been used in cross-cultural training of normal subjects; since in both programs the basic goal is to change degrees of differentiation, the experience gained in one area may be adapted to the other area.

The treatment of cognitive deviance does not necessarily require the development of entirely new forms of therapy. We have already suggested that several current therapies may implicitly result in cognitive modifications; it seems sufficient to make this goal explicit and to focus the treatment more sharply toward achieving it. The integration of current types of treatment with a cognitive conceptualization of mental disturbances is exemplified in a study on the relationship between behavior therapy and cognitive structures (Edna Foa, 1973), which will be considered briefly.

Cognitive Structures in Behavior Therapy

In the practice of behavior therapy it is alway necessary to rely on the patient's subjective reports with regard to the degree of anxiety he experiences in different situations. Eliciting this information presents, however, difficulties with some patients: obsessive-compulsives are reluctant to commit themselves to a specific rank order of subjective feelings; other patients have become so skillful in avoiding anxiety-provoking situations that they cannot differentiate among them according to their degree of potential anxiety arousal. Even in the absence of such difficulties it seems desirable to free the therapeutic process as much as possible from reliance on the patient's subjective report. This goal may be facilitated by using the knowledge we have about interpersonal cognitive structures. To illustrate this point, let us consider the application of two specific structures, the structure of resources (Ch. 3) and that of family roles (Ch. 4), to three techniques of behavior therapy: hierarchy construction, shaping behavioral changes and behavioral analysis.

HIERARCHIES. A central concept in behavior therapy is that of hierarchy. When a patient presents non-adaptive anxiety to a class of events, the therapeutic aim is to dissociate the anxiety response from the events by pairing them to an incompatible response such as relaxation (Wolpe, 1958, 1969). This procedure starts with the identification of stimulus-situations to which the patient responds with anxiety, and then classifying them into different themes. For each theme several situations are chosen, varying with respect to the degree of anxiety they elicit in the patient. These situations are then ordered along the dimension of anxiety, from the most to the least anxiety evoking. Thus, proximity of events in the hierarchy indicates similarity in anxiety-evoking potential: the nearer two events are in the hierarchy, the more similar are their respective degrees of anxiety arousal. Apparently, the hierarchy is effective in ordering events on some underlying dimensions, which are relevant to anxiety, so that events similar on these dimensions are placed next to each other. It follows that stimuli which are perceived as similar, evoke a similar degree of anxiety. Construction of a hierarchy thus involves delimitation of a universe of content and ordering of events in this universe along dimensions which are directly related to anxiety arousal.

Frequently the dimensions appearing in a hierarchy are physical: when a patient experiences fear of a given object, such as a spider or a snake, a hierarchy can be based on the physical distance from this object. In this case, events assuming similar values of anxiety will also be similar with respect to the distance between the patient and the feared object (for examples, see Wolpe, 1969, pp. 87–88). Other physical dimensions which often occur in hierarchies are length of time (e.g., five days prior to examination), time duration, height, width, and number of feared objects. The relationship between physical dimensions and anxiety is not always monotonic: being "on the way to the university on the day of an examination" was found, for example, as anxiety-arousing as being "in the process of answering an examination paper" (Wolpe, 1969, p. 117). Nevertheless, these dimensions provide an objective guideline for hierarchy construction.

Physical dimensions may prove to be less useful when interpersonal or social anxiety is considered (Wolpe, 1969, p. 116). Perhaps in these cases, anxiety level is less related to the physical attributes of the situation than to its social connotations. The anxiety experienced while being at a party may be more influenced by the particular people met there than by the length of staying at the gathering (Wolpe, 1969, pp. 112–113).

Until now, one had to rely on his own intuition and on the patient's report in the search for meaningful social dimensions. Now, however, dimensions of the cognitive structures of social events have been identified; since their generality across people was verified, they may be applied to the construction of hierarchies in the same way that physical dimensions were used so far. There is, indeed, close formal similarity between a hierarchy and a cognitive structure: a hierarchy is a set of events belonging to a given universe of content ordered by their degree of anxiety-arousal; a structure is a set of classes (of events) belonging to a given universe of content, ordered along specific dimensions, which may or may not be related to anxiety-arousal. Two differences can be noted: (1) The dimensions underlying a hierarchy are known to be directly related to anxiety, while this relationship has not been demonstrated, as yet, with regard to dimensions of cognitive structures; (2) The dimensions of a hierarchy are either physical or derived in each case by empirical intuitive considerations; on the other hand, those of a structure are psychological and grounded in theory. The second difference is merely one of practice; it appears, therefore possible to use psychological dimensions of general validity in hierarchy construction. As an example of such usage, let us consider the structure of resources (see Ch. 3). We have seen that resources proximal in the structure are more likely to elicit similar responses in terms of the degree of satisfaction experienced in a positive exchange or in terms of residual aggression left after terminating a negative one (see Ch. 6). These results may be generalized to anxiety, which is an autonomic and cognitive response to a certain stimulus-event. If we know that a given class of events evokes a very high degree of anxiety, we can then hypothesize that its neighboring classes will evoke a somewhat lower degree of anxiety, which will be, however, higher than the level elicited by a remote class. Suppose that a patient manifests high sensitivity to loss of love or rejection, so that any event which contains elements of rejection evokes a high degree of anxiety. On the strength of the structure of resources, we shall expect that expression of disrespect will also evoke anxiety, although less so than does rejection. Being misinformed will produce even less anxiety, while being deprived of money will create the least anxiety, money being the resource most removed from love in the structure. In essence, knowledge of the structure of resources provides a guideline for constructing a hierarchy. At the top of the hierarchy, we shall put items from the class of personal rejection (loss of love), followed by items which convey loss of status; then some items regarding loss of information are to be introduced into the hierarchy and finally some items of money loss.

The structure of resources has two dimensions, particularism and concreteness. For the specific problem of social anxiety, the former dimension seems to be more relevant than the latter. Therefore, in the previous example only one side of the structure was used, varying events on the particularistic dimension; furthermore, the other dimension was kept constant on the symbolic side on the assumption that the more concrete resources may be less easy to present through images.

Another application of resource structure is exemplified by a patient who constantly fears making mistakes which will result in physical discomfort to people: they may get hurt, waste time in searching for objects he misplaced, have to turn off a light he left burning, etc. All these fears belong to the class of services. He never worries about causing a loss of money: the fact that he does not work and thus has to be supported does not bother him; nor does he appear upset by the cost of his therapy, borne by his parents. In the hierarchy of mistakes appropriate to this case, those involving desservices will be at the top, followed by items pertaining to resources progressively more remote from services.

In the first example the actor was another person and the object was the patient; in the last example, the actor was the patient himself while the object was the other. In both examples, the "other" was left unspecified. The notion of particularism indicates, however, that the particular other with whom the interaction takes place is an important factor for the degree of loss or gain perceived and therefore is likely to affect the intensity of anxiety: the more similar two "others" are, the more alike may be the levels of anxiety they elicit. Hence, it is desirable to order the various "others" with whom the patient interacts, with respect to their similarity and differences. The reader is already familiar with the structure among members of the family (Ch. 4): the nearer two roles are in this structure, the more similar are their respective behaviors. If similar behaviors elicit a similar degree of anxiety, then the anxiety experienced in a given role will generalize to neighboring roles more than to remote ones; thus, when the peak of anxiety is established, the relative degree of anxiety attached to other roles can be predicted.

Consider a patient who experiences a high degree of anxiety in his relationship with his father. The structure of roles suggests less anxiety towards his mother and brothers, and still lower anxiety in relationship to his sister. In constructing a hierarchy, events involving his father would be put on top, followed by events involving his mother, his brother and then his sister. Moreover, the dimensions of sex and power may generalize to other significant persons. A friend would elicit less anxiety than the boss; the latter is similar to the father as both involve a same-sex and different-power relationship.

When anxiety toward father heightens on a specific resource, such as the fear of criticism (loss of status), the two structures may be used simultaneously: our patient who fears being criticized by his father for causing him physical discomfort could be presented first with images about his sister criticizing him for making mistakes which caused her loss of money; then one would move gradually along resources as well as along family roles, toward resources and roles of higher anxiety potential.

SHAPING BEHAVIORAL CHANGE. Frequently mental patients have a low rate of emitting certain interpersonal responses. Fear of rejection or criticism may, for example, inhibit a patient from responding negatively when deprived by the other; a similar problem occurs when the patient is unable to express positive feelings toward the other in situations where such expression is appropriate. In behavior therapy *assertive training* is used to treat these problems. The patient is taught, for example, to express love or affection towards those who provide him with a resource and to express disapproval when the other had deprived him of resources.

The application of interpersonal structures to assertive training involves two steps: first the particular resource and roles for which inhibition is strongest are identified. Training then starts from resources and roles which are remote from the highly inhibited ones and proceeds gradually toward the latter through the structural pattern. It may be easier to begin the training of a patient who has difficulty in negative exchanges of love by teaching him to express his negative feelings through depriving the other of money or goods (i.e., presents) when possible; then one would proceed to services and finally to expression of personal resentment. Likewise, the patient who fears his father may find it easier to assert himself with opposite-sex and same-power figures and gradually move towards asserting himself with his boss and father.

Assertive training involves also enriching expression of positive feelings. Again, with those patients who are inhibited in expressions of love it may be more successful to begin the training from resources for which exchanges are easier. This approach may be especially suitable to intimate roles such as parent-child or husband-wife where the positive exchanges of love are crucial for maintaining stable and satisfying relationships, while at the same time there are opportunities for exchanging other resources. Some parents have difficulty in expressing affection for their child, and often the child models on such deficient behavior. It may be easier for the parents to initiate exchanges involving information, such as reading a story or discussing a topic which interests the child. Some other parents may be quite comfortable in doing things to and for their children (i.e., giving services). When these easier positive exchanges have been established, training can be extended to praise (giving status) and finally to expression of personal affection. Thus, as in hierarchy construction, the steps of behavioral change may be planned along known dimensions of social events such as those of resources and of family roles.

BEHAVIORAL ANALYSIS. A frequent problem in assertive training is to teach the patient to discriminate between assertion and aggression. This discrimination is of great practical importance: assertive response to being deprived of resources often results in the other restoring what he had taken or, at least, avoiding repetition of such action in the future; thus the patient is rewarded for being assertive. Aggression, on the other hand, breeds further aggression and the aggressive patient may thus face a loss, greater than the one he incurred before "asserting" himself. Discrimination between aggression and assertion is usually taught by modeling to the patient appropriate responses to critical situations. The analysis of behavior according to cognitive classes may provide a more systematic way for training the patient in the discrimination and for generating the modeled responses. Essentially, assertive behavior in response to deprivation consists of requesting the other to avoid, in the future, a behavior which is upsetting; sometimes restitution of the deprived resource is also requested. For example: "I don't like the way you . . .;" "Could I have my book back?" "I would appreciate being served." A common element of these various forms of assertive behavior in response to deprivation is that they convey some status reduction for the person being assertively addressed; this reduction is, however, moderate, and does not involve resources other than status. A stronger response would probably spread to neighboring resources as well, particularly to love; when the response is intense, generalization to proximal classes is more likely to occur. A larger and more widespread deprivation is indeed often labeled by the recipient as aggression.

Training the patient to take away status without depriving the other of love may involve considerable difficulties because of the close cognitive link between these two classes. Discrimination will, however, become easier by grafting on it another dimension, viz., taking vs. giving. The patient will thus be trained to *take* status from the other, while *giving* him love; one way, for example, is to preface criticism by saying "as much as I hate to hurt you . . ."

Another problem which may benefit from behavioral analysis stems from the fact that often the communication of non-assertive individuals involves both explicit and implicit exchanges. When one is asked for his opinion, the explicit resource involved in the communication is information. Yet, some other resources may enter in a subtle way, through tone of voice, facial expressions and the choice of words. When this subtle communication is positive, no problem arises. However, when these behavioral components are negative and imply a loss for the other, the patient may find himself facing a negative reaction. For example: when providing the other with information (as by giving advice or opinion on a certain issue) the patient may convey at the same time his superiority; the other is then likely to respond aggressively to the deprivation of status. Analysis of such critical situations in terms of resources may help the patient eliminate the negative component of his behavior rather than wonder for the cause of the aggressive reaction with which he was faced. This analysis will also help the therapist to derive, systematically, appropriate responses for modeling, by specifying the classes which should and should not be involved in a given behavior.

In discussing the use of cognitive dimensions in behavior therapy we have illustrated how the developments described in this book can be grafted on current treatment practices, making them more specific and focused. We shall now leave the topic of psychopathology to consider cognitive patterns in some additional deviant groups.

DEVIANT PATTERNS OF DIFFERENTIATION
IN DELINQUENT GIRLS

Parental schedules of reinforcement were found to be erratic and inconsistent in families of juvenile delinquents (Andry, 1960; Barron, 1954; Madoff, 1959), possibly because they are determined by the parent's momentary mood rather than by the child's behavior. When reinforcement is contingent upon parental mood and not on the child's own behavior, the child is expected to exhibit difficulties in forming a self-concept which will be differentiated from the way he perceives his parents. Furthermore, when the parent's reaction depends on his own mood and not on specific behaviors emitted by the child, there is high probability that each parent will react differently to the same behavior, according to his own momentary mood. Under such conditions, the child is more likely to conceptualize the two parental figures as different. In normal families, where parents' reaction is contingent on their child's behavior, they will be perceived as more similar. These considerations have led to the following hypotheses:

1. Differentiation between perceived behaviors of self and those of parents will be *weaker* in delinquents than in normal subjects.
2. Differentiation between perceived behaviors of father and mother will be *stronger* in delinquents than in normals.

These hypotheses were tested by Donnenwerth, Teichman and Foa (1973). The Role Behavior Test (see Appendix A) for child-parents roles was administered to delinquent and normal girls (age 13–16). They were instructed to answer only those questions which pertain to a parent or a parent-substitute with whom they had recent contacts. The delinquent subjects were inmates at the State Training School for Girls, Chillicothe, Missouri; the normal group was a random sample of students attending Jefferson Junior High School and Hickman High School in Columbia, Missouri. The two groups were matched on age and, to some extent, also on socio-economic level. There were 47 normals and 17 delinquents for Daughter-Father Role; 51 normals and 34 delinquents answered Daughter-Mother test.

The correlations between the girl's perception of her behavior toward the parent and her perception of the corresponding behavior emitted by the parent toward her, were computed for each behavioral class. These coefficients for normals and delinquents are given in Table 64.

In all eight comparisons the correlation for delinquents was higher than for normals, an indication of *lower* differentiation in delinquents. The difference between the mean correlations of the two groups was significant beyond the .01 level. When each comparison was tested separately, there were significant differences for all behaviors involving

Table 64

CORRELATIONS BETWEEN PERCEIVED DAUGHTER'S BEHAVIORS
TOWARD PARENTS AND PARENT'S BEHAVIOR TOWARD HER

Correlated Variables	Delinquent	Non-delinquent	Difference
Father gives Status to Daughter and Daughter gives Status to Father	.95	.65	.30
Father gives Love to Daughter and Daughter gives Love to Father	.86	.65	.21
Father takes away Status from Daughter and Daughter takes Status from Father	.85	.58	.23
Father takes Love from Daughter and Daughter takes Love from Father	.87	.60	.27
Mother gives Status to Daughter and Daughter gives Status back	.74	.65	.09
Mother gives Love to Daughter and Daughter gives Love back	.76	.62	.14
Mother takes Status from Daughter and Daughter takes Status from Mother	.63	.59	.04
Mother takes Love from Daughter and Daughter takes Love from Mother	.72	.52	.20
Mean correlation	.82	.61	.21

the father; only one correlation of mother-daughter—taking love—approached significance.

A similar picture was obtained by correlating the subject's perception of *herself* with her perception of the parent's behavior toward her. Here too, delinquents differentiate less than normals, particularly in the daughter-father role. Thus, actor's differentiation between self and parent and especially between self and father is stronger in normal girls than in delinquents.

The second hypothesis proposed that the delinquent girl will differentiate more between the behaviors of father and of mother. Hence, it was expected that the correlations between the perceived behaviors of the two parents will be lower in delinquent than in normal girls. The relevant coefficients, presented in Table 65, were all in the predicted direction; the mean correlations of the two groups were different, beyond the .01 level of significance.

In summary, the perceived behaviors of father and mother are somewhat more differentiated in delinquent than in normal girls. On the other hand, the delinquent girl's self image appears less differentiated from the parental image, particularly from the father's image. The finding that delinquent girls differ from normals in daughter-father role supports the proposition advanced by Biller and Weiss (1970) that

Table 65

CORRELATIONS BETWEEN PERCEIVED FATHER'S AND MOTHER'S
BEHAVIOR TOWARD THE GIRL

Variable	Delinquents	Non-delinquents	Difference
Giving status to daughter	.32	.57	−.25
Giving love to daughter	.34	.62	−.28
Taking love from daughter	−.11	.25	−.36
Taking status from daughter	.00	.22	−.22
Mean correlation	.14	.47	−.33

the father, rather than the mother, is the main reinforcing agent for girls.

It is of interest to note that erratic parental behavior has also been held as leading to hostile and non-compliant behavior of the delinquent child toward his parents (Bandura and Walters, 1958 and 1959; Cowie, Cowie and Slater, 1968). These findings suggest that inconsistent parental behavior results in less dependency at the *behavioral* level; our data, on the other hand, indicate more dependency at the *cognitive* level. These two sets of results would seem contradictory if one assumes that cognition and behavior should always point in the same direction. However, Piaget (1954) has suggested that differentiation begins at the behavioral level before becoming cognitively established; obviously in this developmental stage behavior and cognition will be incongruent; as noted in Chapter 2, a cognitive differentiation which is still incomplete is likely to be exercised often at the behavioral level. Hence the extremely independent and rebellious overt behavior of the juvenile delinquent may constitute an attempt to achieve the appropriate level of cognitive differentiation between self and other, which was not attained in the past because of inconsistencies in parental reinforcement. In view of the difficulty encountered by delinquent girls in achieving self-other differentiation, it is perhaps not surprising that their behavioral efforts should be so strong and dramatic. In fact, youth "rebellion" in general may be seen as a means to achieve a more independent self-image. Primacy of overt behavior over cognition appears to characterize a developmental stage; once this stage terminates, overt behavior will be guided by the cognitive structure, so that both will point in the same direction. Thus, divergency between the two levels may indicate a forthcoming change in the cognitive structure, or may be taken as a sign of developmental difficulties.

Attempts to replicate these results with delinquent boys proved unsuccessful: no clear-cut difference between them and normals was found with respect to degree of differentiation; it is possible that the male sample was composed of sub-groups having contrasting differentiation patterns which on the average would cancel each other. Differences between delinquent and normal boys have been reported by other investigators. Teichman (1971,b) found that delinquent boys differentiate between the viewpoint ascribed to father and that ascribed to mother more than do normals. Both Deitz (1969) and Teichman (1971,b) reported higher differentiation between viewpoints of self and parent in delinquent than in non-delinquent boys. Finally, McDavid and Schroder (1957) showed that delinquents have more difficulties than normals in differentiating between behaviors which are socially approved and those which are disapproved.

COGNITIVE DIFFERENTIATION IN THE DEAF AND BLIND

The importance of studying the cognition of mental patients and delinquents stems from the fact that both groups exhibit deviant patterns of behavior. If, as we have assumed throughout this volume, responses are mediated by cognitive processes, then the presence of deviant behavior should lead to the search for deviant cognitive structure. The deaf and blind, however, do not necessarily show gross behavioral deviance. Why would we then suspect that their cognition will differ from the normal pattern?

Interpersonal messages are received through the sense organs; verbal communication stimulates auditory receptors while facial expressions and bodily gestures are received through vision. These messages carry structural information which is required by a young child for the development of his own structure. Deficiency in a given sense organ deprives the child of the particular structural information which is transmitted through these receptors; this deficit, in turn, will be reflected in his cognitive development.

Suppose, for example, that differentiation along a certain dimension is provided mainly through verbal messages; the born-deaf will under-differentiate among the elements of this dimension. Thus, comparison between normal and deaf subjects may help clarify the relationship between cognitive dimensions and verbal communication. The same rationale holds for the study of cognitive differentiations in the blind. Here any systematic differences between these subjects and normals may identify dimensions acquired through visual messages.

The Role Behavior Test (see Appendix A) for son-to-mother role, was administered to 28 young males, deaf-mutes from birth, who received professional and sign-language training at the Jewish Employment and Vocational Service in St. Louis, Missouri. The test was administered in sign-language by an expert interviewer. An equal number of blind male subjects from the same residential area, was also investigated with the same instrument; most of them, however, were not born blind. Apparently, blind people who never experienced vision constitute only a small proportion of the blind population and we were unable to locate a sufficient number of them.

Although a non-verbal form of communication was used in eliciting responses from deaf subjects, their structural pattern of behavioral classes was identical to the one found in normal and abnormal subjects. This result indicates that verbal communication is not required for establishing the behavioral structure or for its investigation.

With regard to degree of differentiation, the clearest finding was obtained in the "level" dimension: deaf subjects showed comparatively scarce differentiation between perception of actual behavior and ideal behavior. This difficulty was also apparent from non-formal observation of the interviews: the interviewer, although very skilled in sign language (she later became a leading actress in a mute troupe) had to make special efforts when translating the notion of ideal behavior. The data on differentiation between actual and ideal level confirmed the intuitive impression that the deaf underdifferentiate on this dimension. Thirteen of the sixteen correlations between actual and ideal were higher for deaf than for normal subjects. Table 66 gives the mean correlations of the four behavioral classes—giving and taking, love and status—for the specified actors and objects. The correlations for blind subjects showed the opposite pattern: all sixteen correlations, except one, were *lower* than those found in normals: their averages for each given actor and for objects are also given in Table 66.

Table 66

MEAN CORRELATION BETWEEN ACTUAL AND IDEAL LEVEL

Actor	Object	Normal	Subjects Deaf	Blind
Son	Son	.65	.70	.44
Son	Mother	.66	.72	.52
Mother	Mother	.64	.85	.59
Mother	Son	.66	.70	.43
Number of subjects		(50)	(28)	(28)

These results suggest that verbal communication is predominant in the acquisition of actual-ideal differentiation. The deaf who are deprived of verbal messages appear to be underdifferentiators, while blind subjects tend to overdifferentiate, possibly because of their heightened attention to verbal communication. In other dimensions handicapped subjects tend to differentiate somewhat less than do normals; this trend is more noticeable for the deaf than for the blind. On the whole the comparison of handicapped with normals seems to indicate that most differentiations of interpersonal cognition are based on a combination of verbal and visual messages, with the former being predominant, and particularly so with respect to the actual-ideal differentiation.

SUMMARY

Interpersonal encounters with mental patients are characterized by high degree of miscommunication. If, as suggested in the previous two chapters, communication failures are due to cognitive differences among communicators, patients' cognition should differ from that of normal individuals. Two types of communication failures were previously proposed: mismapping and mismatching. Mismapping occurs when individuals use different mapping rules in assigning behaviors into cognitive classes. Mismatching occurs when individuals differ in their degree of differentiation among certain classes. Is the difficulty to communicate with mental patients due to mismapping or mismatching? Hypotheses for both types of miscommunication have been proposed in the literature of psychopathology. Empirical investigation of interpersonal communication in schizophrenics has been intensively conducted by Longabaugh and his associates, employing direct observation of staff-staff, staff-patient and patient-patient interaction. They found that the frequency of resource exchanges was greatest among staff members, lowest among patients, with staff-patient exchanges occupying an intermediate position. In staff-patient interactions, the staff member was more likely to be the provider of resources, while the patient was more likely to seek them. Moreover, staff members were more efficient in their interactions, particularly when communicating with other staff members: they were more likely to obtain the resource they sought and to give the other the resource he sought. Patients were more efficient in interaction with staff members than when communicating to other patients. Since these results were recorded by a "normal" observer, they seem to reflect the extent to which the observer's mapping was different from the ones employed by the various observed interactors. The fact that the observer ascribed to staff more success in resource exchange, indirectly suggests that some mismapping was involved in the communication failure of patients. Further studies have indicated that the more disturbed the patient was, the less consistent was the behavior of staff members when interacting with him. It seems that staff changed their behavior toward the patient unsystematically in an effort to "hit" the correct class of his cognition, thus attempting to overcome differences in mapping.

Deviances in degree of differentiation (mismatching) were investigated by comparing mental patients with normals. In all the three cultures studied (India, Senegal and U.S.A.), schizophrenics were found to underdifferentiate between self and other, thus confirming the long standing notion that they suffer from "weak ego boundaries." On the other hand, schizophrenics had low correlations among non-reciprocal roles. This last finding, however, seems to indicate erratic mapping rather than high degree of differentiation, because of the low consistency found between their responses to equivalent instruments. Erratic mapping may also account for the large number of deviations found in the structural pattern of schizophrenics.

The evidence regarding the existence of mismapping and mismatching in mental patients explains their difficulty to communicate. Such difficulty should, in turn, lead to deficiency in interpersonal resources, since these are transmitted through successful encounters. Indeed, it was found that more disturbed patients reported lower frequency of positive exchanges and higher frequency of negative exchanges than did mildly disturbed and normal subjects. Moreover, highly disturbed patients reported more self-rejection and less self-acceptance than did other subjects.

The conception of psychopathology proposed in this book—anomalous mapping rules and deviant degree of cognitive differentiation, resulting in communication difficulties and hence paucity of positive resource exchanges—suggests that treatment should aim at cognitive modification. An increase in resource provision may be desirable, particularly when it leads to cognitive changes. By itself, however, it is unlikely to produce long lasting effects; if communication difficulties persist, the resource deficit will reappear. Most of the research on the effects of psychotherapy was aimed at studying changes in resource accumulation. Yet a close analysis of the processes involved in current practices suggests that cognitive changes do take place through the course of treatment. In general, any modification in reinforcement contingencies will tend to produce changes in degrees of differentiation. On the other hand, modification of mapping rules seems to require manipulation such as behavioral analysis. In the present state of affairs, most of the cognitive changes produced through psychotherapy are induced either accidentally or unsystematically. As we progress in discovering specific patterns of cognitive deviance, their reduction becomes a clearer goal for treatment. Techniques for inducing cognitive changes may be developed by adopting methods already used in cross-cultural training (see Ch. 9) as well as by integrating current types of psychotherapy with the cognitive conceptualization of mental patients developed here. For example, the use of cognitive structure may facilitate the construction of hierarchies in behavior therapy and the adoption of the classification system developed in the book may prove useful in behavioral analysis.

Different, but still deviant patterns of behaviors are emitted by juvenile delinquents. The search for cognitive deviances in this group was influenced by previous findings that juvenile delinquents were exposed in early childhood to erratic and inconsistent schedules of reinforcement. It seems that in these families the delivery of reinforcements and punishments are determined by the parent's mood rather than by the child's behavior. Such practice should lead to underdifferentiation between self and other as actors and to overdifferentiation between mother and father. This cognitive pattern was indeed found in delinquent girls, particularly in the Daughter-Father role.

If patterns of interpersonal communication in childhood influence the degree of differentiation found later on, it becomes of interest to explore the relationship between different modes of communication (i.e., verbal, visual) and specific differentiations. Such an attempt was made by comparing the cognitive structure of the deaf and blind with that of normal subjects. Deaf subjects showed comparatively scarce differentiation between perception of actual behavior and ideal behavior, while blind subjects overdifferentiated in this dimension. These results suggest that verbal communication is predominant in the acquisition of actual-ideal differentiation. In other dimensions handicapped subjects, particularly the deaf tend to differentiate somewhat less than do normals. On the whole, it seems that most differentiations of interpersonal cognition are based on a combination of verbal and visual messages, with the former being predominant.

┌───┐
│ EPILOGUE: MAN AND HIS SOCIETY │
└───┘

Overview

THE READER WHO HAS accompanied us through this book may
wonder whether the knowledge he has acquired here may contribute to a better understanding of human behavior and to the solution
of the many problems existing in the relationship of man to man. This
final chapter constitutes an attempt to answer these questions by clarifying the relevance of resource theory to current problems in our society.

We have conceptualized two types of man's needs, the need for
resource accumulation and the need for confirmation of structure; the
former is satisfied through interpersonal exchanges while the latter
safeguards man's ability to enter these exchanges. Social organization,
in turn, has been perceived as the mechanism for regulating the satisfaction of these needs. In any given society certain needs are better
satisfied than certain others so that social problems arising out of unful-
filled needs differ from one society to another. An attempt to solve
such problems should begin with the development of tools for measuring the performance of society and locating areas of shortage in need
satisfaction. By overcoming methodoligical difficulties which still exist
in the development of social indicators we shall be able to gain a
clearer understanding of the proposed relationship between unsatisfied
needs and social pathology. This line of investigation will spur the
search for new forms of social organization providing optimal need
satisfaction for the largest possible number of individuals.

MAN THE STRUCTURER

Man classifies stimuli and organizes their classes; in this process
the environment acquires meaning for him and the experiences of
the past enable him to understand the present and to predict the future.
We have examined the development and organization of cognitive
structures pertaining to the social environment, noting the manner
in which they differ from one society to another, their deviance in

mental patients and the role they play in interpersonal communication. In this cognitive network the structure of resource classes deserves a special place; in a sense other structures are ancillary to it—tools in establishing the web of interpersonal relations through which resources are obtained and supplied, thus providing for the mutual satisfaction of needs among exchange partners. Indeed, role differentiation as well as the learning of social norms and viewpoint of the others, enable the individual to engage in those interpersonal transactions which will provide the resources he needs.

Seeking Resources

Psychological theorists have long recognized that interpersonal behavior is resource seeking. In the past, however, each scholar has stressed a particular class of resources while de-emphasizing the others. Love is preeminent in the Freudian conception of human motivation; Adler has seen interpersonal relations as a struggle for the acquisition of status; Karl Marx has taught us that man seeks economic resources—money and goods. More recently the conception of man as a processor of information has raised interest in psychology. Thus, there is hardly a resource class which has not served as the pivot of a theory on human behavior.

It has also been argued that man has a dual nature—rational and irrational: Economic man is rational, his goals are recognizable and his behavior predictable; Man the lover and the hater is irrational, a mystery to himself. The structure of resources goes beyond this dualistic conception: it suggests that motivational states are ordered and interrelated; moreover, their rules of exchange vary gradually with the position of the resource in the structure. Thus love is not less rational than money, it just follows a different logic, better known to poets than to accountants. The logic of other resource classes is more similar to money or to love, depending on whether they are nearer to the latter or to the former in the structure of resources.

If resource classes are ordered and if the rules of exchange depend on their position in the structure, then little justification is left for partial theories like economics which deal only with certain types of exchanges. The growing realization, particularly among economists, that economic and psychological problems inter-act and cannot be solved in isolation, requires integration at the theoretical level; perhaps the structure of resources will provide a point of departure toward this goal.

The Dialectics of Stability vs. Change

The structuring activity of man bears important consequences in determining the relationships between stability and change in viewing his environment. We have noted that events, not less than cognitions, contain structures in which the relationship among their component element is reflected; the structure of social events such as interpersonal messages, usually reflects the cognitive structure of their originator. Indeed, the cognitive development of the child results from perceiving sequences of events which have a fairly constant relationship among their component elements. Once the developing cognition, which reflects the structural constancy of past events, becomes established the problem of its fitness to successive events arises: if the world changes the pre-existing cognition will no longer represent it adequately. But how do we know that the environment has changed? Obviously a single dissonant event will not be sufficient evidence of change; the perception of such an event is usually modified to fit the observer's cognition. Cognitive structures are indeed resistant to change and perceptual modification satisfies the need for cognitive stability. Thus cognition acts as a stabilizer of our view of the world. If, however, later events continue to show the same deviant pattern, then it will become increasingly difficult to brush them off through perceptual modification.

The necessity for cognitive changes does not always stem from changes in the environment; the environment may remain constant, yet the individual may expand his field of experience by bringing into his observation phenomena which were previously excluded. In this case cognitive modification will usually consist of a further differentiation leading to the creation of new conceptual classes. The most common instance of this type of change is provided by the cognitive growth of the child. Artistic creation and scientific discovery also seems to result from such cognitive changes which provide a broader understanding of the environment, but do not necessarily imply that the environment has actually changed. On the contrary, scientific research assumes that no change will occur in the structure of the subject matter being investigated; "God is crafty but not mean" said Einstein when expressing the belief that the order of the physical universe remains invariant. A similar view regarding the stability of the social environment is suggested here: we have seen, indeed, that the structure of basic interpersonal cognitions is invariant across cultures. Yet, this consistancy does not rule out changes in degree of differentiation or the appearance of new dimensions. In fact the occurrence of such cognitive changes may solve conflicts among various needs. One type of conflict appears when the structure interferes with the acquisition of resources. For the individual who has been constantly exposed to failure, success is experienced as a dissonant event, threatening the stability of his cognition. Stability can be maintained by perceiving the event as a failure or by decreasing the value of success—in both cases the individual would fail to benefit from the resource with which he was provided. More generally, mental patients often experience difficulty in interpersonal communication because of cognitive deviance, with consequent reduction in their ability to obtain resources through social exchange. Psychotherapy, then, becomes a procedure by which the individual's conflict between the need for cognitive stability and the need for resources is solved. This conflict appears at the societal level as well, albeit in a different form: when a given society or certain segments of it are deficient in some resources, pressure will generate to change the social fabric toward the satisfaction of these needs. For example, a strive toward economic resources may results in redistribution of income through taxation, nationalization of means of production and economic development. These changes, in turn, lead to the transformation of traditional societies into modern ones. But modern society, while providing more economic resources, also results in environmental changes which create dissonance and strain the ability of cognition to reflect accurately outside events. Thus the conflict between maintaining stability and increasing provisions of resources occurs both at the individual and the societal levels, and is prominent in modern culture.

The Dilemma of Traditional vs. Modern Society

Another conflict which exists at the individual and the societal levels involves the various resources; it stems from their differential environmental requirements. We have noted that resources differ with respect to the type of environment in which they can be best exchanged: particularistic resources require prolonged and repeated encounters in small group; the less particularistic resources are more efficiently exchanged in large groups and their exchange does not require long time nor repeated encounters. It so happens that conditions favoring particularistic exchanges are often found in traditional societies, while the environment provided by modern mass society is favorable to economic transactions. Furthermore, at least in some traditional societies the various institutions are less differentiated with respect to the resource classes appropriate for exchange. In these societies the range of resources transacted in a social institution is wider than in modern culture where more institutions are found, each specializing in the exchange of a few resources. The modern person will not seek emotional support from his boss, as will the member of a traditional culture; he will rather approach an intimate friend, a member of his family or perhaps a psychiatrist. Both institutional specialization and the conditions of the urban environment have concurred in making modern society richer in economic resources but poorer in particularistic ones. Those members of modern society who have not shared the general increase of wealth are in the worst situation of all, having lost emotionally without gaining economically. Thus, while developing nations struggle to achieve economic growth and disregard the particularistic losses involved, technologically advanced countries discover that high standard of living is not a sure recipe for happiness.

The reactions to love poverty in modern society has resulted in efforts to increase particularistic exchanges which have taken mainly two directions: attempts for love exchanges in spite of unfavorable environmental conditions (e.g. youth festivals, blind dates, group sex) and creation of new institutions specializing in emotional exchanges (e.g. sensitivity groups, marathons, encounters). The hope is often voiced that once individuals learn to increase particularistic exchanges in these specialized institutions they will eventually transfer the newly acquired skills to other institutions as well, thus reducing the trend toward resource specialization of the latters. Much of the work on community mental health is essentially based on similar principles.

More subtle is the solution adopted by various protest groups advocating drastic changes in modern society; their ideology varies from the religious to the political and their methods range from gentle persuasion to violence. Yet all these groups have a significant element in common: they offer a suitable setting for satisfying the particularistic needs of their members. Emotional fulfillment, in a society where love is scarce, provides the most immediate dividend for the dissident; it gives him the feeling that he has found an answer to the ills which beset the society he opposes. But this may be a satisfactory solution for certain individuals; it does not provide a pattern extendible to society at large.

In the search for solutions of more general applicability there has been an increasing interest in the development of social indicators, i.e. indices designed to measure the quality of life much as economic indicators represent the state of the economy.

SOCIAL INDICATORS

The growing attention paid to measuring quality of life stems from at least two factors. One factor involves the realization that a high level of economic production and consumption is not sufficient for securing human welfare; gross national happiness includes variables which are not covered by the gross national product. A second factor reflects the recognition that there is a close interplay between economic and social elements in society and therefore they should be considered jointly in attempts to solve societal problems.

The Economic Cost of Non-Economic Poverty

There is not point in dwelling on the economic cost of social problems such as crime and welfare which have reached staggering proportions in some countries; they are already well recognized. If, however, these problems result from deficiency in non-economic resources, then an indirect link would have been established between the shortage of non-economic resources and the expenditure of economic ones. Moreover, this link also manifests itself in the many instances where an unsatisfied non-economic need creates a demand for economic resources: workers striking for higher wages are not always short of money; they may also, as many studies have shown, be deprived of information or status; patients going to a physician may seek sympathy and support rather than treatment; a person feeling rejected and unloved may console himself by buying something he does not actually need; "The most powerful, the loudest and the most persistent command in our society is the command to buy" (Reich, 1971, p. 179).

One may wonder why people needing non-economic resources will not seek them rather than settle for economic ones which leave the original need largely unsatisfied. As stated earlier, economic resources are more readily available in modern society; not only are they relatively abundant, but there are many specialized institutions for their provision and they are considerably more accessible than the few social institutions which provide non-economic resources. Furthermore, there is more awareness of economic needs and it is easier to verbalize them than the non-economic ones. All these considerations lead to the proposition that non-economic shortages result in economic costs, as well as in plain human suffering.

The Non-Economic Cost of Economic Development

The other side of the coin is the influence of the economic resources on the non-economic ones. We have noted that environmental conditions which facilitate economic growth seem to hinder non-economic exchanges (the large metropolis is a typical example of this type of environment). Consequently some actions which reduce economic costs may increase non-economic deficits and in the long run the ultimate economic cost may be greater than the original saving. A larger school, hospital, industrial plant, a taller housing development often results in lower cost per unit than a smaller project. In this large scale environment, however, the exchange of particularistic resources become more difficult. The resulting shortage of these resources reflects in turn in economic costs, as we have seen previously.

These reciprocal effects among various resources suggests the necessity of a social accounting system in which the costs and rewards of any given option will be considered in terms which are not merely economic. The first problem in developing appropriate indicators is to decide what items they should include or how to define "quality of life." A detailed list of all the events and conditions which make life pleasant and worthy would be unmanageably long; on the other hand the global notion of "quality of life," being so vague and general, is not amendable to measurement. We have to settle somewhere in the middle with a classification which is detailed enough to pin-point essential differences, and at the same time simple and parsimonious.

An answer to the question of which items contribute to the "quality of life" has been provided by the identification of resource classes and by the discovery of their relationship. All six classes of resources contribute to the "quality of life," so that when any of them falls below a minimum level, "quality of life" is impaired. Still, resources close in the order can compensate for one another; a person poor in love may still be reasonably happy if he acquires status or is pampered with personal services. On the other hand, a resource remote from the needed one does not constitute an efficient substitute.

Some Methodological Problems

Can we measure how much love one has deposited with his wife or how much status is credited to him by his boss in the same way we count the money deposited at the bank? Obviously the research work described in this volume could not have been done in the absence of techniques for observation and for measurement. Yet the instruments used, given in the appendix, constitute only a beginning and in many aspects they are too crude and cumbersome. The goal of producing observation instruments, which are both simple to use and fairly precise, requires the solution of several methodological problems.

1. At the most, we can find out that A has more love than B and B has more than C; but, at the present state of knowledge, we cannot speak in absolute terms. Our measurement regarding quantities of money is more precise: the person who possesses ten dollars not only has more money than the one having five dollars, but he owns twice as much as the second person.

2. People are more aware of the need for certain resources than for some others: individuals know if they need money and usually have no difficulty in expressing such need verbally; the person who needs love or status is often unaware of it, he may just feel a vague discontent which cannot be easily translated into words: the language of love is mostly non-verbal—it consists of facial and bodily expressions which we have barely begun to understand.

3. Acknowledging the existence of particularistic needs may be hin-

dered by cultural norms, thus preventing people from expressing them even when they are aware of their need. The last two differential characteristics of recourses may also explain why people needing particularistic resources demand non-particularistic ones.

Lack of awareness and obstacles to verbalization, as well as the inability to measure precise amounts, constitute serious problems in the quantification of non-economic needs, but not insolvable ones. Partial contributions to their solutions are already available from socio-psychological research in other areas as for example, forced-choice techniques which overcome effects of social desirability. For other aspects of these problems, further research is needed to develop instruments which are reasonably reliable and suitable for mass use.

The Use of Social Indicators

Social indicators will enable us to assess the amount of resources possessed not only by society as a whole, but also by specific groups, strata and classes. The next step will be to investigate the relationship between the need state of various segments of society and social pathology. Working on the general proposition that resource deficiency results in inadequate social performance, it is possible to formulate more specific research questions: Is deficiency in love a factor in drug addiction? Do status-deprived people commit more crimes? Are they more likely to rely on welfare rather than being self-supporting? What is the effect of the welfare system on their status need? If welfare increases this need, then the system perpetuates the dependency of welfare clients on public money rather than leading them toward self-sufficiency. Are some antisocial acts such as political assassination committed as an attempt to gain status? This interpretation is supported by the fact that at least in the United States, these assassins often share a long history of past failures which presumably results in an extreme need for status.

We often hear that black Americans have fewer economic opportunities than whites; where do blacks stand in other resource needs? How do these other needs affect their well being and performance? Furthermore, are patterns of economic consumption related to non-economic needs? People striving for status may, for example, choose goods according to their status value rather than their functionality.

This line of research will provide us with a more precise and detailed knowledge about the resource needs existing in various segments of society, as well as of their effects on social performance.

TOWARD NEW SOCIAL FORMS

Identifying resource deficits and realizing their consequences will have a profound influence on our way of thinking about social problems. It may then strike us as a paradox that in our society a person in economic strictures can apply for relief, while the individual who needs love or status is often left to his own devices unless he first becomes an alcoholic or a drug addict. Providing first-aid for particularistic needs on a large scale may be helpful to some extent, yet it will not obviate the necessity of re-examining the structure of society in an attempt to find out ways of modifying it to optimize the satisfaction of all resource needs. This is not an easy task in view of the contradictory environmental requirements of particularistic and economic exchange: We have seen that particularistic resources require a small, stable, unhurried social environment, while economic resources demand mass production and mass consumption. Is it possible to devise social forms in which all types of exchange would thrive?

A modest step in this direction is provided by attempts to organize industrial production around groups of workers who assume autonomous responsibility for a limited sequence of the production process. In this way the group, rather than the individual worker, becomes a unit in the production line; at the same time the group provides a suitable environment for satisfying the particularistic needs of its members. A critical problem in these experiments is whether the autonomy delegated to the group is large enough to sustain its functioning, but not too large as to make production uneconomical. This type of two-tier organization could be extended to other institutions as well: residential planning, for example, could be organized around small groups of families choosing to live in proximity to one another. A main disadvantage of this solution lies in the fact that the individual is still required to have multiple membership in a variety of institutions conflicting not only for his time, as in present modern society, but for his emotional attention as well. This disadvantage may be overcome by extending the two-tier notion to society as a whole: individuals will be members of fairly permanent small social groups providing particularistic resources; these groups, in turn, will constitute the units of larger social systems which will be concerned mainly with economic exchanges.

Evolution toward forms of social organization which will offer a more balanced supply of resources is not merely a matter of developing technologies for the production and distribution of particularistic resources to complement the technics we already possess for economic production and distribution. An integrated approach to the complex socio-economic problems of modern society can hardly succeed in the absence of a unified science of man, integrating emotional, social and economic aspects of his resource seeking behavior. With this book we hope to have provided a small beginning toward such a goal.

APPENDICES

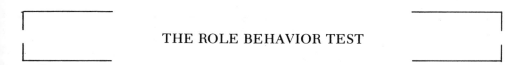

THE ROLE BEHAVIOR TEST

T HIS INSTRUMENT IS designed to elicit the picture a person has of his exchanges of love and status with another person in a specific role relationship. The example given here refers to the wife-husband role-pair. To adapt the instrument to other roles it is merely necessary to change appropriately the role names appearing in the test.

The instrument consists of a series of statements describing the behavior of the wife (or husband) in giving (or taking away) love (or status) to (from) self and husband (wife). Three statements are provided for each variable. Each statement is followed by four questions dealing respectively with actual and ideal behavior from the viewpoint of subject and from the viewpoint of the other person in the role pair. The two latter questions were omitted in more recent versions of the instrument, which thus did not provide information on the viewpoint ascribed to the other. The same questions follow each statement; therefore, in the example provided they appear only after the first statement, to save space. Statements pertaining to the same variable (e.g., the wife giving love to the husband) do not follow one another in the text, but are randomized to minimize sequential effects.

WIFE-HUSBAND RELATIONSHIP

The purpose of this questionnaire is to help you to form as faithful and sharp a picture as possible of the relationship between you and your husband.

This is not a test. There are no right or wrong answers. Just answer the way you feel. This questionnaire will be kept in strict confidence.

On the following pages, you will find a number of brief statements describing behavior between husband and wife. Each statement is followed by some questions. For each question, quickly choose the answer which best reflects your situation and put a mark (X) on the line in front of the answer you have chosen. Please answer each question, but give only one answer to each question; then go on immediately to the next statement.

EXAMPLE:

Judy spends most weekends out in the yard taking care of the garden.

Do you act this way?   __X__ almost never

_____ seldom

_____ sometimes

_____ often

_____ almost always

If you almost never act this way, you would place an (X) next to that answer.

(1) Pat shows her husband she loves him and cares for him; she tries to please him and do the things he likes.

A. Do you act this way when you are with your husband?

0 _____ almost never
1 _____ seldom
2 _____ sometimes
3 _____ often
4 _____ almost always

B. When she's with her husband, do you think a wife should act the way the wife in the story does?

0 _____ definitely not
1 _____ perhaps not
2 _____ perhaps yes
3 _____ yes
4 _____ absolutely yes

C. Would your husband say that you act this way with him?

0 _____ almost never
1 _____ seldom
2 _____ sometimes
3 _____ often
4 _____ almost always

D. Would your husband say that a wife should act as the wife in the story does?

0 _____ definitely not
1 _____ perhaps not
2 _____ perhaps yes
3 _____ yes
4 _____ absolutely yes

(2) Sue gives respect to her husband; she shows him she admires whatever he does.

(3) When she is with her husband, Sandy treats herself with dignity; she shows she respects herself by the way she talks and acts.

(4) When she is with her husband, Carol is a gloomy person who acts unhappy with herself.

(5) Dotty does not give love to her husband; she ignores his feelings and shows him she does not like him.

(6) Bobbie treats her husband with disrespect; she does not look up to him, and she downgrades whatever he does.

(7) When she is with her husband, Kate shows disrespect for herself and acts as if she thinks she is useless.

(8) Janet proves her love for her husband by helping him and sharing things with him.

(9) Ann shows she is proud of what her husband can do; she tells him he is worth a lot and that he can do things very well.

(10) When she is with her husband, Mary shows a lot of respect toward herself; she makes known her self-respect by what she says and does.

(11) Polly acts spitefully toward herself in front of her husband and does not try to please herself.

(12) Marie downgrades herself when she is with her husband; she does not show respect for herself and acts as if she cannot do anything right.

(13) Rose does not have pride in herself; she belittles herself in front of her husband and criticizes her abilities.

(14) Peggy does not show respect for her husband; she criticizes him and tells him he is useless.

(15) Barbara shows her husband she does not like him; she does things he dislikes, and she will not try to please him.

(16) When she is with her husband, Betty is a cheerful wife who acts pleased with herself.

(17) May belittles her husband when she talks to him; she looks down on his abilities and tells him he does not do things right.

(18) Margie acts as if everything her husband does is very important; she praises whatever he does.

(19) Jean is a happy person when she is with her husband; she acts like a wife who knows she is a nice, likable person.

(20) June gives her husband a lot of love; she shows trust in him and is very affectionate with him.

(21) Betsy acts spiteful toward her husband; she lets him know she dislikes him and cannot stand him.

(22) When she is with her husband, Terry acts displeased with herself and does not seem happy with herself.

(23) When she is with her husband, Sarah praises herself for her ability; she acts like a wife who does things very well.

(24) When she is with her husband, Terry acts contented with herself and seems to be satisfied with herself.

Now we turn to some statements about the behavior of a husband when he is with his wife:

(25) Dick shows his wife he likes her and cares for her; he tries to please her and do the things she likes.

A. Does your husband act this way
    when he is with you?

    0 _____ almost never
    1 _____ seldom
    2 _____ sometimes
    3 _____ often
    4 _____ almost always

B. When he is with his wife, do you
    think a husband should act the
    way the husband in the story
    does?

    0 _____ definitely not
    1 _____ perhaps not
    2 _____ perhaps yes
    3 _____ yes
    4 _____ absolutely yes

C. Would your husband say that he
    acts this way with you?

    0 _____ almost never
    1 _____ seldom
    2 _____ sometimes
    3 _____ often
    4 _____ almost always

D. Would your husband say that a
    husband should act as the husband
    in the story does?

    0 _____ definitely not
    1 _____ perhaps not
    2 _____ perhaps yes
    3 _____ yes
    4 _____ absolutely yes

(26) When he is with his wife, Bob shows disrespect for himself and acts like he thinks he is useless.

(27) James treats his wife with disrespect; he does not look up to her, and he downgrades whatever she does.

(28) Al proves his love for his wife by sharing things with her and helping her.

(29) When he is with his wife, Jack is a gloomy husband who acts unhappy with himself.

(30) William downgrades himself when he is with his wife; he does not show respect for himself and acts like he cannot do anything right.

(31) Mike acts spitefully toward himself in front of his wife, and does not try to please himself.

(32) Edward does not have pride in himself; he belittles himself in front of his wife and criticizes his abilities.

(33) Larry shows his wife he does not like her; he does things she dislikes, and he will not try to please her.

(34) David gives his wife a lot of love; he shows trust in her and is very affectionate with her.

(35) When he is with his wife, Peter acts displeased with himself and does not seem happy with himself.

(36) Gary does not show respect for his wife; he criticizes her and tells her she is useless.

(37) Robert acts as if everything his wife does is very important; he praises whatever she does.

(38) Richard belittles his wife when he talks to her; he looks down on her abilities and tells her she does not do things right.

(39) Joe is a happy husband when he is with his wife; he acts like a husband who knows he is a nice, likable husband.

(40) Dan acts spiteful toward his wife; he lets her know he dislikes her and cannot stand her.

(41) Chuck shows he is proud of what his wife can do; he tells her she is worth a lot and that she can do things very well.

(42) John gives respect to his wife; he shows her he admires whatever she does.

(43) Fred does not give love to his wife; he ignores her feelings and shows her he does not like her.

(44) When he is with his wife, Bill acts contented with himself and seems to be satisfied with himself.

(45) When he is with his wife, Paul praises himself for his abilities; he acts like a husband who thinks he does things very well.

(46) When he is with his wife, Tom is a cheerful husband who acts pleased with himself.

(47) When he is with his wife, Harry shows a lot of respect toward himself; he makes known his self-respect by what he says and does.

(48) When he is with his wife, Jim treats himself with dignity; he shows he respects himself by the way he talks and acts.

ADMINISTRATION. Although the instrument is suitable for self-administration in most studies reported in this book, it has been administered by a skilled interviewer who read the statements and questions to the subject and recorded his answers on an answer sheet.

SCORING. The score on any given variable is simply the sum of the weights of the answer to a particular question (A, B, C, or D) for the three statements pertaining to the given variable. The lowest score is thus 0 (zero) indicating low frequency (or desirability) of the behavior described in the statements; the highest possible score is 12. The grouping of the statements according to the variable to which they belong is shown in Table 67.

Table 67

STATEMENTS OF TEST CLASSIFIED ACCORDING TO
THEIR VARIABLE

Variable	Statement Number	
	Behavior of Wife	Behavior of Husband
Giving status to other	2, 9, 18	37, 41, 42
Giving love to other	1, 8, 20	25, 28, 34
Giving love to self	16, 19, 24	39, 44, 46
Giving status to self	3, 10, 23	45, 47, 48
Taking status from self	7, 12, 13	26, 30, 32
Taking love from self	4, 11, 22	29, 31, 35
Taking love from other	5, 15, 21	33, 40, 43
Taking status from other	6, 14, 17	27, 36, 38

STATEMENTS DESCRIBING BEHAVIORS OF GIVING

FOR VARIOUS RESOURCE CLASSES

FOR EACH ONE OF the six resource classes three statements are provided indicating the giving of the resource to the other.

Love: I feel affection for you; I care about you; I enjoy being with you.

Status: You are a very important person; You do things very well; I admire and respect you.

Information: Here is the information; Here is my opinion; Here is my advice.

Money: Here is your pay; Here is a check for you; Here is some money for you.

Goods: Here is some merchandise for you; Here is a new product you may try; Here is a package for you.

Services: I repaired it for you; I ran that errand for you; I will do that for you.

SOCIAL INTERACTION INVENTORY FOR EXCHANGES

OF GIVING

THIS INVENTORY IS designed to record preferences for re-ceiving a certain resource in return for the resource given by the subject to the other. The resource assumedly given by the subject is described at the top of each list. The resources which can be received in return are presented in pairs; all the possible 15 pairs are given, so that each resource class appears five times, but each time is described by a different statement. The 15 pairs are in random order which varies for different resources given, i.e., for the resource described at the top of the list. The order of presentation of the resource given varies randomly across subjects.

The preference score for each resource desired in return for any given one is the number of times a given resource is chosen over the other ones paired with it. The lowest score is therefore 0 (zero) when the resource is never chosen and the highest score is 5, which is obtained when the resource is chosen every time it appears. Since 15 choices are made in each list the sum of the scores for any such list is always 15. This artificial interdependence of the score may be undesirable for certain analytic purposes (e.g., in computing correlation coefficients among preferences). This artifact was avoided in an alterna-tive form of the inventory; in it every statement describing a resource which could be received in return was rated on a five-point scale from "highly desirable" to "not at all desirable;" in this rating three statements for each resource were presented. Thus, each score ranged, in this case, from 0 (zero) to 12.

SOCIAL INTERACTION INVENTORY
(Giving)

Please read carefully the following *instructions:*

In this questionnaire you are given six hypothetical situations in which you do something for another person. Each of the six situations is presented at the top of a separate page. Listed below each situation are pairs of possible things which the person could do for you in return. From each of the fifteen pairs you are to choose either A or B as the alternative which you would prefer most. Indicate your preference by placing an X in the slot provided to the left of each item. Be sure to choose *only* one item from *each* pair.

Be certain that you are indicating your preference with respect to the particular situation which is given at the top of the page on which you are working. Refer to the situation as often as necessary to keep it strong and clear in your mind. There are no right or wrong answers, we are interested only in your preferences. Even if neither of the two alternatives seems appealing, or if both seem equally appealing you are still to choose one alternative from each pair. Please work carefully and at your own speed. There is no time limitation.

EXAMPLE:

You let a person use your automobile. In return you would prefer that:

_____ A. The person thanks you for being so generous and considerate.

___X___ B. The person buys you a gift.

If you feel that in this situation you would prefer that the person buy you a gift, you would place an (X) next to that alternative.

You are helping a person by providing certain services for them. In return you would prefer that:

_____

_____ A. The person provides you with the opportunity to acquire some new information.
_____ B. The person says that he is very fond of you.

_____ A. The person tells you that he respects you.
_____ B. The person provides you with some desirable wares.

_____ A. The person gives you the feeling that you are very likable.
_____ B. A money order is made out to you by the person.

_____ A. The person does something for you.
_____ B. You are given new information.

_____ A. You receive some object you like from the person.
_____ B. You are made to feel that the person enjoys your company.

_____ A. You receive a check from the person.
_____ B. The person runs an errand for you.

_____ A. The person tells you something that you didn't know beforehand.
_____ B. The person praises you.

_____ A. The person repairs something for you.
_____ B. You receive affection from the person.

_____ A. The person makes you familiar with new facts.
_____ B. The person gives you a certain product.

_____ A. The person tells you that he has confidence in your abilities.
_____ B. The person gives you money.

_____ A. The person gives you some merchandise.
_____ B. The person makes himself available to do some work for you.

_____ A. The person indicates that he wants to be your friend.
_____ B. The person expresses his esteem for you.

_____ A. You receive cash from the person.
_____ B. The person gives you the benefit of his familiarity with a certain subject.

_____ A. The person gives you prestige.
_____ B. The person provides you with some service.

_____ A. You receive a payment from the person.
_____ B. You receive some goods from the person.

You convey to a person that you enjoy being with them and feel affection for them. In return you would prefer that:

_____

_____ A. The person gives you a certain product.
_____ B. The person does something for you.

_____ A. The person gives you the feeling that you are very likable.
_____ B. The person expresses his esteem for you.

_____ A. You receive cash from the person.
_____ B. The person gives you the benefit of his familiarity with a certain subject.

_____ A. You are told that the person has confidence in your abilities.

———— B. The person makes himself available to do some work for you.

———— A. You receive payment from the person.
———— B. The person provides you with some desirable wares.

———— A. The person makes you familiar with new facts.
———— B. The person indicates that he wants to be your friend.

———— A. The person praises you.
———— B. You receive some object you like from the person.

———— A. You are made to feel that the person enjoys your company.
———— B. You receive a check from the person.

———— A. The person runs an errand for you.
———— B. The person tells you something that you did not know beforehand.

———— A. The person gives you some merchandise.
———— B. You receive affection from the person.

———— A. The person gives you money.
———— B. The person provides you with some service.

———— A. The person provides you with the opportunity to acquire some new information.
———— B. The person gives you respect.

———— A. The person repairs something for you.
———— B. The person says that he is fond of you.

———— A. The person gives you new information.
———— B. You receive some goods from the person.

———— A. The person gives you prestige.
———— B. A money order is made out to you by the person.

You provide a person with some money to meet a temporary need. In return you would prefer that:

———————————————————————————————————

———— A. The person makes himself available to do some work for you.

———— B. The person indicates that he wants to be your friend.

———— A. The person gives you the benefit of his familiarity with a certain subject.

_____ B. You receive some goods from the person.

_____ A. The person praises you.
_____ B. A money order is made out to you by the person.

_____ A. The person provides you with some desirable wares.
_____ B. The person runs an errand for you.

_____ A. You receive affection from the person.
_____ B. The person expresses his esteem for you.

_____ A. You receive cash from the person.
_____ B. The person makes you familiar with new facts.

_____ A. The person gives you prestige.
_____ B. The person does something for you.

_____ A. The person gives you money.
_____ B. The person gives you some merchandise.

_____ A. The person gives you new information.
_____ B. The person says he is fond of you.

_____ A. You are told that the person has confidence in your abilities.
_____ B. You receive some object you like from the person.

_____ A. You are made to feel that the person enjoys your company.
_____ B. You receive a check from the person.

_____ A. The person repairs something for you.
_____ B. The person tells you something that you didn't know beforehand.

_____ A. The person gives you a certain product.
_____ B. The person gives you the feeling that you are very likable.

_____ A. You receive a payment from the person.
_____ B. The person provides you with some service.

_____ A. The person provides you with the opportunity to acquire some new information.
_____ B. The person gives you respect.

You give a person certain objects that you possess. In return you would prefer that:

_____ A. The person gives you some merchandise.
_____ B. The person says that he is fond of you.

_____ A. You receive cash from the person.
_____ B. The person does something for you.

_____ A. The person makes you familiar with new facts.
_____ B. The person gives you prestige.

_____ A. The person repairs something for you.
_____ B. You receive affection from the person.

_____ A. The person gives you some new information.
_____ B. The person gives you a certain product.

_____ A. The person gives you respect.
_____ B. You receive a check from the person.

_____ A. You receive some object you like from the person.
_____ B. The person runs an errand for you.

_____ A. The person gives you the feeling that you are very likable.
_____ B. The person expresses his esteem for you.

_____ A. A money order is made out to you by the person.
_____ B. The person gives you the benefit of his familiarity with a certain subject.

_____ A. The person praises you.
_____ B. The person makes himself available to do some work for you.

_____ A. The person gives you money.
_____ B. You receive some goods from the person.

_____ A. The person provides you with the opportunity to acquire some new information.
_____ B. You are made to feel that the person enjoys your company.

_____ A. You are told that the person has confidence in your abilities.
_____ B. The person provides you with some desirable wares.

_____ A. The person indicates that he wants to be your friend.
_____ B. You receive a payment from the person.

_____ A. The person provides you with some service.
_____ B. The person tells you something that you didn't know beforehand.

You convey to a person your respect and esteem for his talents. In return you would prefer that:

_____

_____ A. The person gives you prestige.
_____ B. The person provides you with some desirable wares.

_____ A. You are made to feel that the person enjoys your company.
_____ B. A money order is made out to you by the person.

_____ A. The person does something for you.
_____ B. The person tells you something you didn't know beforehand.

_____ A. You receive some object you like from the person.
_____ B. The person says that he is fond of you.

_____ A. The person gives you money.
_____ B. The person makes himself available to do some work for you.

_____ A. The person provides you with the opportunity to acquire some new information.
_____ B. The person expresses his esteem for you.

_____ A. The person runs an errand for you.
_____ B. The person gives you the feeling that you are very likable.

_____ A. The person gives you the benefit of his familiarity with a certain subject.
_____ B. The person gives you some merchandise.

_____ A. The person praises you.
_____ B. You receive a check from the person.

_____ A. The person gives you a certain product.
_____ B. The person provides you with some service.

_____ A. You receive affection from the person.
_____ B. You are told that the person has confidence in your abilities.

_____ A. You receive some cash from the person.
_____ B. The person makes you familiar with new facts.

_____ A. The person gives you respect.
_____ B. The person repairs something for you.

_____ A. You receive payment from the person.
_____ B. You receive some goods from the person.

_____ A. The person gives you new information.
_____ B. The person indicates that he wants to be your friend.

You provide certain information to a person. In return you would prefer that:

_____ A. The person gives you prestige.
_____ B. The person makes himself available to do some work for you.

_____ A. You receive cash from the person.
_____ B. You receive some goods from the person.

_____ A. The person gives you new information.
_____ B. The person gives you affection.

_____ A. You are told that the person has confidence in your abilities.
_____ B. The person provides you with some desirable wares.

_____ A. The person indicates that he wants to be your friend.
_____ B. A money order is made out to you by the person.

_____ A. The person provides you with some service.
_____ B. The person tells you something that you did not know beforehand.

_____ A. The person gives you a certain product.
_____ B. The person says that he is fond of you.

_____ A. You receive a check from the person.
_____ B. The person runs an errand for you.

_____ A. The person makes you familiar with new facts.
_____ B. The person gives you respect.

_____ A. The person repairs something for you.
_____ B. You are made to feel that the person enjoys your company.

_____ A. The person provides you with the opportunity to acquire some new information.
_____ B. The person gives you some merchandise.

_____ A. The person expresses his esteem for you.
_____ B. You receive a payment from the person.

_____ A. You receive some object you like from the person.
_____ B. The person does something for you.

_____ A. The person gives you the feeling that you are very likable.
_____ B. The person praises you.

_____ A. The person gives you money.
_____ B. The person gives you the benefit of his familiarity with a certain subject.

THIS INVENTORY IS identical in format with the one de-scribed in Appendix C, except that it deals with exchanges of taking, rather than with giving. It thus records preferences for depriving the other of a given resource in retaliation for each resource of aggression used by the other.

SOCIAL INTERACTION INVENTORY
(Taking)

Please read carefully the following *instructions:*

In this questionnaire you are given six hypothetical situations in which another person expresses some form of interpersonal hostility toward you. Each of the six situations is presented at the top of a separate page. Listed below each situation are pairs of alternative ways in which you might respond to the person who misbehaved toward you. From each of the fifteen pairs you are to choose either A or B as the alternative which you would prefer most. You are to indicate your preferred response by placing an X in the appropriate slot to the left of each item. Be sure to choose *only* one item from *each* pair of alternatives.

Be certain that you are indicating your preference with respect to the particular situation which is indicated at the top of the page on which you are working. Feel free to refer to the situation as often as necessary to keep it strong and clear in your mind. There are no right or wrong answers, assume that all alternatives are equally permissible and legitimate. We are interested only in *your preferred* responses. Even if neither of the two alternatives seems appealing, or if both seem equally appealing, you are still to choose one alternative from each pair. Please work carefully and at your own speed.

EXAMPLE:

A person who could provide you with much needed transportation refuses to do so. Your most preferred response would be to:

__X__ A. Avoid further association with the person and be unfriendly toward him.

_____ B. Refuse him assistance when he requested a favor of you.

If you feel that in this situation you would be most likely to behave unfriendly and avoid further association with the person, you would place an (X) next to that alternative.

A person degrades or belittles you. He lets you understand that you are worthless and that you don't do things well. Your most preferred response would be that:

_____ A. You convey to the person that you have a low regard for him.

_____ B. You help yourself to some of the other person's belongings.

_____ A. You let the person feel that you dislike him.

_____ B. You refuse to give money to the person when expected.

_____ A. You will be physically hostile to the other person.

_____ B. You tell the person things that will lead him to the wrong decision.

_____ A. You would confiscate goods belonging to the other person.

_____ B. You make the person realize that you would rather avoid his company.

_____ A. You help yourself to money belonging to the person.

_____ B. You cause inconvenience to the person, or damage his belongings.

_____ A. You provide the person with knowledge that leads him to wrong conclusions.

_____ B. You belittle the person.

_____ A. You disturb the person's comfort through some disservice on your part.

_____ B. You convey to the person that you are displeased with him.

_____ A. You deliberately give the person wrong instructions.

_____ B. You take possession of goods belonging to the other person.

_____ A. You convey to the person that you hold him in low es-
           teem.
_____ B. You withhold money that should be given to the person.

_____ A. You seize objects belonging to the other person.
_____ B. You physically harm the person.

_____ A. You convey to the person that you do not want to asso-
           ciate with him.
_____ B. You let the person feel that you don't respect his abili-
           ties.

_____ A. You make the person lose some money.
_____ B. You provide the person with bad advice.

_____ A. You make unflattering remarks to the person.
_____ B. You withhold aid causing hardship to the person.

_____ A. You manage to gain possession of some money belonging
           to the person.
_____ B. You would assume ownership of things that belong to the
           other person.

_____ A. You deceive the person regarding information he re-
           quests from you.
_____ B. You convey to the person that you resent him.

A person confiscates goods or objects which belong to you. Your most
preferred response would be that:

_____

_____ A. You would assume ownership of things that belong to the
           other person.
_____ B. You convey to the person that you are displeased with him.

_____ A. You refuse to give money to the person when expected.
_____ B. You withhold aid causing hardship to the person.

_____ A. You deceive the person regarding information he requests
           from you.
_____ B. You convey to the person that you have a low regard for
           him.

_____ A. You disturb the person's comfort through some disservice
           on your part.
_____ B. You make the person realize that you would rather avoid
           his company.

_____ A. You deliberately give the person wrong instructions.
_____ B. You would confiscate goods belonging to the other person.

_____ A. You make unflattering remarks to the person.
_____ B. You withhold money that should be given to the person.

_____ A. You help yourself to some of the other person's belongings.
_____ B. You cause inconvenience to the person, or damage his belongings.

_____ A. You convey to the person that you do not want to associate with him.
_____ B. You convey to the person that you hold him in low esteem.

_____ A. You manage to gain possession of some money belonging to the person.
_____ B. You tell the person things that will lead him to the wrong decision.

_____ A. You belittle the person.
_____ B. You physically harm the person.

_____ A. You make the person lose some money.
_____ B. You seize objects belonging to the other person.

_____ A. You provide the person with bad advice.
_____ B. You convey to the person that you resent him.

_____ A. You let the person feel that you don't respect his abilities.
_____ B. You take possession of goods belonging to the other person.

_____ A. You let the person feel that you dislike him.
_____ B. You help yourself to money belonging to the person.

_____ A. You will be physically hostile to the other person.
_____ B. You provide the person with knowledge that leads him to wrong conclusions.

A person cheats you by taking or withholding money which belongs to you. Your most preferred response would be that:

_____

_____ A. You disturb the person's comfort through some disservice on your part.
_____ B. You convey to the person that you do not want to associate with him.

_____ A. You deliberately give the person wrong instructions.
_____ B. You help yourself to some of the other person's belongings.

_____ A. You convey to the person that you have a low regard for him.
_____ B. You manage to gain possession of some money belonging to the person.

_____ A. You seize objects belonging to the other person.
_____ B. You physically harm the person.

_____ A. You convey to the person that you resent him.
_____ B. You belittle the person.

_____ A. You make the person lose some money.
_____ B. You tell the person things that will lead him to the wrong decision.

_____ A. You let the person feel that you don't respect his abilities.
_____ B. You will be physically hostile to the other person.

_____ A. You refuse to give money to the person when expected.
_____ B. You take possession of goods belonging to the other person.

_____ A. You deceive the person regarding information he requests from you.
_____ B. You make the person realize that you would rather avoid his company.

_____ A. You convey to the person that you hold him in low esteem.
_____ B. You would confiscate goods belonging to the other person.

_____ A. You let the person feel that you dislike him.
_____ B. You withhold money that should be given to the person.

_____ A. You cause inconvenience to the person, or damage his belongings.
_____ B. You provide the person with knowledge that leads him to wrong conclusions.

_____ A. You would assume ownership of things that belong to the other person.
_____ B. You convey to the person that you are displeased with him.

_____ A. You help yourself to money belonging to the person.
_____ B. You withhold aid causing hardship to the person.

_____ A. You provide the person with bad advice.
_____ B. You make unflattering remarks to the person.

A person conveys to you that he dislikes you. He is unfriendly and avoids your company. Your most preferred response would be that:

_____ A. You would confiscate goods belonging to the other person.
_____ B. You withhold aid causing hardship to the person.

_____ A. You let the person feel that you dislike him.

_____ B. You make unflattering remarks to the person.

_____ A. You manage to gain possession of some money belonging to the person.

_____ B. You deliberately give the person wrong instructions.

_____ A. You convey to the person that you have a low regard for him.

_____ B. You will be physically hostile to the other person.

_____ A. You help yourself to money belonging to the person.

_____ B. You help yourself to some of the other person's belongings.

_____ A. You tell the person things that will lead him to the wrong decision.

_____ B. You convey to the person that you resent him.

_____ A. You convey to the person that you hold him in low esteem.

_____ B. You would assume ownership of things that belong to the other person.

_____ A. You convey to the person that you do not want to associate with him.

_____ B. You withhold money that should be given to the person.

_____ A. You cause inconvenience to the person, or damage his belongings.

_____ B. You provide the person with knowledge that leads him to wrong conclusions.

_____ A. You seize objects belonging to the other person.

_____ B. You make the person realize that you would rather avoid his company.

_____ A. You make the person lose some money.

_____ B. You disturb the person's comfort through some disservice on your part.

_____ A. You deceive the person regarding information he requests from you.

_____ B. You let the person feel that you don't respect his abilities.

_____ A. You physically harm the person.

_____ B. You convey to the person that you are displeased with him.

_____ A. You provide the person with bad advice.

_____ B. You take possession of goods belonging to the other person.

_____ A. You belittle the person.

_____ B. You refuse to give money to the person when expected.

A person gives you false or distorted information. His deceit leads you to make bad decisions in matters which are important to you. Your most preferred response would be that:

_____ A. You convey to the person that you hold him in low esteem.
_____ B. You disturb the person's comfort through some disservice on your part.

_____ A. You help yourself to money belonging to the person.
_____ B. You would assume ownership of things that belong to the other person.

_____ A. You tell the person things that will lead him to the wrong decision.
_____ B. You convey to the person that you are displeased with him.

_____ A. You belittle the person.
_____ B. You take possession of goods belonging to the other person.

_____ A. You convey to the person that you resent him.
_____ B. You manage to gain possession of some money belonging to the person.

_____ A. You will be physically hostile to the other person.
_____ B. You provide the person with bad advice.

_____ A. You would confiscate goods belonging to the other person.
_____ B. You make the person realize that you would rather avoid his company.

_____ A. You refuse to give money to the person when expected.
_____ B. You physically harm the person.

_____ A. You deceive the person regarding information he requests from you.
_____ B. You convey to the person that you have a low regard for him.

_____ A. You cause inconvenience to the person, or damage his belongings.
_____ B. You convey to the person that you do not want to associate with him.

_____ A. You deliberately give the person wrong instructions.
_____ B. You seize objects belonging to the other person.

_____ A. You let the person feel that you don't respect his abilities.
_____ B. You withhold money that should be given to the person.

_____ A. You help yourself to some of the other person's belongings.
_____ B. You withhold aid causing hardship to the person.

_____ A. You let the person feel that you dislike him.
_____ B. You make unflattering remarks to the person.
_____ A. You make the person lose some money.
_____ B. You provide the person with knowledge that leads him to wrong conclusions.

A person injures you or gives you bad services. His behavior results in inconvenience or damage to you or your belongings. Your most preferred response would be that:

_____ A. You deliberately give the person wrong instructions.
_____ B. You convey to the person that you do not want to associate with him.

_____ A. You make unflattering remarks to the person.
_____ B. You help yourself to some of the other person's belongings.

_____ A. You let the person feel that you dislike him.
_____ B. You manage to gain possession of some money belonging to the person.

_____ A. You disturb the person's comfort through some disservice on your part.
_____ B. You deceive the person regarding information he requests from you.

_____ A. You would confiscate goods belonging to the other person.
_____ B. You convey to the person that you resent him.

_____ A. You make the person lose some money.
_____ B. You cause inconvenience to the person, or damage his belongings.

_____ A. You tell the person things that will lead him to the wrong decision.
_____ B. You let the person feel that you don't respect his abilities.

_____ A. You will be physically hostile to the other person.
_____ B. You convey to the person that you are displeased with him.

_____ A. You provide the person with knowledge that leads him to wrong conclusions.
_____ B. You take possession of goods belonging to the other person.

_____ A. You belittle the person.
_____ B. You withhold money that should be given to the person.

_____ A. You would assume ownership of things that belong to the other person.

_____ B. You withhold aid causing hardship to the person.

_____ A. You make the person realize that you would rather avoid his company.

_____ B. You convey to the person that you have a low regard for him.

_____ A. You help yourself to money belonging to the person.

_____ B. You provide the person with bad advice.

_____ A. You convey to the person that you hold him in low esteem.

_____ B. You physically harm the person.

_____ A. You refuse to give money to the person when expected.

_____ B. You seize objects belonging to the other person.

┌─────────────   ─────────────┐
│   GROUP INTERACTION INVENTORY   │
└─────────────   ─────────────┘

THIS INSTRUMENT RECORDS the expectations of a task-team member regarding the behavior of the most and least preferred team-mate in giving to the subject or depriving him of the three resources of love, status, and information. Each type of behavior (giving or taking one of the three resources) is represented in the test by four statements. Each was rated on a five-point scale ranging from 0 (zero) for "almost never" to 4 for "almost always." These ratings were added up for the four statements pertaining to any given type of behavior yielding a score between 0 (zero)—when expectation was lowest—and 16 for the highest expectation.

GROUP INTERACTION INVENTORY

Please read carefully the following *instructions:*

Our group is divided into eight (8) teams, and each team has to fulfill a given task, previously agreed upon by the team.

You have interacted previously with your fellow team members and have some impressions of them. You may prefer some of the team members more than some others.

In this questionnaire you are asked to rate your *EXPECTATIONS* of the *most* preferred and *least* preferred team members. Indicate your choice by placing an X in one of the slots. Be sure to choose *only* one possibility for each item.

PLEASE, DO NOT WRITE THE NAMES OF THESE GROUP MEMBERS.

EXAMPLE: How much of the following behavior would you *expect* from the person you *preferred most* of your team?

	almost never	seldom	sometimes	often	almost always
Would buy you a gift	____	X	____	____	____

How much of the following behaviors would you *expect* from the person you *preferred most* of your team?

	almost never	seldom	sometimes	often	almost always
1. Would make you familiar with new facts.	____	____	____	____	____
2. Would tell you things that would lead you to the wrong decision.	____	____	____	____	____
3. Would call you and give you relevant reference for your paper.	____	____	____	____	____
4. Would express esteem for you.	____	____	____	____	____
5. Would convey to you that he dislikes you.	____	____	____	____	____
6. Would make you realize that he would rather avoid your company.	____	____	____	____	____
7. Receiving affection from the person.	____	____	____	____	____
8. Would give you prestige.	____	____	____	____	____
9. Would give you the feeling that you are very likable.	____	____	____	____	____
10. Would give you false information.	____	____	____	____	____
11. Would praise you.	____	____	____	____	____
12. Would convey to you that he is fond of you.	____	____	____	____	____
13. Would deceive you regarding information you request from him.	____	____	____	____	____
14. Would let you understand that you do not do things well.	____	____	____	____	____
15. Would convey to you that he resents you.	____	____	____	____	____
16. Would let you feel he does not respect your abilities.	____	____	____	____	____
17. Would make unflattering remarks.	____	____	____	____	____
18. Would indicate that he wants to be your friend.	____	____	____	____	____
19. Would convey to you that he has a low regard for you.	____	____	____	____	____
20. Would be unfriendly toward you.	____	____	____	____	____
21. Would give you respect.	____	____	____	____	____
22. Would give you new information.	____	____	____	____	____
23. Would deliberately give you wrong instructions.	____	____	____	____	____
24. Would tell you something that you did not know beforehand.	____	____	____	____	____

How much of the following behaviors would you *expect* from the *least preferred* person of your team?

	almost never	seldom	sometimes	often	almost always
1. Would make you familiar with new facts.	———	———	———	———	———
2. Would tell you things that would lead you to the wrong decision.	———	———	———	———	———
3. Would call you and give you relevant reference for your paper.	———	———	———	———	———
4. Would express esteem for you.	———	———	———	———	———
5. Would convey to you that he dislikes you.	———	———	———	———	———
6. Would make you realize that he would rather avoid your company.	———	———	———	———	———
7. Receiving affection from the person.	———	———	———	———	———
8. Would give you prestige.	———	———	———	———	———
9. Would give you the feeling that you are very likable.	———	———	———	———	———
10. Would give you false information.	———	———	———	———	———
11. Would praise you.	———	———	———	———	———
12. Would convey to you that he is fond of you.	———	———	———	———	———
13. Would deceive you regarding information you request from him.	———	———	———	———	———
14. Would let you understand that you do not do things well.	———	———	———	———	———
15. Would convey to you that he resents you.	———	———	———	———	———
16. Would let you feel he does not respect your abilities.	———	———	———	———	———
17. Would make unflattering remarks.	———	———	———	———	———
18. Would indicate that he wants to be your friend.	———	———	———	———	———
19. Would convey to you that he has a low regard for you.	———	———	———	———	———
20. Would be unfriendly toward you.	———	———	———	———	———
21. Would give you respect.	———	———	———	———	———
22. Would give you new information.	———	———	———	———	———
23. Would deliberately give you wrong instructions.	———	———	———	———	———
24. Would tell you something that you did not know beforehand.	———	———	———	———	———

REFERENCES

Adams, H.B.: "Mental illness or interpersonal behavior?" *Am Psychol, 19:*191–197, 1964.

Adams, J.S.: Inequity in social exchange. In Berkowitz, L. (Ed.): *Advances in experimental social psychology.* New York, Academic Press, 1965, vol. 2.

Adler, A.: *The Neurotic Constitution.* New York, Dodd, Mead, 1926.

Albert, R.S.: The role of mass media and the effects of aggressive film content upon children's aggressive responses and identification choices. *Genet Psychol Monogr, 55:*271–285, 1957.

Alexander, C.N. & Simpson, R.L.: Balance theory and distributive justice. *Sociol Inquiry, 34:*183–184, 1964.

Allison, J. & Hunt, D.E.: Social desirability and the expression of aggression under varying conditions of frustration. *J Consult Psychol, 23:*528–532, 1959.

Allport, B.W.: *Personality: A Psychological Interpretation.* New York, Holt, 1937.

Andrew, R.J.: The origins of facial expressions. *Sci Am, 213:*88–94, 1965.

Andry, R.: *Delinquency and Parental Pathology.* London, Methuen, 1960.

Arieti, S.: Schizophrenia: The manifest symptomatology, psychodynamics and formal mechanism. In Arieti, S. (Ed.): *American Handbook of Psychiatry.* New York, Basic Books, 1959, vol. I.

Aronfreed, J.: *Conduct and Conscience.* New York, Academic Press, 1968.

———: The concept of internalization. In Goslin, D.A. (Ed.): *Handbook of Socialization Theory and Research.* Chicago, Rand McNally, 1969.

Aronson, E.: The effects of effort on the attractiveness of rewarded and unrewarded stimuli. *J Abnorm Soc Psychol, 63:*375–380, 1961.

———: The theory of cognitive dissonance: current perspective. In Berkowitz, L. (Ed.): *Advances in Experimental Social Psychology.* New York, Academic Press, 1969, vol. 4.

———: Some antecedents of interpersonal attraction. In Arnold, W.J. and Levine, D. (Eds.): *1969 Nebraska Symposium on Motivation.* Lincoln, Nebraska, University of Nebraska Press, 1970.

———, & Linder, D.: Gain and loss of esteem as determinants of interpersonal attractiveness. *J Exp Soc Psychol, 1:*156–171, 1965.

———, & Mills, J.: The effect of severity of initiation on liking for a group. *J Abnorm Soc Psychol, 59:*177–181, 1959.

———, Willerman, B., & Floyd, J.: The effect of a pratfall on increasing interpersonal attractiveness. *Psychonomic Sci, 4:*227–228, 1966.

Asch, S.E.: The doctrine of suggestion, prestige, and imitation in social psychology. *Psychol Rev, 55:*250–276, 1948.

———: Effects of group pressure upon the modification and distortion of judgment. In Guetzow, H. (Ed.): *Groups, Leadership and Men.* Pittsburgh, Carnegie Press, 1951.

———: The metaphor: A psychological inquiry. In Tagiuri, R. and Petrullo, L. (Eds.): *Person Perception and Interpersonal Behavior.* Stanford, Stanford University Press, 1958.

Ayer, J.G.: Effects of success and failure of interpersonal and task performance upon leader perception and behavior. Unpublished M.A. thesis, University of Illinois, Urbana, 1968. (a)

418

————: Semantic-game study: Progress report. Unpublished manuscript, 1968. (b)

Bailey, E.D.: Social interaction as a population-regulating mechanism in mice. *Can J Zool, 44:*1007–1012, 1966.

Baker, J.W., & Schaie, K.W.: Effects of aggressing "alone" or "with another" on physiological and psychological arousal. *J Pers Soc Psychol, 12:*80–86, 1969.

Baldwin, A.L.: *Theories of Child Development.* New York, Wiley, 1967.

————: A cognitive theory of socialization. In Goslin, D.A. (Ed.): *Handbook of Socialization Theory and Research.* Chicago, Rand McNally, 1969.

Baldwin, J.M.: *Mental Development in the Child and the Race.* New York, MacMillan, 1894.

Bales, R.F., & Strodtbeck, F.L.: Phases in group problem-solving. *J Abnorm Soc Psychol, 46:*485–495, 1951.

Bandura, A.: Social learning through imitation. In Jones, M.R. (Ed.): *Nebraska Symposium on Motivation.* Lincoln, Nebraska, University of Nebraska Press, 1962.

————: Vicarious processes: A case of no-trial learning. In Berkowitz, L. (Ed.): *Advances in Experimental Social Psychology.* New York, Academic Press, 1965, vol. 2.

————: Social learning theory of identificatory processes. In Goslin, D.A. (Ed.): *Handbook of Socialization Theory and Research.* Chicago, Rand McNally, 1969.

————, Ross, D., & Ross, S.A.: A comparative test of the status envy, social power, and secondary reinforcement theories of identification learning. *J Abnorm Soc Psychol, 67:*527–534, 1963.

————, & Walters, R.: Dependency conflicts in aggressive delinquents. *J Soc Issues, 14* (3):52–65, 1958.

————: *Adolescent Aggression.* New York, Ronald Press, 1959.

————: *Social Learning and Personality Development.* New York, Holt, Rinehart and Winston, 1963.

Bannister, D., & Fransella, F.: A grid test of schizophrenic thought disorder. *Br J Soc Clin Psychol, 5:*95–102, 1966.

————, & Agnew, J.: Characteristics and validity of the grid test of thought disorder. *Br J Soc Clin Psychol, 10:*144–151, 1971.

Barker, R.G., & Wright, H.F.: *Midwest and Its Children.* Evanston, Ill., Row, Peterson, 1955.

Barron, M.L.: *The Juvenile in Delinquent Society.* New York, Alfred A. Knopf, 1954.

Barron, N.M.: The effect of leadership style and leader behavior on group creativity under stress. Unpublished Master thesis. Department of Psychology, University of Illinois, Urbana, 1967.

Barry, H., Bacon, M.K., & Child, I.L.: A cross-cultural survey of some sex differences in socialization. *J Abnorm Soc Psychol, 55:*327–332, 1957.

Bateson, G., Jackson, D.D., Haley, J., & Weakland, J.H.: Toward a theory of schizophrenia. *Behav Sci, 1:*251–264, 1956.

Benoit, E.: Status, status types, and status interrelations. In Biddle, B.J., & Thomas, E.J. (Eds.): *Role Theory: Concepts and Research.* New York, Wiley, 1966.

Benzinger, T.H.: The human thermostat. *Sci Am, 204:*134–147, 1961.

Berger, E.M.: The relation between expressed acceptance of self and expressed acceptance of others. *J Abnorm Soc Psychol, 47:*778–782, 1952.

Berkowitz, L.: *Aggression: A Social Psychological Analysis.* New York, McGraw-Hill, 1962.

————: The concept of aggression drive: Some additional considerations. In Berkowitz, L. (Ed.): *Advances in Experimental Social Psychology.* New York, Academic Press, 1965, vol. 2.

———: On not being able to aggress. *Br J Soc Clin Psychol, 5:*130–139, 1966.

———: Social motivation. In Lindzey, G., & Aronson, E. (Eds.): *The Handbook of Social Psychology,* 2nd ed. Reading, Mass., Addison-Wesley, 1969, vol. 3. (a)

———: The frustration-aggression hypothesis revisited. In Berkowitz, L. (Ed.): *Roots of Aggression.* New York, Atherton, 1969. (b)

———, & Daniels, L.: Affecting the salience of the social responsibility norm. *J Abnorm Soc Psychol, 28:*275–281, 1964.

———, & Geen, R.G.: Film violence and the cue properties of available targets. *J Pers Soc Psychol, 3:*525–530, 1966.

———, Green, J.A., & Macaulay, J.R.: Hostility catharsis as the reduction of emotional tension. *Psychiatry, 25:*23–31, 1962.

———, & Holmes, D.S.: A further investigation of hostility to disliked objects. *J Pers, 28:*427–442, 1960.

———, Lepinski, J.P., & Angulo, E.J.: Awareness of own anger level and subsequent aggression. *J Pers Soc Psychol, 11:*293–300, 1969.

Berlyne, D.E.: *Conflict, Arousal and Curiosity.* New York, McGraw Hill, 1960.

———: *Structure and Direction in Thinking.* New York, Wiley, 1965.

Berscheid, E., Boye, D., & Walster, E.: Retaliation as a means of restoring equity. *J Pers Soc Psychol, 10:*370–376, 1968.

———, & Walster, E.: When does a harm-doer compensate a victim? *J Pers Soc Psychol, 6:*435–441, 1967.

———: Attitude change. In Mills, J. (Ed.): *Experimental Social Psychology.* New York, MacMillan, 1969.

———: *Interpersonal Attraction.* Reading, Mass., Addison-Wesley, 1969.

Bettelheim, B.: Joey: A "mechanical boy." *Sci Am, 200* (3):116–127, 1959.

Biddle, B.J., & Thomas, E.J.: *Role Theory: Concepts and Research.* New York, Wiley, 1966.

Biller, H.B., & Weiss, S.D.: The father-daughter relationship and the personality development of the female. *J Genet Psychol, 116:*79–93, 1970.

Blake, R.R., & Mouton, J.S.: Conformity, resistance, and conversion. In Berg, I.A. & Bass, B.M. (Eds.): *Conformity and Deviation.* New York, Harper, 1961.

Blau, P.M.: *Exchange and Power in Social Life.* New York, Wiley, 1967.

Bleuler, E.: *Dementia Praecox; or The Group of Schizophrenias.* New York, International University Press, 1950. (Translated from the German edition, 1911).

Blum, R.H.: A cross-cultural study. In Blum, R.H. and Associates (Eds.): *Society and Drugs.* San Francisco, Jossey-Bass, 1969.

Blumstein, P.W., & Weinstein, E.A.: The redress of distributive injustice. *Am J Sociol, 74:*408–418, 1969.

Bolles, R.C.: Species-specific defense reactions and avoidance learning. *Psychol Rev, 77:*32–48, 1970.

Bramel, D.: A dissonance theory approach to defensive projection. *J Abnorm Soc Psychol, 64:*121–129, 1962.

Brehm, J.W., & Cole, A.H.: Effect of a favor which reduces freedom. *J Pers Soc Psychol, 3:*420–426, 1966.

Bresnahan, J.L., & Blum, W.L.: Chaotic reinforcement: a socioeconomic leveler. *Dev Psychol, 4:*89–92, 1971.

Breznitz, S., & Kugelmass, S.: Intentionality in moral judgment: developmental stages. *Child Dev, 38:*469–479, 1967.

Brim, O.G.: Family structure and sex role learning by children: a further analysis of Helen Koch's data. *Sociometry, 21:*1–16, 1958.

Brislin, R.W.: The content and evaluation of cross-cultural training programs. Arlington, Va.: Institute for Defense Analyses, 1970.

Bronowski, J.: *Science and Human Values.* London, Hutchinson, 1961. Quoted by Koestler, 1964.

Brown, D.G.: Sex-role development in a changing culture. *Psychol Bull, 54:*232–242, 1958.

Brown, R.W.: Language and categories. Appendix to Bruner, J.S., Goodnow, J.J. & Austin, G.A. (Eds.): *A Study of Thinking.* New York, Wiley, 1956.

Brown, R.W.: How shall a thing be called? *Psychol Rev, 65:*14–21, 1958.

Bruner, J.S., Goodnow, J.J., & Austin, G.A.: *A Study of Thinking.* New York, Wiley, 1956.

Buhler, C.: Basic theoretical concepts of humanistic psychology. *Am Psychol, 26:*378–386, 1971.

Burnet, F.M.: *Self and Not-Self.* New York, Cambridge University Press, 1969.

Burnstein, E., & Worchel, P.: Arbitrariness of frustration and its consequences for aggression in a social situation. *J Pers, 30:*528–540, 1962.

Buss, A.H.: *The Psychology of Aggression.* New York, Wiley, 1961.

———: Physical aggression in relation to different frustrations. *J Abnorm Soc Psychol, 67:*1–7, 1963.

———: Instrumentality of aggression, feedback and frustration, as determinant of physical aggression. *Journal of Personality and Social Psychology, 3:*153–162, 1966.

Butler, J., & Haigh, G.: Changes in the relationship between self concepts and ideal concepts consequent upon client-centered counseling. In Rogers, C.R. & Dymond, R. (Eds.): *Psychotherapy and Personality Changes.* Chicago, University of Chicago Press, 1954.

Byrne, D.: Response to attitude similarity-dissimilarity as a function of affiliation. *J Pers, 30:*164–177, 1962.

———: Attitudes and attraction. In Berkowitz, L. (Ed.): *Advances in Experimental Social Psychology.* New York, Academic Press, 1969. vol. 4.

———, Ervin, C.R., & Lamberth, J.: Continuity between the experimental study of attraction and real-life computer dating. *J Pers Soc Psychol, 16:*157–165, 1970.

Calhoun, J.B.: Population density and social pathology. *Sci Am, 206:*139–146, 1962.

Cannon, W.B.: *The Wisdom of the Body* (Rev.). New York, Norton, 1939.

Capehart, J., Tempone, V.J., & Hebert, J.: A theory of stimulus equivalence. *Psychol Rev, 76:*405–418, 1969.

Carlsmith, J.M., Collins, B.E., & Helmreich, R.L.: Studies in forced compliance: I. the effect of pressure for compliance on attitude change produced by face-to-face role playing and anonymous essay writing. *J Pers Soc Psychol, 4:*1–3, 1966.

———, & Gross, A.E.: Some effects of guilt on compliance. *J Pers Soc Psychol, 11:*232–239, 1969.

Carpenter, C.R.: Societies of monkeys and apes. In Southwick, C.H. (Ed.): *Primate Social Behavior.* Princeton, New Jersey, Van Nostrand, 1963.

Carr, J.E.: Differentiation similarity of patient and therapist and the outcome of psychotherapy. *J Abnorm Psychol, 76:*361–369, 1970.

Carson, R.C.: *Interaction Concepts of Personality.* Chicago, Aldine, 1969.

———, & Heine, R.W.: Similarity and success in therapeutic dyads. *J Consult Psychol, 26:*38–43, 1962.

Cartwright, D.: A field theoretical conception of power. In Cartwright, D. (Ed.): *Studies in Social Power.* Ann Arbor, University of Michigan, 1959. (a)

———: Power: a neglected variable in social psychology. In Cartwright, D. (Ed.): *Studies in Social Power.* Ann Arbor, University of Michigan, 1959. (b)

————, & Zander, A.: Power and influence in groups: Introduction. In Cartwright, D. & Zander, A. (Eds.): *Group Dynamics: Research and Theory.* New York, Harper and Row, 1968.

Cattell, R.B.: *Personality: A Systematic Theoretical and Factual Study.* New York, McGraw-Hill, 1950.

————: Personality structure: the larger dimensions. In Semeonoff, B. (Ed.): *Personality Assessment.* New York, Penguin, 1966.

————, & Warburton, F.W.: *Objective Personality and Motivation Tests: A Theoretical Introduction and Practical Compendium.* Urbana, Ill., University of Illinois Press, 1967.

Centers, R., & Granville, A.C.: Reciprocal need gratification in intersexual attraction: a test of the hypotheses of Schutz and Winch. *J Pers, 39:*26–43, 1971.

Chemers, M.M., Lekhyananda, D., Fiedler, F.E., & Stolurow, L.M.: Some effects of cultural training on leadership in heterocultural task group. *Int J Psychol, 1:*301–314, 1966.

————, & Skrzypek, G.J.: An experimental test of the contingency model of leadership effectiveness. *J Pers Soc Psychol, 24:*172–177, 1972.

Chomsky, N.: *Syntactic Structures.* The Hague, Mouton, 1957.

————: Explanatory models in linguistics. In Nagel, E., Suppes, P., & Tarsky, A. (Eds.): *Logic, Methodology and Philosophy of Science.* Stanford, Stanford University Press, 1962.

————: Linguistic structure and cognitive processes. Paper read at Western Psychology Association meeting, Santa Monica, 1963.

Christie, R.: The Machiavellis among us. *Psychol Today, 4:*82–86, 1970.

Christie, R., & Geis, F.L.: *Studies in Machiavellianism.* New York, Academic Press, 1970.

Cohen, A.R.: Social norms, arbitrariness of frustration, and status of the agent of frustration in the frustration-aggression hypothesis. *J Abnorm Soc Psychol, 51:*222–226, 1955.

————: Situational structure, self-esteem and threat-oriented reactions to power. In Cartwright, D. (Ed.): *Studies in Social Power.* Ann Arbor, University of Michigan, 1959.

Cohn, R.: Differential cerebral processing of noise and verbal stimuli. *Science, 172:*599–601, 1971.

Cole, M., & Bruner, J.S.: Cultural differences and inferences about psychological processes. *Am Psychol, 26:*867–876, 1971.

Cone, C.D.: Observations of self-induced mitosis and autosynchrony in sarcoma cell networks. *Cancer Research, 28:*2155–2161, 1968.

Conn, L.K., & Crowne, D.P.: Instigation to aggression, emotional arousal and defensive emulation. *J Pers, 32:*163–179, 1964.

Cooley, C.H.: *Human Nature and the Social Order.* New York, Scribner, 1902.

Cooley, W.W., & Lohnes, P.R.: *Multivariate Procedures for the Behavioral Sciences.* New York, Wiley, 1962.

Coopersmith, S.: *The Antecedents of Self-Esteem.* San Francisco, W.H. Freeman, 1967.

Cowie, J., Cowie, C., & Slater, E.: *Delinquency in Girls.* London, Heinemann, 1968.

Coyle, G.L.: *Social Process in Organized Groups.* New York, R.R. Smith, 1930.

Crandall, V.J., & Bellugi, U.: Some relationships of interpersonal and intrapersonal conceptualizations to personal-social adjustment. *J Pers, 23:*224–232, 1954.

Cronbach, L.J.: The two disciplines of scientific psychology. *Am Psychol, 12:*671–684, 1957.

Crowne, D.P., & Marlowe, D.A.: A new scale of social desirability independent of psychopathology. *J Consult Psychol, 24:*349–354, 1960.

————: *The Approval Motive.* New York, Wiley, 1964.

Day, R.H.: Visual spatial illusions: a general explanation. *Science, 175:*1335–1340, 1972.

deCharms, R., & Wilkins, E.J.: Some effects of verbal expression of hostility.*J Abnorm Soc Psychol, 66:*462–470, 1963.

Deese, J.: Behavior and fact. *Am Psychol, 24:*515–522, 1969.

Deitz, G.E.: A comparison of delinquents with non-delinquents on self-concept, self-acceptance and parental identification.*J Genet Psychol, 115:*285–295, 1969.

Deutsch, M., & Gerard, H.B.: A study of normative and informational social influences upon individual judgement.*J Abnorm Soc Psychol, 51:*629–636, 1955. Quoted by French and Raven, 1959.

Devereux, E.C., Bronfenbrenner, U., & Rodgers, R.R.: Childrearing in England and the United States: a cross-national comparison. *J Marriage Family,* 1969, *31:*257–270, 1969.

Dinwiddie, F.M.: *An Application of the Principle of Response Generalization to the Prediction of Displacement of Aggressive Responses.* Washington, Catholic University of America Press, 1955.

Dollard, J., Doob, L., Miller, N., Mowrer, O., & Sears, R.: *Frustration and Aggression.* New Haven, Yale University Press, 1939.

Donnenwerth, G.V.: Effect of resources on retaliation to loss. Unpublished doctoral dissertation. University of Missouri, Columbia, Missouri, 1971.

————, Teichman, M., & Foa, U.G.: Cognitive differentiation of self and parents in delinquent and non-delinquent girls. *Br J Soc Clin Psychol, 12:*144–152, 1973.

Dulany, D.E., Jr.: The place of hypotheses and intentions: an analysis of verbal control in verbal conditioning. In Eriksen, C.W. (Ed.): *Behavior and Awareness.* Durham, N.C., Duke University Press, 1962.

Duncan, S.D., Jr.: Nonverbal communication. *Psychol Bull, 72:*118–137, 1969.

Egeth, H., Marcus, N., & Bevan, W.: Target-set and response-set interaction: implications for models of human information processing. *Science, 176:*1447–1448, 1972.

Ekman, P.: Pan cultural elements in facial display of emotion. *Science, 164:*86–88, 1969.

————: Universal and cultural differences in facial expressions of emotion. In Cole, J. (Ed.): *1971 Nebraska Symposium on motivation.* Lincoln, Nebraska, University of Nebraska Press, 1972.

Eldred, S.H., Bell, N.W., Sherman, L.J., & Longabaugh, R.H.: Classification and analysis of interaction patterns on a ward for chronic schizophrenics. *Disord Communication, 42:*381–386, 1964.

Emmerich, W.: Young children's discriminations of parent and child roles.*Child Dev, 30:*403–419, 1959.

————: Family role concepts of children ages six to ten. *Child Dev, 32:*609–624, 1961.

————: Personality development and concepts of structure. *Child Dev, 39:*671–690, 1968.

————, Goldman, K.S., & Shore, R.E.: Differentiation and development of social norms. *J Pers Soc Psychol, 18:*323–353, 1971.

English, H.B., & English, A.C.: *A Comprehensive Dictionary of Psychological and Psychoanalytical Terms.* New York, Longmans, Green, and Co., 1958.

Epstein, S., & Taylor, S.P.: Instigation to aggression as a function of degree of defeat and perceived aggressive intent of the opponent.*J Pers, 35:*265–289, 1967.

Feather, N.T.: Organization and discrepancy in cognitive structures. *Psychol Rev, 78:*355–379, 1971.

Federn, P.: *Ego Psychology and the Psychoses.* New York, Basic Books, 1952.

Feshbach, S.: The drive-reducing function of fantasy behavior. *J Abnorm Soc Psychol,* 50:3–11, 1955.

———: The catharsis hypothesis and some consequences of interaction with aggressive and neutral play objects. *J Pers, 24:449–462,* 1956.

———: The stimulating versus cathartic effects of a vicarious aggressive activity. *J Abnorm Soc Psychol, 63:*381–385, 1961.

Festinger, L.: An analysis of compliant behavior. In Sherif, M. and Wilson, M.O. (Eds.): *Group Relations at the Crossroads.* New York, Harper, 1953.

———: A theory of social comparison processes. *Hum Relations, 7:* 117–140, 1954.

———: *A Theory of Cognitive Dissonance.* Evanston, Row, Peterson, 1957.

———, & Carlsmith, J.M.: Cognitive consequences of forced compliance. *J Abnorm Soc Psychol, 58:*203–210, 1959.

———, Schachter, S., & Back, K.: *Social Pressures in Informal Groups.* New York, Harper, 1950.

Fiedler, F.E.: A contingency model of leadership effectiveness. In Berkowitz, L. (Ed.): *Advances in Experimental Social Psychology.* New York, Academic Press, 1964. vol. I.

———: The effect of leadership and cultural heterogeneity on group performance: A test of the contingency model. *J Exp Soc Psychol, 2:*237–264, 1966.

———: *A Theory of Leadership Effectiveness.* New York, McGraw-Hill, 1967.

———: Personality and situational determinants of leader behavior. Technical Report #71–18, University of Washington, Seattle, June, 1971. (a)

———: On the death and transfiguration of leadership training. Paper read at the American Psychological Association meeting, Washington, D.C., September, 1971. (b)

———, Meuwese, W., & Oonk, S.: An exploratory study of group creativity in laboratory tasks. *Acta Psychol, 18:*100–119, 1961.

———, Mitchell, T.R., & Triandis, H.C.: The culture assimilator: an approach to cross-cultural training. *J Appl Psychol, 55:*95–102, 1971.

Flanagan, T.C.: Techniques for developing critical requirements from critical incidents. *Am Psychol, 4:*236, 1949.

Foa, E.B.: Schizophrenics and neurotics: some differences in their interpersonal cognitive organization. Unpublished master's thesis, University of Illinois, Urbana, 1970.

———: The use of cognitive structures in behavior therapy. Unpublished manuscript, 1973.

———, Turner, J.L., & Foa, U.G.: Response generalization in aggression. *Hum Relations, 25:*337–350, 1972.

Foa, U.G.: Types of formal leaders: their role perception and ingroup contacts. *Transactions of the Second World Congress of Sociology.* 1954. vol. 1.

———: The contiguity principle in the structure of interpersonal relations. *Hum Relations, 11:*229–238, 1958. (a)

———: Empathy or behavioral transparency? *J Abnorm Soc Psychol, 56:*62–66, 1958. (b)

———: Some correlates of the empathy of the workers with the foreman. *J Appl Psychol, 44:*6–10, 1960.

———: Convergences in the analysis of the structure in interpersonal behavior. *Psychol Rev, 68:*341–352, 1961.

———: A facet approach to the prediction of communalities. *Behav Sci, 8:*220–226, 1963.

———: Workers satisfaction in four disciplinary climates. In Riley, M.W. (Ed.): *Sociological Research.* New York, Harcourt, Brace and World, 1963.

————: Cross-cultural similarity and difference in interpersonal behavior. *J Abnorm Soc Psychol*, 68:517–522, 1964.

————: New developments in facet design and analysis. *Psychol Rev*, 72:262–274, 1965.

————: Perception of behavior in reciprocal roles: the ringex model. *Psychol Monogr*, 80:(15, Whole No. 623), 1966.

————, & Chemers, M.M.: The significance of role behavior differentiation for cross-cultural interaction training. *Int J Psychol*, 2:45–48, 1967.

————, & Donnenwerth, G.V.: Love poverty in modern culture and sensitivity training. *Sociol Inquiry*, 41:149–159, 1971.

————, Mitchell, T.R., & Fiedler, F.E.: Differentiation matching. *Behav Sci*, 16:130–142, 1971.

————, & Lekhyananda, D.: Cultural differences in reaction to failure. *Int J Psychol*, 4:21–25, 1969.

————, Triandis, H.C., & Katz, E.W.: Cross-cultural invariance in the differentiation and organization of family roles. *J Pers Soc Psychol*, 4:316–327, 1966.

Frankl, V.E.: *Man's Search for Meaning*. Boston, Beacon Press, 1962.

Freedman, J.L.: Attitudinal effects of inadequate justification. *J Pers*, 31:371–385, 1963.

French, J.R.P., & Raven, B.: The bases of social power. In Cartwright, D. (Ed.): *Studies in Social Power*. Ann Arbor, University of Michigan, 1959.

Freud, A.: *Normality and Pathology in Childhood*. New York, International University Press, 1965.

Freud, S.: *An Outline of Psychoanalysis*. New York, Norton, 1949.

Fromm, E.: Selfishness and self-love. *Psychiatry*, 2:507–523, 1939.

Gambaro, S., & Rabin, A.I.: Diastolic blood pressure responses following direct and displaced aggression after anger arousal in high- and low-guilt subjects. *J Pers Soc Psychol*, 12:87–94, 1969.

Ganz, L., & Riesen, A.H.: Stimulus generalization to hue in the dark-reared macaque. *J Comp Physiol Psychol*, 55:92–99, 1962.

Geen, R.G.: Effects of frustration, attack, and prior training in aggressiveness upon aggressive behavior. *J Pers Soc Psychol*, 9:316–321, 1968.

————, & Berkowitz, L.: Name-mediated aggressive cue properties. *J Pers*, 34:456–465, 1966.

————: Some conditions facilitating the occurrence of aggression after the observation of violence. *J Pers*, 35:666–676, 1967.

Gerard, H.B. & Mathewson, G.C.: The effects of severity of initiation on liking for a group: a replication. *J Exp Soc Psychol*, 2:278–287, 1966.

Gergen, K.J.: *The Psychology of Behavior Exchange*. Reading, Mass., Addison Wesley, 1969.

Gewirtz, J.L.: Mechanisms of social learning: some roles of stimulation and behavior in early human development. In Goslin, D.A. (Ed.): *Handbook of Socialization Theory and Research*. Chicago, Rand McNally, 1969.

————, & Baer, D.M.: Deprivation and satiation of social reinforcers as drive conditions. *J Abnorm Soc Psychol*, 57:165–172, 1958.

Goldstein, A.P., Heller, K., & Sechrest, L.B.: *Psychotherapy and the Psychology of Behavior Change*. New York, Wiley, 1966.

Goldstein, J.H., & Arms, R.L.: Effects of observing athletic contests on hostility. *Sociometry*, 34:83–90, 1971.

Goodenough, E.W.: Interest in persons as an aspect of sex difference in the early years. *Genet Monogr*, 55:427–439, 1957.

————: Componential analysis. *Science*, 156:1203–1209, 1967.

————: Frontiers of cultural anthropology: social organization. *Proceedings of the American Philosophical Society, 113:*329–335, 1969.

Goranson, R.E., & Berkowitz, L.: Reciprocity and responsibility reactions to prior help. *J Pers Soc Psychol, 3:*227–232, 1966.

Gouldner, A.W.: The norm of reciprocity: a preliminary statement. *Am Sociol Rev, 25:*161–179, 1960. Reprinted in Hollander, E.P. & Hunt, R.G. (Eds.): *Current Perspectives in Social Psychology,* 2nd ed. New York, Oxford University Press, 1967.

Graham, F.K., Charwat, W.A., Honig, A.S., & Weltz, P.C.: Aggression as a function of the attack and the attacker, *J Abnorm Soc Psychol, 46:*512–520, 1951.

Guilford, J.P.: *The Nature of Human Intelligence.* New York, McGraw-Hill, 1967.

Hall, E.T.: *The Silent Language.* Greenwich, Conn., Fawcett, 1963.

Hall, K.R.: Observational learning in monkeys and apes. *Br J Psychol, 54:*201–226, 1963.

Halpern, F.: Emotional reactions and general personality structure. La Guardia Report, as reprinted in Solomon, D. (Ed.): *The Marihuana Papers.* New York, Signet Books, 1968.

Halverson, H.M.: Complications of the early grasping reactions. *Psychol Monogr, 47:*47–63, 1936.

Halwes, T., & Jenkins, J.J.: Problem of serial order in behavior is not resolved by context-sensitive associative memory models. *Psychol Rev, 78:*122–129, 1971.

Hamblin, R.L., Buckholdt, D., Bushell, D., Ellis, D., & Ferritor, D.: Changing the game from "Get the teacher" to "Learn." *Transaction,* January, 1969, 20–31.

Hamlin, R.M., & Lorr, M.: Differentiation of normals, neurotics, paranoids and non-paranoids. *J Abnorm Psychol, 77:*90–96, 1971.

Handfinger, B.M.: Effect of previous deprivation on reaction time for helping behavior. Paper presented at E.P.A. annual meeting, 1973.

Hardy, K.R.: Determinants of conformity and attitude change. *J Abnorm Soc Psychol, 54:*289–294, 1957.

Hare, A.P.: *Handbook of Small Group Research.* New York, Free Press of Glencoe, 1962.

Harlow, H.F.: Mice, monkeys, men and motives. *Psychol Rev, 60:*23–32, 1953.

————: The nature of love. *Am Psychol, 13:*673–685, 1958.

————, & Suomi, S.J.: Nature of love—simplified. *Am Psychol, 25:*161–168, 1970.

————, & Zimmerman, R.R.: Affectional responses in the infant monkey. *Science, 130:*421–432, 1959.

Harman, W.W., McKim, R.M., Mogar, R.E., Fadiman, J., & Stolaroff, M.J.: Psychedelic agents in creative problem solving: a pilot study. In Tart, C.A. (Ed.): *Altered States of Consciousness.* New York, Wiley, 1969.

Harrow, M., Fox, D.A., & Detre, T.: Self-concept of the married psychiatric patient and his mate's perception of him. *J Consult Clin Psychol, 33:*235–239, 1969.

————, Markhus, K.L., Stillman, R., & Hallowell, C.B.: Changes in adolescents' self-concept and their parents' perception during psychiatric hospitalization. *J Nerv Ment Dis, 147:*252–259, 1968.

Hartman, O.P.: Influence of symbolically modeled instrumental aggression and pain cues on aggressive behavior. *J Pers Soc Psychol,* 280–288, 1969.

Harvey, O.J., Hunt, D.E., & Schroder, H.M.: *Conceptual Systems and Personality Organization.* New York, Wiley, 1961.

Hatherington, E.M.: Effects of paternal absence on sex-typed behaviors in Negro and white, preadolescent males. *J Pers Soc Psychol, 4:*87–91, 1966.

Heider, F.: Consciousness, the perceptual world, and communications with others. In Tagiuri, R. & Petrullo, L. (Eds.): *Person Perception and Interpersonal Behavior.* Stanford, California, Stanford University Press, 1958.

Helmreich, R., Aronson, E., & LeFan, J.: To err is humanizing—sometimes: effects of self-esteem, competence and a pratfall on interpersonal attraction. *J Pers Soc Psychol, 16:*259-264, 1970.

———, & Collins, B.E.: Studies in forced compliance: IV. Commitment and magnitude of inducement to comply as determinants of opinion change. *J Pers Soc Psychol, 10:*75–81, 1968.

Henry, A.F.: Family role structure and self blame. *Social Forces, 35:*35–38, 1956.

Higgins, J.: Inconsistent socialization. *Psychol Rep, 23:*303–336, 1968.

Hillson, J.S., & Worchel, P.: Self-concept and defensive behavior in the maladjusted. *J Consult Psychol, 21:*83–88, 1957.

Hokanson, J.E.: The effects of frustration and anxiety on overt aggression. *J Abnorm Soc Psychol, 62:*346–351, 1961.

———, & Burgess, M.: The effects of three types of aggression on vascular processes. *J Abnorm Soc Psychol, 64:*446–449, 1962.

Hollander, E.P.: Conformity, status and idiosyncrasy credit. *Psychol Rev, 65:*117–127, 1958.

Hollister, L.E.: Marihuana in man: three years later. *Science, 172:*21–29, 1971.

Homans, G.C.: *Social Behavior: Its Elementary Forms.* New York, Harcourt, Brace & World, 1961.

Hornberger, R.H.: The differential reduction of aggressive responses as a function of interpolated activities. Paper presented at meeting of American Psychological Association. Cincinnati, Ohio, September, 1959. (Quoted by Berkowitz, 1962, p. 219).

Hovland, C., & Sears, R.: Minor studies in aggression: VI. Correlation of lynchings with economic indices. *J Psychol, 9:*301–310, 1940.

Hsu, F.L.K.: Kinship and ways of life: an exploration. In Hsu, F.L.K. (Ed.): *Psychological Anthropology, Approaches to Culture and Personality.* Homewood, Ill., Dorsey Press, 1961.

Hull, C.L.: *Principles of Behavior.* New York, Appleton-Century-Croft, 1943.

Humphreys, L.D., Ilgen, D., McGrath, D., & Montanelli, R.: Capitalization on chance in rotation of factors. *Educ Psychol Measurement, 29:*259–271, 1969.

Hunt. J. McV.: *Intelligence and Experience.* New York, Ronald Press, 1961.

Hutt, S.J., & Hutt, C.: *Direct Observation and Measurement of Behavior.* Springfield, Ill., Charles C Thomas, 1970.

Iversen, S.D.: The contribution of the ventral temporal lobe to visual analysis in the monkey. Paper delivered at the XIX International Congress of Psychology, London, August, 1969.

Jackson, D.D.: The question of family homeostasis. *Psychiatr Q [Suppl], 31:*79–90, 1957.

——— (Ed.): *Human Communication.* Palo Alto, Calif., Science and Behavior Books, 1969, vols. 1 & 2.

Jakobovitz, L.A.: Comparative psycholinguistics in the study of cultures. *Int J Psychol, 1:*15–37, 1966.

Janis, I.L.: *Air War and Emotional Stress: Psychological Studies of Bombing and Civilian Defense.* New York, McGraw-Hill, 1951.

———, & Rife, D.: Persuasibility and emotional disorders. In Hovland, C.I. & Janis, I.L. (Eds.): *Personality and Persuasibility.* New Haven, Conn., Yale University Press, 1959.

Jenkins, H.M.: Sequential organization in schedules of reinforcement. In Schoenfeld, W.N. and Farmer, J. (Eds.): *Theory of Reinforcement Schedules.* New York, Appleton-Century-Croft, 1971.

———, & Harrison, R.H.: Effects of discrimination training on auditory generalization. *J Exp Psychol, 59:*246–253, 1960.

Jessor, R., & Richardson, S.: Psychosocial deprivation and personality development. In *Perspectives on Human Deprivation: Biological, Psychological and Sociological.* U.S. Department of Mental Health, Education and Welfare, 1968.

John, E.R., Shimokochi, M., & Bartlett, F.: Neural readout from memory during generalization. *Science, 164:*1519–1521, 1969.

Johnsgard, P.A.: *Animal Behavior.* Dubuque, Iowa, Brown, 1967.

Johnson, M.M.: Sex role learning in the nuclear family. *Child Dev, 34:*319–333, 1963.

Jones, E.E.: *Ingratiation: A Social Psychological Analysis.* New York, Appleton-Century-Croft, 1964.

———, Bell, L., & Aronson, E.: The reciprocation of attraction from similar and dissimilar others: a study in person perception and evaluation. In McClintock, C.C. (Ed.): *Experimental Social Psychology.* New York, Holt, Rinehart and Winston, 1972.

———, & Gerard, H.B.: *Foundations of Social Psychology.* New York, Wiley, 1967.

———, Gergen, K.J., & Davis, K.E.: Some determinants of reactions to being approved or disapproved as a person. *Psychol Monogr, 76:*(No. 2, Whole No. 521), 1962.

Jones, S.C.: Some determinants of interpersonal evaluating behavior. *J Pers Soc Psychol, 3:*397–403, 1966.

———: Self and interpersonal evaluation: Esteem theories versus contingency theories. *Psychol Bull, 79:*185–199, 1973.

Jordan, J.E.: Attitude-behavior research on physical-mental social disability and racial-ethnic differences. *Psychol Aspects Disability, 18:*5–26, 1971.

Jourard, S.M.: *The Transparent Self.* Princeton, N.J., Van Nostrand, 1964.

Katz, E., Blau, P.M., Brown, M.L., & Strodtbeck, F.L.: Leadership stability and social change. *Sociometry, 20:*36–50, 1967.

Katz, E.W.: A study of verbal and non-verbal behaviors associated with social roles. Technical Report No. 20, November 1964, University of Illinois, Department of Psychology and Institute of Communication Research, Contract NR 177–472, Nonr-1834 (36), Advanced Research Projects Agency.

Kelley, H.H.: The process of causal attribution. *Am Psychol, 28:*107–128, 1973.

Kelly, G.A.: *Psychology of Personal Constructs.* New York, Norton, 1955.

Kiesler, C.A., & Kiesler, S.B.: *Conformity.* Reading, Mass., Addison-Wesley, 1969.

Kiesler, S.B.: The effect of perceived role requirements on reactions to favor-doing. *J Exp Soc Psychol, 2:*198–210, 1966.

———, Baral, R.L.: The search for a romantic partner: the effects of self-esteem and physical attractiveness on romantic behavior. In Gergen, K.J. & Marlowe, D. (Eds.): *Personality and Social Behavior.* Reading, Mass., Addison-Wesley, 1970.

Killian, L.M.: The significance of multiple group membership in disaster. *Am J Sociol, 57:*309–314, 1952.

Kimble, G.A.: The facts and a set of pressures. *Contemporary Psychol, 16:*59–63, 1971.

Kinney, E.E.: A study of peer group social acceptability at the fifth grade level in a public school. *J Educ Res, 47:*57–64, 1953.

Koch, S.: Psychology cannot be a coherent science. *Psychol Today, 3:*14 & 64–68, 1969.

Koestler, A.: *The Act of Creation,* New York, MacMillan, 1964.

————: *The Ghost in the Machine.* New York, MacMillan, 1968.

Kohlberg, L.: Stages and sequence: the cognitive-developmental approach to socialization. In Goslin, D.A. (Ed.): *Handbook of Socialization Theory and Research.* Chicago, Rand McNally, 1969. (a)

————: *Stages in the Development of Moral Thought and Action.* New York, Holt, Rhinehart and Winston, 1969. (b)

Kregarman, J.J., & Worchel, P.: Arbitrariness of frustration and aggression. *J Abnorm Soc Psychol, 63:*183–187, 1961.

Lana, R.E.: Manipulation-exploration drives and the drive-reduction hypothesis. *J Gen Psychol, 63:*3–27, 1960.

————: Exploratory phenomena and the drive-reduction hypothesis. *J Gen Psychol, 67:*101–104, 1962.

————: Pretest sensitization. In Rosenthal, R. & Rosnow, R.L. (Eds.): *Artifacts in Behavioral Research.* New York, Academic Press, 1969.

Landfield, A.W., & Nawas, M.M.: Psychotherapeutic improvement as a function of communication and adoption of therapist's values. *J Counseling Psychol, 11;*336–341, 1964.

Larson, L.L., & Rowland, K.M.: Leadership style and cognition complexity. College of Commerce and Business Administration. University of Illinois, Urbana-Champaign, 1972. (a)

————: Leadership style, stress and behavior in task performance. College of Commerce and Business Administration, University of Illinois, Urbana-Champaign, 1972. (b)

Latané, B., & Darley, J.M.: Bystander "apathy." *Am Sci, 57:*244–268, 1969.

Laufer, L.: *Israel and the Developing Countries: New Approaches to Cooperation.* New York, Twentieth Century Fund, 1967.

Leary, T.: *Interpersonal Diagnosis of Personality.* New York, Ronald Press, 1957.

Leavitt, H.J.: Some effects of certain communication patterns on group performance. In Barlund, D.C.: *Interpersonal Communication.* Boston, Houghton Mifflin, 1968.

Leventhal, G.S.: Influence of brothers and sisters on sex-role behavior. *J Pers Soc Psychol, 16:*452–465, 1970.

————, Allen, J., & Kemelgor, B.: Reducing inequity by reallocating rewards. *Psychonomic Sci, 14:*295–296, 1969.

————, & Anderson, D.: Self-interest and the maintenance of equity. *J Pers Soc Psychol, 15:*57–62, 1970.

————, & Bergman, J.T.: Self-depriving behavior as a response to unprofitable inequity. *J Exp Soc Psychol, 5:*153–171, 1969.

————, & Lane, D.W.: Sex, age, and equity behavior. *J Pers Soc Psychol, 15:*312–316, 1970.

————, & Michaels, J.W.: Extending the equity model: perception of inputs and allocation of reward as a function of duration and quantity of performance. *J Pers and Soc Psychol, 12:*303–309, 1969.

Levine, M.: Hypothesis Theory and nonlearning despite ideal S-R reinforcement contingencies. *Psychol Rev, 78:*130–140, 1971.

Levine, S.: Psychotherapy as socialization. *Int J Psychiatry, 8:*645–655, 1969.

Levinger, G.: The development of perceptions and behavior in newly formed social power relationships. In Cartwright, D. (Ed.): *Studies in Social Power.* Ann Arbor, University of Michigan, 1959.

Lévi-Strauss, CL: *Structural Anthropology.* New York, Basic Books, 1963.

————: *The Savage Mind.* Chicago, The University of Chicago Press, 1966.

Lewin, K.: *Principles of Topological Psychology.* New York, McGraw-Hill, 1936.

Lewis, H.B.: Studies in the principles of judgments and attitudes: IV. the operation of prestige suggestion. *J Soc Psychol, 14*:229–256, 1941.

Lewis, O.: The culture of poverty. *Sci Am, 215*:19–25, 1966.

Linder, D.E., Cooper, J. & Jones, E.E.: Decision freedom as a determinant of the role of incentive magnitude in attitude change. *J Pers Soc Psychol, 6*:245–254, 1967.

Longabaugh, R.: A category system for coding interpersonal behavior as social exchange. *Sociometry, 26*:319–344, 1963.

———: The structure of interpersonal behavior. *Sociometry, 29*:441–460, 1966.

———: Sources of interactional uncertainty and their relationship to pre-morbid schizoid prognosis of schizophrenics: an exploratory study. Unpublished manuscript, 1971.

———, Eldred, S.H., Bell, N.W., & Sherman, L.J.: The interactional world of the chronic schizophrenic patient. *Psychiatry, 29*:78–99, 1966.

———, & Whiting, J.W.M.: A transcultural test of the Leary grid. Paper read at American Psychological Association, Philadelphia, 1963.

Lorenz, K.: *On Aggression.* New York, Harcourt, Brace and World, 1966.

———: Der Kumpan in des umwelt des Voegels. *J für Ornithologie, 83*:137–213 and 289–413, 1935. Quoted by Salzen, 1970.

Lovaas, O.I.: Effect of exposure to symbolic aggression on aggressive behavior. *Child Dev, 32*:37–44, 1961.

Luria, A.R.: *Higher Cortical Functions in Man.* New York, Basic Books, 1966.

———, Simernitskaya, E.G., & Tubylevich, B.: The structure of psychological processes in relation to cerebral organization. *Neuropsychologia, 8*:13–19, 1970.

Lynn, D.B.: *Parental and Sex Role Identification.* Berkeley, McCutchan Publishing Corp., 1969.

———, & Sawrey, W.L.: The effects of father-absence on Norwegian boys and girls. *J Abnorm Soc Psychol, 59*:258–262, 1959.

MacKay, D.M.: Psychophysics of perceived intensity: a theoretical basis for Fechner's and Stevens' laws. *Science, 139*:1213–1216, 1963.

Madoff, J.M.: The attitudes of mothers of juvenile delinquents toward child rearing. *J Consult Psychol, 23*:518–520, 1959.

Madsen, K.B.: *Theories of Motivation.* Cleveland, Allen, 1961.

Mallick, S.K., & McCandless, B.R.: A study of catharsis of aggression. *J Pers Soc Psychol, 4*:591–596, 1966.

Maltzman, I., Langdon, B., & Feeney, D.: Semantic generalization without prior conditioning. *J Exp Psychol, 83*:73–75, 1970.

Mandler, G.: From association to structure. *Psychol Rev, 69*:415–427, 1962.

Marlowe, D., & Gergen, K.J.: Personality and social interaction. In Lindzey, B. & Aronson, E. (Eds.): *The Handbook of Social Psychology.* 2nd ed. Reading, Mass., Addison-Wesley, 1969, vol. 3.

Maslow, A.H.: Deprivation, threat and frustration. *Psychol Rev, 48*:364–366, 1941.

Mason, W.A.: Early social deprivation in nonhuman primates: Implications for human behavior. In Glass, D.C. (Ed.): *Environmental Influences.* New York, The Rockefeller University Press and Russell Sage Foundation, 1968.

Masserman, H.: Is uncertainty a key to neurotigenesis? *Psychosomatics, 11*:391–402, 1970.

McClelland, D.C. (Ed.): *Studies in Motivation.* New York, Appleton-Century-Croft, 1955.

———, Atkinson, J.W., Clark, R.A., & Lowell, E.L.: *The Achievement Motive.* New York, Appleton-Century-Croft, 1953.

McDavid, J., & Schroder, H.M.: The interpretation of approval and disapproval by delinquent and non-delinquent adolescents. *J Pers, 25:*539–549, 1957.

McDougall, W.: *The Energies of Men: A Study of the Fundamentals of Dynamic Psychology.* London, Methuen, 1932.

McGuire, W.J.: The nature of attitude and attitude change. In Lindzey, G. and Aronson, E. (Eds.): *The Handbook of Social Psychology,* 2nd ed. Reading, Mass., Addison-Wesley, 1969, vol. 3. (a)

———: Suspiciousness of experimenter's intent. In Rosenthal, R. & Rosnow, R.L. (Eds.): *Artifact in Behavioral Research.* New York, Academic Press, 1969. (b)

McNeill, D.: Developmental psycholinguistics. In Smith, F. & Miller, G.A. (Eds.): *The Genesis of Language.* Cambridge, M.I.T. Press, 1966.

Mead, G.H.: *On Social Psychology; Selected Papers.* Edited and with an introduction by A. Strauss. (Rev. ed.). Chicago, University of Chicago Press, 1964.

Merton, R.K.: *On Theoretical Sociology.* Glencoe, Ill., Free Press, 1967.

Michaelsen, L.K.: Leader orientation, leader behavior, group effectiveness, and situational favorability: an extension of the contingency model. Technical Report, Institute for Social Research, University of Michigan, Ann Arbor, Michigan, September, 1971.

Milgram, S.: The experience of living in cities. *Science, 167:*1461–1468, 1970.

Miller, G.A., Galanter, E., & Pribram, K.H.: *Plans and the Structure of Behavior.* New York, Holt, 1960.

Miller, H., & Bieri, J.: An informational analysis of clinical judgment. *J Abnorm Soc Psychol, 67:*317–325, 1963.

Miller, N.E.: Theory and experiment relating psychoanalytic displacement to stimulus-response generalization. *J Abnorm Soc Psychol, 43:*155–178, 1948.

———: *Effects of Group Size on Group Process and Member Satisfaction.* Ann Arbor, University of Michigan, 1950.

———: Liberalization of basic S-R concepts: extensions to conflict behavior, motivation and social learning. In Koch, S. (Ed.): *Psychology: A Study of a Science.* New York, McGraw-Hill, 1959, vol. 2.

———, & Bugelski, R.: Minor studies of aggression: the influence of frustrations imposed by the in-group on attitudes expressed toward out-groups. *J Psychol, 25:*437–442, 1948.

Miller, P.H., Kessel, F.S., & Flavell, J.H.: Thinking about people thinking about . . . : a study of social cognitive development. *Child Dev, 41:*613–623, 1970.

Mirsky, A.: Communication of affects in monkeys. In Glass, D.C. (Ed.): *Environmental Influences.* New York, The Rockefeller University Press and Russell Sage Foundation, 1968.

Mitchell, T.R.: Leader complexity and leadership style. *J Pers Soc Psychol, 16:*166–174, 1970.

———, & Foa, U.G.: Diffusion of the effect of cultural training of the leader in the structure of heterocultural task groups. *Aust J Psychol, 21:*31–43, 1969.

Mogar, R.E.: Psychedelic research in the context of contemporary psychology. *Psychedelic Rev, 8:*96–104, 1966.

———, & Savage, C.: Personality changes associated with psychedelic (LSD) therapy. *Psychotherapy, 1:*154–162, 1964.

Money, J.: Sex hormones and other variables in human eroticism. In Young, W.C. (Ed.): *Sex and Internal Secretions.* Baltimore, Williams and Williams, 1961.

Moreno, J.L.: *Who Shall Survive?* Washington, D.C., Nervous and Mental Diseases Publishing Co. Monograph No. 58, 1934.

Morin, R.E., Hoving, K.L., & Konick, D.S.: Are these two stimuli from the same set? Response times of children and adults with familiar and arbitrary sets. *J Exp Child Psychol,* 10:308–318, 1970.

Mosher, L.R.: Schizophrenic communication and family therapy. *Fam Processes,* 8:43–63, 1969.

Mosher, D.L., Mortimer, R.L., & Grebel, M.: Verbal aggressive behavior in delinquent boys. *J Abnorm Psychol,* 73:454–460, 1968.

———, & Proenza, L.M.: Intensity of attack, displacement and verbal aggression. *Psychonomic Sci,* 12:359–360, 1968.

Mowrer, O.H.: Freudianism, behavior therapy and "self-disclosure." *Behav Res Ther,* 1:321–337, 1964.

Mucchielli, R.: *Introduction à la Psychologie Structurelle.* (Psychologie et Sciences Humaines.) Brussels, Dessart, 1966. English version: New York, Funk and Wagnalls, 1970.

Muller, H.P.: Relationship between time-span of discretion, leadership behavior, and Fiedler's LPC score. *J Appl Psychol,* 54:140–144, 1970.

Murdock, G.P.: World ethnographic sample. *Am Anthropol,* 59:664–687, 1957.

Murray, H.A.: *Explorations in Personality.* New York, Oxford University Press, 1938.

Mussen, P., & Rutherford, E.: Parent-child relations and parental personality in relation to young children's sex role preferences. *Child Dev,* 34:589–607, 1963.

Nord, W.R.: Social exchange theory: an integrative approach to social conformity. *Psychol Bull,* 71:174–208, 1969.

Nye, F.I., Carlson, J., & Garrett, G.: Family size, interaction, affect and stress. *J Marriage Fam,* 32:216–226, 1970.

Omwake, K.: The relationship between acceptance of self and acceptance of others shown by three personality inventories. *J Consult Psychol,* 18:443–446, 1954.

Osgood, C.E.: Semantic differential technique in the comparative study of cultures. *Am Anthropol,* 66:171–200, 1964.

———: Speculations on the structure of interpersonal intensions. *Behav Sci,* 15:237–254, 1970.

O'Toole, R., & Dubin, R.: Baby feeding and body sway: an experiment in George Herbert Mead's "Taking the role of the other." *J Pers Soc Psychol,* 10:59–65, 1968.

Parsons, T.: *The Social System.* Glencoe, Ill., Free Press, 1951.

———: Family structure and the socialization of the child. In Parsons, T. & Bales, R.F. (Eds.): *Family, Socialization and Interaction Process.* Glencoe, Ill., Free Press, 1955.

———: A note on some biological analogies. Appendix A in Parsons, T. & Bales, R.F. (Eds.): *Family, Socialization and Interaction Process.* Glencoe, Ill., Free Press, 1955.

Pastore, N.: The role of arbitrariness in the frustration-aggression hypothesis. *J Abnorm Soc Psychol,* 47:728–731, 1952.

Pepitone, A.: Some conceptual and empirical problems of consistency models. In Feldman, S. (Ed.): *Cognitive Consistency: Motivational Antecedents and Behavioral Consequences.* New York, Academic Press, 1966.

———: The role of justice in interdependent decision making. *J Exp Soc Psychol,* 7:144–156, 1971.

———, Maderna, A., Caporicci, E., Tiberi, E., Iacono, G., DiMaio, G., Perfetto, M., Asprea, A., Villone, G., Fua, G., & Tonucci, F.: Justice in choice behavior, a cross-cultural analysis. *Int J of Psychol,* 5:1–10, 1970.

———, & Reichling, G.: Group cohesiveness and the expression of hostility. *Hum Relations,* 8:327–337, 1955.

Peterson, D.R.: *The Clinical Study of Social Behavior*. New York, Appleton-Century-Croft, 1968.

Peterson, N.: Effect of monochromatic rearing on the control of responding by wavelength. *Science, 136:*774–775, 1962.

Piaget, J.: *The Origins of Intelligence in Children*. New York, International Universities Press, 1952.

————: *The Construction of Reality in the Child*. New York, Basic Books, 1954.

Pirojnikoff, L.A.: Catharsis and the role of perceptual change in the reduction of hostility. Unpublished dissertation, 1958.

Premack, D.: Reinforcement theory. In Levine, D. (Ed.): *1964 Nebraska Symposium on Motivation*. Lincoln, Nebraska, University of Nebraska Press, 1965.

Pribram, K.H.: A review of theory in physiological psychology. *Ann Rev Psychol,* 1960.

Pruitt, D.G.: Reciprocity and credit building in a laboratory dyad. *J Pers Soc Psychol,* 8:143–147, 1968.

Reich, C.A.: *The Greening of America*. New York, Bantam Books, 1971.

Rescorla, R.A.: Pavlovian conditioning and its proper control procedures. *Psychol Rev, 74:*71–80, 1967.

Rice, R.W. & Chemers, M.M.: Predicting leadership emergence using Fiedler's contingency model of leadership effectiveness. *J Appl Psychol, 57:*281–287, 1973.

Rodgers, D.A., & Ziegler, F.J.: Cognitive process and conversion reactions. *J Nerv Ment Dis, 144:*155–170, 1967.

Roethlisberger, F.J., Dickson, W.J., & Wright, H.A.: *Management and the Worker: An Account of a Research Program Conducted by the Western Electric Company, Hawthorne Works, Chicago*. Cambridge, Mass., Harvard University Press, 1939.

Rogers, C.R.: *Client-Centered Therapy*. Boston, Houghton Mifflin, 1951.

Rosen, B.C., & D'Andrade, R.: The psychosocial origins of achievement motivation. *Sociometry, 22:*185–218, 1959.

Rosen, S.: The comparative roles of informational and material commodities in interpersonal transactions. *J Soc Psychol, 2:*211–226, 1966.

Rosenbaum, M.E., & deCharms, R.: Direct and vicarious reduction of hostility. *J Abnorm Soc Psychol, 60:*105–111, 1960.

Rosenthal, R. & Jacobson, L.: *Pygmalion in the Classroom: Teacher's Expectation and Pupils' Intellectual Development*. New York, Holt, Rinehart and Winston, 1968.

Rosenzweig, S.: An outline of frustration theory. In Hunt, J. McV. (Ed.): *Personality and the Behavior Disorders*. New York, Ronald Press, 1944.

Rosnow, R.L.: A "spread of effect" in attitude formation. In Greenwald, A.G., Brock, T.C., & Ostrom, T.M. (Eds.): *Attitude Change: Theory and Research*. New York, Academic Press, 1968.

————, & Robinson, E.J.: Irradiation effects. In Rosnow, R.L. & Robinson, E.J. (Eds.): *Experiments in Persuasion*. New York, Academic Press, 1967.

Rothaus, P., & Worchel, P.: The inhibition of aggression under nonarbitrary frustration. *J Pers, 28:*108–117, 1960.

Rothbart, M.K., & Maccoby, E.E.: Parents' differential reactions to sons and daughters. *J Pers Soc Psychol, 4:*237–243, 1966.

Rotter, J.B.: *Social Learning and Clinical Psychology*. New York, Prentice-Hall, 1954.

Ruesch, J.: Analysis of various types of boundaries. In Grinker, R.R. (Ed.): *Toward a Unified Theory of Human Behavior*. New York, Basic Books, 1956.

————: *Disturbed Communication*. New York, Norton, 1957.

————: *Therapeutic Communication.* New York, Norton, 1961.

Salzen, E.A.: Imprinting and environmental learning. In Aronson, L.R., Tobach, E., Lehrman, D.S., Rosenblatt, J.S. (Eds.): *Development and Evolution of Behavior.* San Francisco, W.H. Freeman, 1970.

Sampson, E.E.: *Social Psychology and Contemporary Society.* New York, Wiley, 1971.

————, & Insko, C.A.: Cognitive consistency and performance in the autokinetic situation. *J Abnorm Soc Psychol, 68:*184–192, 1964.

Santrock, J.W.: Paternal absence, sex typing, and identification. *Dev Psychol, 2:*264–272, 1970.

Sarbin, T.R., Taft, R. & Bailey, D.E.: *Clinical Inference and Cognitive Theory.* New York, Holt, Rinehart and Winston, 1960.

Sawyer, J., & Levine, R.A.: Cultural dimensions: a factor analysis of the world ethnographic sample. *Am Anthropol, 68:*708–731, 1966.

Schachter, S.: *The Psychology of Affiliation.* Stanford, Stanford University Press, 1959.

Schaller, G.B., & Emlen, J.T.: The ontogeny of avoidance behavior in some precocial birds. *Anim Behav, 10:*370–381, 1962.

Stent, G.S.: Prematurity and uniqueness in scientific discovery. *Sci Am, 227:*84–93, 1972.

Schopler, J., & Thompson, V.D.: Role of attribution processes in mediating amount of reciprocity for a favor. *J Pers Soc Psychol, 10:*243–250, 1968.

Schroder, H.M., Driver, M.J., & Streufert, S.: *Human Information Processing.* New York, Holt, Rinehart, & Winston, 1967.

Schutz, W.C.: *FIRO: A Three-Dimensional Theory of Interpersonal Behavior.* New York, Holt, 1958.

Scott, W.A.: Cognitive complexity and cognitive flexibility. *Sociometry, 25:*405–414, 1962.

————: Cognitive complexity and cognitive balance. *Sociometry, 26:*66–74, 1963.

Sears, P.S.: Doll-play aggression in normal young children: influences of sex, age, sibling status, father's absence. *Psychol Monogr, 65:*(6, Whole No. 323), 1951.

Sears, R.R., Maccoby, E.E., & Levin, H.: *Patterns of Child Rearing.* Evanston, Ill.; Row, Peterson, 1957.

————, Pintler, M.H., & Sears, P.S.: Effect of father separation on preschool children's doll play aggression. *Child Dev, 17:*219–243, 1946.

Secord, P.F., & Backman, C.W.: Personality theory and the problem of stability and change in individual behavior: an interpersonal approach. *Psychol Rev, 68:*21–32, 1961.

————: An interpersonal approach to personality. In Maher, B.A. (Ed.): *Progress in Experimental Personality Research.* New York, Academic Press, 1965, vol. 2.

Seeman, M.: On the meaning of alienation. *Am Sociol Rev, 24:*783–791, 1959.

Seligman, M.E.P.: Control group and conditioning: a comment on operationism. *Psychol Rev, 76:*484–491, 1969.

Sherif, M.: An experimental study of stereotypes. *J Abnorm Soc Psychol, 29:*371–375, 1935. (a)

————: A study of some social factors in perception. *Arch Psychol, 27:* No. 187, 1935. (b)

Shima, H.: The relationship between the leader's modes of interpersonal cognition and the performance of the group. *Jap Psychol Res, 10:*13–30, 1968.

Shuval, J.T.: *Social Functions of Medical Practice: Doctor-Patient Relationship in Israel.* San Francisco, Calif., Jossey-Bass, 1970.

Siegel, S.: *Nonparametric Statistics for the Behavioral Sciences.* New York, McGraw-Hill, 1956.

Sigall, H., & Aronson, E.: Liking for an evaluator as a function of her physical attractiveness and nature of the evaluation. *J Exp Soc Psychol, 5:*93–100, 1969.

Skinner, B.F.: *Science and Human Behavior.* New York, MacMillan, 1953.

Slagle, J.R.: *Artificial Intelligence: The Heuristic Programming Approach.* New York, McGraw-Hill, 1971.

Solomon, R.L., Turner, L.H., & Lessac, M.S.: Some effects of delay of punishment on resistance to temptation in dogs. *J Pers Soc Psychol, 8:*233–238, 1968.

Stafford, P.G., & Golightly, B.M.: *LSD the Problem Solving Psychedelic.* New York; Award Books, 1967.

Stagner, R., & Karwoski, T.F.: *Psychology.* New York, McGraw-Hill, 1952.

Staub, E., & Sherk, L.: Need for approval, children's sharing behavior, and reciprocity in sharing. *Child Dev, 41:*243–252, 1970.

Stock, D.: An investigation into the intercorrelations between the self concept and feelings directed toward other persons and groups. *J Consult Psychol, 13:*176–180, 1949.

Stolurow, L.: Idiographic programming. *Nat Society Programmed Instruct J,* October, 1965, 10–12.

Stotland, E.: Peer groups and reaction to power figures. In Cartwright, D. (Ed.): *Studies in Social Power.* Ann Arbor, University of Michigan, 1959.

Strickberger, M.W.: *Genetics.* New York, MacMillan, 1968.

Sullivan, H.S.: *Clinical Studies in Psychiatry.* New York, Norton, 1956.

Sutton-Smith, B., & Rosenberg, B.G.: Age changes in the effects of ordinal position on sex-role identification. *J Genet Psychol, 107:*61–73, 1965.

Tajfel, H.: Social and cultural factors in perception. In Lindzey, G., & Aronson, E. (Eds.): *The Handbook of Social Psychology.* 2nd ed. Reading, Mass., Addison-Wesley, 1969, vol. 3.

Tanaka, Y.: Cross-cultural comparability of the affective meaning systems. *J Soc Issues, 23:*27–46, 1967.

Tasch, R.J.: The role of the father in the family. *J Exp Educ, 20:*319–361, 1952.

————: Interpersonal perceptions of fathers and mothers. *J Genet Psychol, 87:*59–65, 1955.

Taylor, S.P.: Aggressive behavior and physiological arousal as a function of provocation and the tendency to inhibit aggression. *J Pers, 35:*297–310, 1967.

Teichman, M.: Unpublished manuscript, 1970.

————: Antithetical apperception of family members by neurotics. *J Individ Psychol, 27:*73–75, 1971. (a)

————: Ego defense, self-concept and image of self ascribed to parents by delinquent boys. *Percept Mot Skills, 32:*819–823, 1971. (b)

————: Satisfaction from interpersonal relations following resource exchange. Unpublished doctoral dissertation, University of Missouri, Columbia, Missouri, 1971. (c)

Teichman, Y., Bazzoui, W., & Foa, U.G.: Changes in self-perception following short-term psychiatric hospitalization. In preparation.

Thibaut, J.W., & Coules, J.: The role of communication in the reduction of interpersonal hostility. *J Abnorm Soc Psychol, 47:*770–777, 1952.

————, & Kelley, H.H.: *The Social Psychology of Groups.* New York, Wiley, 1959.

Tiller, P.O.: Father-absence and personality development of children in sailor families: a preliminary research report. *Nordisk Psychologi,* No. 9, 316–320, 1958.

Tolman, E.C.: A psychological model. In Parsons, T., and Shils, E.A. (Eds.): *Toward a General Theory of Action.* Cambridge, Mass., Harvard University Press, 1951.

Tomkins, S.S.: *Affect, Imagery, Consciousness. Vol. 1. The Positive Affects.* New York, Springer, 1962.

————: Affect and the psychology of knowledge. In Tomkins, S.S., & Izard, C.E. (Eds.): *Affect, Cognition and Personality*. New York, Springer, 1965.

Triandis, H.C.: Cognitive similarity and interpersonal communication in industry. *J Appl Psychol, 43*:321–326, 1959.

————: Cognitive similarity and communication in a dyad. *Hum Relations, 13*: 175–183, 1960. (a)

————: Some determinants of interpersonal communication. *Hum Relations, 13*:279–287, 1960. (b)

————: Exploratory factor analyses of the behavioral components of social attitudes. *J Abnorm Soc Psychol, 68*:420–430, 1964.

————: Interpersonal relations in international organizations. *J Organization Behav Hum Perform, 2*:26–55, 1967. (a)

————: Toward an analysis of the components of interpersonal perception. In Sherif, M., Sherif, C., & Kent, D.P. (Eds.): *Attitudes, Ego Involvement and Attitude change*. New York, Wiley, 1967. (b)

————: *Attitude and Attitude Change*. New York, Wiley, 1971.

————: A broad theoretical framework on which we may be able to build. Unpublished manuscript, 1972.

————, & Vassiliou, V.: A comparative analysis of subjective cultures. In Triandis, H.C., Vassiliou, V., Vassiliou, G., Tanaka, Y., Shanmugam, A.V. (Eds.): *The Analysis of Subjective Culture*. New York, Wiley-Interscience, 1972.

————, Vassiliou, V., & Nassiakou, M. Three cross-cultural studies of subjective culture. *J Pers Soc Psychol Monogr, 8*:(4, pt. 2, 1–42), 1968.

Tuckman, B.W.: Personality structure, group composition, and group functioning. *Sociometry, 27*:469–487, 1964.

————: Group composition and group performance of structured and unstructured tasks. *J Exp Soc Psychol, 3*:25–40, 1967.

Turner, J.L.: For love or money: pattern of resource commutation in social interchange. Unpublished Master thesis. University of Missouri-Columbia, Columbia, Missouri, 1971.

————, Foa, E.B., & Foa, U.G.: Interpersonal reinforcers: classification, interrelationship, and some differential properties. *J Pers Soc Psychol, 19*:168–180, 1971.

Uzgiris, I.C., & Hunt, J.McV.: Toward ordinal scales of psychological development in infancy. Unpublished manuscript, 1972.

Vannoy, J.S.: Generality of cognitive complexity-simplicity as a personality construct. *J Pers Soc Psychol, 2*:285–296, 1965.

Varble, D.L., & Landfield, A.W.: Validity of the self-ideal discrepancy as a criterion measure for success in psychotherapy—a replication. *J Counsel Psychol, 16*:150–156, 1969.

Vieru, T.: Quelques considerations sur la notion de "structure" dans la psychotherapie. *Ann Med-Psychol, 2*:(126), 487–492, 1969.

Wallace, A.F.C.: The psychic unity of human groups. In Kaplan, B. (Ed.): *Studying Personality Cross-Culturally*. New York, Harper and Row, 1961.

Walster, E., Walster, B., Abrahams, D., & Brown, Z.: The effect on liking of underrating or overrating another. *J Exp Soc Psychol, 2*:70–84, 1966.

Walters, R.H.: On the high magnitude theory of aggression. *Child Dev, 35*:303–304, 1964.

————, & Thomas, E.L.: Enhancement of punitiveness by visual and audio-visual displays. *Can J Psychol, 17*:244–255, 1963.

Wechsler, H., & Pugh, T.F.: Fit of individual and community characteristics and rates of psychiatric hospitalization. *Am J Sociol, 73*:331–338, 1967.

Weil, A.T., Zinberg, N.E., & Nelsen, J.M.: Clinical and psychological effects of marihuana in man. *Science, 162:*1234–1242, 1968.

Weinstein, E.A., Beckhouse, L.S., Blumstein, P.W., & Stein, R.B.: Interpersonal strategies under conditions of gain and loss. *J Pers, 36:*616–634, 1968.

———, DeVaughan, W.L., & Wiley, M.G.: Obligation and the flow of deference in exchange. *Sociometry, 32:*1–12, 1969.

White, R.: Motivation reconsidered: the concept of competence. *Psychol Rev, 66:*297–333, 1959.

Whiting, J.W.M.: Effects of climate on certain cultural practices. In Goodenough, W.H. (Ed.): *Explorations in Cultural Anthropology.* New York, McGraw-Hill, 1964.

———, & Child, I.L.: *Child Training and Personality.* New Haven, Yale University Press, 1953.

Wickens, D.D.: Encoding categories of words: an empirical approach to meaning. *Psychol Rev, 77:*1–15, 1970.

Wiggins, J.S.: Personality structure. *Annu Rev Psychol, 19:*293–350, 1968.

Winch, R.F.: *Mate Selection.* New York, Harper, 1958.

———: Another look at the theory of complementary needs in mate-selection. *J Marriage Fam, 29:*756–762, 1967.

Wohlford, P., Santrock, J.W., Berger, S.E., & Liberman, D.: Older brothers' influence on sex-typed, aggressive, and dependent behavior in father-absent children. *Dev Psychol, 4:*124–134, 1971.

Wolpe, J.: *Psychotherapy by Reciprocal Inhibition.* Stanford, Calif., Stanford University Press, 1958.

———: *The Practice of Behavior Therapy.* New York, Pergamon, 1969.

Worchel, P.: Catharsis and the relief of hostility. *J Abnorm Soc Psychol, 55:*238–243, 1957.

———: Personality factors in the readiness to express aggression. *J Clin Psychol, 14:*355–359, 1958.

———: Status restoration and the reduction of hostility. *J Abnorm Soc Psychol, 63:*443–445, 1961.

Worchel, S., & Mitchell, T.R.: An evaluation of the effectiveness of the culture assimilator in Thailand and Greece. Technical Report 70–13, Department of Psychology, University of Washington, Seattle, 1970.

Wylie, Ruth C.: *The Self Concept.* Lincoln, University of Nebraska Press, 1961.

Wynne, L.C., & Singer, M.T.: Thought disorders and family relations of schizophrenics; II. A classification of forms of thinking. *Arch Gen Psychiatry, 9:*199–206, 1963.

Yates, A.J.: *Frustration and Conflict.* New York, Wiley, 1962.

Young, P.T.: *Motivation of Behavior.* New York, Wiley, 1936.

Zajonc, R.B.: The concepts of balance, congruity and dissonance. *Public Opinion Q, 24:*280–296, 1960.

———: Cognitive theories in social psychology. In Lindzey, G., and Aronson, E. (Eds.): *The Handbook of Social Psychology,* 2nd ed. Reading, Mass., Addison-Wesley, 1968. vol. 1.

Zelditch, M., Jr.: Role differentiation in the nuclear family: a comparative study. In Parsons, T., & Bales, R.F. (Eds.): *Family Socialization and Interaction Process.* Glencoe, Ill., Free Press, 1955.

Zimbardo, P.G.: The human choice: individuation, reason and order versus deindividuation, impulse and chaos. In *1969 Nebraska Symposium on Motivation, 17:*237–307, 1970.

Zimet, C.N., & Schneider, C.: Effects of group size on interaction in small groups. *J Soc Psychol, 77:*177–187, 1969.

AUTHOR INDEX

SUBJECT INDEX

A

Abstraction, 27
Acceptance, (*see* Giving)
Accommodation, 26
Actor,
  as dimension, 33, 94
  as self vs. other, 44–45
  in differentiation, 54–56
  in perceptual class, 56
  in vicarious aggression, 228, 234–235
  of behavior, 33, 94–95
Adaptation, level of, 7
Aggression, 184, 224
  as deprivation of resources, 225
  behavior of, 314
  classification by resources, 225
  definitions of, 225–226
  displacement of, 229–234
    and particularistic resources, 231
    and power of objects, 230
    and similarity between objects, 230
    symbolic, 233–234
  effects of watching movies, 235
  exposure to violent behavior, and, 235
  in resource theory, 227
  in restoring homeostasis, 132
  physical vs. verbal, 226
  residual, 195–199
  response generalization, and, 186, 228
  tolerance for, 313
  towards self, 231–232
  vicarious, 234–235
    as change of actors, 234
    cathartic effect of, 234–235
Alienation, 171
  as self-estrangement, 172
  resource exchange, and, 172
Ambivalence, 63
Anxiety, 366
  evoking potential, 366
  in obsessive compulsive, 366
  social roles and, 369
  structure of, 368
Arab, (*see* Cultural training, Culture)
Arousal, 128, 191
Assertive training,
  applications of interpersonal structures to, 369
  discrimination from aggression, 370

Assimilation,
  generalizing, 26
  recognitory, 26
  vs. accommodation, 8
Assimilator, (*see* Cultural training)
Attitude change, 297
  primacy vs. recency, 8
Attraction, attractiveness, 240
  interpersonal encounter and, 240
  liking and, 241
  pratfall, and, 241
  reciprocation in, 245
  redefinition of, 240
  resources and, 243
  self-esteem and, 242
Attribution theory, 11

B

Balance, (*see* Dissonance)
Behavior, (*see also* Aggression, Dimensions)
  classes of, 31
  comparison of verbal and overt, 190–192
  differential, 101
  dyadic, 53
  in different institutions, 322
  of helping, 168, 199
  repertoire, 28
  sequence of, 52–54
  structure of, 61
Behavior therapy,
  assertive training, 370
  construction of hierarchies, 366
  contingency in, 155
Blinds, cognitive differentiation in, 375–376
Boundary, (*see also* Differentiation)
  cognitive, 30
Brain lesions, mental functions and, 14–15

C

Catharsis, 192, 227–228, 234
Child training, 308 (*see also* Development)
City, (*see* Urban society)
Clinical inference, 11
Cognition, 5–9 (*see also* Differentiation, Structure),
  as stabilizer, 382
  awareness, and, 8–9
  boundary, 30
  changes in success and failure, 329–330

445